GEOGRAPHIES: An Intermediate Series

EDITED BY PROFESSOR R. W. STEEL, B.Sc. M.A.

LATIN AMERICA

GEOGRAPHIES: AN INTERMEDIATE SERIES
Edited by Professor R. W. Steel

LATIN AMERICA
G. J. Butland

AFRICA AND THE ISLANDS
R. J. Harrison Church, J. I. Clarke, P. J. H. Clarke and J. H. Henderson

THE COUNTRIES OF NORTH-WESTERN EUROPE
F. J. Monkhouse

PHYSICAL GEOGRAPHY
R. K. Gresswell

MAP STUDIES AND FIELD EXCURSIONS
A. H. W. Robinson and K. L. Wallwork

THE WORLD OF MAN
R. H. Buchanan

Latin America

A REGIONAL GEOGRAPHY

by Gilbert J. Butland, B.A. Ph.D., D.Litt.
Emeritus Professor of Geography
and formerly Foundation Professor and Pro Vice-Chancellor
in the University of New England
Armidale, New South Wales

Third Edition

LONGMAN

LONGMAN GROUP LIMITED
London
Associated companies, branches and representatives throughout the world

First Published 1960
Second Edition 1966
Third Edition 1972
Second Impression 1977
ISBN 0 582 31076 8

Printed in Hong Kong by
Wing Tai Cheung Printing Co Ltd.

Preface

IN spite of the fact that Latin America is still the most neglected of all the world's major regions, from the point of view of both the British general reader and its treatment in schools, the demand for a text-book on its regional geography has been steadily growing. It is in an effort to supply this need that this volume has been written. The emphasis throughout the book is on regional description, as it is here that the deficiency is greatest. The aim has been to give VIth form and Training College students and those taking up a study of the continent at First Year University level a comprehensive picture of the principal components of the Latin American mosaic. For these students a number of good general treatments are available, and for many of them a basic study of the structural, climatic and vegetational patterns has already formed a part of their geographical work. No attempt has been made, therefore, to do more than provide a brief physical, historical and economic setting for the regional studies which follow.

Because the author feels that the national individuality of the twenty republics is growing rather than declining in importance, the basis of these regional studies is constructed on the framework of each separate national state, although broad linking introductions are provided to the five larger groupings of these republics. One of these great semi-continental areas, that of Middle America, accounts for nearly one-third of the book, a proportion not unjustified when one contemplates its significance in American affairs and the appalling ignorance displayed concerning the lands which compose it. This latter defect is due in no small measure to these middle lands 'falling between two stools', many books dealing with South America only and others with North America, which far too often stops short at the Río Grande. Nor do the syllabuses of most examination boards encourage the student to devote much attention to Middle America. The combined result is that too often it is dismissed inaccurately as 'Central America', or treated as an awkward appendix to the lands lying to the north or south.

Although the author fully subscribes to the fundamental geographical concept that the cores of geographical regions are more significant than their boundaries, he has risked the division of the national states into major regions by means of firm and definite lines on maps which act as a guide to the reader as each republic is considered. The justification, based partly on nearly thirty years' teaching experience, is that a student has a firmer grasp of a region's content if he is aware of its peripheral limits and can see it as a component of a larger whole. No one is more aware than the author of the defects and generalizations of such boundary drawing; nor does the process follow a uniform criterion. In some cases (as with Brazil) the use of state boundaries is more convenient; in others (as with the Pacific republics) physical criteria of relief, climate or vegetation are employed; while in another group economic considerations of land use may be more fundamental in shaping the regional consciousness of the area's people. In this way the reader is made fully aware of the complexity of the geography of a diverse region which cannot and should not be confined within the strait-jacket of a uniform plan.

The text is not loaded with statistical material, much of which rapidly becomes out of date. The emphasis has been a comparative one, to set a state or region in its continental significance. The good teacher and student will always be supplementing regional description with readily available figures to illustrate trends and principles. Some statistics, in summary form, framed so they can be used for comparative purposes, are, however, included for purposes of reference at the end of each chapter.

The author, hopeful that readers of the book will pursue further studies of Latin America, has not hesitated to introduce them to Spanish and Portuguese geographical terminology which often cannot be adequately or accurately translated by one English word. A glossary of these terms is provided, and its use in regional description helps to convey a fuller understanding of areal characteristics, not least in the intelligent interpretation of large and even small-scale maps of the lands being studied.

Many people have co-operated in the publication of the book. These include Mr D. W. Oliver, who has drawn the maps, Miss O. R. Daniell, who has typed the text, Professor R. W. Steel, whose editorial comments have been invaluable, the staff of Longmans, Green & Co, whose patience has permitted the author to spread the work over several years, and the representatives of many of the twenty republics who have generously given information. To all these the author is very grateful. Without them the book would not have been possible. Acknowledgment is also made to the companies and institutions which have provided illustrative material, and to the Geographical Association's kindness in permitting the publication of some of the author's maps previously used in their journal *Geography*.

September 1959   GILBERT J. BUTLAⅠ.

PREFACE TO THE SECOND EDITION 1966

While much of the social and cultural geography of enormous areas of the continent remains remarkably static, the development of transport (particularly since the larger republics have established and expanded their motor car industries) and the continued rapid growth of population are producing significant alterations in the relative importance of many features of Latin American geography. This new edition endeavours to incorporate the more important of these changes, such as the economic re-orientation of Cuba since the 1959 revolution. All the statistics in the summaries and throughout the text have been revised and brought as up to date as figures are available. In addition there has been much revision of detail consequent upon the author's visit to most of the countries of South America during 1964.

He is also most appreciative of help received from geographers and others both in Latin America and elsewhere regarding detailed information on many developments in the continent. No one person can be equally conversant with every part of such a vast and complex region, and without such co-operation the task of presenting a comprehensively accurate account would have been almost impossible.

September 1965   GILBERT J. BUTLAND

PREFACE TO THE THIRD EDITION 1972

Continued rapid population growth throughout most of Latin America has resulted in a great variety of social, economic and political reactions to the many problems facing the continent. In many states dictatorships have come and gone, a new socialist economy has begun to evolve in Chile, once-progressive Uruguay faces relative economic stagnation, yet authoritarian Brazil forges a tremendous pace of economic growth, Venezuela leaps forward into the leading group of industrial republics, the ex-colonial dependencies grapple with the problems of their new independence, and Mexico resolutely programmes the seventh decade of its revolution. These are but a few of the facets which reflect the conditions surrounding the lives of the 300 million Latin Americans of the 1970s; and this new edition endeavours to assess the prospects and problems in their geographical setting. This has been done by a new concluding section to each chapter, by a thorough revision of all material, statistical and otherwise, throughout the book, and by the addition of numerous relevant new maps, diagrams and statistical tables. A further visit to Middle America enabled the author personally to evaluate some of the developments and trends taking place in that major area.

Once again he is appreciative of help received from geographers and others both in Latin America and elsewhere regarding detailed information on many developments in the continent. He acknowledges with gratitude particularly, the invaluable assistance afforded by regular monthly *Bulletins of the Bank of London and South America*, the weekly political and economic reports of *Latin America*, published by Latin American Newsletters Ltd, and the *Statistical Abstract of Latin America* published annually by the Latin American Center of the University of California at Los Angeles.

The help of Mrs Caroline Mitchell in typing corrections and additional material and of Mrs Marion Schofield in preparing maps and diagrams has also been invaluable in the production of the new edition.

June 1971   GILBERT J. BUTLAND

Contents

Chapter   *Page*

INTRODUCTION

1 The Historical Endowment   1
2 The Physical Endowment   9
3 The Economic Endowment   17

PART I

MIDDLE AMERICA

4 General Introduction to Middle America   33
5 Mexico   35
6 The Central American Republics   87
7 The West Indies   115

PART II

THE NORTH ANDEAN REPUBLICS AND THE GUIANAS

8 General Introduction to the Northern Andes and Guiana   173
9 The Guianas   178
10 Venezuela   189
11 Colombia   211
12 Ecuador   233

PART III

THE PACIFIC REPUBLICS

13 General Introduction to the Pacific Republics   247
14 Peru   252
15 Bolivia   276
16 Chile   286

PART IV

THE PLATA REPUBLICS

17	General Introduction to La Plata Republics	309
18	Argentina	313
19	Paraguay	354
20	Uruguay	361
21	The Falkland Islands	372

PART V

PORTUGUESE AMERICA

22	Brazil	377

Trade and Production Statistics	437
References	444
Glossary of Spanish and Portuguese Geographical Terms	451
Conversion information and factors	454
Index	457

Maps

Figure		*Page*
1	The colonial divisions and administration of Latin America	2
2	Principal indigenous linguistic groups of the Andes	4
3	Ethnic framework of Latin America	6
4	The relief of Latin America	10–11
5	The physiographic regions of Latin America	12
6	The forests of Latin America	13
7	The sedimentary basins and oilfields of Latin America	19
8	The distribution of population in Latin America	20
9	Total population of major states	22
10	Population increase in Latin America	23
11	The international railway systems of Latin America	25
12	The international road links of Latin America	26
13	Single commodity dependence in Latin America	27
14	G.N.P. per capita, Latin America	28
15	Economic co-operation and U.S. investment in Latin America	29
16	Steel production in Latin America	30
17	The regions and states of Mexico	37
18	The trunk railway system of Mexico	38
19	The vegetational zones of Mexico	40
20	The regions of Eastern Mexico	43
21	The regions of Western Mexico	49
22	Central Mexico	58
23	The road and rail network of Central Mexico	61
24	Mexico City	66
25	Southern Mexico	73
26	The lands of the Mayas	78
27	The physiographic provinces of Central America	88
28	The regions of Central America	96
29	The regions of the West Indies	116
30	Mountain trend lines of the Caribbean lands	119

31	Jamaican parishes and Cuban provinces	122
32	The social revolutions of Latin America	126
33	The relief units of Hispaniola	129
34	Jamaica. Bauxite and sugar	134
35	Trinidad. Oil and sugar	153
36	Middle America. Sugar, bananas and bauxite	175
37	The regions of the Guianas	179
38	The economic development of the Guianas	181
39	The regions of Venezuela	190
40	Western Venezuela	191
41	The altitudinal zones of the Sierra de Mérida	195
42	Central Venezuela	197
43	Eastern Venezuela	201
44	Irrigation in the Venezuelan Llanos	202
45	The regions of Colombia	212
46	Roads and railways in Colombia	215
47	The distribution of coffee cultivation in Colombia	217
48	The regions of Ecuador	234
49	The regions of Peru	253
50	The departments of Peru	256
51	Petroleum exploration in Peru's Montaña	271
52	Colonization areas of Latin America	272
53	The regions of Bolivia	277
54	The regions of Chile	287
55	The Tierra del Fuegian oilfield	298
56	Chile. Magallanes field industrialization	299
57	Central Chile. Industrialization of petroleum	300
58	Sugar beet cultivation in Central Chile	302
59	The regions of Argentina	314
60	Relief units of Northern and Central Argentina	316
61	Sub-regions of Northern and Central Argentina	317
62	The railways of Argentina	338
63	Buenos Aires	340
64	Patagonia	342
65	Paraguay, oriental and occidental	355
66	The regions of Uruguay	363
67	The sections of Brazil	378
68	The serras and structural elements of Eastern Brazil	380
69	Brazil's Northeast	382
70	The Paulo Afonso hydro-electric power plant	393
71	The Southeast and South of Brazil	408

72 The Frontier zone of Paraná   416
73 Brazil's Central States   419
74 Brazilian Amazonia   424
75 The railway systems of Brazil   429
76 Transverse and longitudinal road systems of Brazil   430

PLATES

		page
1	A shanty-town in Venezuela	24
2	Winnowing wheat in Mexico	42
	Grinding sugar cane at Montemorelos in the eastern region of Mexico	42
3	Cultivated fields near México City	59
4	The dome of Popacatapetl in Mexico	67
5	Carrying pots to Toluca market	68
6	A Mayan hieroglyphic column at Copán, Honduras	90
7	The pyramid of Zacaleu, Honduras	97
8	Open-cast bauxite mining in Jamaica	136
9	A village market in Jamaica	137
10	Resettlement housing, San Juan, Puerto Rico	142
11	Arrowroot is grown in St. Vincent	146
12	The dome of Micotrin in Dominica	148
13	Digging a drainage ditch on a Guyana sugar estate	
	Cutting planting lines for bananas in Honduras	183
14	The Bolívar oilfield of Lake Maracaibo	192
15	Cocoa in east-facing valleys of Venezuela	196
16	Caracas, Venezuela	198
17	Orinoco *llanos*, Venezuela	199
18	Loading ore at Palua for shipment to Baltimore	203
19	The Cerro Bolívar iron hill	205
20	Packaging milk and rolling hides in Venezuelan factories	206
21	Apartment blocks and new highways in Caracas, Venezuela	208
22	A village in eastern Colombia	213
23	The hazardous braided course of the Magdalena, Colombia	218
24	In the *oriente* of Ecuador	
	The interior of Zulia State, Venezuela	240
25	Inca ruins	249
26	A watercourse in the Peruvian desert seen from the air	254
27	Two scenes in Cuzco province, Peru	262
28	Huancayo in central Peru	264
29	An Andean valley near Ayacucho, Peru	265

30	El Misti near Arequipa, Peru	267
31	Inca terraced farmland of Machu Picchu, Peru	270
32	Chuquicamata, Latin America's greatest copper plant	290
33	Mediterranean Chile: the hill slopes of the coastal range and the flat acres of the central plain	292
34	Semi-arid land in the Andean fringe of Catamarca province	320
35	Harvesting wheat on the Argentine pampa	334
36	Buenos Aires	341
37	Patagonia is Argentine's greatest area of sheep pastoralism	345
38	Argentine wool and Peruvian cotton are two examples of raw material production	347
39	Hereford cattle in Uruguay	367
40	Montevideo harbour	369
41	Carnauba wax trees in Ceara State	387
42	Ouro Preto, in Minas Gerais State	399
43	A scene in Rio de Janeiro	406
44	Brasilia	422
45	Brasilia: residential blocks form neighbourhood units	432

We are grateful to the following for permission to reproduce photographs: Aluminium Company of Canada for Plate 8; the Anglo-Argentine Society for Plate 34; Bethlehem Steel Company, U.S.A. for Plate 18; Booker Brothers, McConnell & Co. for Plate 13 (*upper*); Brazilian Government Trade Bureau for Plates 41, 42; the Chilean Embassy for Plate 33; Chilex Ltd for Plate 32; Grace Line for Plates 28, 31; Orinoco Mining Company for Plate 19; Revista La Chacre—Buenos Aires, República Argentina for Plate 35; United Fruit Company, New York for Plates 6, 7, 13 (*lower*); Ministerio de Fomento, Venezuela for Plates 14, 15; Government Geologist's Office, Windward Islands for Plate 12. Plate 9 is Crown copyright reserved and Plates 20, 22, 23, 24 are Shell photographs; Plate 44 is by Aerofilms; Plate 11 by Anne Bolt; Plates 36, 40 by J. Allan Cash; Plate 39 by Pictorial Press; Plates 2, 3, 4, 5, 25, 26, 27, 29, 30, 37 and 38 by Paul Popper Ltd; and Plate 17 by Hamilton Wright. The following photographs were supplied by Camera Press: Plate 45 by Mike Andrews; Plates 1, 21 by Francois Chalais; Plate 43 by Armand Latourre and Plate 16 by Nick de Morgoli. Plate 10 is from a photograph by the author.

CHAPTER ONE

The Historical Endowment

THE term 'Latin America', embracing all the lands south of the Mexican-United States boundary, and made up of twenty-four independent republics and some fourteen ex-colonial dependencies, stresses the Latin characteristics of the peoples and settlements of these lands. These involve language, religion, customs, institutions and economic ideas, all of which can be traced, to a greater or less degree, to European origins in Spain and Portugal, and in a few areas to France and Italy too. This common heritage is a continuing legacy of the last four hundred and eighty years, initiated by Columbus's discovery of the New World in 1492. Within fifty years from that event there were few parts of habitable Latin America which had not been visited by Spanish or Portuguese explorers, and although the potential development of some regions had not been foreseen, it is surprising how many of the major settlements had been established in that half century, as the following list will show:

Panamá City	1519	Asunción	1537
México City	1521	Bogotá	1538
Quito	1534	Sucre	1538
Lima	1535	Santiago	1541

It is inevitable, therefore, that the impress of such a long period should be a strong one, and the common characteristics of even very dissimilar countries are sufficient to give a broad unity to Latin America. This does not mean to say that the much older basis of an indigenous Indian population can be ignored. This is indeed one of the most fundamental contrasts with North America, where the original inhabitants of the continent play a very minor role in the human geography of the United States and Canada. In Latin America there are large areas occupied almost entirely by Indian peoples, and others where they contribute largely and often predominantly to the ethnic make-up of the inhabitants. The term 'Indo-America', therefore, can have·some significance, especially in

1

Fig. 1. *The colonial divisions and administration of Latin America*
The present political divisions have evolved from the colonial pattern of the
16th, 17th and 18th centuries

those parts of the continent where Indian languages, institutions and ways of life still persist.

The evolution of the present political pattern began almost immediately upon the discovery of the continent. The line of Tordesillas, a papal partition of 1494, effectively divided the new lands into a Spanish empire and a large Portuguese colony (Fig. 1). The latter was to grow thirty-five years later into the largest political unit of Latin America, Spain ceding Amazon territory to it in exchange for the Portuguese Philippines. Settlement in Brazil, however, remained largely coastal in character, and although large east–west strips were allocated in feudal *capitanias* stretching towards the interior, the plantations and towns of the coastal areas laid the basic population pattern which even still dominates the distribution of Brazilians today. Dutch, French and British attacks on a 4,500-mile coastline had periods of success, and for thirty years in the 17th century the Dutch held the best provinces of Brazil with Pernambuco as their capital. Their activities were finally forced northward into the remote region beyond the Amazon mouths, and the three Guiana colonies (the largest non-Latin fragments of Latin America) were the legacy of their intervention in the continent.

The process of Portuguese colonization was a gradual penetration westward, in which the scattered Indian peoples were incorporated or subdued without a major clash. The Spanish occupation of the rest of the continent was of a very different character, involving four principal conquests of pivotal regions of Indian resistance, and the subsequent spread of military, colonizing and missionary enterprise from these centres to the surrounding areas. The leaders or *conquistadores* of these expeditions, Cortés, Pizarro, Quesada and Valdivia, in thirty years (1520–50) subdued the Aztecs of Mexico, the Incas of Peru, the Chibchas of Colombia and the Araucanians of Mediterranean Chile (Fig. 2). Only by this means were colonial administrations established and great areas of territory consolidated into the Spanish domains. The areas of greatest Indian development and culture became the zones of effective Spanish colonization and exploitation of mineral and agricultural wealth. México City, Lima, Bogotá and Santiago became centres of primary administration, and a network of settlements grew from northern Mexico and the Spanish Main through Panamá and the Spanish ocean to the western outposts of Argentina in the Andean piedmont.

Upon the basis of conquest was established the Spanish colonial system which pervaded the social, economic and political life of

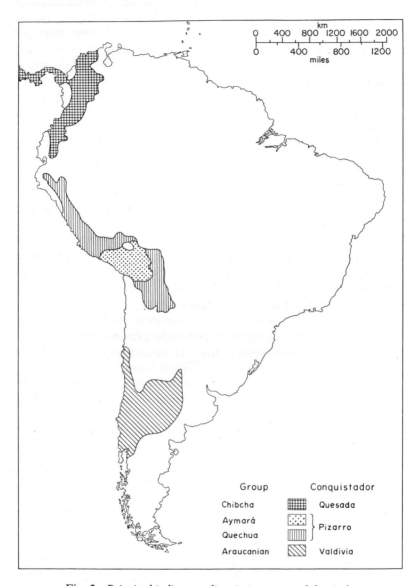

Fig. 2. *Principal indigenous linguistic groups of the Andes*
The areas occupied by these groups were the key zones in the conquest of
Spanish South America

Hispanic America. An administrative pattern took shape which in essence shaped the present political distribution of the continent today (Fig. 1). A system of large estates, of a landed minority and landless peasants grew up, which provides not only the *latifundia* problems from Guatemala to Chile but the basic social pattern in much of rural Latin America now. The dominance of the capital city in population and political and economic power began the centralist control and metropolitan concentrations which characterize most of the Latin American states at the present time. The religious, cultural and educational institutions were moulded on those of Spain.

The coming of Independence in the first thirty years of the 19th century at first changed this long-established colonial system but little. Allegiance to Spain was broken, but the pattern of social and economic life remained relatively unaltered. Slowly in many parts autocratic rule has given way to greater democracy; gradually a middle class has evolved; and in this century, the old pattern of primary agricultural and mineral production has been invaded by a growing industrialization. In the process, and as a result of varying factors of location, ethnic composition and physical endowment, the Latin American nations have tended to develop their own individual characteristics, so that in spite of their fundamental historical unity increasingly divergent forces separate them into some two dozen nations.

One of the major distributions essential to an understanding of the political and economic development of these nations is that of their racial composition (Fig. 3). In Latin America as a whole six classifications of principal ethnic ingredients together form the population, but in many states one or two only of these are significant. In Brazil alone do all six contribute sizeable numbers to its total 95 million people. The elements in order of their appearance on the Latin American scene are:

1. THE INDIANS

Differing greatly in the degree of their cultural development and ranging from stone age hunters to the once advanced Maya people of southern Mexico and Guatemala, the Indians still form the basic element over large areas of Amazonia, the Andes and Middle America. Today they probably number some 40 millions, fairly equally divided between South and Middle America.

Fig. 3. *Ethnic framework of Latin America*
Racial diversity is greater than that in any other continent

2. THE IBERIANS

The three centuries of Spanish and Portuguese colonial occupation and the continuing attraction of republics with a common language and cultural tradition have made the people from the Iberian peninsula the most numerous European element in the continent. While estimates are little more than intelligent guess-work, it is probable that the pure descendants of Portuguese and Spaniards do not exceed the total of the Indians, a third of their number being in Argentina and Uruguay.

3. THE NEGROES

Finding in many areas the Indian labour supply insufficient for the plantation system they were establishing, the Iberians imported large numbers of African slaves. In north-east Brazil, the West Indies and the Caribbean coastlands the descendants of these immigrants form a substantial proportion of the population, and in all Latin America they number probably 35 millions.

4. THE MIXED ELEMENTS

It is, however, the blending of these three principal types, Indian, Iberian and Negro, that accounts for the majority of Latin Americans today. The *mestizo* or Iberian-Indian mixture is the largest single element in the continent's population, numbering some 110 millions or one-third of the total. The mixtures obviously vary considerably from those predominantly Indian to those largely Iberian, the average Paraguayan or Mexican mestizo, for example, being more Indian than the Chilean or Uruguayan type. The Iberian-Negro mixture, or *mulatto*, is less numerous and is chiefly represented in Brazil and the West Indies, a product of the plantation system in those areas. An estimate of 30 millions is an approximation, but the varying degrees of mixture ranging from almost complete Iberian to 99 per cent Negroid make such estimates open to a big margin of error. The Indian-Negro mixtures known as *zambos* or *cafusos* represent but a relatively small proportion of the Latin Americans, for the fact that Negroes were imported into areas lacking an adequate supply of Indian labour indicates that rarely did these two groups exist in large numbers together. Where the Negroes have moved westward in Brazil and in other frontier areas zambos occur more abundantly.

5. THE NEW EUROPEAN IMMIGRANTS

Since Independence, and especially in the last hundred years, considerable numbers of other European immigrants have peopled the continent, in addition to the steady flow of Iberians, which has been a persistent and permanent characteristic throughout four and a half centuries. Italians have been the largest single national group, but Germans, Poles, Swiss, French, British and many from south and eastern Europe have all contributed to the movement. While relatively small numbers of these are found in every Latin American state, the main concentrations are in southern Brazil, Uruguay, Argentina and south middle Chile, lands which have been largely settled and opened up by this new tide of immigrants. Because these areas were for the most part empty and neglected by the early Iberian colonists, and because their sparse Indian populations have been greatly reduced or eliminated, the new immigrants form the great mass of the population and there is relatively little racial mixture with the other ethnic elements. They number another 40 millions.

6. THE NEW ASIATIC ELEMENTS

Even more recently, and particularly in the 20th century, Brazil especially has received an influx of Japanese colonists who have settled mainly in the state of São Paulo. With the abolition of slavery in the British and Dutch Empires, Indians from India, Chinese and Javanese were imported to form a labour supply for the plantations of Trinidad and British and Dutch Guiana. Chinese and Japanese occur in most of the principal ports, and a widely-representative gathering of Middle-Eastern Asiatic groups, Syrians and Lebanese especially, form an element in the principal capital cities. These new Asiatic groups probably total some three million people.

The complexity of this ethnic distribution is increased by the widespread scale of the racial mixture which has taken place. As a result there are few racial antagonisms of any significance. The differences which do occur are largely the outcome of social classes, based on economic, educational and cultural distinctions. Latin America is thus singularly fortunate in being relatively free of the racial problems which beset so much of the world.

CHAPTER TWO

The Physical Endowment

I T is inevitable that Latin America, created as a result of historical forces, should overlap a number of major structural regions and distinct physical environments. Outstanding in this respect is the contrast between the north–south trending mountain system of the Andes and the east–west relief lines of the major islands of the West Indies and their continuations into Middle America. Farther north the predominant pattern of North America, continued south across the United States–Mexican boundary, dominates the physique of most of Mexico.

It is within this three-fold composition that the physical basis of the continent can be outlined (Figs. 4, 5 and 6).

1. THE NORTH AMERICAN CONTINUATION

The long trend lines of Lower California and the Sierras Madre Occidental and Oriental emphasize that the Río Grande merely cuts obliquely across a region which in essentials of physical landscape is the same on both sides of the boundary. It is a region of folded and faulted blocks separated either by deep troughs such as the Gulf of California or by extensive plateaux like that of northern Mexico. Similarly, the coastal plain of the Gulf of Mexico forms a unity on both sides of the frontier, in spite of its more narrow and restricted area south of Texas.

The natural resources of metals in the highlands and of petroleum in the coastal zone emphasize the economic implications of the bisection of this one major region. It is worth recalling that not much more than a century ago Latin America spread considerably farther north into this structurally unified region, these extensions being lopped off by the westward expansion of the United States across the continent.

Climatically the extension of desert conditions into the north-western and central zones of northern Mexico shows a unity with the deserts of Arizona and south-eastern California. The rainier conditions of the Sierra Madre Occidental are similar to the western sierras

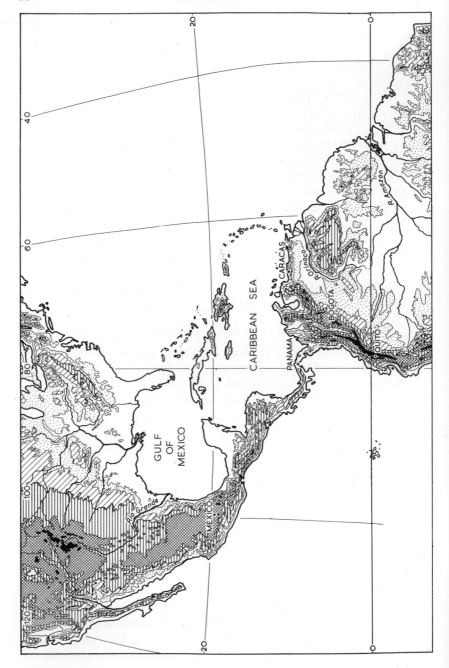

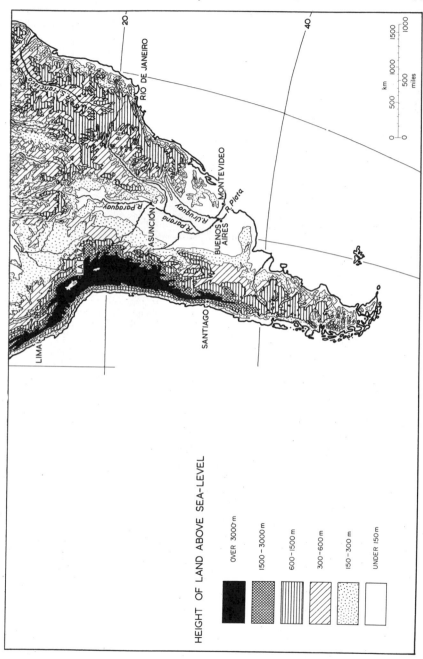

Fig. 4. *The relief of Latin America*

Fig. 5. *The physiographic régions of Latin America*
This attempts to convey the major types of landscape, based on relief and
vegetational cover

Fig. 6. *The forests of Latin America*
Vast expanses of hardwoods cover much of the continent

of the United States, and the eastern Mexico coastal plain receives the same indraught of rain-bearing winds from the Gulf as do the plains of eastern Texas.

2. THE ANTILLEAN COMPLEX

Approximately on the parallel of 18°N. latitude a new pattern establishes itself, a pattern of east–west ranges, of island arcs, of limestone platforms and all the associated phenomena of tectonic instability, volcanoes, earthquakes and deep submarine troughs from which tower great mountain ranges. The structural evolution of this zone of Middle America is but imperfectly known, but the foundering of an old central continental area and the creation of folded and block mountains on its margins is the basis of the resulting pattern.

Within the tropics and invaded by the Caribbean sea and all its branches, there is a certain uniformity of climatic conditions giving high and equable temperatures and a generally plentiful rainfall from the north-east trade winds. The Pacific coastlands are somewhat drier, but in only a few areas is shortage of water a problem. Of more significance are the variations dependent on altitude and windward and leeward aspects. Hurricanes are a common peril, but the West Indian islands athwart their paths receive the most frequent impact of these tropical storms.

3. SOUTH AMERICAN CORDILLERA, PLATEAUX AND PLAINS

The South American component of Latin America is relatively simple in its construction, consisting of the great Cordillera of the Andes, the plateaux of Brazil–Guiana and the intervening river plains of the Orinoco, Amazon and Paraná–Paraguay.

(a) *The Cordillera of the Andes*

This great mountain system stretching from eastern Venezuela to Cape Horn, for thousands of miles over 10,000 feet in height (and exceeding 23,000 feet in Aconcagua) and rarely less than 200 miles wide, is one of the greatest mountain regions of the world. Strewn with volcanoes, torn into separate ranges by violent river torrents, and capped by glaciers and ice sheets, the basic structure is that of a great longitudinal western batholith paralleled by an eastern zone of sedimentary and metamorphic rocks. The areas most favourable to settlement are the mountain-surrounded basins formed either by the work of rivers or by tectonic forces.

A great zone of aridity sweeps diagonally across the system from the Pacific shores through Peru, Chile, Bolivia and Argentina to the Atlantic margins of Patagonia; but in its northern and southern extensions the Cordillera receives a plentiful precipitation from convectional and westerly winds respectively. Variations of temperature through 5,000 miles of latitude are made even more complex by variations of altitude and aspect, a mosaic equally reflected in the vegetational distributions which result.

(b) The Plateaux of Brazil and Guiana

The crystalline foundation of the continent is revealed in the plateaux of Brazil and Guiana, great elevated and peneplained surfaces, which by their altitude make large areas within the tropics available for human settlement. Once part of a much larger land mass, the Brazilian plateau is now truncated by a bold Atlantic-facing scarp which inevitably makes access to the interior from the coast a difficult matter. It is over this scarp that the São Francisco river, after a sluggish course on the plateau, plunges seaward at the Paulo Afonso falls.

The highest parts of the plateau are in Venezuelan Guiana, where often great residual areas stand abruptly above the general plateau level. Other resistant rounded hills stand out as sandstone sierras above the gneisses, schists and granites of its foundation, evidence of a once much more extensive sedimentary cover.

Like the Andean Cordillera these highland areas are great storehouses of mineral wealth, ranging from the vast iron reserves of Brazil and Venezuela to the bauxite mines of the Guianas.

Covering such a vast area there can be little climatic unity, but over much of this plateau expanse savana conditions, as represented by the Venezuelan *llanos* and the Brazilian *campos*, reflect the predominantly summer rainfall of a major region which for the most part receives adequate precipitation.

(c) The River Lowlands

Three great river systems draining eastward to the Atlantic have built up an almost continuous riverine lowland which laps on to the gently dipping margins of the Brazilian–Guianan plateaux and fronts abruptly the mountain walls of the Cordillera. Most of the drainage of these two highland regions finds its way into these rivers, either into the great northward-flowing tributaries of the Amazon draining the heart of the Brazilian plateau, or by their southern counterparts into the Paraná–Paraguay, while the rushing torrents of the west tear into the Bolivian *yungas* and Peruvian *montaña* and so dissect the Cordillera.

The interfluves between Orinoco and Amazon and Paraguay are such inconspicuous features that the headwaters intermesh and, as in the renowned case of the Casiquiare, river capture can be seen in process. Changing from north to south through savana, equatorial forest and scrub forest to temperate grasslands, these lands represent some of the least used and least accessible portions of Latin America. The boundaries of eight of the republics meander through the unpopulated areas of this vast interior zone.

CHAPTER THREE

The Economic Endowment

THE combination of historical and physical environments has given rise to a cultural landscape developed by and related to a colonial economy. This is the essential concept in considering the economic endowment of Latin America. The historical trends, the physical resources and the political development all led to an economic structure based on exploitation. At first this meant the production of minerals, but later foodstuffs and raw materials in animal and vegetable form were channelled to the export markets. This picture is still the typical one of most of the Latin American republics, each state linked to one, and sometimes two, forms of primary production (Fig. 13). For Chile it is copper, Bolivia tin, Venezuela oil, Brazil coffee, Cuba sugar; and although variations have taken place within this pattern, the pattern has remained unaltered. Chile's copper has replaced its nitrates, while Brazil's agricultural booms have jumped from crop to crop, its monopoly of world rubber production early in this century being merely one example.

This heritage of primary raw material production will persist for a long time to come, but already two world wars and a great economic depression have contributed to a process of change. Latin America, finding its export markets so vulnerable to world catastrophes, and the sources of its manufactured imports cut off, has speeded the industrial revolution whereby it could become more self-sufficient in industrial products, often utilizing its own raw materials. The motives and the means by which it has accomplished the industrialization have been varied, but the twin objectives of freeing the economies of the republics from dependence on one product and of raising their standard of living have been dominant (Fig. 16).

The impact on the various republics has varied according to their size, resources, location and economy. Argentina, Brazil, Chile and Mexico have gone farthest on the road to industrialization, with Colombia, Venezuela, Peru and Cuba following in their steps. On a continental basis the supplies or potential supplies of most mineral, pastoral and agricultural raw materials are adequate for the growth of industry; and fuel and power resources in oil, natural gas and hydro-electric power are by no means small, although not always well distributed (Fig. 7). Except for Mexico and Colombia coal resources appear quite limited. A labour supply will be available, although increasing technical education will be needed to utilize it. It is in shortage of capital where the chief difficulties lie, as the possibilities of internal investment are as yet limited. Hence in most cases imports are controlled to protect and permit the growth of Latin America's industries, and the United States and many European nations are helping to provide the financial loans and capital equipment for a variety of industrial programmes.

Most progress has been made in the food-processing and textile industries which are the obvious and natural starting points, but in the post-war years modern integrated iron and steel plants have begun to supply the essential basis for a variety of other metal-using industries, especially in Brazil, Mexico, Argentina, Venezuela and Chile. Compared with the world's major industrial nations these are as yet but small beginnings, although their significance for the future is considerable. Apart from supplying their own domestic needs, export markets and inter-Latin American trade are slowly developing, and the first steps have been taken towards the establishment of a continental free-trade area.

The proximity of the United States has led to the growth of strong commercial and investment links between that country and Latin America, so that over one-third of all the continent's exports go to the United States which provides more than 40 per cent of all Latin America's imports. This is not an evenly distributed trade in respect of all the republics. The Middle American states, for example, with their greater proximity and output of tropical produce have closer commercial dependence on North America than the pastoral and agricultural producing republics of Argentina and Uruguay, which send only 10 per cent of their exports to the United States. The United Kingdom and the European Economic Community are the largest European buyers of Latin American exports, taking approximately 6 and 20 per cent of the total respectively. The EEC countries supply about 18 per cent and the United Kingdom about 5 per cent of the continent's needs. The larger purchases of commodities by the United Kingdom are principally accounted for by its trading connections with Argentina, Uruguay, Venezuela and the Caribbean islands. Western Germany is, however, a greater trading partner with Brazil, Mexico, Central America and all the Pacific republics.

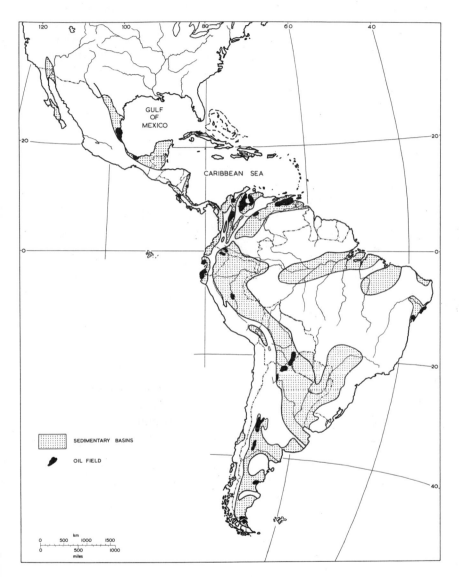

Fig. 7. *The sedimentary basins and oilfields of Latin America*
The basins are potentially petroliferous. The areas of the oilfields have
been exaggerated to indicate their location

Fig. 8. *The distribution of population in Latin America*
The high population densities of Middle America contrast with the empty
heart of the southern continent

Another factor of great importance in the total economic framework of Latin America is its rapidly growing population, increasing at a faster rate than that of any other continent. By 1975 population will total 330 millions which is approximately twice the number of Latin Americans in 1950. The agricultural labour force is not likely to increase, for further mechanization will reduce the demand for workers, and the most likely employment opportunities will be in industry.

There are, however, considerable differences both in the rate of population growth and the present population distribution in the major sections of Latin America, as the following summary indicates:

Area	Annual growth rate 1963–70	Density per square mile
Tropical South America	3·1	26
Mainland Middle America	3·5	65
Temperate South America	1·8	23
Caribbean	2·3	267

The pattern of population distribution in the continent still reveals the sparsely settled interior, and confronts Latin America with another problem, that of providing the incentives, transport and financial means whereby its undeveloped lands may also contribute to the economic growth of the continent (Figs. 8, 9 and 10). The problem of relatively underdeveloped countries providing housing, education, food and other services for an additional 8 million folk annually, in addition to the task of combating deficiencies in all these fields for their present populations, is, however, a continuous brake on the availability of finance for further economic development.

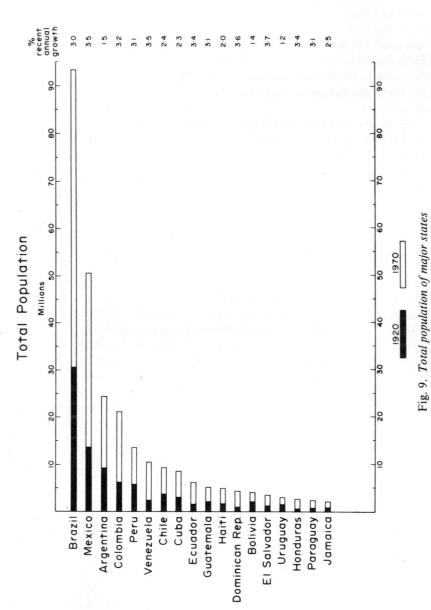

Fig. 9. *Total population of major states*

Most republics have tripled their population in the last half century, Argentina, Uruguay and Bolivia being the major exceptions

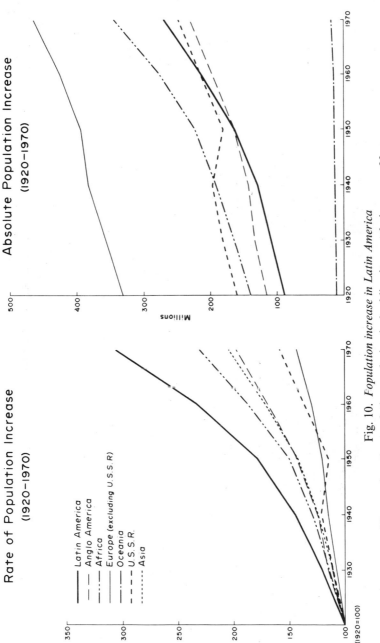

Rate of Population Increase (1920–1970)

Absolute Population Increase (1920–1970)

Latin America
Anglo America
Africa
Europe (excluding U.S.S.R.)
Oceania
U.S.S.R.
Asia

Fig. 10. *Population increase in Latin America*

The continent's population explosion is doubling its population every 23 years

Plate 1. *Rural-urban migration has created on the fringes of most large cities vast shanty-towns which now house 30 million Latin Americans. A Venezuelan example*

Fig. 11. *The international railway systems of Latin America*
Only in the extra-tropical areas are international rail links important. There
are few transcontinental railways and many countries have no rail connections with their neighbours

Fig. 12. *The international road links of Latin America*

Although the Pan-American Highway has many important gaps, the road connections linking the twenty republics have developed considerably in this century

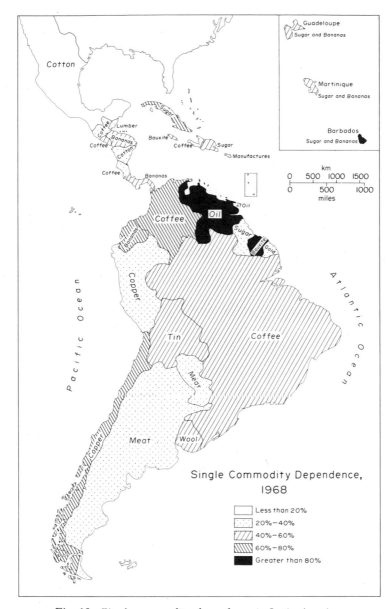

Fig. 13. *Single commodity dependence in Latin America*
Of the major republics only Mexico has a diversified export pattern

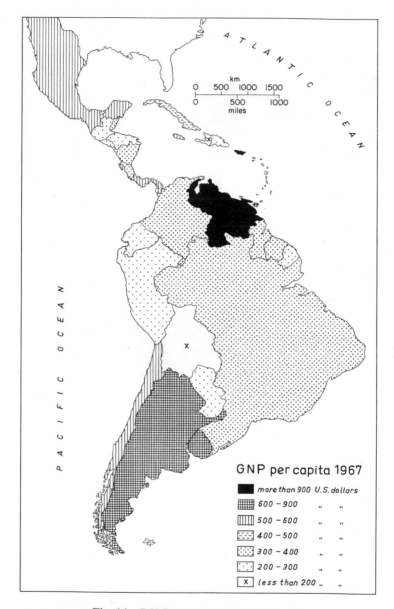

Fig. 14. *G.N.P. per capita, Latin America*
Economic production in most republics has only just kept pace with
population growth

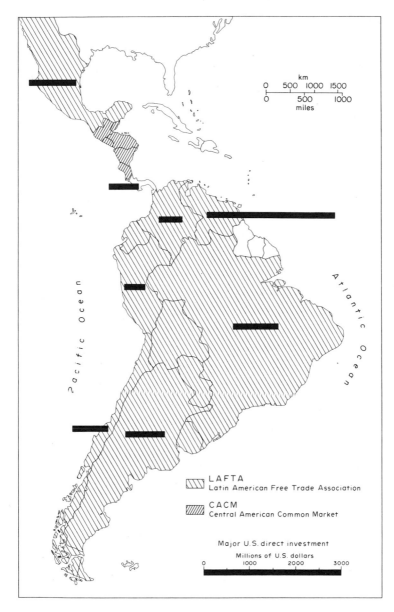

Fig. 15. *Economic co-operation and U.S. investment in Latin America*

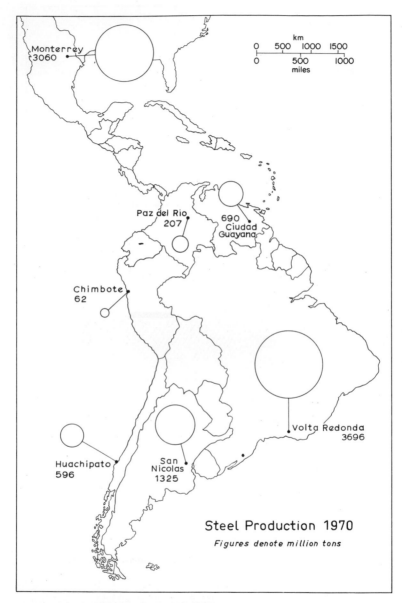

Fig. 16. *Steel production in Latin America*
Each of the major republics has developed heavy industry since the Second
World War

PART I

MIDDLE AMERICA

CHAPTER FOUR

General Introduction to Middle America

I T is important to distinguish the term 'Middle America' from the more common use of 'Central America', which refers only to the six small republics and one colony between Mexico and Colombia. Middle America embraces Central America and Mexico and the West Indies, and thus includes nearly one-third of all Latin Americans and its second most populous nation. Containing structural features associated both with North America and the Antilles, and a very wide range of climatic and vegetational zones dependent on great variations of altitude and aspect, it can in no sense be considered as one physical region. It is a major human unit of Latin America in which the impact of historical events since the days of Columbus has resulted in a certain unity of experience. These are the lands of the Spanish Main, where Spanish control was first introduced, where new settlements were first established and where a new political system was imposed on a varied basis of indigenous Indian cultures. Until 1914 (and to a large extent even since) these lands have been united by their common orientation to the Caribbean. Only in a few exceptional cases do the Pacific coastlands participate in the significant stages of historical, economic and political development; and the realization of their potentialities is a most recent chapter in the evolution of the region.

Into this Caribbean scene have infiltrated throughout the centuries Anglo-Saxon, French, Dutch and North American interests, commercial, economic, colonizing and strategic; and they have succeeded to a greater or less extent in changing the typical Latin American characteristics of the region. This process has gone farthest in the case of the smaller islands of the West Indies, but the influence of alien penetration can be seen in the banana plantations of Central America, and in the mainland colony of Belize. The external influences indeed altered the political map by the secession of Panama from Colombia, and the dismemberment of the peripheral regions of northern Mexico, from which were created the south-western states of the United States. In no other region of Latin

America has foreign intervention in internal political struggles been so frequent and undisguised.

This association with North America and Europe has profoundly affected the social, economic and political geography of the whole region. The presence of a large negroid population, the legacies of slavery and plantation agriculture, strategic bases, the tourist trade, an inter-oceanic canal and the birth of new nations are all examples of the developments related to those external influences.

Middle America has been likened to the Mediterranean of the Old World, and indeed on its shores arose the oldest and most advanced civilization of Latin America, that of the Mayas. When the Panama Canal was cut, the Caribbean was transformed into a great through route (as the Suez Canal did for the Mediterranean) which increased outside interest and influence in the region.

Yet the area in its fundamentals of an indigenous Indian foundation on which the framework of the Spanish colonial system was built, remains Latin American. It symbolizes in fact the variety and range of Latin American developments in the political, social and economic fields. Here are the first scenes of European colonization and the last remnants of the system; here occurred the first and last emancipations from Spain; here are examples of old-fashioned military dictatorships and progressive democracies; here survive the feudal *haciendas* and the new *ejidos* or community farms which have replaced them; here exist primitive slash-and-burn agriculture and modern mechanized farming; side by side occur modern steelworks and long-established domestic handicrafts, the modern arterial road and the village footpath, dependence on mineral extraction and increasingly successful diversified economies.

In one particular way its problems are more urgent than those of the rest of Latin America, in that the pressure of population on the region's resources is greater than in the continent to the south. There are less unoccupied lands, more areas of chronic over-population, and faster growing numbers in most of the states constituting the region.

CHAPTER FIVE

Mexico

WITH an area exceeding three-quarters of a million square miles Mexico is the third largest country of Latin America, only Brazil and Argentina being larger. With a population of 50 millions it stands second only to Brazil, which has approximately twice that number of people. Before the annexation of Texas in 1845 and the war of 1846–7 with the United States, the area of Mexico was more than twice as great, extending over the area now included in the states of Texas, New Mexico, Arizona, Colorado, Utah, Nevada and California. Its present northern boundary was defined only some one hundred and twenty years ago, in 1853, and the similarity of culture, language, peoples and economic interests on both sides of this boundary is still striking in spite of the differing political evolution in the past century. The land frontier of over 1,600 miles, however, is more than a boundary between two independent republics. It is a zone where Latin America ends and Anglo-America begins, and the links between the Mexican and American peoples are far weaker than those between the United States and its northern neighbour, Canada. Unlike the zone of the Canadian-United States boundary, the Mexican-United States boundary runs for the most part through empty territory and is a barrier rather than a zone of contact (Fig. 8). There is only one major exception to this, along the route of the Inter-American highway to México City, where with increased motor transport North American influences are spreading into Mexico as they have spread across the northern frontier into Canada (Fig. 12). Although in terms of physical geography Mexico is largely a southward continuation of the United States, in terms of human geography it is a northward continuation of Latin America, and its historical, cultural and economic affinities with the twenty-three republics south and east of it are clearly dominant.

Structurally, the extension southward of the major physical units of the western United States dominates the build of the northern half of Mexico. All the physical units north of the boundary, between

Texas and California, have their counterparts south of the international frontier, in the following manner:

United States	*Mexico*
Texas coastal plain	Gulf coastal plain
The Rockies	Sierra Madre Oriental
Basin and Range Province	North Mexican plateau
Salton Trough	Gulf of California
Sierra Nevada	Baja California
Pacific Coast Ranges	Sierra Santa Clara

Between 18° and 20°N. a transverse east–west zone of volcanic peaks, known as the Sierra Volcánica Transversal terminates this parallel alignment of north–south structural units. From the point of view of structure North America can be considered to end in this range, for south of it the great structural trend lines are east–west, and, physically, Southern Mexico is thus closely linked with Central America and the West Indies (Figs. 25 and 30). Its southern boundary with Guatemala is in every sense an artificial one (Fig. 26).

It is not easy, therefore, to delineate a scheme which permits a consideration of the major regional units of Mexico without being aware of the many drawbacks of any such classification. Although containing many important sub-divisions, the country will be divided into eight large units as indicated in Figure 17:

   (i) The Gulf Coastal Plain and Sierra Madre Oriental.
  (ii) The Northern Plateaux.
 (iii) The Sierra Madre Occidental.
 (iv) The North–west Pacific Coast.
  (v) Lower California.
 (vi) The Central Mesetas.
(vii) Southern Mexico.
(viii) The Yucatán peninsula.

THE GULF COASTAL PLAIN AND
SIERRA MADRE ORIENTAL

The coastal plain of eastern Mexico is a region very different from all the other regions of the country (Fig. 20). As so frequently occurs in the predominantly highland republics of Latin America, the recognition and utilization of the economic assets of this lowland

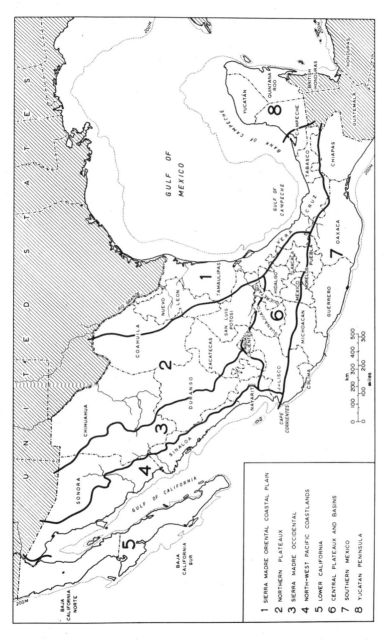

Fig. 17. *The regions and states of Mexico*

1 SIERRA MADRE ORIENTAL COASTAL PLAIN
2 NORTHERN PLATEAUX
3 SIERRA MADRE OCCIDENTAL
4 NORTH-WEST PACIFIC COASTLANDS
5 LOWER CALIFORNIA
6 CENTRAL PLATEAUX AND BASINS
7 SOUTHERN MEXICO
8 YUCATAN PENINSULA

portion is largely a feature of the 20th century. For Cortés it was a region to be passed through as quickly as possible, and for centuries the disadvantages of the *tierra caliente*, especially exemplified in the danger of yellow fever, were powerful deterrents to settlement.

Partitioned into the three coastal states of Tamaulipas, Veracruz and Tabasco, the plain extends for more than 750 miles from Piedras Negras on the Río Grande to Ciudad del Cármen where it opens out into the Yucatán peninsula. It is widest at these two extremities, adjoining the Río Grande and along the southern shores of the Gulf of Campeche, north-east of the isthmus of Tehuantepec. Towards its central southern portion it is considerably narrower, and between Tampico and Veracruz it rarely exceeds 20 miles in width. Fringed throughout much of its length by mangrove swamps, off-shore sand bars, lagoons and coral reefs, the coast is not an hospitable one, and the two major ports created upon it, Tampico and Veracruz, are the result of heavy expenditure to prevent their silting up. Laguna de la Madre in the northern part of the plain and Laguna de Tampico are

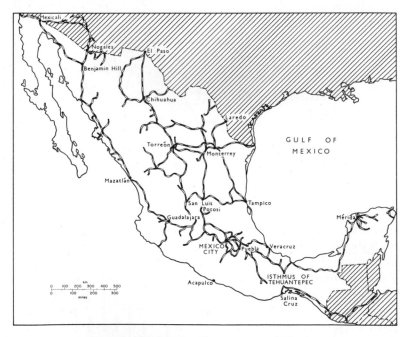

Fig. 18. *The trunk railway system of Mexico*

Half of Mexico's trade enters and leaves the country across its boundary with the United States. Only Argentina and Brazil have a greater mileage of lines

examples of the amphibious nature of the coast; and the many rivers discharge their loads of sediment into these and on the continental shelf, thus slowly extending its width seaward. In historical times the Tamesi and Pánuco rivers have united their mouths south of Tampico. Aided by small vertical uplift, deposition throughout Tertiary and Quaternary times has been the method of formation of the plain, and masses of sediments, alluvial and marine, partially mantle the last easternmost folds of the Sierra Madre Oriental and the volcanic necks and laccoliths which become more and more frequent as the plain approaches the great volcanic Sierra Volcánica Transversal. The Tuxtla volcano is the most conspicuous example in the far south standing out above the river plains and lagoons of Papaloapan and Coatzacoalcos.

The upper courses of the many rivers crossing the northern plain often reveal the underlying north–south orientation of the outer folds, but their lower courses form a series of parallel streams which drain the eastern sierra to the Gulf and divide the plain into rectangular sub-regions progressively rainier and hotter towards the Gulf of Campeche, as these statistics indicate:

AVERAGE TEMPERATURE (°F.)

	January	July	Annual	Rainfall (inches)
Corpus Christi	57	83	70	28
Tampico	66	82	75	45
Veracruz	70	81	77	60

Three-quarters of the rain falls in the months June–October.

There is likewise a progressive deterioration in vegetation as one passes from the selva and semi-deciduous forests of Tabasco through the savana of Veracruz to the grasslands and dry steppes of northern Tamaulipas (Fig. 19). It is this climatic and vegetational differentiation of the plain which strongly influences its present land utilization.

Of the three states making up the coastal plain, Veracruz is most important, the scarcity of rain in Tamaulipas and its excess in Tabasco proving deterrents to widespread occupance. Much of the tropical produce of Mexico is derived from Veracruz. Crops of maize, beans, rice, oranges, tobacco and tropical fruits are of very great importance, and the banana plantations of the Coatepec area, the vanilla production of Papantla, the coffee estates of Coatepec and Córdoba, where the trees are grown in the shade of orange trees, are among the most important in Mexico; and the republic obtains a

Middle America

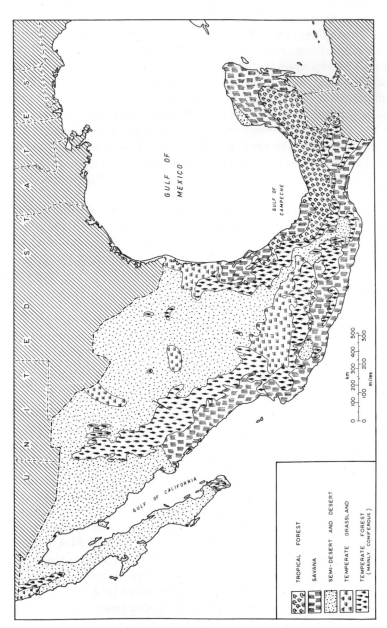

Fig. 19. *The vegetational zones of Mexico* (after Vivó)

great proportion of its sugar supply from this region. It is also one of the major cattle and pig-raising areas.

In Tabasco crops of cocoa, rice, bananas and coconuts dominate the agricultural scene, while in the drier conditions of Tamaulipas cotton grown under irrigation from the Río Grande in the Matamoros area and sugar cane in the El Mante district are the principal arable products.

While in some cases such as cotton, cocoa and coffee, yields are high, the region suffers like so many Latin American regions from lack of means to modernize its agriculture, and there is little doubt that with mechanization, improved seeds, soil surveys, land drainage and generally improved housing and health facilities this region (especially areas with volcanic-derived soils) could become one of the greatest zones of tropical agriculture in the Americas, besides supplying a far greater proportion of the food requirements of the Mexican people than it does at present.

Nor is its economic value limited to agriculture and pastoralism, for this is the zone from which is derived Mexico's not inconsiderable production of petroleum and natural gas. The principal oilfield is that of Poza Rica in the state of Veracruz south of Tuxpan, which accounts for approximately 31 per cent of Mexican output. Faja de Oro produces about 8 per cent, Ebano-Pánuco 3 per cent and the new Tabascan fields together some 28 per cent (Fig. 20).

This great oilfield was the first major oil-producing area of Latin America, and in the second decade of this century its expansion was remarkably rapid. By 1921 Mexico was exporting more than one-fifth of world exports of petroleum. During the following quarter-century there was a considerable decline so that production in the 1940s was less than a quarter that of 1921. This was due to the exhaustion of the producing wells, the lack of development of other areas, and difficulties between the Mexican Government and the American and British companies which controlled 95 per cent of the industry before the expropriation of their interests in 1938.

Lacking trained personnel and adequate equipment, for ten years the industry experienced a period of arrested development, but in recent years the Mexican oil company, Petróleos Mexicanos, with the help of contract drilling by other foreign concerns, has expanded production very considerably, and it continues to grow by some 10 per cent annually. The principal achievement of the last decade has been the opening up of Tabasco as a major oil-producing state, four large fields now being located there. The submarine extensions

Plate 2. *The methods employed on many of Mexico's farms are still primitive.* (Left) *Winnowing wheat, and* (below) *grinding sugar cane at Montemorelos in the eastern region*

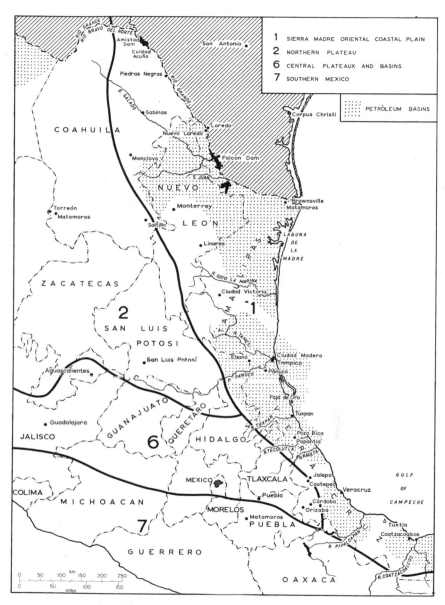

Fig. 20. *The regions of Eastern Mexico*

of the Gulf fields, off the mouths of the Pánuco and Tuxpan rivers, now yield one-quarter of Mexico's annual output. Although this represents only about 1¼ per cent of world production (and is still about 70 per cent of the volume obtained in 1921), the republic is Latin America's second producer of petroleum.

Figures 7 and 20 indicate the considerable areas which are potentially oil-bearing, and the proved reserves in 1968 indicate adequate petroleum for a further twenty years at present rate of production. All but 10 per cent of present output is now consumed within Mexico, the Government encouraging its use in industry and for domestic fuel to reduce deforestation for charcoal production, which has caused so many problems of soil erosion and lack of water conservation. The principal port for the export of petroleum is Tampico, and all except two of Mexico's refineries are situated in the coastal zone.

The significance of the coastal zone in the commercial life of the republic is indicated by the fact that half of Mexico's imports enter its ports and frontier points, Nuevo Laredo on the Río Grande accounting for 32 per cent and Veracruz for another 20 per cent (Figs. 11, 12 and 18). Over one-third of the country's exports also pass through the four towns of Matamoros (10 per cent), Veracruz (13 per cent), Tampico (8 per cent) and Nuevo Laredo (6 per cent). Thus the trade across a land frontier is as great as that entering or leaving maritime ports, a unique phenomenon in Latin America. Veracruz (200,000) is by far Mexico's greatest seaport, and until rail and road transport orientated more trade northward its relative significance was even greater, stemming from its historical impetus as the terminus of the Spanish fleet's annual trading voyage to supply all its northern and trans-Pacific empire. Overcoming by means of breakwaters its site on a reef and silt-encumbered coast, its flat location has given it unlimited scope for expansion. Fundamental however has been its proximity to the capital and the crowded populations of the Mesetas Centrales which are served by the railway via Jalapa (Fig. 23).

In a similar way Tampico (155,000), with the great petroleum centre of Ciudad Madero (138,000) adjoining it, serves as the port of Northern Mexico, and its rail connections with the mining and industrial cities of San Luis Potosí (190,000) and Monterrey (1,200,000) have been important influences in determining this. The petroleum exploitation adjoining the city in this century has been another factor in its rapid growth.

On the coastal plain and the sierra slopes there developed in the earliest period of Mexico's indigenous cultures the most advanced group of La Venta, and the influence of its later populations, Olmecs, Toltecs, Náhuas and Aztecs, on the Highland and Maya cultures was of considerable significance.

Veracruz is the most densely peopled of all the coastal states of Mexico, containing 3¾ million people with an average density of 130 per square mile, but there are considerable variations. The *tierra templada*, especially around Jalapa (66,000) and Orizaba (80,000) and on the lower slopes away from the level lowland, support larger numbers than the *tierra caliente*, and the southern coastal extensions of the state are more thinly peopled than its north and centre. The integrated Papaloapan development scheme is already ensuring a fuller use of these potentially rich lands of the south, and a beginning has been made with a similar plan in the Grijalva–Usumacinta basin in the states of Tabasco and Chiapas (Fig. 52).

Tamaulipas has over 1½ million people and Tabasco 800,000. The latter state with its *selvas* conditions suffers from the disabilities for agricultural use inherent in such areas, but it is not unlikely that further discoveries of petroleum there will increase its economic significance if not its population and settlement. Tamaulipas was relatively neglected until the last half-century of the colonial period, when a Spanish cattle hacienda economy replaced the hunting pattern of its indigenous inhabitants. The region is now being more fully utilized and a new irrigation scheme using the waters of the Soto la Marina will enable more productive use of 100,000 acres there. In the valley of the Río Grande and its tributaries the Salado and San Juan considerable crops of cotton, maize and string beans are raised, and many thousands of acres are irrigated, the largest scheme being completed in 1953 by which the Falcón Dam waters 700,000 acres on the Mexican side of the international boundary. A similar scheme providing flood control and irrigation in the area round Ciudad Acuña, the Amistad Dam, was completed in 1969. These developments are leading to new settlements and increased population, and the growing importance of Mexico's two land ports, Nuevo Laredo (142,000) and Matamoros (176,000), where several 'export only' industries have been set up add to the economic strength of Tamaulipas. The state's population increased by over 60 per cent during the 1950–60 decade, almost twice the average rate of increase for the nation as a whole; a further 45 per cent increase occurred in the 1960–70 decade.

Few Europeans live in this coastal region, and they are concentrated mainly in the ports and coffee plantations. The bulk of the population is mestizo with an important Negro and mulatto element.

The eastern slopes of the Sierra Madre Oriental are best included as an extension of the Gulf coastal plain, for although rising to 12,750 feet in the latitude of the Tropic, the influence of the Gulf climatic and vegetational conditions is maintained. Structurally the use of the word sierra is rather deceptive, for nowhere is it the bold and continuous range of the Cordillera Madre Occidental, but rather a faulted, broken and eroded folded scarp margin of the plateau, its edges rising little above the level of the plateau on the west, and its eastern slopes mantled with coastal deposits. The down-throw of this great north–south fault limiting the plateau is believed to be as much as 4,000 feet. A complex series of east–west and north–south rugged limestone ranges have been deeply dissected by the rivers draining eastward, and in these depressions and valleys occur the principal settlements. Two considerations favour this location, firstly, that the humid conditions of the Gulf coast spread into these valleys, permitting the cultivation of tierra templada crops. Rainfall is not abundant but with careful use, and aided by irrigation south of Monclova, it is sufficient for agriculture. Secondly, the dissection of the plateau edge has not made communications with the plateau easy, and it is by means of the depressions that transport routes are funnelled through passes westward from the Texas and Tamaulipas Gulf plain. Linares and Victoria occupy such entrance sites permitting plateau–lowland communication, and the route from Tampico up the Pánuco valley to San Luis Potosí is another such artery which links the highland mining camps with the Gulf. Another from the Río Grande passes southward through Monclova, but the rapidly expanding city of Monterrey is the best example of such a route centre, for its dominance became certain when the international railway from Texas via Nuevo Laredo utilized the gap it controlled to reach the plateau. It is now a great route centre controlling roads in many directions, including the Inter-American highway (Fig. 12). Other factors which have contributed to make Monterrey the third city of Mexico and second in industrial output are connected with its location in respect of mineral resources. It is the largest centre for lead production, which for long was Mexico's principal metal export. Output continues to decline, although it is still second only to silver in importance. Far more important however is Monterrey's development as the great iron and steel manufacturing centre of

Mexico (second only in production in Latin America to that of Brazil's Volta Redonda), and together with Monclova producing nearly all the republic's iron and steel output (Fig. 16). The iron ore is brought from the Cerro de Mercado in Durango state, which is Mexico's largest reserve (estimated to exceed 70 million tons), and from Golondrinas in Nuevo León. It is smelted with coal from Sabinas in Coahuila, which, while Secondary in age, is of good coking quality. Total production of iron and steel in 1969 exceeded 3,750,000 tons, almost one-third of Latin American output. A great network of manufacturing industries has also been established in Monterrey, producing consumer goods such as cigarettes, beer, furniture, glassware and tiles, and it has undoubtedly become the great urban nucleus of all northern Mexico, receiving the agricultural and mineral production of a vast zone and distributing manufactured and imported goods in return.

Extending over the eastern part of the states of Coahuila and San Luis Potosí and throughout Nuevo León, the Sierra Madre Oriental supports few settlements other than the mining, manufacturing or route centres already indicated. Subsistence farming is practised on the steep slopes of the ridges forming the Sierra, and market gardening on the slopes between Monterrey and Linares, growing crops of wheat, oranges, sugar cane and vegetables for the urban populations of the zone. The Montemorelos region is the premier orange-growing district of Mexico.

South of the Pánuco basin the Sierra swinging south-eastward, with peaks rising to over 10,000 feet, merges into the volcanic ranges of the Sierra Volcánica Transversal, and the steep slopes of the Orizaba region approach close to the coast in the Veracruz area. Here, with its abundant rainfall, is one of the regions of greatest hydro-electric power potential in Mexico, and 16 per cent of the republic's reserves occur in the Tuxpán, Tecolutla and Nautla basins, a similar potential occurring in the river basins south of this zone.

THE NORTHERN PLATEAUX

This great north-central region of Mexico (Figs. 20 and 21) stretches from the northern boundary to the high volcanic plateaux of central Mexico, and is enclosed on east and west by the Sierras Madre Oriental and Occidental. It includes the greater part of the states of Chihuahua, Coahuila, Durango, Zacatecas and San Luis Potosí, and is thus in area the largest of the great natural regions of Mexico.

Structurally it consists of great mesetas or uplifted blocks in some ways resembling the Great Basin of Utah. The height of the plateaux of which it is composed is extremely variable, ranging from 1,150 feet in Coahuila to 8,240 feet in Zacatecas, indicating arid peneplanation, with each unit reaching its own base level. Such desert weathering and erosion is still at work throughout most of the region. Crossing the plateaux, especially in the north, are folded and faulted block ranges, mainly of Cretaceous age and aligned principally on the dominant north-west–south-east strike, except where laccoliths have displaced this axis. The latter evidence of vulcanism is more prevalent in the north, while in the south outpourings of lava often mask the underlying structures. Some of the block mountains rise 5,000 feet above the intervening *bolsones* especially on the plateau's southern margins.

Throughout the region there has been extensive sedimentation which is still in process either in the form of æolian deposition in the north or in the form of great alluvial fans and desert screes deposited by the many rivers in the lower parts of the mesetas; and the region's western and southern surfaces are largely mantled with these recent products of erosion of the Sierra Madre Occidental.

More important than structure in giving the region a unity are the qualities of aridity and interior drainage. Its climate is characterized by its low rainfall, which rarely exceeds 20 inches as these statistics indicate:

Town	inches
Saltillo	17·6
San Luis Potosí	13·9
Chihuahua	15·4
Durango	18·0
Zacatecas	20·2

Amounts increase westward and southward, and it is increasing rainfall which is largely the factor delimiting it from the Central Plateaux, south of 22°N. Most of the rain occurs during July, August and September in heavy downpours, the air masses from the Gulf of Mexico releasing the greatest quantities on the inner slopes of the Sierra Madre Occidental by orographic uplift. It is the combination of marked summer maximum rainfall, large diurnal temperature ranges, and low humidity which mark these north Mexican plateaux as one of the finest examples in the world of semi-desert conditions (Fig. 19).

Vegetation varies considerably from the steppes of the southern margins through the xerophytic yucca and cactus scrub of the north to the coniferous forests of the Sierra Madre Occidental, the grass-chaparral of the upper Nazas valley in the sierra piedmont and in the Conchos valley, and the sand dunes of the boundary zone west of Ciudad Juárez. All the drainage is derived from the western sierra, the eastern bolsones of Mapimi and San Luis Potosí being largely devoid of surface streams. With the exception of the Conchos river system which has been captured by the Río Grande, nearly all this drainage from the west never reaches the sea, but after cutting its way through the limestone and volcanic mountains which are scattered across the plateaux surface, finds its way to perennial or

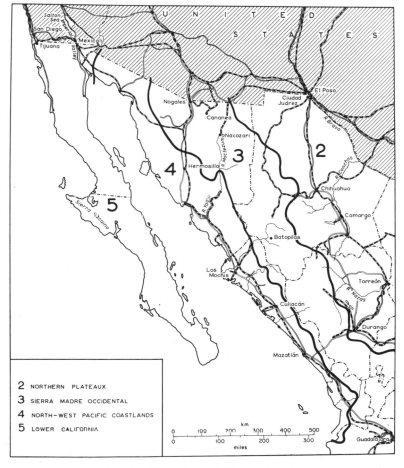

Fig. 21. *The regions of Western Mexico*

temporary shallow lakes, or merely peters out either by evaporation loss or porosity of the surface. These great inland drainage basins, or bolsones, vary considerably both in size and in fertility, largely dependent on the amount of river water they receive, that of Mayrán being well watered with the important Nazas river. The Río Bravo (Grande) itself drains a large bolsón on both sides of the international boundary, cutting its way eastward through several ranges to reach its confluence with the Pecos tributary.

Unlike the advanced and early civilizations which grew up in the coastal plain and in the highlands to the south, the indigenous cultures of Mexico's -northern plateaux were of the hunting and collecting type, and the tribes of Apaches and Comanches never accepted Spanish colonial rule. Resistance to effective incorporation within the national life of Mexico continued until the end of last century, and delayed settlement and utilization of the region.

Throughout four centuries it has been the mineral wealth of the region which has been the great magnet of settlement and land occupance, and nearly all the urban centres owe their origin to the quest and exploitation of these resources. The intense metamorphism and fracturing of the rocks of the mesetas favoured lode mineralization in an abundance typical of the western Cordillera of North America. The profusion and variety of mining sites on the Mexican plateaux and in the Sierra Madre Occidental is unequalled in Latin America. To detail them produces a catalogue of the great centres scattered throughout the five states of the region. Sixty-eight per cent of present mineral production is made up of lead, zinc, silver, copper and gold, but the importance of the iron reserves and the output of such additive metals as antimony and cadmium are also noteworthy.

The following table indicates the position of Mexico in world production of some of these resources:

	Percentage of Mexican metal production	Percentage of world production	Position in world production	Principal centres
Lead	18	6	5th	Widespread in five states of plateaux
Zinc	24	5	7th	Chihuahua, Zacatecas, San Luis Potosí
Silver	14	17	2nd	Widespread throughout Mexican plateaux
Antimony	1	6	5th	Chihuahua and Sonora
Cadmium	1	18	3rd	Centres mining zinc

Durango City itself is built on the great iron reserves of Cerro de Mercado, and the mining of over 1 million tons of coal annually in the Coahuila zone places Mexico fourth among the Latin American coal-producing countries. Increasing attention is also being paid to the processing of the mineral production, a refining plant at Torreón producing large quantities of refined zinc and sulphuric acid.

While it is now the premier mining zone of Mexico, Chihuahua alone producing one-third of the republic's minerals, its economy is no longer confined to mineral exploitation, and the cultivation of cereals, vegetables, fruits and textile crops has increasing significance, both on a commercial and a subsistence scale. First and foremost is the rich oasis-like area in the Bolsón de Mayrán known as the Laguna district, where the waters of the Nazas and Aguanaval can be used to irrigate some 400,000 acres in the south-west of Coahuila, north-east of Durango. Here some 60 per cent of the cotton crop of Mexico is grown, and in terms of value of its agricultural produce it is the richest zone in the republic. Yields are high and most of the crop is grown on the new ejido collective holdings which replaced the former extensive haciendas in 1936, and the intensive utilization of these lands supports one of the densest agricultural populations in Mexico. Apart from subsistence crops wheat is also grown over considerable areas, and in pre-ejido days wheat was more important than cotton.

Other areas of agricultural importance are the Camargo district in the middle Conchos basin and on the Río Grande downstream from Ciudad Juárez. Both areas use the waters of these two rivers to irrigate considerable areas of high-grade cotton, and the Conchos valley and the wetter areas of the eastern piedmont of the Sierra Madre Occidental grow also crops of wheat and maize.

The most widespread utilization of this vast region, however, is for pastoralism, and great numbers of cattle, goats and sheep find sufficient pasture especially in the wetter piedmont areas and in the valleys of the principal streams. This is particularly true of the surviving Indian communities on the upper Nazas headstreams where a mixed pastoral-agricultural economy prevails, but since 1951 with the eradication of foot-and-mouth disease in the area, great packing plants have been established at Chihuahua to convert the cattle into an economic asset.

Although covering nearly one-third of the area of Mexico the total population of less than 7 millions is but one-seventh of the national total. A quarter of the people are concentrated in the large towns of the region such as San Luis Potosí (190,000), Torreón (283,000),

Ciudad Juárez (522,000) and Chihuahua (347,000) and these urban concentrations are a notable feature of the population distribution in an area otherwise scantily peopled. They are either old-established mining towns which have become administrative centres such as San Luis Potosí, Chihuahua and Durango (145,000), new agricultural centres such as Torreón and Gómez Palacio (61,000) or important road and rail communications centres as Ciudad Juárez and Saltillo (135,000). Indeed, in such a vast region, all these centres have acquired a significance in respect of transport links. Torreón and Durango, for example, occupy key positions in relation to north–south and east–west routes from Mexico City to the United States and from Atlantic coast to Pacific coast respectively.

Compared with the routes of the eastern coastal region the commercial significance of the international routes via Ciudad Juárez and Piedras Negras to and from the United States is small, and together they account for less than 7 per cent of the international trade of Mexico.

Apart from the large urban centres the pattern of population distribution is extremely light, and consists of small mining or agricultural-pastoral communities, the latter being closely related to accessibility to water. These statistics, which include the city populations, indicate the relatively sparse distribution:

	Total population (1969)	Per square mile
Chihuahua	1,826,000	19·2
Coahuila	1,225,000	21·0
Durango	959,000	20·7
San Luis Potosí	1,436,000	59·3
Zacatecas	1,082,000	37·3

THE SIERRA MADRE OCCIDENTAL

The region of the Sierra Madre Occidental stretches southward for 800 miles from the border with the United States, along the western portions of the states of Chihuahua and Durango, and in parts attains a width of 200 miles. This great series of parallel intensely folded and faulted ranges aligned on a north-north-west–south-south-east axis, peneplained and mantled over extensive areas with volcanic outpourings, is the most rugged and mountainous region of Mexico. Except in the extreme north it is everywhere over 6,000 feet in height and rises to over 10,000 feet in the centre and south. The longitudinal valleys are in many cases synclinal in structure, and their depth has been increased both by faulting and rapid and devastating river erosion. Receiving rains from east and west, there originate here all the rivers which permit the economic utilization of the northern plateaux and the Pacific coastal region. A score of these rivers have torn deeply incised gorges through the lava-topped ranges of the Sierra and have thus united by short transverse canyons the longitudinal valleys.

Crowned by the greatest expanses of coniferous forests in Mexico, with mixed deciduous and evergreen woods on their lower slopes, these are the largest forest reserves the country possesses (Fig. 19).

Sparsely peopled still by Indian tribes who eke out a living based on agricultural patches won from the forested valleys, the region has been a refuge for the more backward groups, and the impact of Spanish-Mexican culture on their lives has been of little effect. This is one region where the hacienda never gained sway and where the backward Indian communal holdings and villages have persisted into the 20th century. The only other settlements are those of mining communities such as Batopilas, which after two centuries is still one of the richest silver mines in Mexico, or Las Coloradas in western Durango, the richest gold zone still worked. They are illustrative of the considerable deposits of silver, gold, lead, zinc and copper introduced by the vulcanism which this region experienced.

Apart from its reserves of water and timber, the Sierra Madre Occidental's greatest influence on Mexican life is the great barrier it is to east–west transport (Fig. 18). Nowhere does a railway cross it, and only between Durango and Mazatlán has an all-weather road penetrated its rugged fastnesses. Viewed from the northern plateau its elevation is not outstanding, but the succession of mountain ridges, deep longitudinal valleys and transverse canyons which separate the plateau from the coast is a wild and inhospitable region to cross. Within a considerable network of internal airways, the Durango–Mazatlán route is the only one crossing the Cordillera.

THE NORTH-WEST PACIFIC COASTLANDS

There are some important similarities and contrasts between the north-western Pacific coastlands (Fig. 21) and the Gulf Coastal Plain. Like the latter it consists of three states, in this case Sonora, Sinaloa and Nayarit; and like its eastern counterpart it receives a plentiful rainfall in the south and becomes progressively more arid in its northern extensions. The period of maximum rainfall in both

cases is the summer, and few places on eastern and western coasts
of a continent show such similar conditions:

	January temperature (°F.)	July temperature (°F.)	Percentage rainfall June–October	Total (inches)
Tampico	66	82	76	44·9
Mazatlán	68	83	86	30·2

On the north-western Pacific coastal region, however, forests
occur only in the extreme south of Nayarit state and the northward
change through savana and steppe to hot desert is a much more
rapid transition than on the Gulf plains, which are nowhere so arid
as in Sonora state.

These Pacific coastal lowlands vary considerably in width. Rarely
do the sierras restrict it to a fringe less than 6 miles, yet where the
flat-bottomed transverse valleys extend eastwards stretches of lowland some 50 miles wide occur. The relief pattern, therefore, is a
series of lava-covered mesetas subdivided from each other by the
transverse river valleys which contain the numerous rivers born in
the Sierra Madre Occidental. The northern state of Sonora, west of
the Sierra, contains numerous faulted blocks related both to the
tectonic trough of the Gulf of California and the similar basin and
range units across the international boundary in Arizona and
southern California.

In Sonora, except near the water courses, a meagre pastoral existence is possible for a few tribes who survive especially where the
interior height and increasing precipitation give better grazing for
their herds. Otherwise rainfall is so scanty and evaporation so great
that the surface consists of true yucca and cactus desert, and alkali
flats close to the rivers in the valleys. Irrigation schemes to control
and regulate the availability of water in the valley bottoms permit
considerable agriculture despite the aridity. The southern valleys of
the state are the principal wheat-growing areas of Mexico and the
ones with the highest yield; the Yaqui valley is an important rice
producer contributing 45 per cent of the Mexican rice crop; and
considerable quantities of linseed are also grown.

It is in the southern states of Sinaloa and Nayarit that the combination of summer heat, more plentiful rainfall, and well-watered
valleys permits both subsistence and commercial agriculture of an
increasingly profuse nature as one passes southward. In respect of

the cash crops, the Los Mochis and Culiacán areas of Sinaloa share with central Veracruz the major part of the sugar cane production of the country, while most of Mexico's tomatoes are grown in the valleys of northern Sinaloa, and most of the tobacco in Nayarit.

It is in the intensive use of all the available irrigated acres for subsistence farming of the traditional Mexican crops of maize, squash, beans and chile on the numerous ejidos established in these two states that this region is now most important, for this type of agriculture has grown at the expense of the old commercial production raised on the former haciendas. Nearly half the total population of Nayarit live on ejidos, which here and in south Sinaloa stretch continuously along the coastal plain and eastward into the valleys.

The mineral riches of Sonora, which for the most part have only been exploited in this century, are varied. It is the principal copper producing area of Mexico, the chief centres being Cananea, Nacozari and La Colorada and these mines are linked by rail with the United States by which they were developed. Coal is mined in the Yaqui valley and some iron occurs at El Volcán.

More than 3 million people live in these three states, the density of population in Sinaloa and Nayarit being three times greater than that of Sonora, which includes such great areas of mountainous and desert country. While this total population is not large, it is predominantly rural and dependent on agriculture in a relatively restricted terrain. Large towns are few, and only three in the whole region have a population exceeding 100,000. They are Culiacán (140,000) in northern Sinaloa, which in the Spanish expansion northwestward was a frontier base for the *misiones* beyond, Mazatlán (175,000) the principal port not only of the region but of Pacific Mexico, and the terminus of the only road linking it with the east, and Hermosillo (196,000) an orange-growing and meat-packing centre of the Sonora valley.

The isolation of this coastal region, imposed upon it by the great barrier of the Sierra Madre Occidental, and the frequency of the valley and coastal settlements have resulted in a longitudinal pattern of communications by road and rail linking them in the north to the United States and in the south to the Central Plateaux via Guadalajara. It was by means of this old colonial road that much of this region was settled, and now, aided by the railway, it effectively incorporates this otherwise isolated region into Mexican economic life (Figs. 11, 12, 18 and 23).

BAJA CALIFORNIA

This 700-mile long peninsula (Fig. 21) rising in the northern part to over 10,000 feet in height may be considered to be a continuation of the structural province of the Sierra Nevada block in the United States. It is a mountainous zone of folded Cretaceous rocks, capped by great volcanic outpourings and faulted, fractured and tilted westward to present a series of mesetas and small coastal plains facing the Pacific and forbidding cliffs to the Gulf of California. The Sierra Santa Clara range forming a projection on the west coast is analogous to the most westerly structural province of North America, the Coast ranges of western California and Oregon. The Gulf of California is a great structural trough between the Baja Californian block and the numerous block mountains of Sonora which flank the Sierra Madre Occidental on the west.

Climatically it is a long arid zone of transition from the winter régime rains of California to the summer rainfall régime of Sinaloa and Pacific South Mexico. Thus only its northern and southern extremities are of use for pastoralism and agriculture. The great central core is a land of xerophytic vegetation, rugged mountain scree country devoid of rivers, awaiting the discovery of petroleum on the Los Angeles scale to rescue it from desolation and unproductivity.

Thé southern clusters of population are surviving remnants of settlements established as Franciscan and Dominican *misiones*. The backward indigenous peoples have now all disappeared completely, and the mestizo populations carry on small subsistence farms with cattle raising and fishing. Two small copper-mining centres have a fluctuating production. The total population is less than 125,000.

The northern settlements are more flourishing and support a population six times as great, for this includes the Mexican portion of the Colorado delta and Imperial valley, where, with irrigation, crops of alfalfa, wheat, cotton and linseed constitute an important economic basis to life in this zone. The relatively small area of the Imperial valley in Mexico is part of the Salton trough, most of which lies in the United States. This closed basin was the northernmost part of the Gulf of California which was severed from the Gulf by the Colorado delta, and it is renowned for its fertile soil. Mexicali is the centre of this valuable oasis region, and alone accounts for 450,000 of the population. Tijuana (354,000), another frontier settlement, in the extreme north-west of the republic, is the largest centre outside the Colorado–Imperial oasis area, and claims to have the world's largest desalination plant with a daily capacity of 28 million cubic litres. Together these two towns receive nearly 9 per cent of Mexico's imports, Mexicali being linked to the longitudinal Pacific coastal railway which unites it with the capital, México City. No other area of Mexico grew so rapidly in population during the 1950–70 decades as did northern Baja California. Most of Mexico's 'export only' or 'in bond' industries (see final section of this chapter) specializing in electrical and electronic goods and textiles are located in this peninsula; and beginning in 1970, a five-year programme of land distribution, the construction of a road through the entire length of the peninsula, and the erection of eight tourist centres involving marinas and hotel facilities will further enhance the importance of the state.

The tuna, albacore, sardine and crab fisheries off the west coasts of Sonora, Sinaloa and Lower California are amongst the richest in Mexico and account for 80 per cent of national production. Much of this fishing is carried on by United States vessels, but sardines and shrimps are tinned at several points on Mexico's north Pacific coast.

THE CENTRAL MESETAS

The southernmost portion of the great Mexican plateau (Fig. 22) is structurally a continuation of the northern plateaux already described. It is differentiated from it on three grounds. Firstly, it is more favoured climatically, having considerably more rainfall; secondly, although containing one basin of inland drainage, the Valle de México, it is for the most part drained by considerable rivers such as the Lerma and Santiago to the Pacific and by the Moctezuma and Pánuco to the Gulf of Mexico; and, thirdly, it is bounded in the south by the great east–west active volcanic belt of the Sierra Volcánica Transversal stretching from near Veracruz to Cape Corrientes.

Otherwise the basic structural foundation is of Cretaceous limestones and shales, folded, faulted, peneplained, covered with extensive lava flows, uplifted and tilted northwards. Along the high southern margin of this great highland fault block have occurred the vast lava flows and volcanic eruptions of which the east–west group of magnificent cones of Orizaba, Ixtaccíhuatl, Popocatépetl, Toluca, Jorullo and Colima are the most impressive evidence. Although Orizaba exceeds 18,000 feet there are many lower peaks of great beauty, and of special interest is the new cone of Parícutin born in 1943 which now rises 1,700 feet above the plateau level. In only a few places is the basic Cretaceous plateau relief revealed.

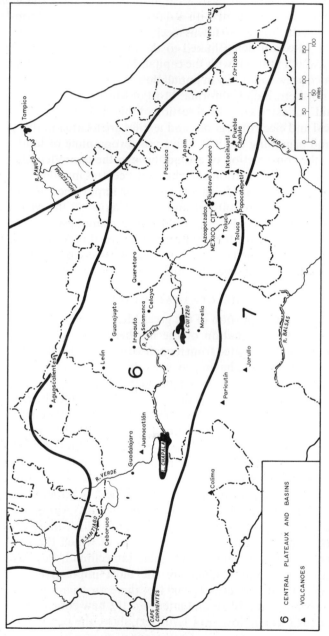

Fig. 22. *Central Mexico*

A maze of Tertiary and Quaternary lava outpourings, thousands of feet thick, mesa-like hills, cinder cones, basalt flows, crater lakes and plugs form this zone, partially blocking river exits torn by erosion and damming up basins, many of which have been filled in recent geological and historical time by deposition of material eroded from the surrounding highlands. Between these basins is undulating hilly volcanic country into which the headwaters of rivers draining to the Pacific and Gulf of Mexico have cut deep narrow valleys in their competition to capture the drainage of these volcanic basins.

As the whole region exceeds at least 5,000 feet in height the effect of altitude on temperatures experienced is marked. Only exceptionally do mean monthly summer temperatures exceed 70°F. and those of the winter months vary between 50 and 60°F. Rainfall, while by no means abundant, is usually adequate, being often dependent on local conditions relative to the disposition of the high land. Sites with exposure to Gulf influences receive the maximum amounts. At least 75 per cent of the precipitation occurs from June to October, and usually an even higher proportion. This fairly uniform climatic

Plate 3. *Cultivated fields near Mexico City. The mountain-enclosed basins support most of Mexico's people*

régime of cool dry winters and warm wet summers is summarized in these figures from some of the major centres in all parts of the Meseta:

	Altitude (feet)	January (°F.)	July (°F.)	Annual rainfall (inches)	June–October rainfall (inches)
León	5,900	57	69	25	22
Pachuca	8,000	53	59	14	10
México City	7,500	54	63	23	19
Puebla	7,100	54	63	35	28
Guadalajara	5,100	60	69	40	36

Under natural conditions the mountainous parts of the region support coniferous forest, and the intermont basins grassland, but both deforestation and agriculture have over the centuries greatly changed this simple distribution.

The region is the most densely populated part of Mexico, for here on less than one-seventh of the area of the republic live half of its 50 million people. This is the heart of Mexico, in which are concentrated a wealth of natural and industrialized resources which such occupation has developed. Here is a great network of communications, road, rail and air, linking together the region internally, and connecting it with all the other regions of Mexico (Fig. 23). Here are concentrated most of the cattle, half the farm land, and most of the industry of the republic. Yet, outside the great urban sprawl of the capital and its satellite towns within the Federal District, there are only five cities with a population exceeding 100,000: Guadalajara, 1,352,000; Puebla, 384,000; León, 341,000; Aguascalientes, 167,000; and Morelia, 154,000.

The population is in fact predominantly rural-agricultural in composition, and although the soil resources are by no means exceptional, in places it reaches very high densities. In the states of México, Morelos and Tlaxcala these exceed 170 per square mile.

This great concentration of settlement long antedates the Spanish conquest and occupation of Mexico, for this region was in turn the home of the Teotihuacán, Toltec and Tenochtitlán cultures, advanced civilizations which held sway over the greater part of the area of present-day Mexico. Once its capital fell to Cortés in 1521 Mexico became the property of Spain and the process of more extended settlement and occupation merely a matter of time. Here were the twin objectives of the Spanish imperial quest, mineral wealth and an adequate labour force to work in field and mine and to be converted

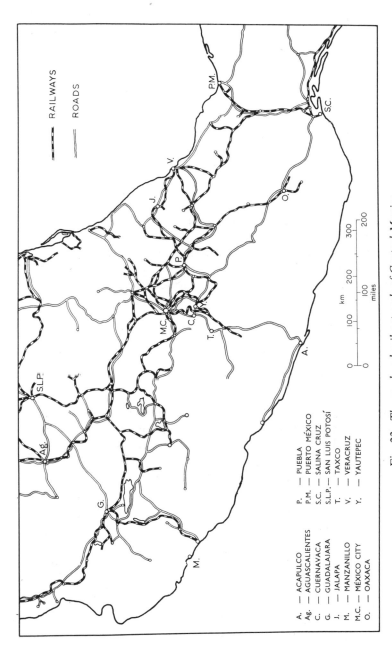

Fig. 23. *The road and rail network of Central Mexico*

This system serves the most closely settled region of Middle America, and contrasts with the few transport facilities of southern Mexico

A. — ACAPULCO
Ag. — AGUASCALIENTES
C. — CUERNAVACA
G. — GUADALAJARA
J. — JALAPA
M. — MANZANILLO
M.C. — MÉXICO CITY
O. — OAXACA

P. — PUEBLA
P.M. — PUERTO MÉXICO
S.C. — SALINA CRUZ
S.L.P. — SAN LUIS POTOSÍ
T. — TAXCO
V. — VERACRUZ
Y. — YAUTEPEC

RAILWAYS
ROADS

to Christianity. Most of the early settlements were established on or accessible to discoveries of rich lodes of gold and silver. Pachuca, Morelia, Guanajuato and Aguascalientes are such examples in the Central Mesetas, and the restless search for more carried the colonists into the mining centres of the northern plateaux already described. The abundance of this mineral wealth was unequalled in Latin America, for now after more than four centuries of fluctuating but continuous exploitation, most of these mining towns are still important producers, Pachuca, for example, being the richest silver centre in the world.

In the surrounding country the Spanish established vast cattle haciendas which also continued in basic format unaltered into the 20th century, and only the agrarian reform of the 1930s converted the greater part of these large properties into the ejido, the typical Mexican land holding of today.

In the midst of this mining-pastoral economy the dense Indian populations carried on subsistence agriculture, based on the cultivation of maize; and despite the changes which have come to Mexico in over four centuries, this economic pattern remains fundamentally unchanged. Maize is the basic staple of the Mexican people; some 6 million acres are devoted to the cultivation of the crop in these Central Mesetas, far more than the combined acreage devoted to all other crops; and the similarity between the distribution of maize and that of population is a striking one.

Yet in spite of the important part that it plays in feeding the Mexican people, the yields are very low. This is due in large measure to primitive cultivation methods, the meagre use of fertilizers and poor seed, but there is little doubt that the widespread cultivation of maize in this region over vast areas is not the best and most economic method of land utilization. Maize is a crop which is easily adapted to a variety of climates. Hence its widespread use throughout all Mexico. The cool summers of the Central Mesetas, often lacking in sufficient rain for luxuriant growth of the plant, and lands in many cases exhausted by its constant cultivation do not provide the ideal environment for maize, and form a considerable contrast to the ideal conditions of the United States corn belt. It is not easy, however, to change long-established traditional farming and eating habits of millions of people, and Mexico continues to import maize to make up the deficiency in her needs. Much progress is, however, being made, and the National Maize Commission, devoting its attention to this most widespread and serious agricultural problem, has produced for sale a dozen tested varieties of disease-resistant maize seed with a growing season adapted to various altitudes. About a quarter of the 20 million acres devoted to maize in Mexico is now sown with these varieties.

Although there is a wide distribution of population throughout this region in the numerous valleys and clustered around the fertile soils at the bases of the great volcanoes, settlement avoiding only the highest mountain lands, the greatest concentrations occur in the intermont basins. This is a pattern very typical of Latin America, and it is repeated throughout the Highland zone, in the states of Central America, in Colombia, Ecuador and Peru. In the Mexican basins the lowest areas are usually occupied by lakes, of which Lake Chapala is the largest, or by marshy areas unfavourable to settlement. Most of the villages, farms and cities are therefore concentrated on the margins of the intermont basins and on the surrounding slopes. Only one of the basins, that of México City, has no natural drainage to the sea, and its streams once emptied into Lake Texcoco and several smaller lakes in a similar way to the basins of inland drainage of the northern parts of the plateau already described. Since the 17th century, however, increasingly efficient drainage operations have connected the basin with the upper Pánuco, and the former lake bed has been partly used to extend the city and provide a modern airport close to the city centre.

Although any division of the populated areas of this region must to some extent be an arbitrary one, it is convenient to consider the intermont basins in two groups, an eastern one consisting of the Basins of México, Puebla and Toluca and a western one consisting of El Bajío of Guanajuato and the Aguascalientes valley. Along both the railway connecting México City with Querétaro and the gorge of the Lerma after it leaves the Toluca basin population distribution thins considerably, thus forming a dividing zone between the two groups of concentrations of settlement. Moreover, although varying individually considerably in altitude, all the eastern basins are situated at a much greater elevation than the western group.

The Eastern Basins

The Basin of México is an irregularly shaped region, occupying some 150 square miles, with the capital city located towards its south-eastern fringe. Forming not only the greatest urban concentration in Mexico, it is one of the largest cities of Latin America, only Buenos

Aires and São Paulo exceeding it in size. The city itself has a population of 3½ millions, but the several other urban centres grouped near it, such as Gustavo A. Madero and Azcapotzalco, many of them growths from old Aztec centres, are in themselves larger than most other Mexican cities, and the Federal District may in many ways be considered as a great conurbation with a total population exceeding 7 millions. The rapidity of its growth may be gauged from the fact that in 1925 the city and the conurbation were both one-sixth of their present size. Central Mexico has always been a magnet for population since earliest times, and this latest phase of urbanization, a feature of all its cities, is no exception to this age-long process. In pre-Conquest times the Basin of México was called Anáhuac, and although philologists dispute its exact translation, the interpretations all carry the idea of 'water'. Here was a region possessing sufficiently humid conditions for sedentary agriculture in contrast to the generally pastoral and hunting environments of the north whence came its earliest inhabitants. Despite the lapse of centuries it is still the sedentary agricultural pattern of maize, beans and chile which forms the core of economic life for all except the urban dwellers in the Basin of México, and for that matter, of all the intermont basins to a greater or less degree. Increasing quantities of wheat are being grown, a crop discouraged by Spain in the colonial period to protect its own production, and the changing diet of the urban population provides a ready market for wheat flour. Large numbers of dairy cattle, and plots of alfalfa for fodder are now occupying a greater proportion of the farming lands. This welcome development suffered a severe setback in the foot-and-mouth disease epidemic of 1947–52, but recent importations of Dutch, Swiss and Jersey breeds for crossing with the native cattle breeds have helped to re-establish an industry which is capable of great expansion in the Basin.

In a small north-eastern enclave of the Basin around the town of Apam large crops of maguey are grown, particularly for the conurbation. This plant is an agave from which the fermented drink, pulque, is derived, and which is a principal constituent of the Mexican's diet. Taken in moderate quantities it provides many of the nutritive constituents not obtained from other food eaten. Throughout the central region small patches are devoted to its cultivation, and its manufacture and distribution involve a considerable domestic organization in all the basins.

There seems little real geographical reason, physical or human, why México City should have become the centre which has grown into the great industrial, commercial and administrative metropolis of the republic (Fig. 24). Its selection as the capital of the great empire of Tenochtitlán seems to have been the fortuitous fact which commenced its long progress of increasing dominance over all other cities of the Central Mesetas. Several other centres in several of the other basins have equal, and in some cases superior, physical advantages to México City, but once having been established as the pre-Conquest capital, the historical forces were such as to preserve and strengthen its unique eminence.

This long history is reflected in its urban geography today. It is both an old Latin city of rectangular plan clustered around the central plaza with headquarters of Church and State, and a modern American city with its skyscrapers, large department stores, banks and ugly sprawl of factories and industrial housing estates. The buildings reflect the times when their creators modelled them on Madrid, and then on Paris. Today they look to Chicago and Washington.

The value of the industrial production of the Federal District in 1964 represented about 55 per cent of Mexico's total, and this is a gauge of the importance of its developing industrial structure. México City is by far the greatest industrial city of Middle America. Like all countries in the first stages of industrialization a large share of its industrial structure is concerned with food processing and the preparation of consumer goods such as beer, tobacco, soap, paper, glass, matches, cement and many others. Indeed every encouragement is given in the form of tax reliefs to those establishing new industries to supply home demand, and over 60 per cent of such new factories established between 1940 and 1970 were located in this central region, the majority being in the capital. This increasing concentration has, however, created problems of air pollution, transport congestion, higher labour costs and a consequential rise in the cost of living. The Mexican government, therefore, has decided that no new manufacturing plants will be established in the Federal District after 1975, and none on the periphery of México City after 1980.

Outside the Federal District there is only one other large urban centre in the Basin of México. This is Pachuca (70,000) some 60 miles to the south-east, on the extreme corner of the basin and its hilly edge. It has retained its importance from early colonial times because of the great resources of silver which are still mined there in quantities unequalled elsewhere.

Seventy miles south-east of the Basin of México, is the Basin of

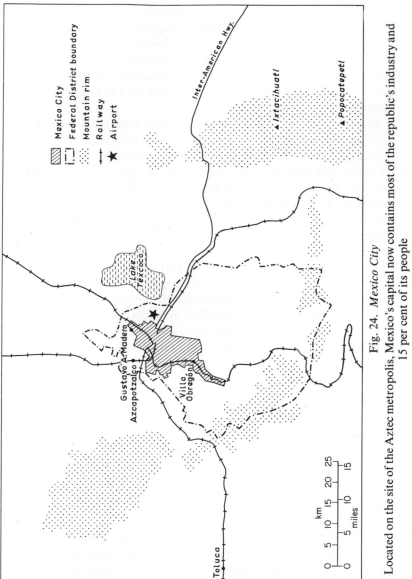

Fig. 24. *Mexico City*

Located on the site of the Aztec metropolis, Mexico's capital now contains most of the republic's industry and 15 per cent of its people

Plate 4. *Popocatapetl (17,887 feet) is a part of the highland rim surrounding the basin of Mexico City*

Puebla, spreading out between the volcanoes of Popocatepetl and Ixtaccíhuatl on the west and Malinche on the east. Some 400 feet lower than the Basin of México it is drained by the Atoyac, a head-stream of the Balsas. Experiencing similar temperature conditions to the metropolitan basin of Anáhuac, it is more favoured in quantity of rainfall, and agriculturally it has altogether a better environment. In addition to the typical maize-beans-maguey economy it has been famous since colonial times for its wheat production, and it is still one of the major zones of the country both for this cereal and for barley.

The concentration of population in the numerous communities of the core of the basin around Puebla is one of the greatest in Mexico, and is indicative of the oasis-like nature of its agricultural wealth. The old pre-Conquest centres of Cholula and Tlaxcala have declined, and Puebla (384,000) has become both the nucleus of the Basin and the sixth city of Mexico. This is not only the result of its function as an administrative, route and agricultural centre, but stems from

Plate 5. *The basic stock of the Mexican people is the indigenous Indian.
Carrying pots to Toluca market*

its significance as Mexico's premier textile city. The cotton spinning and weaving industry is the country's largest single industry accounting for nearly one-fifth of total industrial production; and the majority of the mills making the cotton cloth which clothes most of the Mexican population are concentrated in Puebla, and in Orizaba to the east. Utilizing hydro-electric power from the Atoyac, electricity production in Puebla state is the highest *per capita* in Mexico. Probably no other state in the republic compares with Puebla in its economy based both on agriculture and industry.

The Basin of Toluca, west of Anáhuac, but separated from it by mountains over 10,000 feet in height, is the only one of the eastern group of basins which is drained by the Lerma. Standing over 8,600 feet high, it is the most elevated of the intermont basins of Mexico, and it is only recently geologically that its internal drainage has been captured, for its central portion still contains swamps and a lake, restricting utilization and settlement there. Population distribution is therefore peripheral, close to the encircling hills, but it is dense, and based on the typical subsistence agriculture characteristic of the central basins. Toluca (105,000) is the only large urban centre, and although having a small industrial structure its importance is principally that of a large market town serving the needs of this area of concentrated settlement. Its linkage, however, to México City by a 40 mile eight-lane highway will probably convert its function to that of a satellite of the capital city.

The Western Basins

All the western intermont nuclei of settlement are inter-connected by the Lerma river and its tributaries, but this has materialized in very recent geological time, and the basins still contain lakes, the drainage of which has not been captured by the main stream except in time of excessive rain. They are thus basins with a common river running through them, yet not completely drained by it.

The Mexicans refer to these western basins as 'El Bajío' (the flat), which again implies a unity which is perhaps deceptive, for there are three fairly clear zones of concentrated population rather than one continuously even distribution. It does, however, convey the correct impression that this great intermont 'lowland' is from the point of view of area the greatest in central Mexico.

When the Lerma leaves the Toluca basin it falls ·by means of a narrow gorge a total of 2,600 feet to an elevation of 5,900 feet at the eastern entrance to the Bajío, and then incising itself more and more deeply as it flows westward, passes through another gorge some 400 feet lower.

El Bajío's extensive cultivable area, the rich volcanic soils, including those of the old lake floors north and south of the Lerma, and a longer growing season in which both summer and winter temperatures are higher than those experienced further east have all combined to make it the richest and most productive agricultural area of central Mexico. It is the greatest maize, beans and cattle area of the country, and in addition, important quantities of wheat, chick peas, tomatoes, potatoes, peaches, pears and strawberries are produced on the flat *vegas* of this basin. Some of these crops are exported, such as the chick peas, yields of which are very high, Mexico ranking second only to Chile as a world producer of this crop. In spite of the overwhelming acreage devoted to maize, there is in fact a better diversification of agriculture here than elsewhere in central Mexico. A meat-packing plant at La Piedad, for example, processes 100,000 pigs annually.

Settlement is predominantly rural, in large communities of several thousand people and particularly concentrated in two parallel areas, one running west from Querétaro and swinging north to León, and one spreading out around and east and west of Lago de Cuitzeo. León (341,000) and Morelia (154,000), the two largest urban centres of El Bajío, thus command the northern and southern extensions of the basin, and are becoming industrial centres of some significance, processing the agricultural products in the form of wheat milling and fruit canning. Salamanca (15,000) contains the large Pemex oil refinery serving the needs of the Central Basins, and is the only refinery not located on the Gulf oil fields or the Federal District. Irapuato (128,000) and Celaya (59,000) are the only other large towns, an importance derived from their situation not only as market centres, but as controlling the principal longitudinal railways running north to the United States.

Only Morelia of these large towns of El Bajío ranks as a mining centre; the others in the northern periphery of the basin, such as Guanajuato and Querétaro, where the silver-bearing crystalline schists protrude from their volcanic cover, have all declined as their resources have been worked out.

The second major zone of concentrated population is to the north and north-west of Lago de Chapala in central Jalisco; and this part of the western basins is sometimes called the Basin of Jalisco. Situated at an altitude of 5,000–5,100 feet, it is the lowest of the central Mexican intermont basins, and several small volcanic cones, mud volcanoes and geysers are strewn across its surface. Most conspicuous however is the great cone of Ceboruco dominating its western end and Mexico's largest lake, Chapala, a shallow expanse of 1,500 square miles, which receives the Lerma at its eastern end. Like the area to the east its generally warmer climate permits maximum arable utilization, again for the most part based on the maize-beans-chili subsistence economy. Linseed and oranges are also grown and large herds of cattle are raised on the hill slopes above the basin. Wheat is less in evidence, as rainfall is greater here than in any other of the Mesetas Centrales.

Population densities are great, as this was one of the areas of earliest colonial settlement, and Guadalajara (1,352,000) so far has retained its centuries-old status as Mexico's second city. With the much faster growth of industrial Monterrey, it appears certain that it will soon lose this distinction. A major market city for west central Mexico it has also developed a number of small industries, including textiles, shoes, soap, clothing, tiles, glassware, and it commands the important coastal road and rail route linking the north Pacific nuclei with the central mesetas. This has transformed its position from a cul-de-sac to a unique pivotal point linking the two Mexican regions (Fig. 23).

Lago de Chapala is drained by the Santiago river, as the lower Lerma is now called, and in 270 miles it plunges 5,000 feet to the Pacific in a deeply incised, inaccessible gorge, which effectively delimits further settlement. One of its great waterfalls, that of Juanacatlán, 70 feet high and 524 feet wide, is one of Mexico's most magnificent spectacles.

The third nucleus of settlement in the west is relatively small, being in the upper Verde valley, a tributary of the Santiago, in the small state of Aguascalientes. Here a fairly diverse agriculture based on cereals, fruit and vegetables is the principal activity of the rural areas, but more than half the population is concentrated in the town of Aguascalientes (167,000) which is the principal railway maintenance centre of the Mexican railways, and has several textile mills and food and beverage processing factories.

SOUTHERN MEXICO

The five southern states fronting the Pacific, Colima, southern Michoacán, Guerrero, Oaxaca and Chiapas form a complex structural region where North American trend lines interlock with those of Central America and the West Indies (Fig. 25). The principal relief components within the region are five in number:

(i) The southern dissected slopes and valleys of the Sierra Volcánica Transversal.
(ii) The Balsas Valley.
(iii) The Sierra Madre del Sur.
(iv) The Isthmus of Tehuantepec.
(v) The Highlands of Chiapas.

There are however certain structural characteristics in common, such as the east–west alignment of these features, a feature of the Central American-West Indies build, the continuity of their geological formations, interrupted though it is by rifts, and the fact that the whole region is the most seismic of the Mexican regions.

Most of the region, therefore, is rugged, broken country, and its unity is rather a question of its location, isolation and biogeography than in its surface features.

The precipitous southern scarp face of the Sierra Volcánica Transversal plunges precipitously down from the 3-miles-high snow-capped volcanoes of the central Mexican plateau to the deep and narrow east–west trough of the Balsas. Scarred by the numerous southward draining tributaries of this river and its western affluent the Tepalcatepec, there are few footholds for settlement along its face.

High up on its sides, however, are a few valley basins which have been breached by its streams, and these nuclei set in the midst of rugged cliffs and deep *quebradas* support a thriving agriculture. Sheltered from the excessive precipitation of the eastward facing slopes around Jalapa, and warmer than the high meseta basins above, the climate is almost ideal for a variety of warm temperate and tropical crops. There are a number of such basins strung from west to east along this face (Uruapan, Tacambaro, Juluapan, Yautepec, Cuantla) but the one centred on Cuernavaca (83,000) at 4,500–4,900 feet altitude in the state of Morelos is the most densely peopled. Although less than 40 miles from México City, but 3,000 feet lower down, the diversity of its agriculture is a striking contrast. In addition to the subsistence crops of the mesetas, its sugar cane and rice fields are of considerable importance. Pressure of population on limited land resources led to this area taking full advantage of the new ejido system, and it is also one of the most successful in adapting its agricultural techniques to the physical background, with the aim of soil

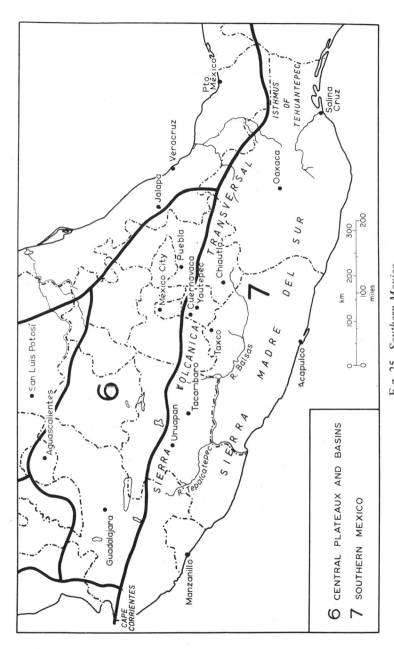

Fig. 25. *Southern Mexico*

The eastern extensions of this region appear on Fig. 26

conservation, so that even new arable acres have been incorporated which were previously thought to be impossible for arable use. This is the area *par excellence* where the proverbial Mexican farmer 'falls out of his fields'. Since colonial times it has supplied sugar for the central region, and still in spite of the greatly increased population, with the help of Sinaloa and Veracruz, it permits the republic to be self-sufficient in this commodity, boasting the largest sugar refinery of Mexico. Its economic links are, therefore, mainly with the plateau basins, although an important motor road now leads south from it to the historic Pacific port of Acapulco, through the silver and tin mining town of Taxco.

Apart from such centres as the Morelos valley, small agricultural communities take advantage of climate and volcanic soils wherever there is sufficient flat land in small valley basins or valley heads, and inevitably such villages are largely self-sufficient units partially isolated from each other and from the dense populations of the intermont basins above them.

The Balsas river, an 800-mile long trough, divides this dissected and ravined slope from the Sierra Madre del Sur on the south, and forms the boundary between the states of Guerrero and Michoacán. Within this depression a fairly large population of Indian farmers practise subsistence agriculture on the rich, volcanic, alluvial plains, all crops of the tierra caliente being possible. Two great disadvantages, however, restrict the full utilization of this zone, isolation and floods. Only one road links the middle part of the valley northward to El Bajío, and within the valley itself and to the Pacific coast communications are of a primitive kind. During the decade 1950–60 a scheme to control the flood waters of the Tepalcatepec part of the valley and permit settlement and utilization of 66,000 acres was implemented. This is an integrated development comparable with that being carried out in the Papaloapan river basin on the Gulf side of the Sierra Madre del Sur. A further scheme, known as the Las Truchas project, involving a major steel plant and hydro-electric development linked by a 75-mile long railway to Puerto Necesidad at the mouth of the Balsas, promises to become one of the largest mining complexes in Mexico (Fig. 52).

The Sierra Madre del Sur which forms the watershed of the Balsas basin on its southern flank is a series of folded ranges aligned east–west, and thus associated with the structural system of Central America and the West Indies. Geologically, however, there are many similarities with the other mountain complexes further north, in that this Sierra is composed largely of folded Cretaceous sediments, many igneous intrusions and the typical lava capping over large areas. Later uplift and widespread faulting have resulted in extensive dissection by rivers such as the Balsas tributaries and the numerous short swift streams of its Pacific slope.

The mountains descend steeply to the Pacific shore, and the extent of lowland between the Isthmus of Tehuantepec and Cape Corrientes is extremely limited except where the Balsas reaches the sea. Moreover, considering the restricted effectiveness of the rainfall received, particularly in the first half of the year with its high temperatures, the region is not favoured climatically, as these statistics show:

	Temperatures:		7 months Winter rainfall:	Total
	January ($^\circ$F.)	July ($^\circ$F.)	November–May (inches)	rainfall (inches)
Manzanillo	75	82	4	36
Acapulco	78	83	5	54
Salina Cruz	76	82	6	39

The greatest disadvantage of the coastal strip, however, is its isolation. Four roads connect it with central Mexico and most of these are of recent construction (Fig. 23), but only in Guerrero state, for 100 miles west of Acapulco (100,000), is there a coastal road. In this part of the lowland cattle are kept, and several irrigation works have been constructed to permit a more reliable agricultural economy. Small quantities of copra, rice and sesame are produced commercially, and further west in Colima, bananas. Manzanillo (26,000) in this state, being the only southern Mexican port linked directly by rail with the central plateaux, has become a little more important than the others, especially since 1964 with the expenditure of 17 million dollars on its improvement, but all together handle an insignificant amount of international trade. However, with the growth of trans-Pacific air and sea passenger movement, especially between Australasia and the United States and Britain, Acapulco has increasingly become an important port of call and international airport on these routes.

It is in the tierra templada, in the highland valleys, that agriculture is more prosperous, and some commercial surplus is available, although here a subsistence economy centred on maize is still the dominant one. Wheat, coffee, oranges and tobacco are typical products, and the meseta of Oaxaca City (98,000), the largest settlement of southern Mexico, is the most important area. Situated at a height of 5,000 feet it is linked by road and rail to México City, thus enabling the products to be transported to the country's chief market. Nearby is Mitla, the ruins of a great pre-Conquest settlement, for southern México was an important area of advanced indigenous Mixtec and Zapotec culture linking the two major nuclei of Anáhuac and the Maya Empire of Chiapas, Guatemala and Yucatán. The region's population is still largely Indian and rural in character, and is heavily concentrated in the tierra templada.

The Sierra Madre del Sur is truncated in the east by a fault scarp which stands sharply above the *graben* of the Tehuantepec isthmus (Fig. 26). Here the Pacific approaches within 130 miles of the Gulf of Mexico and the highest point of land in the rift valley is a saddle block 90 yards wide and 850 feet high. The low undulating country, drained to north and south, is driest on the Pacific coast, but further north, savana gives way to mixed woodland. The Pacific area of the isthmus is much less important than the Gulf plain, and population is sparse. The trans-isthmian railway linking Salina Cruz (35,000) with Coatzacoalcos (Puerto México) (60,000) is of small significance, in spite of its inter-connection with the Guatemalan railways, for it is much easier to transport Central American produce direct by boat to San Francisco than to route it via Puerto México for transport to the east coast of the United States of America.

Continuing the structural and relief features of the Sierra Madre del Sur, eastward of the Tehuantepec graben, the Sierra Madre de Chiapas completes the sub-regions of southern Mexico. This range is separated by a depression parallel with it from another block, some-times called the Sierra del Norte de Chiapas. Six or seven thousand feet below the highlands, this Valley of Chiapas, drained by a tribu-tary of the Grijalva, is really another low intermont basin and has the characteristic concentration of population practising a self-sufficient agricultural-pastoral economy, with a small export of coffee.

Unlike the remainder of southern Mexico, however, the Pacific coastlands at the foot of and on the slopes of the Sierra are relatively important and have a fairly large number of settlements with a thriving tierra caliente agriculture, largely based on more adequate rainfall and made commercially possible by the coastal railway running through the zone.

This is the area growing most of Mexico's cocoa, a crop grown there since Aztec times. With Tabasco, it accounts for 95 per cent of the country's output. The zone is second only to Veracruz and

Tabasco in its yield of bananas and to the Coatepec and Córdoba region of Veracruz in coffee production. All these several parts of southern Mexico have a population approaching a total of 8 millions. Considering its physical background, therefore, it is not scantily peopled, particularly as the region lacks great towns more than any other part of Mexico (with the exception of arid Baja California). This latter characteristic is a reflection of the fact that industrialization to any appreciable extent has not made its appearance in the region. Few areas of Mexico are worse served with communications, and in many ways it seems that the republic faces away from this region, away from its less developed Pacific coast, and away from a tropical economic structure in some respects more akin to the Central American republics it adjoins. To overcome this neglect recent Mexican governments have been endeavouring to turn their attention to the south, and the Tepalcatepec and Papaloapan Commissions are two of the most obvious evidences of this interest. Only by such integrated development will the region contribute more to the nation's economy and permit the absorption of surplus population from less well-endowed regions of the north (Fig. 52).

YUCATAN

The Yucatán peninsula (Fig. 26) is a region totally unlike that of any other Mexican region. Only a very small area in the north centre exceeds 500 feet in height, and in relief it is either lowland or low undulating tableland, practically devoid of all surface drainage. This is not due to lack of rainfall but to its geological composition. The whole region is made up of Tertiary limestones, many of them coralline in nature, and as they decrease in age towards the north, it would appear that the peninsula was uplifted progressively from the south, probably in association with epeirogenic movements of much greater magnitude further west. The Bank of Campeche beyond the wave-built barrier reef off its northern and western coasts is the most extensive part of the Mexican continental shelf, and in this respect and structurally the region bears a strong resemblance to the Floridan-Bahamas region less than 400 miles to the north-east.

There are many karstic phenomena on the peninsula, but the most typical are the *cenotes* or sink holes which occur where the roof of a subterranean drainage channel has collapsed. They thus often appear in lines related to this drainage system, and were strong factors in

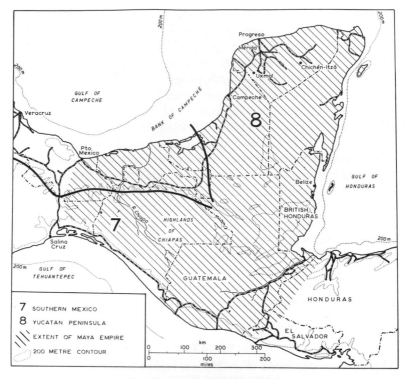

Fig. 26. *The lands of the Mayas*
The area which supported the most advanced of the Pre-Columbian cultures
of Latin America

the siting of Indian settlements for water supply. The ridges and hills
which cross the peninsula from south-east to north-west have been
variously explained as being of æolian origin consisting of indurated
coral débris, or an indication of the last phase of the Tertiary folding
of Middle America.

Climatically, the whole area experiences hot conditions throughout the year; even in the north monthly mean temperatures never fall
below 70°F., and only the Gulf of Tehuantepec coastlands are hotter
than Yucatán. Rainfall, most of which occurs in the hottest months,
is small in the north (35 inches in Mérida), but increases as the highlands of Guatemala–Chiapas are approached. This is reflected in the
natural vegetation pattern as xerophytic scrub in the extreme north-
west gives way to savana over the northern half of the region and
then to tropical forests in the south.

The region was the home of probably the most advanced cultural civilization that the Western Hemisphere knew in pre-Conquest times, that of the Mayas. From the 11th to the 13th century the three cities of Mayapan, Uxmal and Chichén–Itzá developed a political system which permitted great scientific achievements, particularly in astronomy. Its centre before the 5th century was in the southern forested part and in adjacent Chiapas and Guatemala, but a carefully organized and 'staggered' migration to the drier savana country took place in the 5th–6th centuries (Fig. 26). It has been suggested that both the migration and the declining state in which it was discovered in the 16th century were due to soil exhaustion and overpopulation consequent upon the persistence of the shifting agriculture which formed its economic basis.

The population now is still largely Maya Indian, especially in Quintana Roo and Campeche; and in the former territory their resistance to European colonization continued until less than a century ago. There they still practise the economy of the *milpa* (a forest clearing made available for temporary arable use by burning the trees), and maize is again the staple foodstuff. Others are collectors of chicle, the base of chewing gum, Mexico producing 80 per cent of world requirements from this area.

Possessing no mineral wealth, the area was not favoured by the Spanish, and its principal role was as a great pastoral area. In the north large cattle haciendas were established, and Mérida was the cultural, economic and administrative capital of the region. It is in this century that Yucatán has become economically important as the producer of tropical crops such as sugar, oranges, copra and bananas, the latter being grown especially in Campeche. But most of its prosperity is based on the cultivation of henequen, a yucca from which a coarse golden fibre is obtained. This is manufactured into 'binder twine', still a necessity of the mechanized harvesting equipment of the world's great grain producers. The opportunity to establish this industry came with the temporary cessation of supplies of Manila hemp during the Spanish-American war at the close of the 19th century, an economic advantage which Yucatán has maintained ever since despite increasing competition, for Mexico here grows 45 per cent of the world's needs of henequen fibre. It is cultivated in the north-western part of the peninsula, where the semi-arid conditions are most suitable for the plant (Fig. 19), and 350,000 acres are planted under this crop. Although the estates were parcelled out in ejidos at the time of agrarian reform, a method of co-operation between the previous owners and the new *ejiditarios* has been established, by which production and quality have been maintained. In both Yucatán and Campeche the vast majority of the rural population live on ejidos.

Of the three administrative units, nearly 70 per cent of the population live in Yucatán state, and the good rail and road network is indicative of its commercial importance, largely a growth of the 20th century. Mérida (201,000) is the eleventh city of Mexico, and is the only large urban settlement in the peninsula, controlling all its economic affairs. Its port, Progreso, 15 miles to the north, exports nearly 4 per cent of Mexico's exports, largely henequen, now increasingly in the form of manufactured fibres.

Quintana Roo, with less than 95,000 inhabitants, is the most sparsely peopled unit of Mexico, with approximately 5 persons per square mile, which is a striking contrast to rural densities in the henequen zone which exceed 150 persons per square mile.

PROSPECTS AND PROBLEMS

The social and economic transformation of Mexico in the last sixty years, from a feudal rural society dependent on mining and primitive agriculture to a stable, increasingly industrialized state with half its population urbanized, is the most impressive achievement of any Latin American country.

The first thirty years following the 1910 Revolution were, almost inevitably, difficult ones. Revolutionary turmoil, internal opposition from those whose vested interests were threatened, international ostracism and considerable economic dislocation all combined to make the prospects for Mexico's future distinctly unfavourable. However, once the foundations had been laid, the nation has reaped the benefits in the remarkable economic growth of the last thirty years, which is unequalled elsewhere in Latin America, and, for that matter, anywhere else in the underdeveloped world. Credit for this should be given to a high sense of national purpose by the Mexican people, to sound political, financial and economic leadership and to the evolution of a stable political system, all of which have enabled reforms and changes to be introduced in an ordered, dynamic and flexible way.

There has been since 1940 an average real annual growth rate of some 6 per cent, with an average annual *per capita* increase in income of 3 per cent, and this without serious inflation. During the 1960s the gross national production increase was almost 7 per cent annually. A great variety of economic statistics indicate this achievement. During the decade, electricity production more than doubled, 60 per cent of it hydro-electric generated; petroleum production grew by 10 per cent annually; iron and steel output doubled; wheat production did the same; and there were significant increases in the numbers of farm animals and in the output of most food commodities such as sugar, eggs and milk.

Economic progress is matched by social improvement, most evident in the field of education, where illiteracy has been reduced from 80 to something like 20 per cent. To this must be added the greater social contentment and community stability produced by the country's agrarian reform programme, which, whatever its shortcomings, had a greater impact on the transformation of the Mexican nation than that experienced by any other part of Latin America from such measures.

These achievements are all the more remarkable when one considers the inherent difficulties and problems of Mexican geography. As has already been seen in the consideration of the various regions of the country, much of Mexico is either arid or semi-arid, mountainous, isolated or suffers from the problems of humid tropical lands. Less than 12 per cent of the total area can be considered arable, and if to this is added lands suitable for pastoral use, even in a most extensive manner, the total represents only about half of Mexico's land. On the human side there is still the ingrained traditionalism of the Mexican peasant, and this is seen particularly in the cultivation of maize, beans and chili almost irrespective of their suitability to the land producing them or the folk consuming them, simply because this has been for centuries the pattern to follow. There remain, therefore, in many parts of the countryside extremely poor peasant communities living in the old traditional·way on a precarious subsistence level. In addition there are many landless peasants and unemployed or under-employed dwellers in the shanty-towns on the periphery of the growing industrial cities.

These difficulties must be seen against the background of a steady population increase which has doubled the population of Mexico in the last twenty years. The annual $3\frac{1}{2}$ per cent growth rate is one of the largest increases of the major states in the continent; and the 50 million Mexicans now constitute one-sixth of the total population of Latin America.

During the 1960s the labour force increased by nearly 5 millions to a total of 16 millions in 1970, and the absorption of this increasing labour force is one of the republic's major problems, not only to provide additional employment for an extra half million workers annually, but to use it to secure higher productivity and so ensure continued development of the economy. Agricultural production is growing faster than the total manpower employed in agriculture, but in absolute numbers, agricultural population continues to increase. In the past decade the percentage of the labour force employed in agriculture fell from 58 to 50 per cent, and the percentage involved in manufacturing industry grew from 12 to 21 per cent. The relief, therefore, afforded by industrial expansion and tertiary services growth has been considerable, but whether these can continue to absorb the surplus of unskilled land workers is problematical. The availability of relatively low-cost labour has led to the Mexican government initiating a scheme for the establishment of export industries in the U.S. border areas and at the ports and certain points in the interior. The substantially reduced production costs resulting from the abundance of labour offer a considerable incentive to the foreign manufacturers. Several U.S. companies have established twin plants on the frontier between the two countries. Their functions are complementary, the one requiring intensive use of machinery is installed on the U.S. side, and the other, situated on the Mexican side, is involved with the processes requiring a large amount of manual labour. The proximity of the U.S. market for the products of these industries is also, of course, an added advantage.

The land re-distribution programme, involving the more intensive agricultural use of arable land, has also absorbed some surplus rural labour. In addition a steady stream of emigrant workers, both legal and illegal, still crosses into the United States. Those who enter illegally are referred to as 'wetbacks', as a frequent way of entry is to swim the Rio Grande. The total emigration in 1953 is estimated to have passed the 1 million mark, but is much smaller in volume in recent years.

The principal absorber of population growth is, however, the cities with their service industries and expanding manufacturing plants. In contrast to most of Latin America, this industrial expansion is financed to the extent of 90 per cent by domestic savings, a clear indication of the Mexicans' confidence in the future of their country. It is also, contrary to a general impression, based on private investment, much of it foreign capital. A more clearly stated nationalism, however, in recent years has highlighted the financial cost to the republic of this foreign investment, and present policies are designed to control the extent of its growth (Fig. 15).

The efforts sponsored by the *Nacional Financiera* (Industrial Development Corporation) to increase the republic's industrial fabric, to reduce imports of consumer goods, to raise the standard of living and to broaden the basis of Mexico's economic life, have been strikingly successful. Manufacturing has shown recently an annual growth rate of some 8 per cent, and in some industries, such as petrochemicals, the expansion is three or four times this rate of growth. Almost all Mexico's iron and steel consumption is produced internally and about 80 per cent of consumer goods are produced within Mexico. Although the value of the republic's imports is now about 50 per cent higher than that of its exports, over half of the imports are capital goods and another one-third raw materials. In most cases such imports obviously further contribute to continued economic growth.

The balance of payments deficit is largely overcome by the rapidly expanding tourist trade of Mexico which eclipses that of all the rest of Latin America combined. Over 3 million foreign tourists visit Mexico annually and in 1973 they contributed 1,587 million dollars to the reserves. On the other hand Mexicans travel abroad more extensively than any other Latin Americans and the cost of this to the reserves in the same year was 790 million dollars. There is also swelling criticism that an increasing part of Mexico's tourist revenue finds its way back to the United States because of the widespread intrusion of United States capital into all aspects of the tourist industry. Mexico, however, has to live with its 71 per cent dependence on the United States of America as a market and as a provider of imports, and its access to the world's greatest industrial nation and the world's greatest market has undoubtedly contributed to its economic development.

The growth of Mexican exports has largely kept pace with the republic's economic growth, and especially encouraging has been the rising proportion of manufactures to total exports, now contributing some 30 per cent of export income. Fortunately the natural resources of Mexico are more diversified than those of most Latin American countries, and there is, therefore, less dependence on the export of one or two primary commodities. The high proportion of agricultural and mineral products still means, however, that export revenue is still subject to international price fluctuations. Mining output is growing, but at a slower rate than other sectors of the economy, Mexico's position as the world's premier silver producer occasionally being taken by Canada. The value of the fifteen principal mineral exports, however, exceeds 200 million U.S. dollars annually.

The republic's massive agrarian reform programme, centred on the *ejido* as the principal economic and social unit of the country's agricultural system, has been strengthened in recent years. Apart from the increase in agricultural production, its contribution to social and political stability can scarcely be over-emphasized. Striking progress has been made in growing foodstuffs previously imported, and since 1959 the country has been self-sufficient in meeting its needs of wheat.

Mexico's economic programme for the future includes many irrigation and integrated development projects particularly in southern Mexico in order to utilize more fully the thinly inhabited regions of the country, the expansion of the nation's fisheries, which have hitherto been relatively neglected, the investment of large amounts of capital in improved road communications and in improved agricultural techniques and equipment, and increased efforts to house more adequately the growing population. This latter need has become particularly evident with the growth of Mexican cities and the shanty towns which have mushroomed around them.

Despite the remarkable sameness in the character and economy of Mexican rural life, despite the considerable differences which exist between urban affluence and rural poverty, despite the problems of the rapid industrialization of a peasant society, and despite the absorption of much of its economic growth by its continuous growth of population, the achievements of Mexico in the 20th century have no parallel in any other Latin American country, and there is no reason to believe that the prospects are less promising for the future.

STATISTICAL SUMMARY — MEXICO

Area: 760,375 square miles

Population (1970): 50,633,000

Percentage of land

(*a*)	Arable	12%
(*b*)	Pastoral	40%
(*c*)	Forest	22%
(*d*)	Other	26%

Animal numbers

(a)	Cattle	33·8 million
(b)	Sheep	7·9 ,,
(c)	Pigs	16·6 ,,
(d)	Goats	14·3 ,,
(e)	Horses and Mules	6·2 ,,

Communications

(a)	All-season road mileage	40,574
(b)	Railway mileage	14,799
(c)	Air routes	1,325 million passenger miles
		141 ,, ton miles

Principal products

(a) *Agricultural*

Maize	9,264,000 metric tons
Sugar	2,411,000 ,, ,,
Wheat	2,400,000 ,, ,,
Sorghum	2,100,000 ,, ,,

(b) *Mineral*

Petroleum	19,019,000 metric tons
Sulphur	1,700,000 ,, ,,
Coal	1,424,000 ,, ,,
Iron	1,618,000 ,, ,, ⎫
Zinc	214,000 ,, ,,
Lead	168,000 ,, ,,
Copper	74,000 ,, ,, ⎬ metal content
Manganese	31,000 ,, ,,
Antimony	4,000 ,, ,,
Silver	1,249 ,, ,, ⎭

Exports

(a) *Total:* $1,255,000,000

(b) *Percentage share of principal commodities*

Cotton	14%
Sugar	8%
Coffee	6%
Shrimps	4%
Zinc	4%
Lead	2%

MEXICAN EXPORTS, 1966–67*
(*million U.S. dollars*)

Main commodities	1966	1967
Cotton, raw	222	144
Maize	47	73
Sugar, refined	57	67
Shrimps	54	61
Coffee	83	60
Sulphur	35	48
Zinc and concentrates	45	44
Petroleum and derivatives	39	39
Livestock	42	38
Lead and concentrates	28	23
Others	576	546
TOTAL	1,228	1,143

* Including revaluation.
SOURCE: *Informe Anual*, Banco de México S.A.

MEXICAN IMPORTS, 1966–67
(*million U.S. dollars*)

Principal items	1966	1967
Transport equipment:		
Motor cars and parts, chassis, engines	169	169
Railway rolling stock, equipment	21	17
Machinery and parts:		
Machine tools	49	43
Textile	37	50
Tractors	31	32
Internal combustion engines	20	27
Printing and paper making	22	19
Agricultural	10	9
Unspecified industrial	25	32
Plastics and moulding	9	9
Telegraphic and telephone apparatus	31	44
Electricity generators	10	14
Rubber (natural and synthetic)	26	20
Iron and steel bars, tubes, sheets	57	69
Petroleum and derivatives	41	50
Paper and paperboard	32	34
Newsprint	15	18
Wool	20	22
Others	980	1,070
TOTAL	1,605	1,748

SOURCE: *Comercio Exterior*, Banco Nacional de Comercio Exterior S.A.

CHAPTER SIX

The Central American Republics

THE area known as Central America comprises the six states of Guatemala, Honduras, El Salvador, Nicaragua, Costa Rica and Panama, the territory of Belize and the Canal Zone administered by the United States. Such is its political composition, and in the south-east the political boundary closely agrees with physical and human frontiers probably best localized in the Gulf of Darién–Atrato trough. In the north-west, however, there is no such coincidence. The political boundary is very artificial, and the physical and human conditions of the Mexican provinces south of the Sierra Volcánica Transversal, and especially those east of the isthmus of Tehuantepec, have much in common with the rest of Central America (Figs. 26 and 27).

The partition of the region into its present complex political units is largely an historical development of the last one hundred and fifty years, partly consequent upon the achievement of independence from Spain. Previous to this emancipation most of the region for three centuries had been included in the one administrative unit of the Captaincy-General of Guatemala, and even under independence it remained a federation until 1839 (Fig. 1). Several attempts have been made in the 19th and 20th centuries to restore this unity which would enhance the whole region's economic and political strength, but all have foundered on provincial rivalries. Indeed no region of Latin America has suffered more from international wars than these Central American states. As an example, Nicaragua was at war with Honduras on four separate occasions in less than fifty years. The most recent clash was between Honduras and El Salvador in 1969. Yet in spite of these conflicts there remains a community of aspirations, ideas, interests and sentiments.

There is indeed much which unites Central America and much which divides it, and it is useful to consider the bases of these two conflicting tendencies.

Structurally, it is one unit dominated by the east–west trends of the folded and faulted mountain system of the West Indies and

Central America, and relatively distinct from the mountain systems of North and South America. Yet the diversity of landscape included within it is quite large, varying from the flat Atlantic lowlands to the abrupt Pacific slopes, from the deep depressions of the Nicaraguan lakes to the lofty volcanic peaks of Guatemala.

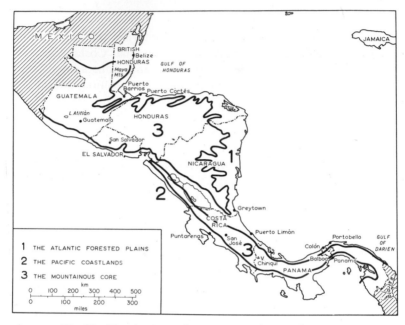

Fig. 27. *The physiographic provinces of Central America*

Climatically, the whole region participates in a general two-season rhythmic framework of coincidence of heavy rains with summer heat, consequent upon the northward swing of the heat equator and the inter-tropical front, so that very few areas receive their maximum rainfall except from May to October. Yet contrasts between the Atlantic and Pacific sides of the region are marked. This is largely due to the persistent prevalence of the north-east trades, so that the Atlantic shore is as much exposed to their rain-bearing qualities as the Pacific shore is sheltered from them. The following statistics, grouped in contrasting pairs working northward from the isthmus of Panama, indicate the wet conditions of the Caribbean coastlands and the semi-aridity of half the year on the opposite shores:

Rainfall amounts in inches:			
	Winter	Summer	Total
Colón	44	84	128
Balboa	19	50	69
Greytown	117	143	260
San Ubaldo	4	70	74
Belize	27	52	79
San Salvador	5	63	68

The important climatic and vegetational changes consequent upon altitude are perhaps of even greater significance, for the tierras caliente, templada and fria with their contrasts in temperature, rainfall, vegetation and crops are a dominating pattern throughout the region.

On the human side, while again bearing the common impress of Spanish colonization and settlement, largely from the two foci of Panamá City and Guatemala City, the historical evolution of the various parts of the region showed considerable diversity, related to the physical conditions, historical forces, and the indigenous peoples. These latter varied from the advanced Maya to the Chocó of Darién, the region being transitional culturally between the Maya and Chibcha civilizations. Certain regions such as the forested Caribbean coastlands repelled settlement, while the highlands of Costa Rica attracted the European colonists. The racial pattern, therefore, is by no means homogeneous either within Central America as a whole, or within the boundaries of each state. Even 20th-century developments, with the growing influence of the United States in the region, have not been equal in their impact throughout the area. The extensive United Fruit Company plantations of Honduras and the lack of such in Nicaragua illustrate this point. There is, however, a unity of American influence in all the area, and this is especially so in the economic field where the United States supplies nearly all the imports, and receives an equally large proportion of the same type of exports from all the area, mainly tropical agricultural produce and forest products. Allied with this economic similarity is the predominance of *rural* settlement throughout the region, with one main metropolitan urban nucleus in each political unit. Finally, although their political development, the outcome of both physical and human conditions, has a unity, it is by no means quite so uniformly revolutionary and dictatorial as is generally believed. Few states of Latin America can compare with Costa Rica in general cultural, political

Plate 6. *A Mayan hieroglyphic column at Copán, Honduras. The Latin American landscape contains many relics of its ancient civilizations*

and democratic stability, glaring as the contrast may be with its northern neighbour's perennial dictatorship.

Yet many of these differences in physical and human geography cut across the political units of which the region is composed. Except for El Salvador and Belize, all the other states straddle the area from Caribbean to Pacific and therefore partake of the contrasting conditions experienced in that transect. It is this transition across the region which is everywhere dominant, although the changes evident in the longitudinal direction from Mexico to Colombia are by no means insignificant.

Before considering the sub-regional and political divisions of Central America, therefore, it is well to indicate the Atlantic-Interior-Pacific basis which is common to the whole region (Fig. 27).

THE ATLANTIC FORESTED PLAINS

From the north of Belize to the Gulf of Darién the outstanding structural movements which seem to have affected these coastlands are those of slight vertical uplift and submergence, but the coral cays or submarine platforms, and river deltas which fringe the shores indicate that a small submergence is the latest phase and is probably still in progress. Off-shore waters are almost everywhere shallow, the continental shelf extending over 150 miles off the northeast Nicaraguan coast, and good natural harbours are non-existent. Built up as a plain of deposition by the numerous rivers which flood and dump their loads of débris and extend their deltas seaward and toward each other, this lowland is the expression of the predominantly Atlantic drainage of all Central America.

The coastal plain rises almost imperceptibly towards the interior and is widest in northern Belize and in Nicaragua, in parts being over fifty miles wide. Along the north coast of Honduras the mountain ranges reach the sea in échelon formation and pinch out the coastal plain into a series of intervening valley mouths, and the narrowing of the isthmus in Costa Rica and Panama likewise considerably restricts its extent. This is the tierra caliente *par excellence* of Central America. Fringed with mangrove swamps and covered with a dense and almost impenetrable jungle of humid high forest with luxuriant undergrowth, temperatures rarely fall below a monthly average of 70°F. Rainfall is abundant at all seasons, and humidity is high.

This combination of physical conditions, trying climate, difficult terrain in respect of vegetation, inhospitable coast and few harbours, proved sufficient deterrents to Spanish settlement without the frequently accompanying drawback of hostile Indian tribes; and except in one or two isolated spots, this plain for two or three centuries remained a *terra incognita*. Although occasionally the highland areas were reached by intrepid adventurers from the Atlantic, in most cases it was from the Pacific slope that settlement emanated. The Caribbean shores were the haunt of buccaneers, pirates and privateersmen, and the exploitation of the forest to secure valuable Campeche wood or logwood, a heavy dyewood, brought the British and Spanish to the Gulf of Honduras coasts.

Only the strategic nature of the Panama isthmus commanding the trans-isthmus route to the Spanish possessions of the Pacific shore compelled utilization of the Caribbean coastland at that point. Here grew up Portobelo, the fortress commanding this route, but no other settlement of any size or importance (except Mérida in the drier north-west Yucatán) marked the Spanish occupation of Caribbean Central America from the Gulf of Darién to Veracruz.

It is only in the late 19th and particularly in the 20th century that its agricultural potentialities for tropical commercial crops have been tapped. Plantations of cocoa, rubber, coconuts, bananas and other tropical fruits have been carved from the forest, and above 1,000 feet, in protected localities where insolation is not too great, coffee groves have been established. With these developments, and making them possible, have come immigrant Negro labour from the West Indies, and from the United States, capital investment in roads, railways and ports for the export of the products. Now the Caribbean coastlands are in some cases linked with the highland interior, as in Costa Rica and Guatemala, and a considerable proportion of Central American exports leaves the new ports of Limón, Puerto Cortés and Puerto Barrios built to handle this trade.

In the late 1930s the spread of sigatoka disease among the Caribbean banana plantations threatened to undo much of the work which had made these shores of use, and many new plantations were laid out on the Pacific coast. Methods of controlling the disease were discovered, however, and although expensive, the heavily capitalized American United Fruit Company found this a practicable method for the richest banana-producing areas of the Atlantic shore. One more permanent effect which has resulted has been the diversification of agriculture, and now crops of abacá, rice, sugar, cacao and oil palms provide not only additional cash products but subsistence foodstuffs.

Not all parts of the lowland are utilized, and especially is this true of the Nicaraguan portion, eastern Panama, and Belize, and in many areas (the latter for example) extraction of forest products, chicle, mahogany and pine is still a major economic activity.

THE PACIFIC COASTLANDS

The Pacific coastlands offer some striking contrasts. The mountains descend abruptly to the sea, and rarely are the coastal plains extensive. Their greatest development occurs where tectonic depressions debouch on the coast, as around the Gulf of Fonseca, or behind the peninsulas of southern Costa Rica and Panama, which are probably the remnants of a previously continuous parallel maritime mountain range. Where they do occur the lowlands are composed for the most part of volcanic débris carried down from the nearby highlands and are remarkably flat antechambers to the abrupt mountain slopes. Unlike the Caribbean, the descent to the ocean is rapid; seas are deep. The shore is tectonic in origin and seismic activity is still pronounced. Although tierra caliente conditions prevail generally, the marked aridity of the November–April period leads to important vegetational differences, and the forest and undergrowth are semi-deciduous, less dense, and broken by tracts of savana. Humidity is less steadily high, and the smaller rainfall means that the tierra caliente extends to only 1,500 feet compared with 2,100 feet on the Caribbean side. Thus apart from the narrowness of the Pacific lowland, the tierra templada of the hilly interior is much more accessible from the Pacific coast, and until recent developments on the Caribbean, the settlements of most of the Central American states were more closely linked with the Pacific. Not that the Pacific coastlands became great areas of intensive settlement. They still repelled population, only to a lesser extent than the Atlantic. Their utilization in a similar form to the Caribbean lowlands was later, as they faced away from the markets demanding tropical produce. In many cases their exploitation is a present continuing process, and they are a substitute region to the disease-invaded Atlantic counterparts. The settlements of the Pacific lowland therefore are not large, with the exception of Panamá City, which is in a separate category. Nor do these ports, such as San José and Puntarenas, handle as much trade as their Caribbean rivals, for obviously the commercial orientation of these states is towards the more industrialized and populated eastern United States, which is both their market and supplier of imports.

THE MOUNTAINOUS CORE

This region of plateaux, internal basins, deep river valleys and volcanic highlands is a complex area, consisting of two major sections. The northern part, comprising a considerable area of Guatemala, Honduras and Nicaragua, consists of two great structural zones. In the first place a system of folded parallel mountain ranges is aligned on a great semi-circular trend concave to the north. Thus in its western section the alignment is north-west–south-east but in the eastern part of Honduras and Nicaragua it swings south-west–north-east, and produces the echelon impingement on the north Honduran coast already described. Tangentially to this semi-circular trend, aligned parallel with the Pacific coast, occur the Volcanic Highlands of Central America which are probably related to the fault line of foundering which determines that coast. Its greatest volcanic manifestation in area, in extent of the lava flows and cones, and in activity is in Guatemala, diminishing southward. The magnificent grouping of cones around Lake Atitlán is one of the finest examples of this zone, some peaks exceeding 13,000 feet in height.

The second constituent, confined to the isthmus south and east of the Nicaraguan lakes, is a typical island-arc type of mountain system consisting of parallel ridges which in Panama become more and more irregular in their disposition. Vulcanism is still present, especially in Costa Rica where the volcanic cones of Turrialba, Poas, Barba and Irazú crown the central range, and exceed 11,000 feet; and eroded cones and craters also exist in Panama.

These highland regions, above 2,000 feet in altitude, are the tierras templada and fria, the former extending to approximately 6,000 feet on the Atlantic aspect and 5,000 feet on the Pacific side. It is the tierra templada, with its higher rainfall and still magnificent forests and its more equable and temperate conditions (64–74°F.) which has become the great zone of settlement in Central America. Favoured by its volcanic soils and similar relief conditions to the internal basins of the Mexican volcanic sierra, nuclei of population raise subsistence and commercial crops of coffee, sugar cane, cotton, tobacco, string beans and maize, while in the mixed woodland of the tierra fria, cultivation of European type fruits and cereals, followed by pastoralism at higher levels above the tree line, completes a varied economy which offers self-sufficiency to countless rural communities.

While once again there are many variations from one part of Central America to another, dependent on local physical and human conditions, it is in this mountainous zone that 80 per cent of the people live; it is here that the great cities of each unit occur; it is here that European, Indian and mestizo in varying numbers and admixtures form an ethnic contrast to the Indian, mulattoes and Negroes of the coastlands.

	Total population (1970)	Density (per square mile)	Indian	European	Mestizo	Negro
			(approximate percentage)			
Belize	122,000	13	17	4	41	38
Guatemala	5,200,000	135	60	5	33	2
Honduras	2,600,000	57	7	1	90	2
El Salvador	3,500,000	396	11	11	78	
Nicaragua	2,000,000	36	5	17	69	9
Costa Rica	1,700,000	83	1	85	12	2
Panama	1,500,000	47	10	11	65	13

It is possible to consider a little more fully the variations within this general pattern of the environments if the components of the Central America scene are treated transversely, in the following sub-regions (Fig. 28):

   (i) Petén–Belize.
   (ii) Caribbean Guatemala, Honduras and Nicaragua.
   (iii) The Pacific Volcanic Region of Central America.
   (iv) Costa Rica–Panama.

Petén and Belize

This British territory, still claimed by Guatemala as the province of Belize, and the north Guatemalan province of Petén (a great northern appendix eccentric to the rest of Guatemala and covering one-third of its area) together form a structural unit distinct from the rest of Central America. They are in fact the southern continuation of the Yucatán peninsula, consisting of relatively low country of slightly undulating folds in a great early Tertiary and Cretaceous limestone platform. The east–west trend lines are evident in the shape of the dominant hills and of Lake Petén. Much of the surface is karst, containing dolines and *siguanes* (*cenotes*), with the Caribbean coast marshy, lagoon-fringed and with coral reefs and keys off-shore.

South of the Sibun river in Belize, the first of the higher hill ranges pushes east-north-east into the colony as the Maya mountains (Cockscomb mountains), reaching in parts over 3,000 feet, with a granitic core overlain on its flanks with Carboniferous slates.

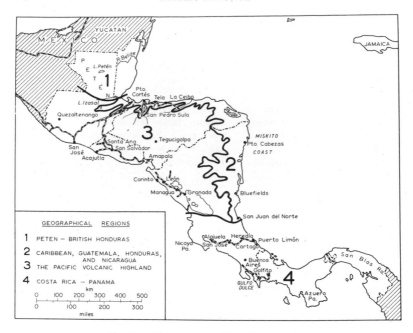

Fig. 28. *The regions of Central America*

Like the rest of southern Yucatán the whole region is forest covered, with a great wealth of trees which still constitutes its major economic importance. From the forests of Petén mahogany, cedar and chicle are extracted and exported via Puerto Barrios. This is by far the richest forest zone of Guatemala, and only a portion of it is fully explored. Until 1960 Belize's economy was also largely linked to forest products, but in the 1960–70 decade the contribution of pine lumber, mahogany logs and lumber, cedar and chicle gum to the country's exports declined from 40 to 7 per cent of the total.

Some subsistence agriculture is carried on by the Maya Indians, descendants of the occupants of the Old Empire which was located in this region. They eke out a living in forest clearings with the assistance of hunting and fishing, and, as in Mexico, maize is the staple crop. In recent years considerable efforts have been made in Belize to extend commercial agriculture both for the home and overseas market. Crops of rice, maize, sugar cane, coconuts, bananas and vegetables are grown, but the most successful enterprise is that of grapefruit, 5,000 acres being devoted to this product, particularly

Plate 7. *The mountain-girdled basins of Central America reveal evidence of settlement since Mayan times. The pyramid of Zacaleu, Honduras*

in the Stann Creek valley where the Maya mountains reach the coastal plain. Citrus is now the second most important export commodity, accounting for approximately 44 per cent of agricultural exports and about 23 per cent of the total export sales. There has also been a considerable expansion in sugar production consequent upon the modernization and construction of sugar mills in the northern third of the country, where sugar cultivation is concentrated.

In order to stimulate the production of staple food commodities to feed Belize's small population of 122,000, concerted efforts have been made to provide agricultural credits, storage, marketing facilities and guaranteed prices. In most years sufficient maize, beans, rice and vegetables are produced to avoid imports of these commodities; and ample supplies of fish are also caught, rock lobsters (crawfish) being an important export.

The whole region is sparsely populated, settlement in the interior being largely dependent on local supplies of water. It is rural in character, Flores, the capital of Petén, having 2,300 inhabitants, while Belize the chief port and capital of Belize has some

54,000. Communications are poor, and the agricultural estates are situated near the coast to avoid transport difficulties. Much timber is floated down the Belize river and the Petén chicle is flown out by air.

Caribbean Guatemala – Honduras – Nicaragua

From the point of view of relief this area embraces the Caribbean coastal plain of these three states, the east–west narrow folded and faulted mountain ranges which impinge upon it, and the numerous longitudinal valleys which separate them. Of the latter, that occupied by the Motagua river is one of the most important, as it connects the Gulf of Honduras with the zone of dense settlement around Guatemala City. Another is the down-faulted depression of the Ulúa valley leading from the Gulf of Honduras, near Puerto Cortés, south to the Gulf of Fonseca.

The climatic and vegetational deterrents to use of the tierra caliente lowlands in the past have been described, and the rugged terrain of the mountain ranges did not favour settlement, for, except in Honduras, the minerals the Spanish were seeking were not evident. Even the population of the indigenous people was sparse, and, especially along the Miskito coast, they were also hostile.

The 20th-century developments have most affected the coastal plain and the deep valleys thrusting westward into the mountains. The highlands for the most part remain thinly peopled and occupied by Indians practising subsistence agriculture, and without major settlements.

Guatemala's seventy-mile seaboard on the Caribbean receives the three deep valley lowlands of the Saratún, Lake Izabal and Motagua, and it is here in the last half-century that the United Fruit Company has established its banana plantations. A close network of light railways serving the estates and a line, following the Motagua river, linking the port, Puerto Barrios (31,000), with the capital have been constructed. Although many of the Company's activities have now been transferred to the Pacific coast, this area is still the more important of the two, and 75 per cent of the imports of Guatemala pass through Puerto Barrios. A road has been built to link Guatemala City with this Caribbean lowland at Santo Tomás de Castilla (formerly called Matías de Gálvez), the site of a modern port. This now provides an alternative route to that provided by the railway system, built by the United Fruit Company, but expropriated by the Guatemalan government in 1968.

Similar developments in tropical agriculture in the valley lowlands leading from the north coast of Honduras have been even more extensive. Elaborate flood control works, land clearing and reclamation, and modern scientific agriculture have converted this jungle coastland into one of the greatest banana-growing areas of the world, and Honduras now ranks as the greatest exporter of bananas in Central America, exporting some 12 million stems annually. Ecuador grows twice as many but is the only exporter of bananas greater than Honduras.

Apart from the 50,000 acres devoted to this crop, an even greater area now grows abacá, oil palms, coconuts, cacao, sugar and tropical fruits; and the United Fruit Company has built a college of tropical agriculture in Zamorano to endeavour to diffuse more modern agricultural practices throughout the region and in Central America generally.

Unlike Guatemala and Nicaragua the zone has become a major population nucleus of the state. San Pedro Sula (160,000) in the Ulúa valley is the second city of Honduras, and its most industrialized centre. It serves as a collecting and distributing centre both for the Caribbean lowland and the Ulúa valley leading to the capital.

Tela (18,000), La Ceiba (35,000) and Puerto Cortés (30,000), are all important nuclei serving banana-producing districts, and more than half of Honduran trade passes through Puerto Cortés. Bananas, once accounting for three-quarters of the country's exports, now rarely represent more than half this proportion.

Far less important is the Nicaraguan lowland, in spite of its very considerable extent, and Bluefields (18,000) is the largest settlement, one of two established by Jamaican Negroes in the 18th century. The Nicaraguan banana plantations were devastated in the 1940s by the sigatoka disease and only small shipments are made from Bluefields. Puerto Cabezas and the coastlands 50 miles north and south of it contain most of the few people on the Caribbean coast, and this is an important timber producing area. Less than 10 per cent of the population of Nicaragua, however, live in the eastern half of the state and the major economic activity is shifting agriculture of the Indian and Negro peasants.

The contrast between the Honduran and Nicaraguan coastlands cannot be explained by physical conditions, but is in part due to the unsettled conditions which for so long have characterized Nicaraguan history, and the inadequacy of a labour supply in the region.

The Pacific Volcanic Highland

Most of the people of Central America are found within this region. The physical advantages for life within the tropics are clearly present here in greater abundance than elsewhere in Central America, and from pre-Conquest times it has contained the settled areas which have grown to be the cores of the four republics of Guatemala, Honduras, El Salvador and Nicaragua.

The faulted and folded structures are here mantled with a great covering of volcanic material, which has produced intermont basins, lava-topped plateau surfaces and rich soil basins on the mountain slopes. Except for the relatively restricted Pacific slope, most of the northern part of the region is within the tierras templada and fria, and its wealth of agricultural diversification has permitted a centuries-old sedentary subsistence agriculture. To this economic basis, particularly in the last century, has been added the commercial crop of coffee, ideally suited to the slopes, soils and climate of the region. In the last twenty-five years the extension and transfer of banana cultivation to the Pacific coastlands has further strengthened its economic activities.

Three great depressions penetrate the highland, those of the Motagua and Ulúa already mentioned, leading south-west and south respectively from the Gulf of Honduras, and a great north-west–south-east corridor from the Gulf of Fonseca on the Pacific to San Juan del Norte on the Costa Rican-Nicaraguan frontier, and partly filled by Lakes Managua and Nicaragua.

This latter zone has become the principal area of settlement in Nicaragua, and thus forms somewhat of an exception to the highland concentrations of the three states to the north. The region, however, is still within the volcanic area, and in Lake Nicaragua itself three cones exceed 5,000 feet in height. In the north-western extension of the depression toward its deepest downthrow, that of the Gulf of Fonseca, intense volcanic activity has strewn the area with cones, many of which are still active, and the fertile ash soils are the basis of the republic's agriculture.

The part of the lowland sheltered by the central mountain wedge stretching south from Honduras is relatively dry and is given over to pastoralism. It is the *rainier* slopes of the area between the lakes and the Pacific which are of greatest economic importance. Here a much diversified agriculture including coffee, cotton, sugar, tobacco, sesame and rice is practised, with maize and beans still of great importance as subsistence staples. Cotton is of greatest importance commercially, accounting for one-third of the exports. Coffee, 75 per cent of which is grown south of Managua, ranks next in importance, and the country is self-sufficient in sugar.

A surprisingly large number of urban settlements occur in this nucleus of population, Managua (300,000), Léon (62,000) and Granada (40,000) being the largest centres. Corinto (10,000) is the principal Pacific port, 60 per cent of Nicaraguan trade passing through it, while Chinandega (37,000) on the route from Corinto to Managua is now the principal banana zone of Nicaragua.

El Salvador, although less than one-quarter the size of Nicaragua, has a much greater population, and the whole state falls within this Pacific volcanic region. Unlike the other Central American republics therefore, there is a homogeneity and cohesion in a land almost uniformly utilized and more than well occupied. The principal relief constituents of the republic are a double chain of volcanic heights parallel to the Pacific shore, flanked on the north-east by a parallel valley, that of the Lempa and Torola, and then rising towards the highlands of Honduras. The Lempa cuts its way through the volcanic region to reach the Pacific. The heaviest concentrations of population occur within the long interior plateau separating the two volcanic ranges.

The pressure of this population on limited land resources has led to much soil erosion. The major agricultural concentration is upon subsistence crops, maize and beans again providing the great staples of diet. Coffee is the principal commercial crop, grown on the highland slopes, and it is estimated that 150 million trees are cultivated on over 300,000 acres in the state. Although ranking, in Latin America, as an exporter third only to Brazil and Colombia, El Salvador is less dependent than formerly on coffee monoculture.

Fortunately high prices for this product have enabled the country to purchase the increasingly large supplies of foodstuffs its growing population requires. Sugar, once exported in considerable quantities, is now imported, and maize, beans and rice are also produced in insufficiently large quantities to meet the demand.

With the possible exception of Uruguay, no other Latin American state so uses the whole of its territory as does El Salvador. Rural density of population is slightly higher in the western and central parts but nowhere is there empty land which is capable of being occupied. The pattern of land tenure is also largely that of small holdings, neither the colonial hacienda nor the modern American capitalized tropical estate being of any importance. These characteristics and the homogeneous ethnic quality of its people make El Salvador unique not only in Central America but in Latin America.

There has also been some development of industry, and textiles, foodstuffs and consumer goods are produced, the use of local henequen supplies to manufacture coffee bags being especially important.

San Salvador (350,000) is the principal urban centre, with Santa Ana (163,000) as the main coffee centre; and although Acajutla (16,000) handles 40 per cent of the country's trade, a considerable amount of its commerce passes through Puerto Barrios to which it is connected by rail.

The Honduran portion of this region comprises an eastern and a western part separated by the deep structural trough which runs from the plain of Sula to the Gulf of Fonseca. The high basins of both sub-regions reach a variety of altitudes permitting a wide range of templada and fria crops including European fruits and cereals, but coffee and tobacco cultivation and the raising of cattle are the outstanding economic activities. The watershed basins between the Lempa and Ulúa drainage systems contain most of the population of the west, that of Copán being especially productive, and a corresponding group is located on the Humuya–Fonseca watershed in the east. In both cases the mineral wealth, including opals, antimony, gold, silver and platinum, attracted settlement, and Tegucigalpa (253,000), the capital, owes its origin to this fact, the silver mine of San Juancito supplying some 5 per cent of the exports.

The rift valley to the south has Comayagua (13,000) in its central zone and is an important pastoral centre. Although the importance of this trans-isthmian route was recognized from the early days of the Spanish conquest, its economic development, like that of all Honduras, is less than would seem to be expected.

Amapala (4,000), founded in the early 19th century, for long remained Honduras's principal port. It is located on the great strategic bay of Fonseca where not only El Salvador, Honduras and Nicaragua meet, but from which great natural routeways lead north, east and west into the hearts of these countries. The closure of the Inter-American Highway between El Salvador and Honduras since 1969 has stimulated the introduction of direct vehicle services, across the Gulf of Fonseca, between El Salvador and Nicaragua. The importance of air transport to overcome the difficulties of roads and few railways in this mountainous country is worthy of note, and Tegucigalpa has become the air hub of Central America.

The high basins of Guatemala, over 6,500 feet in elevation, bear a close resemblance to those of Anáhuac, with their basic maize and string beans and the tierra fria crops of wheat, barley and potatoes. The population, too, is largely Indian, Quezaltenango (51,000) the second city of Guatemala being in the heart of this agricultural zone. Thus the region has close affinities with its northern neighbour in both the physical and human conditions operative there. To the east a lower group of basins, still within the richly fertile volcanic belt, is the most important coffee and sugar zone, especially around Antigua (24,000) and Amatitlán (12,000).

Guatemala City (577,000), located in order to be accessible from Pacific and Atlantic, was built to replace Antigua when that city was destroyed by earthquake in 1773, and is still the greatest city of Central America. San José (6,000), the Pacific port, is chiefly important as the coffee export port, but is an open roadstead.

Guatemala's exports are 55 per cent dependent on coffee and bananas, the high prices of coffee in recent years tending to increase the importance of that crop. Output is fourth of the Latin American states, being exceeded only by the much larger countries of Brazil, Colombia and Mexico. It is produced in the south-western and central highlands from large plantations, many of them Government-owned, which were begun by Spanish landowners and German pioneers of the second half of the 19th century. The influence of the United Fruit Company on the Guatemalan economy, and their development of banana plantations and communications to the Atlantic coast have already been described.

While these export crops are of great and increasing importance it must not be forgotten that most of the Guatemalan people are small subsistence farmers growing crops of maize, beans and other vegetables in a fairly dense network of Indian communities in the western highlands. Increasing pressure of population in this region, consequent upon Guatemala's very high birth rate, means that many of these people are inadequately fed. Their attachment to their home community is so strong, however, that attempts at re-distributing them in the very considerable areas of Guatemala's unused territory have met with little success, and in 1954 attempts to settle them on expropriated lands of large haciendas nearer the large foci of settlement were frustrated by political forces which caused a crisis of international magnitude.

Costa Rica – Panama

Although divided into two political states, this region is one structural unit of a series of mountain ranges aligned on a north-west–south-east axis with their fringing lowlands. Separated from Nicaragua by the Lake Nicaragua–San Juan depression, and from Colombia by the Atrato valley, it consists of an isthmus over 500 miles in length and nowhere much more than 100 miles in width.

On the Caribbean side coastal lowlands are more typical of Costa Rica than Panama. In the north these stretch through the basin of the San Juan and its tributaries for three-quarters of Costa Rica's frontier with Nicaragua, decreasing in width south-eastward until in Panama they rarely extend more than 20 miles from the sea, especially where the San Blas range adjoins the Caribbean.

Drenched with 120 inches of rain spread fairly evenly throughout the year, these coastlands support a luxuriant forest vegetation on the thick alluvial sediments brought down by such rivers as the San Carlos, Sarapiqui and Sixiaola. Indian communities are supported by subsistence farms in clearings, and in the first forty years of this century this was the principal scene of the United Fruit Company's operations in Costa Rica. The attack of Panama disease caused the abandonment of some of these banana plantations and their reversion to second-growth timber. Others were retained for production of cocoa and abacá, and more recently, Costa Rica has again become a major producer of bananas from this zone. In Panama, too, in the San Blas, Colón and Darién districts bananas are still grown on the Caribbean coastlands. Apart from Puerto Limón (20,000) (and Cristóbal and Colón dependent on the Canal zone) there are no important settlements on the northern coast of the isthmus. Likewise, apart from the good rail network developed from Puerto Limón to serve the 85,000 acres of banana plantations (and the Canal zone roads and railway) the region is devoid of all transport facilities. In the widest part of the plain the lower courses of the rivers are navigable and form the main arteries of communication.

Forming the backbone of the isthmus is the range known in the north-west as the Cordillera de Guanacaste, in the heart of Costa Rica as the Cordillera Central, and in Panama as the Sierra de Veragua. Increasing in height and evidence of recent volcanic activity from north-west to south-east, and rising to over 11,000 feet in height, it is crowned by the four great Costa Rican volcanic cones of

Poas, Barba, Irazú and Turrialba and the Panamanian peak of Chirigui.

On the south-west flanks of the central Costa Rican portion of this cordillera occurs the great area of settlement where live 70 per cent of the people of that state. Known as the Meseta Central, its 3,500 square miles of basaltic and ash soils (some probably riverine and lacustrine deposited) support a diversified agricultural pattern of coffee, sugar cane, tobacco, beans, rice, potatoes and maize. David, the centre of a region on the flanks of Chirigui in Panama, has a similar economic basis. In Costa Rica, there are four principal settlements San José (183,000) the capital, Alajuela (29,000), Cartago (22,000) and Heredia (24,000) but for the most part the population is rural in character, and land-holding is in the hands of small peasant proprietors descended from Spanish 16th-century stock.

The Cordillera de Talamanca, a crystalline ridge flanked with sedimentaries, parallels the Meseta Central on the south-west, but as its average height does not exceed 7,000 feet, Pacific influences, notably the December–May dry season, extend into the Meseta Central, except in the Reventazón valley which drains to the Caribbean.

The Pacific slope of the isthmus is less simple and uniform in its structure, relief and vegetation. Consisting of the remnants of other parallel ranges which form the peninsulas of Nicoya, Golfo Dulce and Azuero and many off-shore islands, the low and often marshy intervening plains are the principal areas used. The Guanacaste lowlands, tributary to Puntarenas (31,000), are the scene of considerable cattle raising; the 50-mile depression of the Diquis valley is another such area and grows tobacco near Buenos Aires; and the Golfito and Quepos coastal lowlands are the major areas of banana, cocoa, coconut and African oil-palm production.

While there is considerable evidence of emergence, the drowned estuaries of the Gulf of Panama reveal recent submergence, and the relatively shallow Pacific coastal waters lead to the high tides experienced at Panamá.

Costa Rica's economic existence is largely dependent on exports of coffee and bananas, and Panama's on the Canal zone and the employment and income it offers to many Panamanians. A United States presidential commission has recommended the construction of a sea-level canal across Panama, 10 miles west of the present canal zone. Such a development will even further strengthen Panama's economy.

The zone containing the great ocean highway which dominates the state of Panama forms a great contrast with the rest of the republic. Forming almost a part of United States territory, the towns of Cristóbal and Balboa are the terminal ports, but Colón (68,000) and Panama (389,000) (within the zone but not under its administration) are the principal cities and contain nearly one-third of the population of all Panama.

Otherwise there is no major nucleus of population, and it thus offers a striking contrast to the core of Costa Rica, which ever since the 18th century has been expanding in all directions and slowly filling the adjacent areas and valleys peripheral to the Meseta Central.

PROSPECTS AND PROBLEMS

Central America as a whole reveals characteristics which are common to Latin America, and yet there are features which distinguish it from the rest of the continent. As an example of the latter, its relative poverty in mineral wealth is outstanding and forms a striking contrast with its great neighbour to the north. The only significant mineral production is that of silver in Honduras and more recently, of bauxite in the San Isidro de El General district of Costa Rica where Alcoa is installing an alumina plant of 400,000 tons annual capacity.

Three outstanding conditions dominate the economies of all the political units forming the area. These are the reliance on tropical agricultural exports, especially bananas and coffee, the large share in their development occupied by foreign capital, and in particular that of the United Fruit Company and its subsidiaries, and the dependence of their foreign trade on the United States.

There is also a considerable import of food supplies which could be met in large part, with improved agricultural techniques and planned development, from within the territories themselves. In recent years, all the republics have devoted much attention to this problem, and there have been substantial gains in agricultural, livestock and fisheries production. The shrimp, crawfish and tuna resources off the Pacific coast appear to have considerable potentialities in this respect; and Central America has now become a significant exporter of meat. Sales of this product are exceeded in value only by the long-established exports of coffee, bananas and cotton; and only Australia and New Zealand sell more meat to the United States.

In spite of such developments, however, imports of foodstuffs into

Central America continue to increase, and if no fundamental agricultural reforms occur to increase productivity, such a trend will undoubtedly continue.

A poor communications system, lack of political stability (except in the case of Costa Rica) and a shortage of capital resources to develop its empty lands have been the principal reasons why the Central American region has remained for so long one of the most underdeveloped areas of Latin America. However, the setting-up, in 1958, of the Central American Common Market (CACM) offered the first real hope of economic integration, a more rational use of resources, and co-operative planned development. The 1960s, as a result, were a period of economic boom. Aided by favourable conditions for the export of primary products, by a growth in manufacturing industry, and by the liberalization of intra-regional trade, all five members of CACM (Panama not being a member) experienced unparalleled economic growth. Towards the close of the decade, however, as more fundamental steps had to be taken to build a fully effective common market, the differences between the five states began to impose increasing strains and tensions. Guatemala's superior share (40 per cent) of Central America's population and total production (30 per cent), El Salvador's dynamic industrial development and over-population problems, Costa Rica's physical separation from three of the members of CACM and its relative political maturity, and Nicaragua's and Honduras's economic and political backwardness are but a few of these major differences.

More than one-third of the area's large industrial plants are located in Guatemala, and that country and El Salvador, the next most important manufacturing state, have benefited most from the expansion in intra-regional trade. Nicaragua and Honduras have industrialized much more slowly and run increasing deficits in balance of payments with their partners in CACM.

The economic climate, therefore, to (*a*) eliminate inefficient high-cost manufacturing plants, (*b*) eliminate internal trade barriers, (*c*) impose more control over industrial location was, in any case, scarcely promising. It became almost impossible in July 1969 when war developed between Honduras and El Salvador. The basic cause of the conflict was Honduran resentment against Salvadorean immigrants (estimated to number about 300,000) who had spilled over the border, had settled in Honduras and were actively involved in the economic life of that state. When a land reform act came into force in Honduras many Salvadoreans, without documents and legal claims to the lands they occupied, were expelled. El Salvador's anger at this treatment of its nationals, its difficulty in accommodating about 100,000 refugees, and the added economic burden imposed on El Salvador's over-population and under-employment problems, combined to make the rift with Honduras the most serious frontier crisis in Latin America for some thirty years.

The immediate economic effects of the closure of the Inter-American highway between the two countries have been to close the Honduran market to Salvadorean industrial products and to deprive El Salvador of foodstuffs and raw materials previously supplied by Honduras, but the more serious long-term effect of the conflict has been to imperil the continuance of the CACM. In 1971 Honduras effectively withdrew from membership, and increasing strains developed among the remaining four states. The break-up of the organization would be a serious set-back to the hope of Central American economic development. All five states need the access to a wider market that a fully developed CACM would bring to their existing industries or to those they plan to establish. All realize that they will never overcome their under-development individually, but probably as important as economic integration is the need of the five states to solve many of their social and political problems. Foremost among these, in the case of all except Costa Rica, are the backwardness resulting from archaic social structures, a long-neglected agrarian system and the continuance of dictatorship and internal political violence.

STATISTICAL SUMMARY — GUATEMALA

Area: 42,044 square miles

Population (1970): 5,164,000

Percentage of land

(a)	Arable	19%
(b)	Pastoral	7%
(c)	Forest	50%
(d)	Other	24%

Animal numbers

(a)	Cattle	1·2 million	
(b)	Sheep	0·7	,,
(c)	Pigs	0·5	,,
(d)	Goats	0·1	,,

Communications
    (*a*) All-seasons road mileage   7,080
    (*b*) Railway mileage   603

Principal products
    Agricultural

Maize	690,000	metric tons
Sugar	171,000	,, ,,
Coffee	108,000	,, ,,
Bananas	90,000	,, ,,

Exports
    (*a*) *Total:* $222,000,000
    (*b*) *Percentage share of principal commodities*

Coffee	51%
Sugar	4%
Bananas	3%

STATISTICAL SUMMARY — BELIZE

Area: 8,867 square miles

Population (1970): 122,000

Percentage of land
    (*a*) Arable   2%
    (*b*) Pastoral   1%
    (*c*) Forest   46%
    (*d*) Other   51%

Principal products
    Agricultural
        Sugar and Molasses   88,000 metric tons

Exports
    (*a*) *Total:* $15,000,000
    (*b*) *Percentage share of principal commodities*

Sugar	40%
Citrus	23%
Forest products	7%

STATISTICAL SUMMARY — HONDURAS

Area: 43,277 square miles

Population (1970): 2,573,000

Percentage of land
  (*a*) Arable   7%
  (*b*) Pastoral 31%
  (*c*) Forest   27%
  (*d*) Other   35%

Animal numbers
  (*a*) Cattle   1·7 million
  (*b*) Pigs   0·8   „

Communications
  (*a*) All-seasons road mileage   1,418
  (*b*) Railway mileage   341

Principal products
  Agricultural
    Bananas   850,000 metric tons
    Maize   355,000   „   „

Exports
  (*a*) *Total:* $182,000,000
  (*b*) *Percentage share of principal commodities*
    Bananas   47%
    Coffee   12%
    Wood   8%
    Silver   5%

STATISTICAL SUMMARY — EL SALVADOR

Area: 8,083 square miles

Population (1970): 3,496,000

Percentage of land

   (*a*) Arable   30%
   (*b*) Pastoral   28%
   (*c*) Forest   11%
   (*d*) Other   31%

Animal numbers

   (*a*) Cattle   0·9 million
   (*b*) Pigs   0·3   ,,

Communications

   (*a*) All-seasons road mileage   1,921
   (*b*) Railway mileage   318

Principal products

   Agricultural
      Maize   202,000 metric tons
      Coffee   138,000   ,,   ,,
      Sugar   125,000   ,,   ,,
      Rice   65,000   ,,   ,,
      Cotton   35,000   ,,   ,,

Exports

   (*a*) *Total:* $212,000,000
   (*b*) *Percentage share of principal commodities*
            Coffee   44%
            Cotton   7%

STATISTICAL SUMMARY — NICARAGUA

Area: 57,143 square miles

Population (1970): 1,965,000

Percentage of land

   (*a*) Arable   7%
   (*b*) Pastoral   7%
   (*c*) Forest   36%
   (*d*) Other   50%

Animal numbers
  (a) Cattle   1·3 million
  (b) Pigs   0·4   ,,

Communications
  (a) All-seasons road mileage   2,116
  (b) Railway mileage   250
  (c) Air routes   28 million passenger miles
                                   3   ,,   ton miles

Principal products
  (a) *Agricultural*
       Maize   172,000 metric tons
       Sugar   108,000   ,,   ,,
       Oilseeds   90,000   ,,   ,,
       Rice   38,000   ,,   ,,
       Coffee   33,000   ,,   ,,
  (b) *Mineral*
       Gold   17,400 troy pounds

Exports
  (a) *Total:* $157,000,000
  (b) *Percentage share of principal commodities*
         Cotton   40%
         Coffee   14%
         Meat   10%
         Sugar   4%

STATISTICAL SUMMARY — COSTA RICA

Area: 19,653 square miles

Population (1970): 1,740,000

Percentage of land
  (a) Arable   12%
  (b) Pastoral   18%
  (c) Forest   59%
  (d) Other   11%

Animal numbers
  (a) Cattle   1·1 million
  (b) Pigs   0·1   ,,

Communications

    (*a*) All-seasons road mileage   3,713

    (*b*) Railway mileage   321

Principal products

  Agricultural

Bananas	567,000 metric tons	
Sugar	145,000 ,,	,,
Rice	87,000 ,,	,,
Maize	76,000 ,,	,,
Coffee	76,000 ,,	,,

Exports

    (*a*) *Total:* $172,000,000

    (*b*) *Percentage share of principal commodities*

        Coffee   32%

        Bananas   26%

        Cocoa   2%

STATISTICAL SUMMARY — PANAMA

Area: 29,306 square miles, of which Canal Zone: 553 square miles

Population (1970): 1,458,000 (Canal Zone: 63,000)

Percentage of land

    (*a*) Arable   7%

    (*b*) Pastoral   11%

    (*c*) Forest   80%

    (*d*) Other   2%

Animal numbers

    (*a*) Cattle   1·0 million

    (*b*) Pigs   0·2 ,,

Communications

    (*a*) All-seasons road mileage   4,133

    (*b*) Railway mileage   404

Principal products

Agricultural

Bananas	583,000 metric tons
Rice	151,000 ,, ,,
Cotton	103,000 ,, ,,
Maize	89,000 ,, ,,

Exports

(a) *Total:* $95,000,000

(b) *Percentage share of principal commodities*

Bananas	58%
Refined Petroleum	19%
Shrimps	10%

CENTRAL AMERICAN COMMON MARKET

REGIONAL TRADE, 1968–70

(*million U.S. dollars*)

Imported from	Year	Total	Costa Rica	El Salvador	Imported by Guatemala	Honduras	Nicaragua
Costa Rica	1968	37·7	—	8·9	8·0	6·5	14·2
	1969	36·1	—	8·5	7·5	7·4	12·7
	1970	48·7	—	11·2	11·2	12·4	13·9
El Salvador	1968	84·9	16·0	—	30·8	23·2	14·9
	1969	71·8	14·2	—	33·2	12·4	11·9
	1970	74·6	19·7	—	39·5	nil	15·4
Guatemala	1968	77.5	15·8	34·6	—	14·2	13·0
	1969	86·4	17·6	38·1	—	17·8	12·9
	1970	105·8	21·0	40·6	—	28·5	15·7
Honduras	1968	31·3	5·2	14·8	7·1	—	4·1
	1969	23·9	5·8	7·3	6·0	—	4·7
	1970	18·6	6·7	nil	7·1	—	4·9
Nicaragua	1968	26·9	11·8	6·9	3·5	4·7	—
	1969	30·9	13·6	6·3	4·6	6·4	—
	1970	49·7	19·7	8·8	7·2	14·0	—
TOTAL	1968	258·3	48·8	65·2	49·4	48·7	46·2
	1969	249·0	51·2	60·2	51·4	44·0	42·2
	1970	297·4	67·0	60·6	65·0	54·9	50·0

NOTE: Statistics relate to the value of imports, because the degree of control on imports is greater than on exports.

SOURCE: *Carta Informativa de la Sieca*.

CHAPTER SEVEN

The West Indies

STRETCHING in a vast arc, more than 2,000 miles long, from the peninsulas of Florida and Yucatán to the Venezuelan coast, are spread out the hundreds of islands large and small which together form the West Indies (Fig. 29).

Although less than half the area of Central America they contain 25 per cent more people, and no comparable area of Latin America has such a variety or complexity of physical and human geography. In their structure, relief, soils, vegetation, histories, peoples, economies and political systems differences are everywhere evident, and it is almost necessary to study each island individually. It is possible, however, to subdivide the great archipelago into four main groups on a basis of the structural unity of each, and consider the components of each group. These are:

(i) The Bahamas.
(ii) The Greater Antilles, between the Yucatán channel and the Anegada passage.
(iii) The Lesser Antilles, from the Anegada passage to Grenada.
(iv) The continental islands, including Barbados, Trinidad and the Venezuelan off-shore islands.

THE BAHAMAS, CAICOS AND TURKS ISLANDS

This archipelago of 700 islands, only 30 of which are inhabited, spreads for 900 miles from Florida to the great Brownson deep (27,972 feet), the greatest depth of the Atlantic, north of Puerto Rico. They are low æolian limestone islands scattered on a submarine platform, and are built of shell detritus in hills and ridges aligned along the outer edges of the banks. The highest in the group is Cat Island which rises to 206 feet above sea-level. The long barrier reef protecting the eastern side of Andros is second in size only to the Great Barrier reef off the Queensland coast of Australia. It flanks the western side of a submarine depression known as the Tongue of the Ocean, which is a mile deep for most of its length.

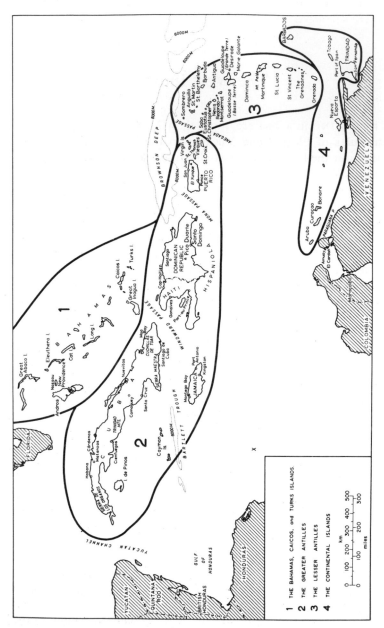

Fig. 29. *The regions of the West Indies*

Andros and Great Abaco are the largest units but together are peopled by only some 15,000 inhabitants. The principal activity in these islands is the exploitation of the yellow pine (mainly for pulpwood and lumber), resources which are estimated to cover 700,000 acres of the Bahamas.

The most important island is New Providence on which the capital, Nassau, is situated. This small island alone has nearly half the total population of the group, which is little more than 175,000, 86 per cent of whom are of negroid origin.

The prosperity of the Bahamas rests principally on the tourist trade, an asset developed from its proximity to the United States and contrastingly mild winter climate. Over 1 million tourists visit the islands annually, the spread of this industry to the lesser known islands or 'Out Islands' being a recent development. More Bahamians earn their living from the provision of services for tourists than from any other sector of the economy; and it is estimated that half the islands' earnings in foreign exchange, or some 150 million dollars annually, is derived from tourism.

Although little more than 1 per cent of the area is under arable use, there has been a considerable expansion in agricultural production in recent years. Now, with fisheries, the islands produce one-third of their food requirements. This expansion is largely the result of the use of modern production techniques, and substantial areas on Abaco and Andros have been cleared mechanically for vegetable production for export. On Abaco a 20,000 acres sugar cane plantation was established in 1969, and dairy farming is carried on in New Providence and Eleuthera islands. Most agricultural output, however, still comes from small subsistence farms varying in size from one half to five acres. Foodstuffs are still the principal import, but local production of poultry products (in which the islands are now self-supporting), tropical and sub-tropical fruits and vegetables significantly contributes to local needs.

In the last decade large scale manufacturing industries have been established, particularly at Nassau and at Freeport on Grand Bahama island. Tax concessions, international banking facilities, good modern harbours, and the nodality of the Bahamas to supply markets throughout the Americas have contributed to the success of its industrialization programme. Using Bahaman limestone and Jamaican bauxite as raw materials, cement output now exceeds 5 million barrels annually and is the islands' principal export commodity. The refining of low sulphur-content fuel oil for areas where air pollution is a severe problem is now carried out at the largest refinery of its type in the world. Pharmaceutical products and rum are other major industrial commodities contributing to Bahaman exports.

The Turks and Caicos islands which are the south-eastern extension of the Bahamas have some 7,000 inhabitants, and are administered by Jamaica. A small quantity of sisal is grown, but the principal export is salt, the combination of low flat islands, high insolation, meagre rainfall and steady trade winds providing an ideal physical environment for its production. The salt industry on Long island in the Bahamas has expanded considerably recently.

All these islands have been in continuous British occupation since the early 18th century, and they can be considered in every way peripheral to Latin America.

THE GREATER ANTILLES

Composed of the four large islands of Cuba, Hispaniola, Jamaica and Puerto Rico, and the smaller structurally associated Virgin islands, the Greater Antilles comprise 90 per cent of the area of the West Indies and an even larger proportion of the region's people.

The early occupation of the western third of Hispaniola by the French and of Jamaica by the British has led to those two areas remaining outside the realm of Spanish colonization, and in language and culture they offer a distinct contrast to the rest of the Greater Antilles.

Structurally, the great west–east arcs of folded and block mountains dominate the relief, and continue the Antillean structures of Guatemala and Honduras (Fig. 30). They are not, however, part of one great mountain range but a series of folds and horsts, described by one writer as the most impressive block-mountain region of the earth. The magnitude of their structure is only fully realized when it is associated with the deep submarine troughs which parallel them, for then their total height above the ocean floor, in several places, exceeds that of Everest, while the descent from the crest of El Yunque in Puerto Rico to the adjacent Brownson deep is more than 31,700 feet.

The complexity of these great ranges, folded, faulted and torn into ridges and deep intervening plains and valleys reaches its maximum in the Cordillera Central of Hispaniola; and Figure 30 indicates the relationship between the ranges of the several islands.

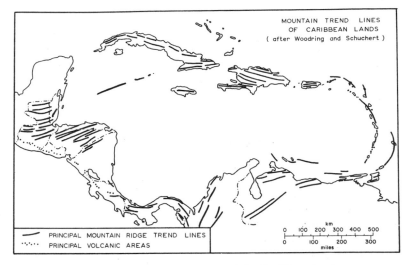

Fig. 30. *Mountain trend lines of the Caribbean lands*
The predominantly east–west trends of the structures of Central America
and the West Indies

The principal submarine depressions are the Bartlett trough extending eastward from the Gulf of Honduras and north of Jamaica
to the Windward passage, truncating the southern face of the Sierra
Maestra of Cuba, and the Atlantic and Brownson trough aligned
parallel to the northern coasts of Hispaniola and Puerto Rico.

CUBA

This island alone (Figs. 29 and 31) is approximately equal in area to
all the remaining West Indian islands, and its population of 8·5 million is similar to that of Venezuela or Chile. Despite a major social
and economic revolution since 1959 its exports by value are equiv-
alent to 70 per cent of those of all the Central American republics
together, and its capital city, Habana (1,566,000) is one of the
greatest ports of Latin America.

Almost 800 miles in length and varying in width from 25 to
120 miles, the island has a greater amount of lowland than any of the
other Greater Antilles. Three relatively small areas of mountain
ranges, progressively higher from west to east, do little to interrupt
these lowlands. The Sierra de los Orgános rising to 2,500 feet
occupies the narrow western Pinar del Río extensions of the island;
the Trinidad mountains with a peak of 3,972 feet overlook the

southern coast for 50 miles east of Cienfuegos; and the Sierra Maestra and Sierra del Cobre culminating in a height of 6,560 feet occupy the broad eastern base of the island and plunge seaward in precipitous cliffs, which form a marked contrast to the otherwise cay- and reef-fringed shallow lowland coasts of the rest of Cuba.

Climatically, therefore, regional differences are small and the whole island experiences sufficiency of rainfall with the heaviest falls from May to October. Temperatures are affected in winter by the influence of the cold air masses centred over North America, but average monthly temperatures vary only between 70 and 82°F. in the coldest and hottest months.

In spite of its favourable physical endowment the four centuries of Spanish occupation resulted in little development of the island. By 1900 the population had reached only 1½ millions, only 3 per cent of the area was cultivated, most of the people were concentrated in Habana province, and communications between this area and the coastal settlements and pastoral estates elsewhere in Cuba were primitive.

Already, however, sugar cane was the principal crop, and after political independence was achieved in 1902, the intensification of sugar cultivation and its spread eastward dominated the agriculture and economic existence of Cuba, until the island became the greatest single source of the world's sugar, producing twice the quantity grown in Brazil.

Within little more than half a century the island made considerable economic progress, a good rail network being constructed to serve the agricultural estates and the foundations of industrialization being laid in the form of light manufacturing for the domestic market. Population grew to four times that of 1900, and without careful curbs on immigration the increase would have been considerably greater.

Four factors were responsible for this rapid economic change, three of which were closely linked to the political transference of power from a Spanish colony to a United States protected republic. The fourth was the great expansion in sugar consumption which coincided with this change and provided an expanding market for the island's great agricultural product.

The three politically derived factors were

(i) the eradication of yellow fever, which had been endemic in the island throughout its history, and which had not only hindered economic progress but sapped the island's demographic growth,

(ii) the preferential tariff on Cuban sugar entering the United States market, and

(iii) the large investment of United States capital to an extent greater than that invested in any other Latin American state. The security of the investments was guaranteed during the period 1903–34 by a treaty provision which enabled the United States to intervene in Cuban affairs to maintain political stability.

As a result the island developed a complete dependence on a one-crop system, 85 per cent of Cuba's exports by value being sugar and molasses. Insufficient maize, rice, beans, potatoes, fats and oils, and dairy products were produced for the needs of the island, in spite of the general fertility and suitability of the republic to the raising of all these foodstuffs.

Pinar del Río, the westernmost province, was the only one of Cuba's six provinces (Fig. 31) which was relatively unimportant in sugar production, and except for the mountainous areas and the southern coastal regions, there were few parts of Cuba which did *not* grow sugar. Although there were considerable fluctuations in area dependent upon the world sugar market, the tendency was for the marginal lands to be devoted to other crops and for sugar to be grown on the *tierra rosa* soils of Habana, Matanzas, Las Villas and the better lands of Camagüey and Oriente.

Large sugar estates owned half the arable land of Cuba and rented an additional 2 million acres, six companies alone occupying 60 per cent of the sugar lands. As with other similar latifundia systems elsewhere in Latin America large areas of these estates were left fallow or as natural pasture. Some 60,000 peasant farmers (*colonos*) grew most of the sugar, on farms varying in size from 500 to 3,000 acres, and the total area under sugar cultivation exceeded 3½ million acres. The grinding of the cane, however, was in the hands of 161 mills and the control which these exercised in respect of the quality, harvesting and demand for the cane was obviously considerable. The larger farms tended to be in the newer areas of production, Camagüey and Oriente, and the smaller farms in the older sugar areas of Habana, Matanzas and Las Villas.

The harvest season from mid-January to June involved a large labour force in cutting, transporting and crushing the cane, and at one time seasonal immigrants from Jamaica and Haiti used to participate in this work. In the second half of the year there was insufficient work on the plantations, and unemployment in Cuba

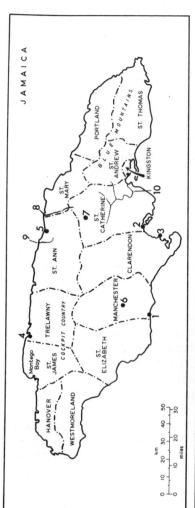

Fig. 31. *Jamaican parishes and Cuban provinces*

1 Alligator Pond
2 Old Harbour
3 Rocky Point
4 Discovery Bay
5 Ocho Rios
6 Mandeville
7 Ewarton
8 White River
9 Roaring River
10 Cobre River

A Santa Cruz
C Camagüey
D Cárdenas
F Cienfuegos
G Guatánamo
M Matanzas
N Nuevitas
S Santa Clara

during this dead season often affected a quarter of the country's labour force. This uneven demand for labour was another bad feature of the sugar monoculture. It also explained the resistance of Cuban labour to the mechanization of the cutting and cultivation parts of the industry, lest these improvements caused a further increase in unemployment.

Apart from the many chronic social consequences of the sugar latifundia, price fluctuations in the world market for sugar caused many crises in Cuba's economy. Although until 1960 it had a fairly assured market for a large proportion of its sugar crop in the United States, it still had to sell to the United Kingdom and Europe to maintain its economic survival, and there were many non-Cuban growers of sugar in a similar position.

The social and economic revolution which occurred in 1959, however, has considerably changed the island's human geography. Of foremost importance is the death of the previous latifundia system and its replacement by agricultural co-operatives and state-run farms. Over 14 million acres of farm land, or 95 per cent of the arable and pasture lands of Cuba have been taken over by the Government as public property, and similar expropriations of the sugar mills have given control of the industry to a National Institute of Agrarian Reform (INRA). The sugar co-operatives have since been reorganized into people's farms on which the workers are employees rather than members of a co-operative enterprise.

A considerable period of economic dislocation inevitably resulted from these rapid changes. The loss of skilled technicians, the inexperience of peasant administrators of the new farms and of the new intensive methods of cultivation designed to increase agricultural diversification, the running down of the internal transport and distributional system, and indiscriminate slaughtering of cattle led to severe food shortages. Prolonged droughts and the United States embargo on trade have further exacerbated the island's problems.

The preferential sugar market in the United States has been cut off, and Cuba's trade increasingly orientated towards the U.S.S.R., Eastern Europe and China. Most of the sugar is exported in an unrefined state, although some is refined for the local market, and rum and industrial alcohol are also produced.

Cuban cigar tobacco is very well known, and exports of this crop account for some 5 per cent of the total of the island's trade. The Vuelta Abajo leaf is the highest quality and is the most famous for the manufacture of cigars within the island, at Habana. Grown in the southern foothills of the Sierra de los Orgános in Pinar del Río province and centred on the town of the same name, it is a crop requiring considerable care and a relatively large supply of labour. Vuelta Arriba leaf from the same district, or Remedios leaf from Santa Clara, are the principal types exported.

The only other important agricultural products are fruits and vegetables, especially grape-fruit and tomatoes from the two western-most provinces and from the Isla de Pinos; cocoa and coffee from Oriente province; some rice from the southern coastal marshlands; henequen on the north coast between Matanzas and Cárdenas, and cedar (for cigar boxes and pencils) from Camagüey and Oriente.

The fairly widespread beef and dairy cattle industry, especially important in Camagüey and Oriente, based on the natural paraná grass pastures, provides the island with most of its meat supplies. Of the total farm area of the island more than half is under pasture, and meat production is second only to sugar in Cuban agriculture. Seventy-five per cent of the cattle are in the three easternmost provinces.

The Cuban fishing industry is by far the largest in the West Indies, and is now organized on co-operative lines.

The island is also important for its mineral wealth in manganese, chromium, copper and iron, much of the latter consisting of natural alloy ores. Most of the mines are located in the Sierra Maestra and in Pinar del Río. The island is the second producer of manganese in the Americas. The recent discovery of rich nickel deposits in the Moa bay region of Oriente province promises to make Cuba one of the largest producers of this mineral. The extraction of salt from sea water is a widespread industry. Although considerable efforts have been made to discover oil, Cuba is still greatly dependent on supplies of imported oil, most of which now comes from the Soviet Union (Fig. 32).

Even before the revolution there had been considerable progress towards industrialization. Aided by considerable United States investment and a fairly large urban local market, the industries were tariff-protected to encourage their growth. They provided employ-ment for many who otherwise would have been seasonally un-employed, 20 per cent of the island's labour force being employed in manufacturing. Many industries use local raw materials, pro-ducing cigars, cigarettes, rope, dairy products, tinned fruit and cement; others use imported raw materials and make tyres, cotton and rayon textiles, footwear, paper, soap and many other consumer goods. Since 1959 there has been increasing governmental control and ownership of industry, and a four-year industrialization plan was launched in 1961. Shortages of raw materials and spare parts have, however, considerably affected industrial production in recent years and the emphasis of the government's economic policies has been switched from industrial to agricultural development.

Most of the manufacturing industry is concentrated in Habana and Santiago de Cuba (250,000). A network of road and rail communications links these two cities, both of which are early 16th-century Spanish sites strategically located in respect of the entrances to the Gulf of Mexico and the Caribbean sea. Both cities situated on easily defended harbours represent the major *raison d'être* of early Spanish interest in Cuba, and they have retained their pre-eminence into the 20th century.

Camagüey (191,000) is centrally situated in the great lowland between the Sierra Maestra and Trinidad mountains, easily accessible to ports on the north and south coasts (Nuevitas and Santa Cruz), and its importance is as a distributing centre in the cattle farming and sugar districts of the lowland. Santa Clara (191,000) occupies a similar position and function for the province of that name, and Cienfuegos (99,000) its port has a flourishing export trade in sugar and tobacco.

Cárdenas (48,000) and Matanzas (82,000) are important sugar ports, and the latter is also a centre of the rayon industry. In common with the rest of Latin America the increasing urbanization of the Cuban population is noteworthy, more than half the people now living in cities. Habana has one-fifth of the population and there are eight other cities with more than 100,000 inhabitants each.

The four-fold increase in Cuba's population (now increasing by 1 million every decade) since 1900 has largely resulted from the prosperity of the sugar industry encouraging immigrants from many European lands, and the principal effect on the ethnic composition of the island's people has been greatly to increase the proportion of white to negro. A century ago 55 per cent of the population were Negro slaves, and still in the coastal areas and ports, especially in Oriente province, negroid and mulatto elements are numerous. Today, however, the negroid proportion in the total population does not exceed 30 per cent, although only rigorous immigration laws prevent a flow of emigrants from the adjoining and much more densely populated islands of Jamaica and Haiti.

Of considerable economic importance until 1959 was the rapidly

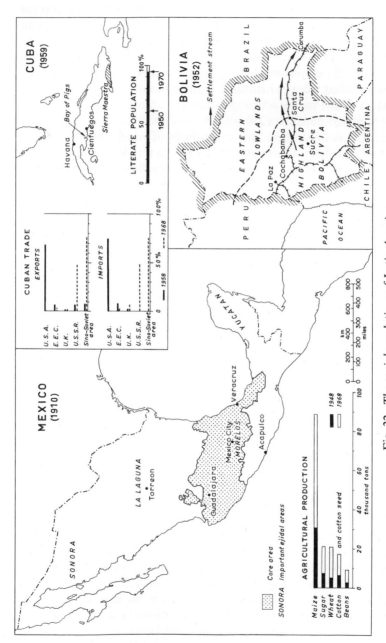

Fig. 32. *The social revolutions of Latin America*

Agrarian reform, internal colonization and social improvement have characterized these revolutions

developing tourist industry (second only in Latin America to that of Mexico) which catered to an annual influx of almost a quarter of a million visitors a year. It is the nearest foreign environment available to the large population concentrations of the eastern United States, and its climate, scenery and exotic life were attractions to a great number of people. Since the revolution the hotels have been nationalized and former private tourist resorts have been taken over as public recreational centres.

Cuba is fortunate among the Greater Antilles in being the island with the smallest pressure of population on land resources, and with increasing diversification of agriculture and a developing industrialization its future prosperity is considerably brighter than that of the other large islands of the West Indies. Like Mexico and Bolivia it has undertaken a radical revolution in an effort to overcome the severe political, social and economic problems which plague most Latin American countries. In so doing it has become involved in a grave international crisis, and has had to defend its new social and economic structure from emigré attack and United States hostility and embargo. To survive it has had to develop close economic ties with Russia, Eastern Europe and China, who now supply 70 per cent of Cuba's imports and take 60 per cent of its exports. The complete overthrow of an economy dominated by United States investment and trade has been the most dramatic upheaval experienced by any Latin American republic. The extent to which the effects of this change will be permanent depends upon the course of future history.

The most important effects of the revolution are in the sociopolitical field, particularly in respect of education, upon which is spent 16 per cent of the national budget. As a result illiteracy has fallen from 26 to 2 per cent of the population. Health facilities have also been greatly improved, unemployment has largely disappeared and there has been a drastic re-distribution of incomes. To avoid the worst effects of population drift to the cities much effort has been expended on the development of rural communities. In fact, despite tremendous problems and many wasteful mistakes, all objective observers of the Cuban scene agree that 'the average Cuban today is better fed, better housed and better educated than he ever was before',[1] and that his standard of living is well above the Latin American average.

[1] Economist Intelligence Unit, 1967.

HISPANIOLA

The second largest of the Greater Antilles, Hispaniola (Figs. 29 and 33) is about three-quarters of the size of Cuba, from which it is separated by the Windward passage. It contains, however, more people than Cuba in a physical environment which is much less favourable. The Antillean mountain system here reaches its maximum development in the islands. Pico Duarte exceeds 10,400 feet in height, and on all sides the surrounding seas plunge into great depths. In Figure 30 the relationship of the mountain ranges of Hispaniola to the similar structural units of Cuba, Jamaica and Puerto Rico is evident. Indeed the whole island consists of a complicated series of east–west faulted mountain blocks with alternating deep-faulted troughs. At least six fairly distinct physical units can be distinguished from north to south. These are:

(i) The northern cordillera, of relatively low altitude, only occasionally exceeding 2,000 feet, and confined entirely to the Dominican Republic.

(ii) The Cibao and Yuna trough, known as the Vega Real and Plaine du Nord in its eastern and western margins respectively.

(iii) The central cordillera, the wide mountainous backbone of the island, known as the Sierra de Ocoa in the Dominican Republic and the Massif du Nord in Haiti. Composed of a medley of volcanic, metamorphic and sedimentary rocks, its ridges, peaks and intermontane valleys occupy one-third of the island.

(iv) A series of ridges and valleys flanking the central cordillera on the south. The several parallel basins are the most important units of this region. They are:

(a) The Plaine Centrale and the Azua lowland.

(b) The Artibonite valley.

(c) The Enriquillo basin and the Plaine du Cul-de-Sac.

The latter has the appearance of a rift valley, which until recent geological times was a marine strait. Parts of its surface are still 150 feet below sea level and are filled with salt lakes.

(v) The southern cordillera or Massif de la Hotte and de la Selle occupying the 240-mile long southern peninsula of Hispaniola, with many peaks exceeding 6,000 feet in height.

(vi) The south-eastern coastal plain of Seibo, the product of emergence from the sea and recent alluvial deposition.

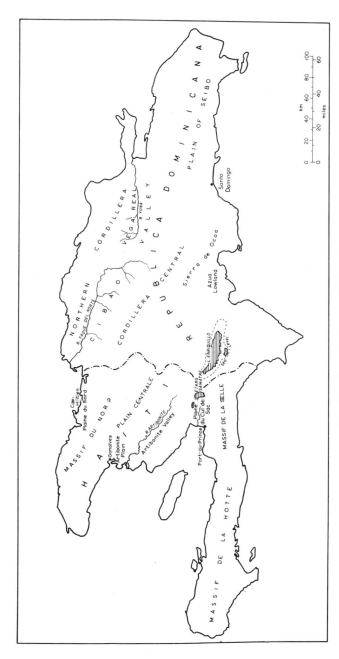

Fig. 33. *The relief units of Hispaniola*
A physical landscape partitioned between two political states

It is not surprising that a region possessing such sharp contrasts of relief within a relatively small area (approximately the size of Scotland) should experience a great variety of climates and vegetation cover. Not only are temperatures affected by elevation and shelter from maritime influences, but there are sharp contrasts in rainfall amounts between exposed coastal regions and deep intermontane valleys in the lee of the transverse mountain ranges. The highest parts of the Central Cordillera are clad in pine forest; evergreen forest covers much of the eastern and south-western peninsulas; and the southern valleys have either a savana or scrub vegetation reflecting semi-arid conditions, where a rainfall total of 50 inches is barely adequate with average temperatures exceeding 75°F. in every month.

Upon this varied physical background two contrasting nations have evolved, Haiti in the western third and the Dominican Republic in the eastern part. From being in the early 16th century the head-quarters of Spanish power in the New World, the island fell first under the influence of pirate buccaneers, and in the 18th century of the French Empire. It is only little more than a century ago that the eastern republic became an independent state, and both nations were occupied for twenty years between the two World Wars by the United States.

The population of the whole island is predominantly negroid or mulatto, descendants of the slaves introduced in the colonial period, although in the Dominican Republic considerable numbers of mestizos and a substantial minority of Europeans, both from colonial days and from recent immigration, differentiate that state from its neighbour. Similarly the Spanish language and the survival of many features of the culture and economic system of the Spanish colonial period make the Dominican Republic more an integral part of Latin America than do the characteristics of French language and African culture and economy typical of Haiti

Although approximately half the area of the Dominican Republic, Haiti has a much larger population, and pressure of people on its resources is an outstanding feature. In contrast, the Dominican Republic, one-third as densely peopled, has been a recipient area for many of the displaced folk of Europe in the chaos caused by the Second World War. Haiti has few empty areas, and no Latin American state has so spread its people over hill and plain almost regardless of terrain. The objective of the people must be largely of a subsistence nature, and the value of its exports rarely exceeds one-quarter of those of the Dominican Republic.

The human geography of the island is in fact a conspicuous example of the effect of differing histories and peoples on a similar physical background, and a more detailed consideration of the regional patterns confirms this contrast.

HAITI

The northern coastal plain of Haiti, centred on Cap Haïtien (30,000), the former capital, was one of the first areas of the island to be settled, and its alluvial soils and hot humid climate still make it one of the most favoured areas. Growing crops of sugar, cotton and sisal on the lowland, and coffee and cocoa on the hill slopes, it contains the most negroid population of the republic and is intensively occupied.

Less favourable is the central plain with its greater aridity and its orientation towards the Azua basin of the Dominican Republic, and its chief utilization is that of cattle raising. The lower Artibonite valley leading seaward to Gonaïves (14,000), with its alkaline soils and mangrove-fringed and scrub-covered lowlands, has raised only poor crops of cotton and been imperfectly utilized. It is an area of some potential relief to Haiti's population problem and a scheme has been put into operation to drain and rehabilitate its lands.

The plain of the Cul-de-Sac, leading out from the Etang Saumâtre to the capital Port-au-Prince (250,000), forms another exceptionally favoured area, which in colonial days was even more extensively irrigated than now. It is still the principal region of sugar-cane cultivation in the republic, and possesses the only railway line, which links its agricultural settlements.

With an average rural density of population exceeding 350 per square mile, there are surprisingly few large centres. Centres of distribution and collection of products are hardly needed. The pattern is one of dispersed agricultural settlement, of farmers, of gardeners growing their patches of coffee, bananas, rice, sugar, maize, manioc, mangoes, oranges and avocado pears, and of the women disposing of the small surplus in the weekly markets at central points on the poor network of tracks connecting the farms.

A little commercial agriculture has appeared in recent years. With the aid of investment from the United States sugar, coffee and sisal are now sold as cash crops. Various vegetable oils and tropical fruits are cultivated, and attempts have been made to establish some of the newer crops such as those from which insecticides are made. Nor has this yet resulted in the growth of a large-estate system.

Some temporary relief on population pressure used to be found in the seasonal migrations to Cuba and the Dominican Republic to help with the sugar harvest, but both countries exerted considerable effort to ensure that the immigrants did not stay. This is a difficult task where a land frontier straggles 160 miles across the mountains of Hispaniola, and there is frequent friction between the two states, as is inevitable.

The only other potential absorption of Haiti's surplus population is likely to come in the future utilization of its mineral resources of copper, lead, silver, zinc and manganese, for even much of its forest land has gone with the demands of agriculture, and soil erosion is severe in many areas. There are undoubtedly significant reserves of minerals and small amounts of copper, gold and iron are mined. Since 1959 some bauxite has been shipped to Texas for refining.

THE DOMINICAN REPUBLIC

In contrast to the fairly even spread of Haitian population, the Dominican Republic has two regions where densities are much higher than elsewhere in the country. These are the Cibao–Vega Real plain of the north, and the south-eastern lowland. The latter area centred on the capital, Santo Domingo (615,000), and the northern lowland, having as its centre Santiago de los Caballeros (330,000), are the great agricultural regions. The Cibao–Yuna Plain has been described as one of 'the most impressively fertile districts in the world'. Endowed with rich alluvial soils, watered by the many tributaries flowing from the Northern and Central cordillera, and liberally supplied with rainfall, its crops of tobacco, cocoa, rice, manioc, maize and sugar are grown on small peasant farms both for subsistence and for export, the country being Latin America's third most important producer of cocoa. Coffee is also of increasing importance. With the collapse of the dictatorship in 1961 some 500 peasant families have been settled on a part of the 1¼ million acres of land previously belonging to the Trujillo family.

In contrast the extensive sugar estates of the south-eastern plain remind one of the haciendas, and this is the most typical land-holding system still in the Dominican Republic. From these estates come the considerable sugar exports which still dominate the country's trade, two companies producing 80 per cent of the total output. In the plain of Azua the drier conditions lead to pastoral farming and sugar can only be grown on the Enriquillo depression with irrigation.

JAMAICA

Jamaica (Figs. 29 and 31) is much smaller than Cuba or Hispaniola, but although less than one-tenth the size of Cuba, it supports over 2 million people, and like Haiti, the pressure of population on limited land resources is the major problem of the island. At its present rate of growth, $2\frac{1}{2}$ per cent annually, numbers will double in the next forty years.

Aligned on an east–west axis 150 miles long and 50 miles wide, the island consists of a mountainous core rising in Blue Mountain peak to over 7,400 feet. This marks the southern line of the Antillean folds continued westward from the south-western peninsula of Haiti and then by a submarine arch into the mountains of Honduras. To north and south the Blue mountains plunge into great ocean depths, the Bartlett trough separating it from the Sierra Maestra of Cuba. These faulted edges of the Jamaica mountains give rise to precipitous cliffs, which along parts of the coast exceed 1,000 feet in height.

Intensely folded and intruded with igneous rocks, the mountainous core is surrounded on all sides by a great dissected limestone plateau which occupies 80 per cent of the area of Jamaica. In parts this is karst country, as in the north-west, where the Cockpit country is a network of collapsed caverns and sink holes; in other areas great solution hollows with fertile tierra rosa soil in the bottom form favourable agricultural regions, the largest such area being the Vale of Clarendon in the south centre of the island. The extensive areas of limestone are also responsible for the generally inadequate surface water supply in spite of the relatively heavy rainfall.

Limited areas of alluvial and raised coral coastal plains fringe the mountain country along the southern coast, the most extensive being west of Kingston.

Many rivers flow north and south from the central mountain ridge, but their descent is so rapid that their principal value is for the development of hydro-electric power, the lower White river, the Cobre, and the Roaring river being the principal ones used in this way.

The mountains contain mineral deposits of manganese, iron and copper, but the exploitation of some of the world's largest deposits of bauxite is the chief development, dating only from 1950 (Fig. 34). The reserves of some 300 million tons occur in depressions in the limestone areas, particularly in the parishes of Manchester, St Elizabeth, Trelawny and St Ann. Two United States companies mine and

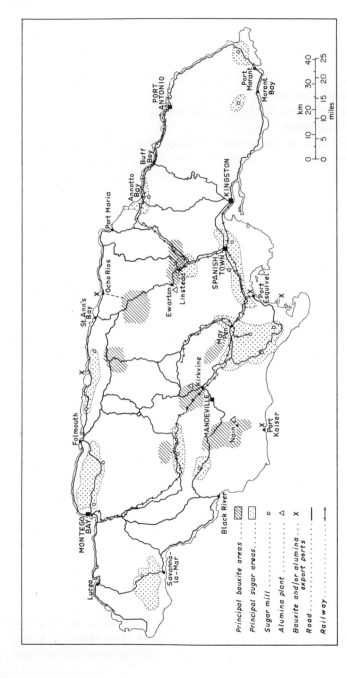

Fig. 34. *Jamaica. Bauxite and sugar*

The two principal export products accounting for three-quarters of the island's export income

ship the dried ore to processing plants in the United States, but a Canadian company processes the bauxite at two plants near Mandeville and Ewarton and then exports the resulting alumina to smelters in Norway and Canada, thus providing employment and saving freight costs. Exports of bauxite which exceed 8 million tons annually, and those of alumina $1\frac{1}{4}$ million tons, make it the world's greatest supplier of aluminium ore. The ports of shipment are Alligator Pond (Port Kaiser), Rocky Point, Discovery Bay (Port Rhoades), Ocho Rios and Old Harbour (Port Esquivel) (Fig. 34). Deposits of gypsum in eastern St Andrew's are exploited commercially, and the limestone provides abundant reserves for cement production.

The northern districts of the island receive the heaviest rainfall from the trades, while those in the rain shadow of the mountain ridge in the south suffer from inadequacy of rainfall, amounts frequently falling below 30 inches annually, and agriculture is in some cases only possible with irrigation.

Most of the population of Jamaica is concerned with agricultural activities, but in addition to subsistence farming on the Haitian model, large amounts of commercial crops are raised, and these still account for 40 per cent of the island's exports, sugar and rum representing 24 per cent and bananas another 8 per cent. Small quantities of cocoa, coffee, tobacco, oranges, grapefruit, pineapples, pimento and ginger make up the remainder.

A quarter of a million acres is devoted to sugar and bananas. The latter are grown on the farms of hundreds of peasant proprietors, and since 1945 an increasing quantity of the sugar is derived from the same source, only 50 per cent of production being now grown on large plantations. Most of the small sugar farmers have less than 20 acres under cane.

Since the Second World War the preferential tariff-protected sugar market and the economic consequences of the Cuban revolution have restored the sugar industry to something of its former importance. Since 1945 production has grown threefold, yields have improved, and the number of sugar factories has been reduced. At the same time the number of sugar farmers has doubled, so the industry is no longer based on the latifundia system of colonial days.

There have been considerable fluctuations in the importance of these two crops in the last three centuries. When Jamaica was first colonized by the British, there was a fairly diversified agricultural pattern of tobacco, indigo, cocoa and sugar, but this rapidly gave

Plate 8. *Jamaica, Guyana and Surinam are the world's major source of bauxite. Ore from this Jamaican open pit is processed into alumina before export, principally to Canada*

way to a commercial monoculture of sugar on the Barbadian model which persisted into the 19th century. In this century the development of the banana industry dominated Jamaican agriculture until by 1937 27 million bunches were sold annually, making the island the largest single source of this fruit in the world. Plant diseases and the Second World War shattered the industry, and its recovery in the post-war years has been restricted by considerable disasters caused by a series of hurricanes, droughts and marketing problems so that

Plate 9. *Subsistence agriculture provides most employment in the West Indies, the surplus being sold at village markets. A Jamaican scene*

the maximum output yet reached since 1945 was 11 million bunches in 1957. Since 1969 all bananas exported have been in island-packed cartons, and output is fairly stationary at 150,000 to 200,000 tons annually, almost all being exported to the United Kingdom.

The principal banana areas are situated along the rainy northern coastlands, especially in the parishes of St Mary and Portland where they are loaded at Oracabessa and Port Antonio. Cocoa, likewise, is favoured by the rainiest districts of the north-east in Portland parish, and coffee in the hills of the eastern part of the Blue mountains. Some sugar is grown in most of the less rainy areas of the island. Half of total production is derived from the parishes of Clarendon and St Catherine; another 20 per cent comes from Westmoreland; and significant amounts from St James, St Thomas and St Elizabeth parishes. It is grown under irrigation in the coastal plain of Kingston, St Andrew's and St Catherine's. This is the most densely populated region of the island accounting for more than one-third of the total population.

Far more important, however, than all these commercial crops, is the widespread subsistence agriculture which feeds the dense rural populations. Distribution of population is uneven. Most of the people live in the coastal areas which generally offer greater possibilities of arable farming than the mountainous and limestone core. The valleys in the plateau with their fertile soils are the major exception to this distributional pattern. Some areas, such as the Yallahs valley, have been seriously eroded by unskilled farming, and efforts are being made to restore their productivity.

The greater part of the area of the island is devoted to pastoral farming, for which the savana on the limestone country is ideally suitable, and much effort is being put into the improvement in quality of the beef and dairy herds.

Relative to its area, road communications are good, and railways link the capital, Kingston, with Montego Bay in the north-west and Port Antonio in the north-east.

The growing population has led to the establishment of industrial and agricultural development corporations to seek additional means of providing a livelihood for the island's people. Agricultural improvements and new crops such as rice in the coastal swamp lands, and industrial developments such as cement, textile, chemical and shoe factories, a paper and cardboard carton mill, an oil refinery and a variety of food processing and other consumer goods plants are some of the steps already taken. Such manufacturing not only meets the increasing local demand for manufactured goods, but provides employment in urban and rural areas, and considerably improves the island's trade balance. Some 25 million dollars worth of manufactured goods are exported annually, but of equal significance is the elimination of imports otherwise needed. For example it is estimated that 60 million dollars worth of cement would have had to be imported into Jamaica in the last thirty years had there been no local manufacture of this product. A growing tourist industry, catering for 400,000 visitors annually, principally centred at Montego Bay, Ocho Rios and Kingston, is also providing alternative employment opportunities, conservatively estimated now to number some 60,000 personnel. Tourist expenditure is some 10 million dollars annually, and the industry is now second only to bauxite as a dollar earner.

Movements of people away from the island have been an important relief to population pressure. For centuries Jamaicans have emigrated to the lands of the Caribbean. They were largely responsible for the colonization of British Honduras, they facilitated the development of the Caribbean coastlands of Central America, they helped construct the Panama Canal, and in recent years many thousands have emigrated to industrial cities of the United Kingdom.

The island was for one and a half centuries under Spanish control but for the last three centuries it is British colonialism which has stamped its political, cultural and social pattern into the island's fabric. The commercial connection with the United Kingdom has been an especially strong one. Thus, although Jamaica participated in the early Spanish colonization and shared the Negro settlement so typical of the Caribbean, it is not in other ways such as language, culture, religion and economic framework a part of Latin America as the other Greater Antilles are. More recently, however, since political independence, the increasing re-orientation of the economy towards industrialization and an emphasis on mineral exports has considerably weakened Jamaica's economic links with the United Kingdom which now supplies and receives only 20 per cent of the island's imports and exports. The United States share of trade with Jamaica is now twice this amount, and in this respect the economic pattern of Jamaica has become more typical of Caribbean Latin America generally.

The Cayman islands, west-north-west of Jamaica, are low limestone faulted blocks continuing the line of Cuba's Sierra Maestra. The small population of 11,000 obtains its livelihood from maritime pursuits, particularly turtle fishing, and there is a developing tourist trade now catering to over 20,000 visitors annually. It has also always been a significant source of emigration from the Caribbean area; and the remitted wages of Cayman seafarers in every part of the world and of men working in the United States and Central America balance out the excess of imports over exports.

PUERTO RICO

Rising from precipitous depths, Puerto Rico and the other small islands between the Mona and Anegada passages (Fig. 29) may be considered as a plateau-like horst, with faulted edges which give the main island its rectilinear shape. Like Jamaica its proportions are 3 : 1 in respect of length and width (105 miles by 35 miles), this axial line being occupied by a mountain mass, most of it over 2,000 feet high, and in El Yunque reaching almost twice that height.

Described by one writer as 'a heap of volcanic débris', intrusive and extrusive rocks occupy the core of the faulted and folded block, but the sedimentary foothills are composed of clays and limestones, in the north-west giving rise to karstic country as in Jamaica. The axis of the mountains is nearer the south coast. Thus the fringing coastal and alluvial plains are narrower there, and most of the drainage is towards the north. Although due partly to structure, this asymmetry also reflects the heavier rainfall of the north and west, giving the streams their greater erosive power.

The contrast between the windward northern and leeward southern districts is even more marked than in Jamaica, the winter dry season being so pronounced in the drier regions that irrigation is necessary for cultivated crops.

With an intensive occupation of more than four centuries most of the natural vegetation has disappeared, although contrasts still exist between the northern forests and the dry chaparral of the south-east.

The last of Spain's New World colonies to be liberated, it was the scene of both 16th- and 19th-century Spanish colonization, in the latter period when the other colonies had achieved their independence. Thus, although it received many thousands of Negro slaves in the 17th and 18th centuries in the characteristic Caribbean absorption in sugar production, the population is far less negroid than that of Hispaniola and Jamaica, and is more comparable with that of Cuba.

In this century, since it fell under the political and economic control of the United States, the outstanding characteristic has been the rapid growth of the island's population, and the problems associated with this increase are similar to those of Haiti or Jamaica. Although only three-quarters the size of Jamaica, Puerto Rico's population already exceeds $2\frac{3}{4}$ millions, and in few places in Latin America is there such comparable pressure on a limited land area. Fortunately, however, in recent years the rate of increase has been dramatically reduced, so that the growth factor of 1 per cent annually is now the lowest in Latin America.

The gravity of this over-population is increased by the lack of unoccupied land, by the unproductive nature of much of the mountainous core, and by the dependence of the people on agriculture. Unfortunately, even the agricultural pattern is not the most suited to give regular employment, for over 300,000 acres are devoted to sugar cane with its uneven seasonal demands on labour. Efficient production of sugar on the best lands of the island has entrenched the latifundia system which characterized the Spanish pastoral estates of colonial days. Absentee land-ownership and uneven distribution of wealth have survived also because the sugar estates find production for the duty-free United States market very profitable. These estates occur in a peripheral distribution along most of the coastal areas of the island, the northern plains being the most favourable.

Likewise, tobacco, grapefruit, oranges and pineapples are commercial crops with a ready sale in the United States, the principal fruit plantations being on the coastal plain west of San Juan and in the northern foothills. Tobacco also grown in the hills is part of a mixed farming economy, the peasants cultivating in addition food supplies of maize, beans and yams.

There is on the poorer lands a large amount of subsistence farming, with cattle and coffee being two of the principal products, but the total food production of the island is inadequate and the deficit is obtained by imports, largely from the United States.

To help meet the difficulties of Puerto Rico's population pressure, an effort has been made, as in Jamaica, to encourage the establishment of industries using local raw materials, and by tax exemptions to persuade United States firms to set up industries in the island. The principal factory manufactures rayon, and others produce foodstuffs and a great variety of consumer goods. Only Argentina, Brazil, Colombia, Mexico and Venezuela have a greater production of cement. Hydro-electric stations have been built to provide the necessary electric power for the industrialization programme, and these together with oil-fuelled stations place Puerto Rico eighth in Latin America in respect of installed capacity of electric energy. No other state in the continent has a larger proportion of its labour force employed in the manufacturing, construction and services sectors, some 71 per cent, contrasted with one-third of that number in agricultural employment.

Plate 10. *By means of its 'operation bootstrap' the economy of Puerto Rico has been transformed in the last quarter century. Re-settlement housing, San Juan*

Fortunately for Puerto Rico, the islanders have taken advantage of their United States citizenship and a steady stream of emigrants flows towards New York City, which now has some three-quarters of a million Puerto Rican citizens. This emigration, similar in its origins and motives, is much greater than the corresponding movement from Jamaica to the United Kingdom.

San Juan (452,000) and Ponce (146,000) on north and south coasts respectively are the major urban centres and account for 20 per cent of the total population.

THE VIRGIN ISLAND GROUP

The easternmost continuation of the Greater Antilles is represented by two submarine banks over 4,000 square miles in extent, from which rise in the north the Virgin Islands and in the south St Croix, as summits of the submerged east–west Antillean ridge represented by Puerto Rico further west. The deep-faulted Anegada passage on the east marks the termination of the mountain chain, and the St Croix bank is a separated fragment produced by geologically recent faulting.

More than three-quarters of the islands are possessions of the United States having been purchased from Denmark in 1917, and the remainder are British. The commercial contacts between these two units are very close, and cattle from the British Virgin Islands, being their main export, all go to St Thomas in the American group, which is the principal urban collecting and distributing centre. Some sugar is also produced on St Croix. The total population is some 80,000, principally negroid.

Their main significance consists of their good harbours and strategic location close to the important entry into the Caribbean from the east.

The decade of the 1960s saw a phenomenal economic expansion in the American Virgin Islands. The value of exports increased twentyfold largely as a result of industrial expansion within the United States tariff wall. The manufacture of watches and pharmaceutical products, and the processing of tungsten ore, petroleum, bauxite and woollen goods were the principal features of this expansion, but tourism is even more important, and over 1 million visitors annually arrive in the islands.

Vieques, the westernmost and largest island of the group, is a part of Puerto Rico, and considerable efforts are being made to develop pineapple and dairy farming there and to encourage Puerto Ricans to emigrate to this island.

THE LESSER ANTILLES

This north–south trending arc of islands, 450 miles long, from Sombrero in the north to Grenada in the south is a festoon of oceanic islands more typical of the Western Pacific than the Atlantic (Fig. 29). It forms a distinct and contrasted group of the West Indies, sharply transverse to the Greater Antilles and the other east–west system of the Venezuelan coastal mountains and islands, and is delimited from them by fault troughs at each end.

Although it has been usual to sub-divide them into Leeward and Windward islands, northern and southern groups separated by the French island of Guadeloupe, this division was only an administrative one with little geographical significance in either the physical or human sense. It is more useful to consider the island festoon as a double line of submarine volcanoes which have grown on the broad top of a mountain arc which narrows in width southward and which itself rises some 7,000 feet above the ocean floor.

The outer or north-eastern line is the older and consists of low dead volcanic peaks and submarine banks which have been much eroded and submerged so that they are in part limestone and sedimentary covered. The newer and inner line is an arc of high active volcanoes, some of which have erupted in recent years. The most disastrous occasion known was that of Mont Pelée in Martinique in 1902, but this arc is a zone of continuing instability, as is evidenced by the fact that as many as a hundred earthquake tremors a day occurred in Nevis in 1951.

The outer arc reaches its maximum elevation above sea level in St Martin (1,360 feet) but most of the islands are lower than this, and the inner arc in Guadeloupe (4,869 feet). The outer arc terminates in Marie Galante, and converges towards the inner arc so that in the island of Guadeloupe the two arcs are represented. Grande Terre is part of the older and lower group, and Basse Terre, separated from it by a mangrove-filled lagoon, and most inappropriately named, thrusts its volcanic cone, Soufrière, high above the Caribbean.

The islands included in the two arcs together with their political connections are as follows from north to south:

The High Islands	The Low Islands
Saba (D)	Sombrero (B)
St Eustatius (D)	Anguilla (B)
St Kitts (B)	St Martin ($\frac{1}{3}$ D, $\frac{2}{3}$ F)
Nevis (B)	St Barthélemy (F)
Redonda (B)	Barbuda (B)
Montserrat (B)	Antigua (B)
Guadeloupe (Basse Terre) (F)	Guadeloupe (Grande Terre) (F)
Iles des Saintes (F)	Désirade (F)
Dominica (B)	Petite Terre (F)
Martinique (F)	Marie Galante (F)
St Lucia (B)	
St Vincent (B)	
The Grenadines (B)	
Grenada (B)	

(B = British; D = Dutch; F = French)

The Low Islands

The principal characteristics of these islands are related to their low relief and porous rock structure. Both factors contribute to a deficiency of water supply both for domestic needs and for agriculture.

Rainfall is small and rarely averages more than 45 inches annually, and the porosity of the limestone surfaces leads to an absence of streams and makes farming precarious. Considerable areas in all these islands, therefore, are devoted to grazing by cattle, sheep and goats, and many of the inhabitants find a living by fishing. Where clay soils occur, as in parts of Antigua and Guadeloupe (Grande Terre), or rainfall amounts are slightly higher, as in Marie Galante and St Martin, sugar is grown, and the cloudless skies (associated with the lack of rainfall) favour high yields.

Sugar is the principal commercial crop of the Low Islands and the economic mainstay of most of the population, Guadeloupe (30,000 acres) and Antigua (12,000 acres) being the main producers. Grown on large estates, it reflects all the disadvantages of the sugar economy, and unemployment is endemic in both islands, although the growth of a flourishing tourist industry in Antigua has absorbed many workers, especially in constructional work. This island has also developed oil-refining to diversify its economic structure.

Following the Second World War high quality sea-island cotton was of increasing importance in Antigua, and in 1958 5,000 acres were devoted to the crop, making it the largest single producer in the Lesser Antilles. Output has now fallen off to less than one-quarter of the average production of the 1950s. St Martin, St Barthélemy and Désirade are other small producers.

The total population of the group is about 300,000, two-thirds of whom are in Grande Terre of Guadeloupe and a further 20 per cent in Antigua. The principal settlements are Pointe à Pitre in the former and St John's in the latter.

The High Islands

All these islands show a remarkable similarity in their physical geography. Although varying considerably in size from the three central large units of Dominica, Martinique and Basse Terre of Guadeloupe to the small islets at each end, the Grenadines and the Dutch islands of Saba and St Eustatius, they are all generally elliptical in shape with a north–south mountain axis dominating the relief.

The physiography of each is characterized by a landscape of high mountains, volcanoes, crater lakes, geysers and an abundance of streams; the climate of each is typified by abundant rainfall, often exceeding 200 inches in the mountainous interior; forests still occupy considerable areas; and the sheltered south-western coasts usually

Plate 11. *St Vincent has almost a world monopoly of arrowroot production*

provide the site for the principal port and settlement of each island. The central mountain cores do not facilitate communications, which in most cases consist of a peripheral road encircling each island.

The favourable climatic conditions of heat and humidity in association with rich volcanic soils permit a variety of agricultural specializations, many of which are due to historical circumstances and the inertia and continuity of commercial contacts for the sale of the produce over the centuries. Thus, St Vincent is the world's principal source of arrowroot, Dominica specializes in lime products (lime juice and oil), Grenada in cocoa, nutmegs and mace, Martinique and St Kitts in sugar, St Lucia in bananas, and Montserrat and Nevis in cotton.

These specializations are so firmly rooted in each island's economy that the introduction of other crops to diversify the agricultural pattern is not an easy process. Much progress has however been made in many islands, and coconut products are now important exports of St Lucia; bananas account for 80 per cent of Dominica's exports and 25 per cent of Grenada's; and copra and bananas are high in

St Vincent's trade. The most common agricultural development in all the islands in the post-war years has been the increasing area devoted to bananas. The clearing of land for this purpose has, however, increased the danger of soil erosion on the steep hillsides; and the industry is, of course, particularly susceptible to the hazard of hurricanes. The four islands of Dominica, St Lucia, St Vincent and Grenada together now produce over 12 million bunches annually, an expansion brought about largely by co-operative marketing and long term contract sales to the United Kingdom market.

There is also considerable variety in the land tenure. Where small properties are the rule, as in Grenada, where there are over 18,000 farms under 25 acres in extent cultivating half the area farmed, subsistence food products in great variety are grown. This is also partly true of St Vincent, and to a less extent of Dominica. Where large estates are predominant, as in Martinique or in St Lucia, only the poorer land is available for food crops and much food is imported and supplemented by fishing. Almost every island has some plantations on which agricultural labourers are employed, and there is also much share-cropping of small properties, as in Montserrat and St Lucia.

There is no mining of any importance, and manufacturing industry is limited to the sugar mills and a few small factories producing goods for local consumption such as soap, cigarettes, baskets and woodwork. Significant developments in the use of Dominica's timber resources and in the growth of the tourist industry in St Vincent and the other islands should further diversify and strengthen the region's economy.

The strategic value of the islands resulted in American bases being established on St Lucia during the Second World War but this was only a transitory development. Since the introduction of larger jet aircraft, however, the former American air base at Vieux Fort has become the island's domestic airport.

The distribution of population is very uneven. Some of the larger units such as Basse Terre of Guadeloupe (90,000) and Dominica (70,000) are relatively thinly peopled and there is some land which is capable of development. Other units such as Martinique (320,000) and Grenada (104,000) are densely peopled, especially when the mountainous character of the islands is taken into consideration.

The total population is some 700,000 fairly equally divided between the two French islands of Basse Terre de Guadeloupe and Martinique, and the six British colonies. The finest harbour is that of

Plate 12. *Most of the high islands of the Lesser Antilles have volcanic cores. The dome of Micotrin (3,891 feet) in Dominica*

Castries on St Lucia,[1] but each island has one principal settlement which is both port and capital; the chief are:

Island	Port and Capital
St Kitts (41,000)	Basseterre
Nevis (16,000)	Charlestown
Montserrat (15,000)	Plymouth
Guadeloupe (Basse Terre) (90,000)	Basse Terre
Dominica (70,000)	Roseau
Martinique (320,000)	Fort-de-France
St Lucia (108,000)	Castries
St Vincent (82,000)	Kingstown
Grenada (104,000)	St George's

Although proportions vary from island to island, Negroes and mulattoes are everywhere the predominant ethnic group, the tendency being for the percentage to be a little less in the northern islands of the group. The present political distribution of the islands

[1] In all the Lesser Antilles, only at Castries and St George's (Grenada) can ships unload direct from ship to wharf.

between France, Britain and the Netherlands dates only from 1815, and while some have been continuously under the control of one of these powers, others have changed ownership many times. Thus the predominant patois of Dominica is still largely French, while that of St Martin is English. The original Carib Indian population has almost disappeared; a few survive in Dominica and St Vincent, but of greater importance economically in the latter island are the groups of East Indians and Portuguese, descendants of those introduced to work the sugar plantations on the abolition of slavery.

Apart from the natural difficulties of earthquake, volcanic eruptions and hurricanes with which the island peoples have to contend, and which have caused appalling disasters in the three centuries since their European colonization, the colonies live under the shadow of many economic disadvantages.

Among the most pressing of these are reliance on single crops, lack of guaranteed markets, and difficulties of inter-island and external communications. After a long period of neglect, much attention is now being paid to all these problems with a view to righting the endemic trade deficits from which most of the colonies suffer. Perhaps the most promising outlook for their future solvency and improved living conditions is to be found in the new political and administrative groupings which have now evolved from their previous colonial status. The establishment, in 1968, of the Caribbean Free Trade Area (CARIFTA) among most of the islands of the British Lesser Antilles, with the object of eliminating all tariffs and quotas between the islands, cannot but help their economic development.

THE CONTINENTAL ISLANDS

Stretching from Aruba off the Gulf of Maracaibo for 700 miles eastward to Barbados is the last group of the West Indian islands. These resume the predominant east–west trend of the Greater Antilles, and are remnants of an outer coastal range of the South American continent, parallel to the North Venezuelan Andes.

They are for the most part isolated horsts, separated from each other by fault troughs, one such being the Gulf of Paria which divides Trinidad from the Paria peninsula of the Sierra de Cumaná. The most important units are the two Dutch islands of Aruba and Curaçao and the two British islands of Trinidad and Barbados.

BARBADOS

The island of Barbados gives striking evidence of the great vertical . movements which have accompanied the mountain building of the Caribbean highland chains. After considerable erosion the island block was submerged to a depth of at least 5,000 feet, covered with sedimentary rocks, and as it was elevated successive coral formations were deposited upon it. Now over 80 per cent of the island's surface is a rolling countryside of an almost English landscape, devoid of surface water, but with considerable areas of fertile soil. Only the northern part, which rises to over 1,000 feet above sea-level and is known as the Scotland district, reveals the folded and faulted basement showing the east-north-east–west-south-west trend of the other islands of this continental group. The contorted sandstones and clays and the scarped north-western coast stand out in sharp contrast to the otherwise typical coral atoll, encircled by its fringing reef. Plentiful supplies of water beneath the coral limestone are pumped to the surface both for irrigation and water supply.

Never occupied by Spain, it is one of the earliest and most continuous examples of British colonization in the Caribbean area. With a moderate rainfall (50–70 inches) and an easily worked landscape free of forest, it proved an amenable environment for white settlers who introduced Negro slaves. The descendants of the latter now outnumber the European-derived group by more than twelve to one, and few agricultural areas in Latin America compare with Barbados in the density of population which now exceeds 1,400 per square mile, the result of continuous occupation of a limited area for over three and a quarter centuries. Its 260,000 people are supported for the most part by an agricultural system which is still predominantly centred around sugar cultivation. Grown in rotation with the typical West Indian subsistence food crops of vegetables, yams, breadfruit, bananas and maize, soil fertility has been maintained to a remarkable extent, on both the large estates and 30,000 peasant farms. Ninety per cent of the area of the island is used for arable and pasture land, and more than half of this is cultivated in large estates. Half the productive land of the island is under sugar at one time.

Although the sugar output of British Guiana, Jamaica and Trinidad is greater, no other island in the eastern Caribbean is so exclusively dependent on the sale of sugar and its products. About £13 million worth of sugar, £1·4 million worth of fancy molasses and

£1 million worth of rum are shipped oversea, and these three products account for over 95 per cent of the exports. To feed such a closely settled population large quantities of the foodstuffs which form their staple diet, flour, rice and salted pork, have to be imported, yet the island supplies a considerable proportion of its own foodstuffs, and a growing tourist industry is helping to diversify its economic basis, but its manufacturing industry is limited to the production of a few consumer goods. Bridgetown (13,000), the principal settlement and port, on the sheltered south-western coast, is of some strategic and commercial importance as the terminus of trans-oceanic cables and because of its control of the south-eastern entrance into the Caribbean basin.

TRINIDAD

In considerable contrast to Barbados, which in few respects is 'Latin American', Trinidad shows both in its physical and human geography close connections with the South American continent of which it is a detached fragment.

The largest island of the West Indies outside the Greater Antilles, approximately 50 miles by 30 miles in size, it consists of three ranges of mountains aligned on an east–west axis with two intervening plains. The three ranges become progressively lower towards the south. The northern range has several peaks over 3,000 feet in height, and is mostly over 1,500 feet, whereas the other two highland areas vary from 500 to 1,000 feet above sea level. The most extensive areas of alluvial lowland are east of Port of Spain and west of Cocos bay.

Outside the prevailing tracks of hurricanes, the trade winds here are predominantly from the east-north-east, and the heaviest rainfall occurs in the eastern parts of the island and especially in the north-east of the northern range, where amounts often exceed 150 inches annually. Considerable forest therefore clothes the eastern parts of the island, and forest industries are already of some importance in the manufacture of matches, crates and building components.

Unlike Barbados, Trinidad was peopled late. Close to the mainland and nominally Spanish, it was neglected by them as having little mineral wealth, and its occupation by rival powers was a risky proposition. Thus the story of its settlement is limited to little more than the last 150 years, and no other island of the West Indies is quite so mixed ethnically. The Europeans are descendants of early Spanish, French and British settlers; large numbers of Negroes were introduced early in the 19th century to work on the sugar plantations; Indians from the hill areas of South India, Chinese, and Portuguese from Madeira were immigrants under contract to replace the slaves after slavery was abolished. Between 1845 and 1917, 150,000 entered Trinidad. Considerable inter-mixture has added to the racial complexity of the population, and an estimate of the constituents is:

Ethnic element	Percentage of total population
Negroes	43
East Indians	37
Europeans	2
Chinese	1
Mixed	17

The island is not so dependent on agriculture as most of the rest of the West Indies, for it is a considerable producer of petroleum. Over 4,000 wells in the southern third of the island, and in the Gulf of Paria, yield over 50 million barrels annually and give direct employment to some 17,000 of the population. An additional 65 million barrels of crude oil from Venezuela, Colombia and Saudi Arabia are also imported for refining in Trinidad. The resulting production, which represents 84 per cent of all Trinidadian exports, is exported from Pointe-à-Pierre and Point Fortin. The existence of oil shows the continuity of the petroliferous structures from Venezuela's eastern basin. The marine Soldado field discovered in 1954 is located on the continental shelf between Venezuela and Trinidad and already accounts for over one-quarter of the island's output (Figs. 7 and 35). Associated with these oil-bearing structures is the famous La Brea asphalt lake in the south-west of the island. This large circular depression, some 100 acres in extent and nearly 300 feet deep in the centre, is a unique and almost inexhaustible supply of road-surfacing material, with an annual production of 175,000 tons, half of which is used locally and the remainder for export.

Sugar is still the dominant crop, and Trinidad's production in recent years has been similar to that of Barbados, with rum as an important by-product. Cultivation is concentrated in the western third of the island on the relatively dry lowlands especially near San Fernando. The sunny weather favours high yields, and the industry is organized on a modern and efficient basis. The crop is grown on large estates and also by peasant farmers, and purchased by the crushing mills. The industry gives employment to some 20,000 people (Fig. 35).

Second in importance is cocoa, which owing to high prices in the post-war years has become of increasing value to the island's economy. Preferring hot, humid, shady conditions, the forested sheltered sections of the mountain ranges, especially in the north, are the principal areas of cultivation. The ravages of witchbroom disease, however, prove a constant menace to the trees. Coffee is also grown in the higher parts of the northern range.

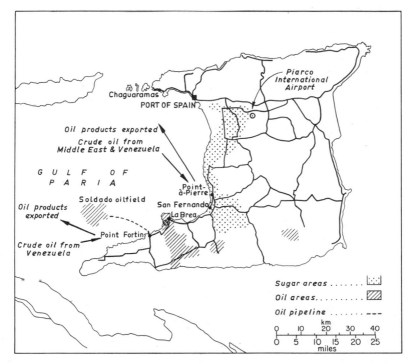

Fig. 35. *Trinidad. Oil and sugar*
Most of the island's export income is derived from the production and processing of these two commodities

Along considerable stretches of the coast, especially the east and south-west, large quantities of coconuts yield several thousand tons of edible oils (lard, margarine and butter substitutes) and soap for local consumption. Another crop utilized locally is rice, which has expanded its area greatly in recent years and is grown chiefly by East Indians. Much expenditure on irrigation in the western lowlands has been devoted to this; parts of the Caroni swamp have been reclaimed and over 20,000 acres of swamp rice are grown in the western and eastern plains.

A co-operative association has encouraged the growth of citrus fruit and large exports of grapefruit, grapefruit juice, oranges, lime juice and lime oil now make these fruit products third only to sugar and cocoa in the agricultural production of the island.

With state encouragement a large number of consumer industries have also been established, supplying a wide variety of the island's needs and assisting the export trade. If one adds a growing tourist industry, and the important transport functions of the island, particularly as an international airport linking Latin America with North America and Europe, it is evident that few West Indian economies are as diversified as that of Trinidad.

Although the sugar districts are densely peopled, the island is in no sense over-populated. Port of Spain (94,000) and San Fernando (40,000) are the principal settlements, and the commercial and administrative functions of the former are leading especially to its rapid growth.

TOBAGO

This dependency of Trinidad lies to the north-east on the continental shelf, and shows the continuation of the axial mountain line of the North Trinidad range, having an igneous core flanked with sedimentary rocks. Rising to over 1,900 feet, the island is similar in its vegetation to the volcanic high islands with a dense forest covering. The coastal areas have been cleared, and cocoa and coconut products are the main exports. Population, however, is scanty (35,000), and it suffers more than the smaller islands from isolation and lack of communications, being dwarfed by the importance of its large southern neighbour.

ARUBA AND CURACAO

These Dutch islands, together with Bonaire support a population of 218,000, Curaçao being of the greatest importance, Willemstadt (46,000) the capital possessing an excellent harbour. Unlike all the other West Indies, where agricultural and rural life dominates the settlement pattern, most of the population of Aruba and Curaçao is urban. This is the combined result of insufficiency of rainfall, typical of the Venezuelan coastal strip (10–20 inches), giving rise to a dry savana vegetation and land offering little opportunity for cultivation, and the dominance of the industrial installations refining Venezuelan oil from the Maracaibo basin. Were it not that petroleum production from this region is continuing to increase, the construction of the canal across the Maracaibo bar and of the refineries on the Paraguaná peninsula might have had serious repercussions on the prosperity of these islands.

PROSPECTS AND PROBLEMS

The basic problems affecting almost all the islands of the West Indies are, firstly, pressure of population on limited areas, and secondly, reliance on the commercial production of one or two primary commodities to the detriment of a more balanced economic system. These two major problems are, of course, inter-related, and an improvement in one of them almost automatically will lead to progress in the other. They are both aspects of the fundamental geographical theme of man – land relationships, and what is most needed in the region is a better adjustment between population and resources.

Only in a few areas, such as the Bahamas and Cuba, are there not high densities of population; and in some areas, such as Haiti and Barbados, there is clearly, by any criteria, over-population. Moreover, because high birth rates and low death rates are the general pattern, the steady growth of population makes the associated problems more difficult year by year. The only island to have tackled the problem of population growth to any successful extent is Puerto Rico, but this by no means indicates that it has been eliminated there. For centuries, therefore, the islands have been sources of emigration – to the Central American mainland, from one island to another, and more recently to the United States, Canada and the United Kingdom. Increasingly stringent immigration restrictions appear, however, to offer little hope that exodus of population will contribute significantly to solving their problems.

Mountainous or hilly terrain imposes considerable difficulties on agricultural development. Only in a few areas, such as most of Cuba, is this not true; and in others, such as Haiti, the misuse of such terrain has made vast areas derelict and productively useless. On the other hand, with the exception of the low islands and predominantly limestone areas, soils generally are of good quality and the climatic environment of adequate heat and moisture at all seasons favours agricultural use of the region, although hurricanes, for most of the islands, have been a constant summer hazard. Occasional droughts, as those in Cuba in the 1960s, have been another handicap. Commercial production of sugar and bananas, and in some islands of certain specialist crops such as tobacco, limes, arrowroot, cotton, coffee, cocoa, ginger and other tropical crops, has been the foundation of their economic existence. Unfortunately, however, with it have persisted all the difficulties of a monocultural system, because few islands developed the cultivation of more than one or two cash crops. The area became, and still largely is, dependent on the fluctuating demand and prices for these products, on estate and company domination of agriculture, on an abundant labour supply with the consequences of under-employment, seasonal unemployment and little incentive to modern production methods if these involve the replacement of manual labour. Even where diversification of, or changes in, commercial production have taken place, many of the original disadvantages of agricultural monoculture have persisted. St Lucia, for example, once a significant producer of sugar on a one-crop basis, has now replaced this with an equally dependent reliance on bananas, and imports a million dollars worth of sugar annually to meet its domestic needs. This is by no means an isolated example, for food imports constitute a significant part of the trade of every island.

Subsistence agriculture on the less valuable land persists throughout the region, and certainly involves most of the population, men, women and children; and once again, the environmental advantages for agriculture have largely enabled the large population to survive. Inefficient farming practices and fragmented holdings, however, have not contributed towards maximum economic output.

Widespread efforts have been made to overcome or reduce the consequences of many of these agricultural problems. Crop diversification, improved marketing arrangements, land redistribution and salvage, and agricultural education have been important features of most of the islands' schemes. Similarly the processing of some of the agricultural commodities to meet the region's needs of certain manufactured products has reduced imports and provided employment. The production of soap and cooking oils from copra, and fibre board from sugar cane bagasse are examples. Where this has been carried out within a pattern of small town or rural industrialization it has also mitigated the worst effects of metropolitan urbanization.

The two most notable changes in economic development that have occurred in the last twenty years have been the exploitation of the region's mineral resources and the growth of the tourist industry. With the exception of Trinidad's petroleum development, minerals contributed insignificantly to the islands' economic pattern. Now the bauxite resources of the area, in particular, and a number of other minerals help the balance of payments by providing important components of some of the islands' export trade. These industries do little towards providing employment, although the part-processing of the minerals, such as bauxite into alumina, does much more in this respect. One of the major chemicals used in producing alumina is caustic soda, and a new plant producing this chemical from raw salt, in Jamaica, is one of the world's largest, providing 170,000 tons annually.

Until the post-war years tourism was largely concentrated in Cuba, Jamaica and the Bahamas. The United States' ostracism of Cuba has destroyed that island's tourist trade, but elsewhere the growth of tourism has been at an accelerating rate, so that few islands have failed to take steps to turn their climatic, scenic and recreational advantages to a profit. Jamaica, Trinidad, the Bahamas, Puerto Rico, the Virgin Islands and many of the Lesser Antilles all have received important economic advantages from the industry. Considerable employment opportunities have been provided, significant revenue has been earned (even when the cost of goods and services from abroad is subtracted from gross earnings), and there are many 'spread effects' in increased land values, business investment and the stimulation of handicraft industries.

Some areas, such as Puerto Rico, Jamaica and the American Virgin Islands are also experiencing an industrial revolution in that important manufacturing and processing plants are producing goods as varied as thermometers, cement and refined tungsten. Many of these industries are based on the use of an abundant supply of labour for the processing of imported raw materials into finished goods for export. Others contribute not only to reducing imports of consumer goods, but to providing additional and more diversified exports and, perhaps most significantly, to absorb surplus rural population into industrial employment. The measure of this industrial expansion can be seen in the facts that exports from the American Virgin Islands grew from $8 million in 1960 to $154 million in 1968, and that the total gross national product of Puerto Rico doubled during the same period.

The region, while having a richly varied cultural, historical and linguistic background, suffers from its political fragmentation, and even attempts to weld together units with relatively common or similar political heritage, such as the British West Indian Federation, have foundered. Similarly groupings of small units such as St Kitts, Nevis and Anguilla have encountered almost unexpectedly great antipathy and strong insular 'nationalism'. More promising has been the growth of economic co-operation in the Caribbean Free Trade Area (CARIFTA). There is scope, undoubtedly, for more coordinated and rational use of resources, to avoid each island endeavouring to develop its own separate but uneconomic industrial units. Fundamental, however, to the growth of co-operation is the provision of inter-island transport services and links between the region and North American ports in particular. Economically viable services between the islands have always been difficult to maintain, because there are so many small and physically separated units, although air transport is now of considerable help in this connection.

The region with its tropical geographical inheritance is largely complementary to its close neighbour, North America, with its largely temperate geographical background; and since many of the colonial links with Europe have been weakened, the paramount importance of trade with the United States and Canada has grown. Against this background, the economic isolation of Cuba from its great neighbour is an absurd contradiction of geographical relationships.

Despite a fairly uniform legacy of negro slavery, which persisted in Cuba until 1886, there are relatively few racial tensions, and the region is thus characteristic of Latin America as a whole. Where it is unlike much of the rest of Latin America is in the absence of an indigenous ethnic foundation. Instead many of its sociological problems can be traced more directly to the consequences of its long plantation-slavery occupance.

Only in the divided island of Hispaniola is there political confrontation between any two units of the West Indies. Friction is deep-seated and dates from colonial times, particularly from the end of the 18th century. The border between Haiti and the Dominican Republic has been closed since 1967. There are some 350,000 Haitian workers in the Dominican republic, a reflection of the former republic's chronic over-population; and political instability there is likely to increase a flow of refugees to a land which already suffers from chronic unemployment. If to this situation is added the United

States' constant fear of another communist state in the Caribbean, the prospects for peace in Hispaniola are less than promising.

STATISTICAL SUMMARY — BAHAMAS

Area: 4,666 square miles (with Turks, Caicos and Cayman islands)

Population (1970): 173,000 (Turks, Caicos and Cayman islands 17,000)

Percentage of land

(*a*) Arable and Pastoral	1%
(*b*) Forest	28%
(*c*) Other	71%

Animal numbers

(*a*) Pigs	11,000
(*b*) Sheep	23,000
(*c*) Goats	14,000

Communications

All-seasons road mileage   700

Exports

(*a*) *Total:* $32,000,000
(*b*) *Percentage share of principal commodities*

Cement	20%
Rum	14%
Pulpwood	12%
Salt	4%
Crawfish	2%

STATISTICAL SUMMARY — CUBA

Area: 44,218 square miles

Population (1970): 8,474,000

Percentage of land
- (*a*) Arable   17%
- (*b*) Pastoral   34%
- (*c*) Forest   26%
- (*d*) Other   23%

Animal numbers
- (*a*) Cattle   6·6 million
- (*b*) Sheep   0·2 ,,
- (*c*) Pigs   1·8 ,,
- (*d*) Goats   0·2 ,,

Communications
- (*a*) All-seasons road mileage   9,820
- (*b*) Railway mileage   8,800
- (*c*) Air routes   203 million passenger miles
     6 ,,   ton miles

Principal products
- (*a*) *Agricultural*

Sugar	5,500,000 metric tons	
Root Crops	533,000	,, ,,
Maize	210,000	,, ,,
Rice	50,000	,, ,,
Tobacco	43,000	,, ,,
Coffee	27,000	,, ,,

- (*b*) *Mineral*

Manganese	24,000 metric tons	
Chrome Ore	18,000	,, ,,
Nickel	18,000	,, ,,

Exports
- (*a*) *Total:* $686,000,000
- (*b*) *Percentage share of principal commodities*
  - Sugar   86%
  - Tobacco   5%

STATISTICAL SUMMARY — HAITI

Area: 10,714 square miles

Population (1970): 4,871,000

Percentage of land

(*a*)	Arable	14%
(*b*)	Pastoral	19%
(*c*)	Forest	25%
(*d*)	Other	42%

Animal numbers

(*a*)	Cattle	0·7 million
(*b*)	Pigs	1·2 ,,
(*c*)	Goats	0·9 ,,

Communications

(*a*)	All-seasons road mileage	1,415
(*b*)	Railway mileage	187

Principal products

(*a*) *Agricultural*

Maize	250,000 metric tons
Root Crops	220,000 ,, ,,
Sugar	59,000 ,, ,,
Rice	44,000 ,, ,,
Coffee	30,000 ,, ,,

(*b*) *Mineral*

Bauxite	370,000 metric tons

Exports

(*a*) *Total:* $36,000,000

(*b*) *Percentage share of principal commodities*

Coffee	38%
Bauxite	12%
Sugar	9%
Sisal	5%

STATISTICAL SUMMARY — DOMINICAN REPUBLIC

Area: 18,816 square miles

Population (1970): 4,329,000

Percentage of land

    (*a*) Arable   22%
    (*b*) Pastoral 18%
    (*c*) Forest   46%
    (*d*) Other   14%

Animal numbers

    (*a*) Cattle   1·0 million
    (*b*) Pigs   1·2 ,,
    (*c*) Goats   1·0 ,,

Communications

    (*a*) All-seasons road mileage   5,124
    (*b*) Railway mileage   786

Principal products

    (*a*) *Agricultural*
        Sugar   819,000 metric tons
        Bananas   318,000 ,,   ,,
        Root Crops 232,000 ,,   ,,
        Rice   148,000 ,,   ,,
        Maize   90,000 ,,   ,,
    (*b*) *Mineral*
        Bauxite   1,092,000 metric tons

Exports

    (*a*) *Total:* $164,000,000
    (*b*) *Percentage share of principal commodities*
        Sugar   54%
        Coffee   13%
        Cocoa   8%
        Bauxite   8%

STATISTICAL SUMMARY — JAMAICA

Area: 4,411 square miles

Population (1970): 1,993,000

Percentage of land

(a)	Arable	22%
(b)	Pastoral	23%
(c)	Forest	19%
(d)	Other	36%

Animal numbers

(a)	Cattle	0·2 million
(b)	Pigs	0·1 ,,
(c)	Goats	0·3 ,,

Communications

(a)	All-seasons road mileage	5,648
(b)	Railway mileage	241

Principal products

(a) *Agricultural*

Sugar	516,000 metric tons
Bananas	327,000 ,, ,,
Root Crops	242,000 ,, ,,

(b) *Mineral*

Bauxite	9,396,000 metric tons

Exports

(a) *Total:* $219,000,000

(b) *Percentage share of principal commodities*

Bauxite and alumina	49%
Sugar and by-products	24%
Bananas	8%

STATISTICAL SUMMARY — PUERTO RICO

Area: 3,435 square miles

Population (1970): 2,773,000

Percentage of land

    (*a*) Arable   30%
    (*b*) Pastoral   35%
    (*c*) Forest   13%
    (*d*) Other   22%

Animal numbers

    (*a*) Cattle   0·5 million
    (*b*) Pigs   0·2 ,,

Communications

    (*a*) All-seasons road mileage   4,288
    (*b*) Railway mileage   266

Principal products

    Agricultural
        Sugar   737,000 metric tons
        Bananas   118,000 ,, ,,

Exports

    (*a*) *Total:* $1,135,000,000
    (*b*) *Percentage share of principal commodities*
        Textiles   25%
        Sugar   21%
        Machines and Vehicles   11%

STATISTICAL SUMMARY — LESSER ANTILLES

(i) BRITISH AND U.S. ISLANDS

Area: 556 square miles

Population: Windward and Leeward Is. (1970): 522,000
Virgin Is. (1970): 68,000

Percentage of land

    (*a*) Arable   36%
    (*b*) Pastoral   1%
    (*c*) Forest   29%
    (*d*) Other   34%

Animal numbers

    (*a*) Cattle   54,000
    (*b*) Sheep   49,000
    (*c*) Pigs   62,000
    (*d*) Goats   59,000

Communications

    All-seasons road mileage   460

Principal products

    Agricultural
      Bananas   71,000 metric tons
      Sugar   52,000 ,,   ,,

Exports

    (*a*) *Total:* $178,000,000
    (*b*) *Percentage share of principal commodities*
        Petrochemicals, alumina, textiles, watches   85%
        Bananas   7%

(ii) GUADELOUPE

Area: 687 square miles

Population (1970): 322,000

Percentage of land

    (*a*) Arable   29%
    (*b*) Pastoral   9%
    (*c*) Forest   33%
    (*d*) Other   29%

Animal numbers

  (*a*) Cattle 70,000
  (*b*) Pigs 30,000
  (*c*) Goats 25,000

Communications

  All-seasons road mileage 270

Principal products

  Agricultural
    Bananas 165,000 metric tons
    Sugar 143,000 ,, ,,
    Root Crops 38,000 ,, ,,

Exports

  (*a*) *Total:* $38,000,000
  (*b*) *Percentage share of principal commodities*
        Sugar and rum 68%
        Bananas 21%

(iii) MARTINIQUE

Area: 425 square miles

Population (1970): 330,000

Percentage of land

  (*a*) Arable 29%
  (*b*) Pastoral 18%
  (*c*) Forest 25%
  (*d*) Other 28%

Animal numbers

  (*a*) Cattle 37,000
  (*b*) Sheep 26,000
  (*c*) Pigs 30,000
  (*d*) Goats 10,000

Communications

  All-seasons road mileage 330

Principal products

> *Agricultural*
> | Bananas | 220,000 metric tons | | |
> |---------|---------|------|------|
> | Sugar | 49,000 | ,, | ,, |
> | Root Crops | 48,000 | ,, | ,, |

Exports

> (a) *Total:* $40,000,000
> (b) *Percentage share of principal commodities*
> | Bananas | 47% |
> |---------|------|
> | Sugar and molasses | 39% |
> | Canned pineapple | 11% |

STATISTICAL SUMMARY — BARBADOS

Area: 166 square miles

Population (1970): 260,000

Percentage of land

> | (a) **Arable** | 65% |
> |---------|------|
> | (b) Pastoral | 11% |
> | (c) Other | 24% |

Animal numbers

> | (a) Cattle | 16,000 |
> |---------|--------|
> | (b) Sheep | 40,000 |
> | (c) Pigs | 27,000 |
> | (d) Goats | 18,000 |

Communications

> All-seasons road mileage 950

Principal products

> *Agricultural*
> Sugar 209,000 metric tons

Exports:
  (*a*) *Total:* $37,000,000
  (*b*) *Percentage share of principal commodities*
      Sugar   77%
      Molasses   9%
      Rum   7%

STATISTICAL SUMMARY — TRINIDAD AND TOBAGO

Area: 1,980 square miles

Population (1970): 1,051,000

Percentage of land
  (*a*) Arable   27%
  (*b*) Pastoral   1%
  (*c*) Forest   45%
  (*d*) Other   27%

Animal numbers
  (*a*) Cattle   55,000
  (*b*) Pigs   41,000
  (*c*) Goats   30,000

Communications
  (*a*) All-seasons road mileage   4,170
  (*b*) Railway mileage   102

Principal products
  (*a*) *Agricultural*
      Sugar   205,000 metric tons
      Oilseeds   19,000 ,,   ,,
      Rice   10,000 ,,   ,,
      Cocoa   5,000 ,,   ,,
  (*b*) *Mineral*
      Petroleum   9,197,000 metric tons

Exports

(*a*) *Total:* $466,000,000

(*b*) *Percentage share of principal commodities*

Petroleum   78%

Sugar   5%

STATISTICAL SUMMARY — NETHERLANDS ANTILLES

Area: 371 square miles

Population (1970): 218,000

Percentage of land

(*a*) Arable   5%

(*b*) Other   95%

Animal numbers

Goats   87,000

Communications

All-seasons road mileage   475

Exports

(*a*) *Total:* $607,000,000

(*b*) *Percentage share of principal commodities*

Petroleum   98%

PART II

THE NORTH ANDEAN REPUBLICS AND THE GUIANAS

General Introduction to the Northern Andes and Guiana

THE three republics of the Northern Andes, Venezuela, Colombia and Ecuador, may be conveniently grouped together as a major region of Latin America, from several viewpoints. There is a certain structural unity in that the Andes, which here split into long distinct ranges and swing north-eastward, dominate the geography, physical and human, of these three states. While each contains a considerable area of river lowland drained either to the Amazon or the Orinoco, it is as yet of small economic importance, and nearly all the people live either on the Andean slopes or in the inter-Andean river valleys and intermont basins, continuing the demographic pattern of pre-Conquest times.

There is also an economic unity in that no other region of South America is linked by ties of international trade so closely to the United States. In each republic one-half of its imports are derived from that source, and a large proportion of their exports are sent to the United States. Economic trends as the result of two world wars are partly responsible for this commercial dependence on North America, and the proximity of these republics to the northern continent, on both the Atlantic and Pacific coasts, has played its part. It is also related, however, to the complementary nature of their tropical and temperate products and their raw material and industrialized economies. This latter feature of their inter-dependence is tending to grow even stronger, for the exhaustion of the United States' high-grade iron ores and its increased consumption of petroleum make Venezuelan iron ore and oil all the more necessary.

It is however their historical unity which is perhaps the greatest justification for considering them as a distinct group of the Latin American states. Even in pre-Conquest times the region had a unity in the negative sense that its indigenous inhabitants had not formed themselves into any closely-knit civilization comparable with the

Incas, Aztecs or Mayas, and the Conquest yielded little treasure in gold or Indian labour comparable with Mexico or Peru. Invaded and settled from north and south, from the Caribbean coastal bases of Coro, Cartagena and Santa Marta and from Pizarro's Peruvian bases, via Quito, Cali and Popayán, the region entered upon a period of slow, steady and balanced development contrasted with the exploitative economy of the great mining regions of Latin America. Its regional unity was recognized in 1718 when it became the Viceroyalty of New Granada, and this endured until 1830 during the first decade or so of independence as Gran Colombia, the political product of Simon Bolívar's struggle in this great theatre of the revolutionary movement of independence (Fig. 1). Although then dividing into the present successor states of the colonial *audiencias*, the concept of Gran Colombia is not dead, and from 1946 to 1954 the Great Colombian Merchant fleet was a unified shipping service of the three republics. In 1948, together with Panama (until 1903 a part of Colombia), the three states signed an agreement binding their Governments to work towards the idea of an economic union. This historical unity is seen in the continuity of settlement in their frontier regions. No three Latin American states are linked so closely by main highways and similarity of settled areas on both sides of international frontiers. The Colombian-Ecuadorean boundary runs through the intermont basin of Tulcán and merely represents the stronger influence of Colombia, at the time of fixing the boundary line, in extending its claims southward. Had the position been reversed it is conceivable that Pasto,.which was first settled from Quito, would be within Ecuador. The Colombian-Venezuelan boundary even more obviously bisects a region with common economic interests, and all the Cúcuta region of Colombia is tributary to the Maracaibo basin.

It is less satisfactory to include the Guiana territories within this same region. They belong obviously to no other major region of Latin America, but have affinities with three regions: the West Indies with which they share a similar historical and political inheritance, Brazil with which they share a similar economic inheritance of plantation agriculture, and Venezuela with which there is a close structural link and several associated characteristics. For the sake of convenience they are included with the three North Andean countries, and there are closer similarities which justify this than may appear at first sight. The greater part of the Guiana plateau falls within Venezuela and the Guiana territories, and even extends west-

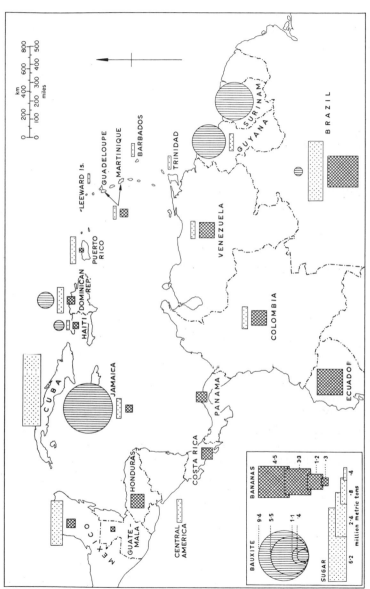

Fig. 36. *Middle America. Sugar, bananas and bauxite*
The principal sources of these three products

ward into Colombia. In contrast to the Andean highlands, this great plateau in all four political areas and in its extension into northern Brazil is scantily populated. Yet this is the classic 'El Dorado' of the New World, and its mineral wealth, whether it be the iron of Venezuela, the diamonds and bauxite of Guyana and Surinam, or the gold of French Guiana, still continues to be the main magnet stimulating its development, and few would deny its potential importance in the future.

This mineral wealth has also led to the development of commercial links between Guiana and North America similar to those already described in the case of the North Andean republics. The aluminium refineries of Canada and the United States depend on this major source of bauxite. This also emphasizes the similarity of Guiana to the remainder of the region in its general lack of industrialization. In all the political units except French Guiana some progress has been made in this direction, even though this may mean only first processing of materials previously exported in their crude state, such as Venezuela's new oil refineries at Amuay and El Cardón, and Surinam's plywood plant. Colombia has done most to create a modern industrial fabric since 1930, and her achievements are impressive particularly in the textile industry which almost supplies the country's needs in this respect, and in her determination to construct an iron and steel industry at Paz del Río in spite of manifold difficulties. In terms of total production and manpower employed, however, the whole region is still overwhelmingly a primary producer of agricultural, pastoral and mineral products, to a greater extent than Mexico, Argentina or Brazil.

Even coastal Guiana has many resemblances to the lower Magdalena, Chocó and Guayas plains and their similar agricultural development, and this unity is reflected in the part played by negroid peoples in all these areas, which differentiates the region from the Pacific and Plata republics south of Ecuador. Ethnically, this whole region may be considered as having a mestizo core in Venezuela and Colombia with negroid coastal fringes (Fig. 3). Ecuador and the Guianas at its two extremities are transitional regions marginal to the adjoining major regions of Peru and Brazil. Highland Ecuador has a great ethnic unity with Highland Peru, whereas Guiana's shortage of labour reminds us of Brazil's *falta da braços*, and in both cases the lack has been made good by polyglot immigrant streams which include an important modern Asiatic component.

The whole region, covering over 1 million square miles, has less than 40 million inhabitants, and is thus relatively thinly peopled. This is especially true of its eastern half, Venezuela and Guiana, which contains less than one-third of the total, and forms a striking contrast to some of the areas of Middle America considered in the previous chapter (Figs. 8, 9 and 10).

CHAPTER NINE

The Guianas

UNTIL the post-war period the three Guiana colonies were the only parts of the mainland of South America which were not politically independent states. Now, Guyana is an independent country within the Commonwealth, Surinam is a part of the Kingdom of the Netherlands, with internal autonomy, and French Guiana is an overseas Department of France. Guyana is almost as large as Great Britain, Surinam approximately five times the size of Holland, and French Guiana one-third that of France; yet their combined population does not exceed $1\frac{1}{4}$ million. More than three quarters of a million live in Guyana, and most of the remainder in Surinam, and this distribution of population is a measure of their respective economic importance.

The region is one of the few coastal areas of Latin America which did not attract Portuguese or Spanish settlement, and following a 17th and 18th-century period in which the Dutch did most to make the coastal plain of use agriculturally, the present political pattern grew out of the Napoleonic Wars settlement, and only in this century have their boundaries with Venezuela and Brazil been demarcated. Structurally there are two clearly marked regions, the Guiana plateau and the coastal plain (Figs. 37 and 38).

THE GUIANA PLATEAU

The plateau slopes northward towards the coastal plain away from the Tumac Humac mountains which form its southern boundary. It is only a part of the great Guiana plateau which stretches westward into Venezuela and southward into Brazil.

Built mainly of granites and gneisses there are stretches, particularly in western Guyana, of massive grey and red sandstones, which have been very resistant to erosion. Sierra Roraima rising to 8,530 feet on the Venezuelan frontier is a part of this formation. Over the sandstone plateau plunge the rivers which create the great waterfalls of Kaietur on the Potaro, and of King George VI on the headwaters of the Mazaruni. Other considerable 'monadnock' features also stand out above the crystalline plateau in both Surinam and French Guiana. One of the lowest saddles is that separating the Branco tributary of the Amazon from the western affluents of the Essequibo, which is savana covered and offered a relatively easy routeway for the Indian peoples of the region. Lines of shell and sand ridges mark the old coastline which fringed the plateau on the north, and these now mark the plateau's boundary with the alluvial coastal plain.

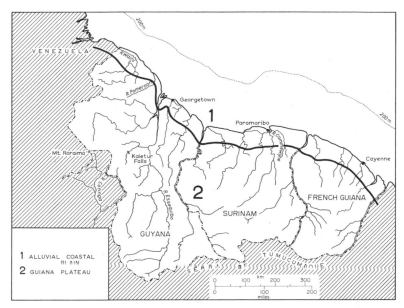

Fig. 37. *The regions of the Guianas*

The rivers are in spate in the first half of the year, and there is a fairly well-marked rainy season from December to April. Except for a few areas such as the Rio Branco savanas, the plateau is a great forested area developed on lateritic soils, and its reserves of timber are probably its greatest potential economic wealth. Commercially, the export of greenheart for lock gates, piers, hulls and keels of ships owing to its resistance to attacks of teredo worm and white ants, accounts for 90 per cent of timber exports. Commercial agriculture is non-existent, but mining is of some importance. The penetration of French Guiana was the result of pioneers searching for alluvial gold in the valleys of the Mana, Aoua, Maroni and Inini. Dredgers on the Mahdia, Potaro and Konawaruk rivers in Guyana produce some 80 per cent of that country's output of gold; another 2,500 workers, particularly in the Mazaruni district, recover half a million pounds' worth of diamonds annually. Since 1914, however, far greater in importance have been the extensive bauxite mining operations in Surinam and Guyana. Their combined annual output of over 13 million tons makes them more important than Jamaica as a major source of aluminium ore. The three countries together supply half of the world's production. Subsidiary companies of the Aluminium Company of America and of the Canadian Aluminium Company mine the ore at Moengo on the Cottica river in Surinam and at Mackenzie at the limit of navigation on the Demerara in Guyana respectively, and it is sent to the United States and Canada for processing. Some 300,000 tons of alumina is processed locally at Mackenzie. Other deposits of bauxite are mined at Kwakwani, 120 miles up the Berbice river, and then taken by barge downstream to Everton for export.

THE COASTAL PLAIN

The great, almost featureless plain varies in width from 15 to 50 miles throughout the 700 miles of the Atlantic seaboard, being widest in Surinam and Guyana. Fringed with mangrove swamps and shallow seas, it has been built up by the deposits of the numerous rivers from the plateau and by sea-borne mud carried westward from the Amazon mouths by the equatorial current. Previous lines of deposition run parallel to the coast in the form of slight narrow hills, tree-covered and standing a few feet above the flooded savana. These deflect the sluggish rivers in their lower courses and create a network of navigable channels. The coastal mud bars frequently extend for over 20 miles parallel to the river estuaries, as in the case of the Waini, Pomeroon and Commewijne rivers. Climatically, a régime of alternate wet and dry seasons of almost equal duration prevails throughout most of the coastal plain, the dry seasons being when the north-east and south-east trades are strongest from February to April and September to October.

The system of reclamation of the tidal marshes behind the mangrove fringe, begun by the Dutch, spread east and west from their principal settlement of Stabrock (now Georgetown) to Pomeroon and French Guiana, and it is in a belt not more than 10 miles wide that all the agriculture of the Guianas takes place. The fertility of the reclaimed lands varies considerably, dependent on the source of the

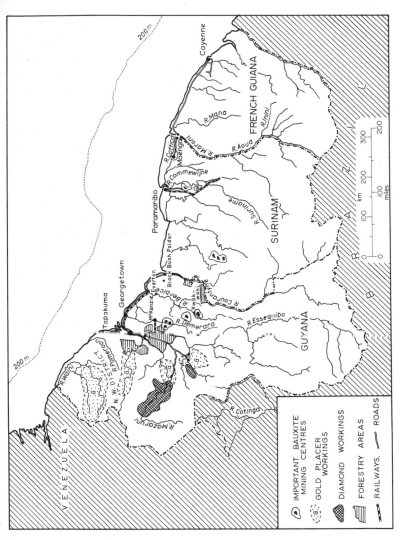

Fig. 38. *The economic development of the Guianas*
The limited penetration of the interior

alluvium of which they are composed. In Surinam some flood fallowing occurs to renew the silt cover. Sugar and rice are the great crops of Guyana, while rice is the staple food crop and most important agricultural export of Surinam, with citrus fruits, especially oranges, as the second most important export crop. French Guiana grows insufficient crops even for its meagre population. The principal agricultural regions extend up the valleys of the Demerara, Berbice, Suriname and Commewijne.

The largest towns are the capitals, Georgetown on the Demerara and Paramaribo on the Suriname, each of which has more than 160,000 people. This represents 20 and 40 per cent respectively of the territories' population. Most of the trade of the region is carried on through these two ports. The entrance to Georgetown is restricted by a river bar and the town itself is protected by a sea wall. Previous to 1804 some estates existed beyond its present defensive position, a vivid illustration of the lowland character of the Guianas coast.

PROSPECTS AND PROBLEMS

For over three centuries the territories have been dependent on exports of sugar, and in the case of Guyana this still constitutes nearly one-third of the value of all exports. Although the value of this crop is three times that of all other crops combined, sugar cultivation is relatively not a large employer of labour. This is because the processes are mechanized and techniques have improved, almost all the sugar being grown on the estates of two large companies. On the other hand, some 30,000 small rice farms of an average size of 7 acres reveal a completely different economic picture. Between 60,000 and 80,000 East Indian peasants and their families cultivate an area twice that devoted to sugar on the clay soils of the coastal plain. There are a number of farmers who each cultivate as much as 500 acres of rice, and two new rice development projects together account for another 35,000 acres, one on the Corentyne coast (Black Bush Polder) and one north of the Essequibo mouth at Tapakuma (Fig. 38).

Although sugar is still so important in the region's economy, there are many problems which continuously face the industry. Because there are two dry and two wet seasons the crop has to be harvested in two separate milling seasons. Moreover, the high rainfall and high water table make for a heavy growth of cane but for lower sucrose content than in drier and better drained countries. Thus 11 tons of Guiana cane is often required to make a ton of sugar compared with

Plate 13. *Tropical agriculture of export crops is the main land use of the Middle American alluvial coastal plains. (Right) Digging a drainage ditch on a Guyana sugar estate; (below) cutting planting lines for bananas in flood-fallowed land in Honduras*

an average of 8 tons elsewhere. The elaborate system of drainage, irrigation and transport canals, estimated to total over 5,000 miles in length, is costly to maintain, and in many cases pumps have to be used to distribute water and then to dispose of it. Drainage by gravity is possible only during low tides. As a result of these difficulties much sugar land in the past was abandoned, but efforts are now being made to reclaim large areas for settlement and agriculture. There is endemic unemployment and underemployment, yet during the harvests there are often difficulties in recruiting an adequate labour supply.

Until about 1926 shortage of labour was the great hindrance to the economic development of the Guianas, and this problem was increased by the abolition of slavery in last century. Indentured and free labour of a variety of races was introduced so that nowhere in Latin America is there a greater variety of ethnic groups. Apart from the indigenous Amerind population of some 35,000, the major elements are 500,000 East Indians, 350,000 Africans, 75,000 Indonesians and 250,000 of mixed race. The European population totals less than 25,000.

With the eradication of malaria since 1940 population in Guyana is now increasing rapidly, and the problem is to extend the development of the many agricultural, pastoral and mineral resources the country possesses to absorb the labour now available. One of the most urgent needs is the provision of a transport system into the interior. In this respect Guyana has made most headway and the navigable rivers have helped to supplement the roads. One of the areas of greatest agricultural potentiality is the North-west District between the Pomeroon river and the Venezuelan frontier, which now has a population density of less than one person per square mile over an area greater than that of Wales. There is, in fact, a strange contrast between the crowded areas of the narrow, developed zone and the vast empty interior. The latter was until recently looked upon as a region which could be developed to absorb the surplus population of many of the overcrowded British West Indian islands, but this would require an enormous amount of capital. At present investment is providing employment only at a rate sufficient to keep pace with the country's own growth of numbers. Unfortunately during the decade 1955–64 political tension, reflected in racial strife (a very rare phenomenon in Latin America) and centred around the colony's effort to secure independence, seriously threatened its economic development.

Few parts of Latin America have such a small percentage of their area relatively undeveloped. To change the situation by improved transport and settlement will require a sustained period of large capital investment. In the same way to diversify the economy of the occupied areas an enormous effort is needed both in agriculture and industry. Guyana alone imports over 12 million dollars' worth of food annually and much of this could be produced within the territory. The opportunities of the CARIFTA market for surplus rice have already been realized, but the use of the interior savana lands for meat production, and the organized development of the territories' forest resources are long overdue. The expansion of the bauxite industry has made the region less dependent on the products of agriculture, but with the considerable hydro-electric potential available an even greater amount of processing into alumina, and eventually into aluminium, is possible. Given political stability and the financial means to implement their opportunities, the Guianas could at last become viable economic states.

STATISTICAL SUMMARY — GUYANA

Area: 82,990 square miles

Population (1970): 770,000

Percentage of land

(a)	Arable	1%
(b)	Pastoral	12%
(c)	Forest	84%
(d)	Other	3%

Animal numbers

(a)	Cattle	332,000
(b)	Sheep	87,000
(c)	Pigs	66,000

Communications

(a)	All-seasons road mileage	558
(b)	Railway mileage	127

Principal products

    (*a*) *Agricultural*

        Sugar   367,000 metric tons

        Rice   198,000 ,,   ,,

    (*b*) *Mineral*

        Bauxite   4,752,000 metric tons

Exports

    (*a*) *Total:* $108,000,000

    (*b*) *Percentage share of principal commodities*

        Sugar and rum   32%

        Bauxite   27%

        Alumina   15%

        Rice   12%

STATISTICAL SUMMARY — SURINAM

Area: 55,129 square miles

Population (1970): 400,000

Percentage of land

    (*a*) Arable   1%

    (*b*) Pastoral 1%

    (*c*) Forest   90%

    (*d*) Other   8%

Animal numbers

    (*a*) Cattle   41,000

    (*b*) Goats   10,000

    (*c*) Pigs   8,000

Communications

    (*a*) All-seasons road mileage   830

    (*b*) Railway mileage   72

Principal products

    (*a*) *Agricultural*

        Rice   118,000 metric tons

        Sugar   17,000 ,,   ,,

    (*b*) *Mineral*

        Bauxite   5,660,000 metric tons

Exports

    (*a*) *Total:* $117,000,000

    (*b*) *Percentage share of principal commodities*

        Bauxite   35%

        Alumina   35%

        Aluminium 12%

        Rice   5%

STATISTICAL SUMMARY — FRENCH GUIANA

Area: 34,740 square miles

Population (1970): 43,000

Percentage of land

    (*a*) Arable   1%

    (*b*) Pastoral 1%

    (*c*) Forest   94%

    (*d*) Other   4%

Animal numbers

    (*a*) Pigs   6,000

    (*b*) Cattle 3,000

Communications

    All-seasons road mileage   170

Principal products

    Mineral

        Gold   1,340 troy pounds

Exports

    (*a*) *Total:* $3,000,000

    (*b*) *Percentage share of principal commodities*

        Shrimps   70%

        Lumber   18%

CHAPTER TEN

Venezuela

WITH an area exceeding 350,000 square miles Venezuela is larger than Great Britain and France combined, yet its total population of approximately 10 millions is less than that of the Greater London area. Yet its population has quadrupled since 1920 and doubled in the last twenty years. Only the small republics of El Salvador and the Dominican Republic have a comparable growth rate of 3·6 per cent annually. This enormous demographic growth in the last half century reflects a change from an economic pattern of four centuries of relative stagnation to one of dynamic change largely based upon its phenomenally great wealth of petroleum and iron ore.

Stretching southward from the Caribbean Sea through 12° of latitude almost to the equator, the country falls into four well-marked major structural and relief regions, increasing in area, but decreasing in economic importance from north to south. These are the Maracaibo lowlands, the Andean mountain ranges, the Llanos of the Orinoco basin and the Guiana Plateau (Fig. 39).

THE MARACAIBO LAKE BASIN

Although it is this area (Fig. 40) that has given the country the name of Venezuela, or 'Little Venice', as the first Spanish explorers named the Indian villages of pile dwellings along the lake shores, the importance of the region in the economy of the republic until the end of the First World War was very slight.

Lake Maracaibo, 120 miles by 60 miles, occupies approximately one-quarter of a great alluvial lowland, enclosed on all sides except its seaward exit by the mountain arms of the Sierras de Perija and Mérida which bifurcate to the north and north-west respectively from the Cordillera Oriental of Colombia. Drained by the eastward flowing Catatumbo and its tributary the Zulia, which has given its name to this province of Venezuela, and by many dozens of rivers from the encircling mountains, the flat surface of the lowland is a network of channels, swamps, lakes and mangrove-fringed coast-lands, especially in the south-west where riverine deposition is at its greatest and the plain its widest. Below these alluvial deposits the lowland is floored by great thicknesses of clay, limestone and sands, its emergence being the result of early and mid-Tertiary withdrawal of the sea by continental uplift.

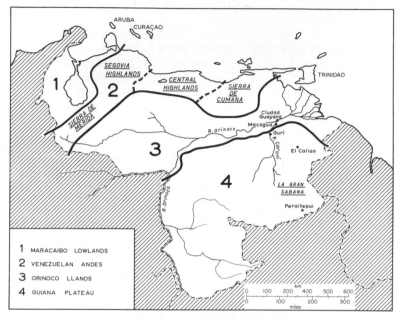

Fig. 39. *The regions of Venezuela*

Except towards the south the lake itself is quite shallow, especially at the bar at its mouth, where a well-marked line delimits the yellowish fresh lake water from the green sea water of the Caribbean. This bar extending for 16 miles (Fig. 40) until recently limited navigation to vessels of less than 13 feet draught. Constant dredging for long maintained a 21-foot channel, but in 1955 this was increased to 25 feet, so permitting ocean vessels to reach Maracaibo city.

The high humidity, the ubiquity of water, its mountain-girt position, and the relative absence of wind not only make the high temperatures oppressive, but aid the growth of luxuriant vegetation. Forests clothe the surface of the lowland, varying from true equatorial selva in the south, through semi-deciduous to dry scrub forest at the seaward margins of the basin, a transition largely dependent on the decrease in the amount of convectional and relief rainfall northward, away from mountain influences. The seasonal nature of the precipitation also varies from a régime of summer maximum near the sea to all-the-year-round precipitation on the encircling mountain slopes. Maracaibo is reputed to have the highest mean temperature of any city of Latin America (82·4°F.).

A few plantations of sugar, cocoa and coconuts exist along the

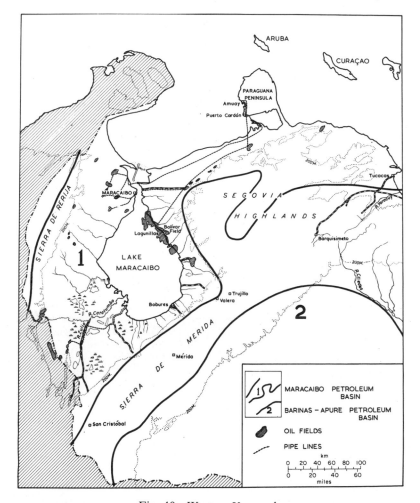

Fig. 40. *Western Venezuela*
Latin America's most productive source of petroleum. The map shows the dyke-protected channel constructed in 1955 to by-pass the Maracaibo bar

southern lake margins, such as at Bobures, but subsistence agriculture, in forest clearings, growing crops of plantains, papayas, cassava, corn and beans, and keeping goats, cattle, pigs, hens and a donkey or two, has long been the principal occupation of the people of the basin, and the lakeside villages supplement their resources with fish, rice and coconuts. A second major occupation, involving folk at many points throughout the lowland, but especially of villages on navigable rivers or on the lake shore, is the transference of cargo, principally coffee, from the surrounding highlands to Maracaibo for export.

Since 1918 the development of one of the world's most productive oilfields has transformed the economic importance of the basin. Three-quarters of Venezuela's production comes from this region, and nearly all of this output is derived from the 6,500 wells of the Bolívar coastal field, the greatest petroleum zone of all Latin America, which occupies the north-eastern coastlands of the lake and extends below its waters (Figs. 7 and 40). More than 2,500 wells have been sunk in the soft mud bottom of the lake, while on the shore the rows of derricks run for thirty miles down the coast like trees planted in an orchard.

Plate 14. *Venezuela is Latin America's greatest source of petroleum, the Bolívar oilfield of Lake Maracaibo*

Almost all the oil is exported by shallow-draught tankers through the shifting sandbanks of the outer exit of the lake, or by pipe lines, to deep-water terminals such as the refining centres of Amuay and El Cardón on the Paraguaná peninsula, and the Dutch West Indian islands of Aruba and Curaçao. The significance of the dredging of the Maracaibo bar thus becomes evident in this connection, for until its completion Curaçao could be considered the outport of Maracaibo. A new development since 1958 has been the increasing exportation of liquid gas.

Statistics of petroleum production rapidly become out of date, but the enormous annual output of 10 per cent of world production and the tremendous reserves, which are 6 per cent of the world's proved reserves, indicate that not only will Venezuela long remain the greatest petroleum producer south of the United States, but that the Maracaibo basin will continue to furnish a large proportion of that output. Most active exploration is taking place in the southern areas of the lake, where a number of concessions were leased in 1969, and in the Gulf of Venezuela, the stretch of water between the Paraguaná and Guajira peninsulas. Much of the drilling penetrates to depths exceeding 12,000 feet, and it is quite possible that the deep Cretaceous La Paz basin to the west of the lake will be an additional source of production.

Apart from the effects such great mineral production has had on Venezuela as a whole, the previously unimportant towns and villages on the oilfields have grown as the industry has prospered. Lagunillas (90,000) has become the centre for the Bolívar field, and Maracaibo (560,000) has grown to be the second largest city of Venezuela. This latter port is the great distributing centre for the basin, and while owing its predominant position very largely to the oil industry, it derives considerable importance from its Andean hinterland. Thus, for example, while the lowland produces no coffee, nearly all the coffee grown in the Andes for export goes through Maracaibo, and the pattern of communications, including the few railways, throughout the lowland is one of routes leading to the lake or navigable rivers for shipment to Maracaibo.

THE VENEZUELAN ANDES

The eastern branch of the Andean cordillera (Figs. 40 and 42) swings north-eastward into Venezuela as the Cordillera de Mérida, and then is aligned on an east–west axis parallel to and adjoining the Caribbean until it terminates in the Paria peninsula facing the island of

Trinidad. Structurally, the northern portions of the mountain system reveal the crystalline core of granites and gneisses while the slopes facing the Orinoco basin have a sedimentary cover, but the present relief is predominantly due to vertical movements post-dating the Andean folding.

Two transverse zones of lower relief break the 750-mile mountain system into three major massifs, the Sierra de Mérida, the Central Highlands and the Sierra de Cumaná. Altitude generally diminishes from west to east, the Sierra de Mérida's snow-capped peaks exceeding 15,000 feet, while the Sierra de Cumaná rarely reaches half that height.

Most of the people of Venezuela live within this highland zone which occupies about one-quarter of the area of the country, the greatest concentrations occurring in the Central Highlands and the coastal cities, many of which were founded over four centuries ago in the early days of Spanish exploration of the Caribbean shores. This relatively close settlement is based on agriculture, on the growing urban occupations connected with the beginnings of manufacturing industry, and on the increasing dominance of the capital city Caracas (1,764,000) in the economic life of Venezuela.

The Sierra de Mérida

This is a great anticlinal structure separating the Maracaibo and Orinoco basins, aligned from north-east to south-west, with a central crystalline core constituting the highest peaks, and overlapped by considerable thicknesses of Cretaceous and Tertiary sandstones. The folding of the Sierra is asymmetrical, and this is reflected in the relief, for the narrow compressed sedimentaries of the north-western flank rise like a wall above the Maracaibo basin while the south-eastern slopes towards the Llanos are wide undulating plateaux.

Land utilization is very largely dependent on altitude with the resulting variety of climates of the four major vertical zones, illustrated in Figure 41. The decreasing temperatures and seasonal range from the tierra caliente to the *páramos* lead to important crop diversification. The coffee zone (tierra templada) and the maize zone (tierra fria) are the most important, as the former produces the principal cash crop of Venezuela, and the latter the staple foodstuff of the people. As a result of the rainfall régime of two rainy seasons (from April to June and from August to November) and two dry seasons, it is possible to grow two crops annually of maize and other subsistence foodstuffs. Better diet and more temperate conditions have probably contributed to the superior vitality of the Indian peoples of this area as contrasted with the inhabitants of the drier Central Highlands or the hot, humid Maracaibo basin.

Most of the settlement occurs in the tierra templada, and the three largest population centres there are San Cristóbal, Mérida and Valera which are situated in intermontane basins aligned along the axis north-eastward from the Colombian-Venezuelan border.

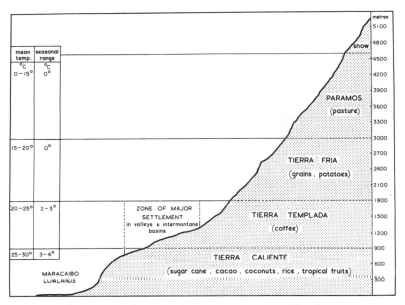

Fig. 41. *The altitudinal zones of the Sierra de Mérida*
The human geography of the Venezuelan Andes is closely related to the conditions dependent on altitude

The great drawback of the Sierra de Mérida is its isolation, and although now connected by road to the Central Highlands and the capital, Caracas, tracks and rivers to the Maracaibo basin still form the chief exit routes for the high-quality coffee, which for over a century has been the only export of this region.

East of Lake Maracaibo and south of the Paraguaná peninsula, with its core of eruptive rocks, the Sierra de Mérida broadens out, north of its main axis, into a series of dissected plateaux and simple folds. The ridges prolonged eastward reach the coast as capes behind which ports have grown up in their shelter on this windward coast.

Plate 15. *High quality cocoa is derived from the east-facing valleys of the Venezuelan Andes*

The intermediate depressions end in marshy plains uninviting for settlement.

This whole area, sometimes referred to as the Segovia Highlands, climatically is less favoured than the Sierra de Mérida proper, for the constant problem is that of inadequate rainfall. This has restricted settlement to the wetter areas, especially the river valleys, which are oases of irrigated cultivation among the semi-arid sterile hills. Cocoa, sugar, sisal and pineapples are the main crops, but as rainfall increases southward coffee plantations on the hill slopes again constitute the main agricultural activity. Population density is less than in the Sierra proper, but Barquisimeto (235,000) has become the great regional capital of this area since the railway from Tucacas was constructed in the late 19th century, and its growth in recent years has been so rapid that it is now the third city of Venezuela. This reflects the increasing importance of this region, and while Barquisimeto is still predominantly an agricultural centre, its manufacturing industries using the raw materials of the region, are of growing significance. The railway originally planned to link Barquisimeto to

Caracas (but completed only to Puerto Cabello) would have also done much to develop the resources of the Segovia Highlands and incorporate this region into the economic life of Venezuela.

The Central Highlands

The Yaracuy–Barquisimeto–Cojedes depression (Fig. 42) delimits the Central Highlands on the west from the area just considered. This central region may be divided into three parallel zones. These are:

- (i) The crystalline coastal sierra of granites, gneisses and schists, flanked in parts by narrow marine terraces, and in others descending abruptly to the Caribbean.
- (ii) A long depression to the south of the coastal sierra, occupied by the Valencia lake basin, the upper Tuy valley and a series of small alluvial basins (Chirgua, Montalban and Nirigua).
- (iii) An interior chain less uniform than the coast range, as the crystalline-sedimentary divide cuts obliquely across it in a north-east–south-west direction.

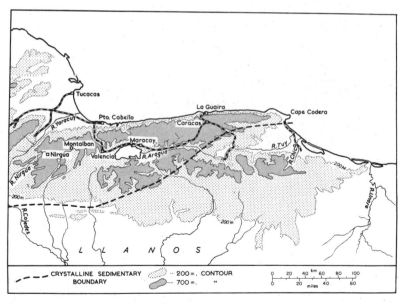

Fig. 42. *Central Venezuela*
The core of Venezuelan settlement

In the heart of the coastal sierra and ten miles from the sea is the alluvium-covered rift basin of Caracas. Reached by a modern road which has overcome the steep ascent from its port La Guaira, Caracas has become the largest and most modern city of Venezuela, containing most of the country's manufacturing industry, and the headquarters of the oil companies.

The relatively short rainy season in November and December results in the coastal sierra being mainly scrub-covered, although forests occur in a narrow zone between the sparse vegetation of the lower slopes and the mountain pastures above 6,000 feet. It is only in the eastward-facing valleys, such as the lower Tuy and the Río Chico plain that there is sufficient rainfall for cultivated crops, especially cocoa.

Plate 16. *The rapidly growing city of Caracas is fast filling the limited space of its small intermontane basin*

Plate 17. *Cattle pastoralism for four centuries has been Venezuela's traditional economy, and with improved stockbreeding and water control the Orinoco llanos offer increased potentialities*

The most productive part of the Central Highlands, and indeed the richest agricultural zone of Venezuela, is the great depression, where there is a varied land use of cattle pastures on the shorelands of Lake Valencia and plantations of cocoa, sugar-cane, cotton and coffee, the latter being grown on the slopes of both coastal and interior sierras above the basin. Although now only half of the country's sugar needs are met from this area, a large proportion of its two high-quality export crops, cocoa and coffee, are derived from here. Cattle are important throughout the region, and it has always been the fattening ground, on both natural and cultivated pastures, for cattle from the Orinoco Llanos. Maracay (142,000) is the principal centre in this connection, and it is now also an important town of the Venezuela cotton textile industry.

The influence of easier lines of communication has had important effects on the settlement pattern, most of the towns being situated either on routes through the highlands to the sea or on the old Valencia–Caracas route linking the two major cities of central Venezuela. The quadrilateral of road and railway communications La Guaira–Caracas–Maracay–Valencia–Puerto Cabello thus dominates the pattern of urban settlement and serves the densest population clusters of the Central Highlands. Valencia has many geographical advantages over the capital, notably that of its productive agricultural environment, and its accessibility to the Caribbean and to the other regions of Venezuela. Only the political and commercial functions of the capital have maintained the lead of Caracas, especially in recent years.

The Sierra de Cumaná

East of Cape Codera the Unare basin breaks the continuity of the Venezuelan Andes and carries to the Caribbean the drainage of part of the Llanos (Fig. 43). To the east the relatively low folded sandstones and limestones of the Sierra de Cumaná constitute a dissected upland with many erosion and rift valleys, the trend of which is emphasized in the double peninsula of Araya and Paria. The Sierra ends on the west in an indented and rugged coastline bordered by rocky islands, and on the east in a low plain bounding the Gulf of Paria and merging into the Orinoco delta. This lowland is important for cocoa cultivation, as it receives considerable rainfall from east winds, but the vegetation changes from bamboo forest through grassland to dry scrub reflect the increasing aridity westward. Barcelona and Cumaná are the two principal towns owing to their importance as outlets for the coffee plantations of the high interior valleys of the Sierra and for the important oilfields of the eastern Llanos which here nearest approach the north Venezuelan coast.

THE LLANOS OF THE ORINOCO BASIN

The great basin of the Orinoco river (Figs. 40 and 43) lies between the Venezuelan Andes and the Guiana massif, but like the Amazon, its upper basin is much more extensive and receives the major tributaries such as the Apure, while its lower basin is relatively narrow with few affluents. The Guiana basement rocks which approach the mesas south of the Sierra de Cumaná actually outcrop north of the river, and, as at Ciudad Bolívar, narrow the channel. The old name of the city, Angostura, or 'Narrows' emphasizes this point.

This great featureless alluvial plain, relieved only by low undulating interfluves, is not homogeneous in its natural vegetation.

Forests enclose the river courses, and over large areas there are scrub forests and palms, but the predominant covering is the savana which results from the marked seasonal rainfall régime of a dry winter (November–March) and a wet summer (April–October). It is not surprising therefore that the continuing economic importance of this region throughout its history has been that of cattle pastoralism, and that the *llanero* or cowboy is still the most legendary Venezuelan.

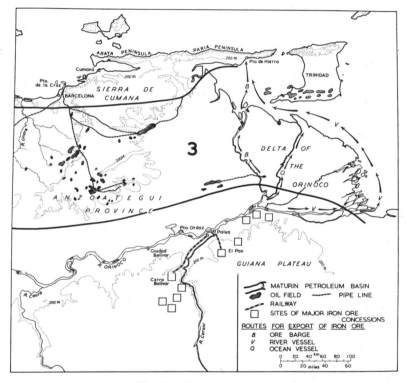

Fig. 43. *Eastern Venezuela*
Latin America's most important post-war mining development has been the opening up of the Caroní iron resources, which now provide the United States with 17 million tons of ore annually

Drought, floods, disease, and lack of communications, and more recently the prosperity based on the exploitation of petroleum, have all prevented this region from becoming a great supplier of meat for the overseas market, in spite of the promise it seemed to hold in the Spanish colonial period.

Since 1930 a new source of economic wealth has transformed the importance of the Llanos, that of petroleum, and the significant proportion (23 per cent in 1963) of the country's production coming from this region, principally from Anzoátequi province, and its more favourable location for utilization for industry and domestic use in Caracas and central Venezuela, suggest that the Llanos will

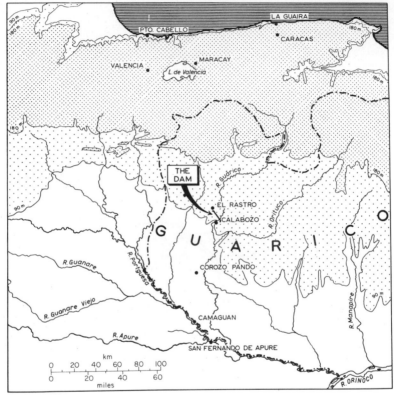

Fig. 44. *Irrigation in the Venezuelan Llanos*
The Calabozo dam on the Guárico is the first of several similar schemes to bring arable farming to a pastoral region

be tied more closely to the main population zone of the country. Using the Unare valley, pipelines carry the petroleum to Puerto La Cruz, east of Barcelona, for export. Contrary to earlier expectations, however, the relative contribution of this eastern region to Venezuela's total petroleum output is tending to decrease. Similarly,

Plate 18. *Venezuela's iron ore exports have made the lower Orinoco an important commercial artery*

although some petroleum is known to exist in the Apure basin, the greater accessibility and development of the Maracaibo basin will maintain for a considerable time its pre-eminence in the nation's oil production. Increasing attention is being paid to the possibilities of oil in the Orinoco delta. If these were to materialize on a large scale, the area would be most favourably located for petroleum export.

Although ships of 400 tons can reach Puerto Ayacucho 750 miles up the Orinoco, it was not until 1951 that the lower course of the river was used as an important commercial routeway for vessels of 15,000 tons. This resulted from the discovery of one of the world's greatest iron ore areas in the tributary basin of the Caroní. United States steel interests now mine this high-quality ore (65 per cent iron content) at El Pao, transport it by rail to Palua, and by means of barges and shallow-draught river vessels, using dredged channels of the Orinoco and its distributaries, take the ore to Puerto de Hierro on the Paria peninsula for export to the Sparrows Point steel industry. Other rich deposits at Cerro Bolívar are sent by road and rail to Puerto Ordáz and then by large ocean vessels of 24 feet draught direct to Morrisville, Pennsylvania (see Fig. 43). Exports soared from 2 million tons in 1953 to over 19 million tons in 1960, but more recently have declined in the face of strong international competition. These developments have also led to a revival in the old market centre of Ciudad Bolívar (64,000), which owes its prosperity to its position as the hub of road, river and air transport. Since 1935 there has been a modern paved highway to Caracas; previously it took merchants from the capital fourteen days to reach Ciudad Bolívar.

The first major effort to overcome the extremes of drought and flood which characterize so much of the Llanos, by a great storage and irrigation dam in the state of Guárico, was completed in 1957. As a result more than 500 ranches growing subsistence crops and specializing in cattle-raising for beef and dairy products have been established. This one scheme has increased the area of land in Venezuela under irrigation by over 50 per cent (Fig. 44). Only in recent years has it been realized that the potentialities of the 9,000 square miles of the flat alluvial land of the Orinoco delta offer enormous scope for tropical agriculture. Since the delta is subject to annual floods a programme of land reclamation has been undertaken to provide 2 million acres of arable land. The indications, therefore, are that the Llanos, occupying one-third of the area of Venezuela, may in the future contribute an increasingly great share to the country's expanding economy.

THE GUIANA HIGHLANDS

South of the Orinoco the Llanos give place gradually to the Guiana massif, a land of mesas and deep narrow valleys largely covered by forest, and in the extreme south-east to a high plateau, almost as large as Switzerland, rising steeply out of the jungle, called the Gran Sabana.

This vast area of the Guiana highlands, comprising a quarter of the area of the country, remained for centuries outside the effective national economy of Venezuela. Little known and accessible only by forest tracks, its only economic importance was in respect of diamond mining at Peraitepui in the upper Caroní valley, and a small gold production at El Callao, which was more important last century than now (Fig. 39).

The great iron-ore mining developments on the northern rim of the plateau, however, have triggered off a remarkable series of events designed to integrate the region more fully into the Venezuelan economy. A special state corporation has been entrusted with a comprehensive survey of the resources of the region and the direction of its integrated development within a national plan. Among the developments have been the establishment of a state steel plant at Ciudad Guayana (which now incorporates the smaller original settlements of Palua and Puerto Ordáz). This is now the fastest-growing iron and steel plant in Latin America, with a productive capacity exceeding a million tons annually. Its largest market is the domestic oil industry's needs of structural steel and iron and steel pipes, but some products are already being exported (Fig. 16).

The vast hydro-electric potential of the Guayana rivers, especially that of the Caroní, is being developed rapidly. Barrages at Macagua and Guri have an installed capacity of 1 million kW and when completed the Guri project will be one of the world's largest hydro-electric plants. Transmission lines already feed the electricity produced to Caracas and other large cities in central and eastern Venezuela.

The abundance of hydro-electric power has made possible the establishment of an aluminium plant, and several other manufacturing industries to meet domestic demand, such as cement and paper pulp have been set up, so that already the region produces about 10 per cent of Venezuela's manufacturing output.

Plate 19. *More iron ore is exported from Venezuela than from any other Latin American republic. The Cerro Bolívar iron hill on the northern fringe of Venezuelan Guayana*

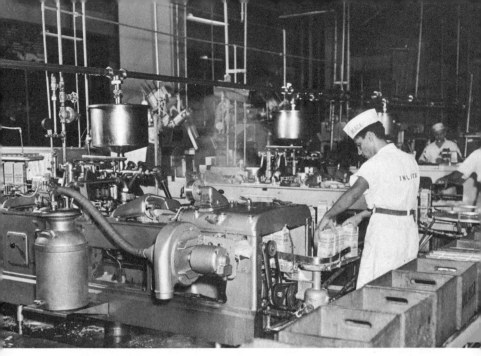

Plate 20. *Although heavy industry has come to the continent in recent years, the processing of raw materials still forms the backbone of the industrial pattern. Packaging milk (above) and rolling hides (below) in Venezuelan factories*

Ciudad Guayana's population of 50,000 in 1962 is expected to be 300,000 by 1975; and the Angostura bridge over the Orinoco at Ciudad Bolívar not only links Ciudad Guayana but the whole Guayana region into the national road network.

It appears that the varied mineral resources of the plateau, which include manganese, nickel and chrome, offer further possibilities for development, and the wealth of nearby coal, petroleum and natural gas reserves could provide power both for domestic and industrial markets.

PROSPECTS AND PROBLEMS

Economically Venezuela is dominated now by the petroleum industry, which accounts for over 90 per cent of its exports, and a large proportion of its imports in the form of capital equipment for the oil companies' activities and consumer goods for its foreign employees. In contrast with its past history the country's greatly favourable balance of trade has enabled it to become the most prosperous state of Latin America, and two-thirds of the Government's revenue stems from taxation of the petroleum industry. The country is, however, using up its reserves at a much faster rate than the other large producers of petroleum, and in spite of continued exploration and fresh discoveries, the ratio of reserves to production is declining. This is scarcely surprising in view of the country's daily output of more than $3\frac{1}{2}$ million barrels, which constitutes two-thirds of total Latin American production and about 7 per cent of total world output in the mid-1970s.

In spite of the importance of the mining industry the proportion of persons employed in it is only $2\frac{1}{2}$ per cent of the working population, and the main effects of the existence of the industry on the Venezuelan people have been increased urbanization and decreased attention to agriculture, as it is cheaper to buy imported foreign food. In spite of its small population and large areas of underdeveloped territory, the country still grows insufficient food for its own needs, even in the products for which it is especially suited. This is partly due to the very rapid increase of population, which has more than doubled since 1950. Its population growth rate of 3·6 per cent annually is the largest in South America. There is an increasing realization of the seriousness of agricultural neglect, and in the decade 1960–70 sugar production has doubled, and none has had to be imported since 1959.

As a result of its high petroleum production the per capita gross

Plate 21. *The rapid growth of Venezuela's population creates continuing problems of housing and transport. Apartment blocks and new highways in Caracas*

national product is the highest in Latin America, but as it is quite possible that the present rate of oil output can be maintained only for some twenty years more, it is imperative that Venezuela's efforts to broaden its economic foundations should be maintained and expanded. To secure the greatest benefit for the future from the exploitation of its valuable mineral resources, Venezuela's programme of 'sowing the petroleum' is utilizing the State's surplus of revenue from the industry to diversify its economy by establishing new manufacturing industries and developing the other natural resources of the country. Much capital has been invested in agriculture, in port facilities, housing, education, health (notably the war against malaria) and in establishing a modern road network to link together the varied regions of the country. In the period 1953–67 electricity production has increased ten-fold, and the Caroní hydro-electric power developments and aluminium smelter are encouraging steps towards greater economic diversification.

Not only is national production growing faster than population increase, but the growth is much greater in the agricultural and manufacturing sectors of the economy than in mining and oil production. Slowly there is increasing self-sufficiency in food supplies, some 200,000 families have benefited from agrarian reform, and there is a steady expansion in utilization of the republic's fishing resources. Much of the industrial development taking place is based on steel and petrochemicals, using thereby the country's two principal mineral raw materials. Even in the export trade of these commodities, some processing reduces bulk, increases value and provides more employment. A briquette plant raising the iron content of Guayana ore from 60 per cent to almost 90 per cent is one such example.

The republic stands alone among Latin American nations not in the need for development, but in possessing the financial means by which it can be accomplished (Fig. 14).

STATISTICAL SUMMARY — VENEZUELA

Area: 352,143 square miles

Population (1970): 10,360,000

Percentage of land

  (*a*) Arable   6%
  (*b*) Pastoral   18%
  (*c*) Forest   53%
  (*d*) Other   23%

Animal numbers

  (*a*) Cattle   6·6 million
  (*b*) Pigs   1·9   ,,
  (*c*) Goats   1·2   ,,

Communications

  (*a*) All-seasons road mileage   22,060
  (*b*) Railway mileage   301
  (*c*) Air routes   542 million passenger miles
                                      27   ,,   ton miles

Principal products

  (*a*) *Agricultural*
       Bananas   1,230,000 metric tons
       Maize   604,000   ,,   ,,
       Root Crops   555,000   ,,   ,,
       Sugar   413,000   ,,   ,,
       Rice   292,000   ,,   ,,
       Beans   70,000   ,,   ,,
       Coffee   62,000   ,,   ,,
  (*b*) *Mineral*
       Petroleum   186,409,000 metric tons
       Iron   17,759,000   ,,   ,,
       Gold   1,600 troy pounds

Exports

  (*a*) *Total:* $2,858,000,000
  (*b*) *Percentage share of principal commodities*
       Petroleum   93%
       Iron Ore   6%
       Coffee   1%

CHAPTER ELEVEN

Colombia

COLOMBIA is one of the most difficult of the Latin American nations to analyse, for the intricate diversity of landscape, climate, peoples and economic conditions creates patterns of great complexity showing few simple inter-relationships. The principal physical reason for this complexity is the fraying of the Andean Cordillera into three great longitudinal ranges, separated by the two deep troughs of the Magdalena and Cauca-Patía (Fig. 45).

The Colombian Andes are narrowest in the south-west adjoining the Ecuadorean frontier. They spread northward as

(i) the Cordillera Oriental, which continues as the Sierras de Perija and Mérida encircling the Maracaibo lowland of Venezuela,

(ii) the Cordillera Central, which terminates south of the Magdalena–Cauca confluence, and

(iii) the Cordillera Occidental, which reaches the Gulf of Darién.

These mountain ranges and the lowlands which penetrate and fringe them on both the Pacific and the Caribbean constitute most of the western half of Colombia, and it is within this setting that most of the 22 million people of the republic live. The eastern half of the country consists of the western extensions of the Amazon and Orinoco plains and the Guiana plateau. While vast in territorial extent, exceeding the area of France and stretching south of the Equator, its economic importance to Colombia is at present negligible. Thus while Bogotá the capital may appear to be ideally situated in the centre of the republic, it is in reality on the periphery of the populated and developed part of the country.

Because of its extreme diversity every division into regional units has its drawbacks, but based on structural differences the country can be considered within the following scheme (Fig. 45):

(i) The Eastern Cordillera.

(ii) The Magdalena Valley.

(iii) The Central Cordillera and Cauca–Patía Valley.

211

(iv) Western Colombia.
(v) The Lower Magdalena Plains.
(vi) The Sierra Nevada de Santa Marta.
(vii) The Orinoco and Amazon Plains.

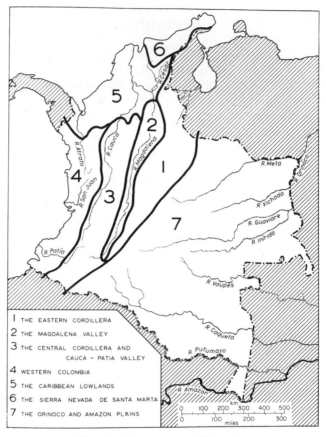

Fig. 45. *The regions of Colombia*

THE EASTERN CORDILLERA

This great range increases in width northward so that approaching the Venezuelan frontier it is over 150 miles from west to east. As vast areas also exceed 6,000 feet, no other part of Colombia has so much land within the tierra fria zone, and the temperatures experienced on the high plateau average 60°F. throughout the year. It is not surprising, therefore, that within this Cordillera live one-third of the people of Colombia, and that it sheltered major nuclei of both the relatively advanced Chibcha Indian civilization and the Spanish colonization which followed it.

This great zone of folded Cretaceous and Jurassic sedimentary rocks appears to have been elevated by enormous vertical movements in post-Tertiary times, and in its northern extensions erosion has stripped the sedimentary cover from the crystalline and granite core. This has been the work of recent Alpine-type glaciers and the great tributary streams of the Amazon, Orinoco, Maracaibo and Magdalena systems. Three tributaries of the Magdalena, the Bogotá, Sogamosa and Suárez in their upper courses occupy, at an average elevation of 8,300–8,550 feet, important intermont basins, in which occur the principal population nuclei of the Cordillera Oriental, those of Chiquinquirá, Sogamosa and Bogotá. Tunja is located in another such smaller upstream extension of the Sogamosa basin.

These plains of deposition are the most distinctive relief feature of the Cordillera, and although their central areas contain shallow lakes, marshes and peat bogs which flood during the rainy seasons, most of their surfaces have fertile well-drained black soil yielding rich crops of food for the dense populations on their fringes. Above these basins are the extensive *páramos* in which bushes such as

Plate 22. *Iberian-type village streets are common in the Andean mountain settlements. A village in eastern Colombia*

rhododendrons give way in the higher parts to short grass steppe. Below the basins are the Cordilleran slopes down which the numerous rivers plunge through forest and llanos after their relatively placid course on the intermont plains.

Even in this one structural region the major climatic differences between north and south, east and west are striking, quite apart from local differences dependent on such factors as elevation, shelter and aspect. Most of the eastern slopes and the northern extensions of the Cordillera have one rainy season during the northern summer from May to October, whereas the slopes draining to the Magdalena and the southern part of the plateau have two maxima from March to May and from September to November. Superimposed upon these rainfall régimes is the general pattern of tierras caliente, templada and fria which influence agricultural activities in Colombia as strongly as in the case of the Venezuelan extension of this Cordillera, the Sierra de Mérida.

Except for the llanos savana below 5,000 feet on the Orinoco slopes of the Cordillera, the treeless intermont basins, and considerable areas of the páramos, the general pattern of natural vegetation is one of humid forest, becoming more arid in character in the deeper depressions such as that of Cúcuta.

The obvious natural advantages of the intermont basins therefore stand out. Level, treeless, fertile lands, well-watered and inhabited by a concentrated Indian population, the Spaniards established major settlements within them, one of which has grown to be the capital of the nation, Bogotá, a city with a population of 2,148,000. Apart from the increasing industrial occupations accompanying the growth of great cities, the major activity of the people of these high basins is subsistence agriculture, and as they lie within the tierra fria, crops of maize, wheat, barley and potatoes are the staple produce, supplemented by the pastoral activities of the surrounding páramos. The two rainy seasons permit a system of double cropping with harvests in August and December.

Settlement has since spread from these basins of Cundinamarca and Boyacá with their dense rural populations into other tributary valleys at lower altitudes such as Bucaramanga, Cúcuta and Ocaña, and, stimulated by transport routes from the Bogotá region to the Magdalena, on to the western slopes of the Cordillera between Girardot and Puerto Salgar. In each case the forests have been cleared, and as all these areas fall within the tierra templada, coffee is the principal crop, although Ocaña specializes in cocoa production,

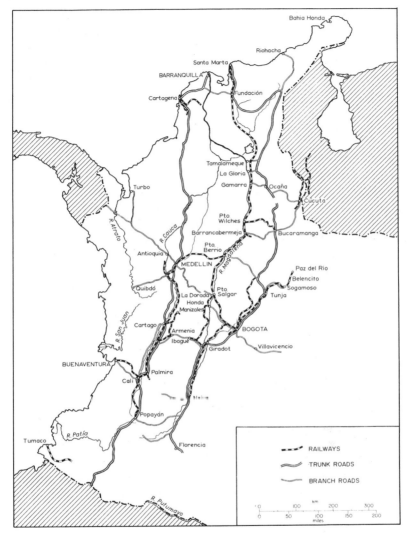

Fig. 46. *Roads and railways in Colombia*
Surface transport is the most difficult economic problem of Colombia

and around Bucaramanga considerable quantities of tobacco are grown.

On the valley slopes of the Cordillera Oriental of Bogotá (or of Cundinamarca) there is also a fairly dense population, with Indian subsistence farming occupying the prime economic role. As the summer rains there delay the harvest until October numerous peasants work first on the earlier harvest of the large arable estates of the Bogotá basin.

Apart from the service industries of Bogotá and many other industrial establishments related to the capital, Bucaramanga (270,000) has textile mills and straw-hat factories and is an important distributing centre for imported goods, Zipaquira has been famous for its salt for centuries, and the emerald mines of Muzo, south-west of Chiquinquirá, are the most productive in the world. At Paz del Río is located Colombia's only integrated iron and steel plant. Utilizing local supplies of iron ore, limestone and coal, it is becoming the nucleus of several associated industries such as wire, rails and fertilizers. The supplies of coal are probably the largest reserves in Latin America, and the annual output of 3·1 million tons is the greatest of all the republics.

Cúcuta (205,000), on the Venezuelan frontier, is situated in a deep alluvial valley and gathers the coffee grown on the slopes of the many tributary valleys of the Zulia river, for export via Encontrados and the lower Catatumbo to Maracaibo. The development of an oilfield at Petrólea, north of Cúcuta on the Colombian portion of the Maracaibo lowlands, has done something to link the north-eastern slopes of the Cordillera with the rest of Colombia, a road having been constructed to La Gloria on the Magdalena, and an oil pipeline to Coveñas on the Caribbean (Fig. 47).

The people occupying the Cordillera are mostly mestizos, the product of Spanish admixture with the large indigenous population living there at the time of the Conquest, while the capital and some other large centres have received considerable influxes of Europeans, particularly in this century.

Road communications on the plateaux and between the intermont plains are a fairly close network not exceptionally difficult to construct, but the links with the Magdalena valley and the Amazon–Orinoco plains are fewer. Thus, this structural region by reason of its semi-isolation has become a distinct human region in spite of its diverse constituents.

THE MAGDALENA VALLEY

The great vertical forces which raised the Eastern Cordillera were probably responsible for the post-Tertiary faulting which delimits the rift valley of the Middle Magdalena, producing the wide and deep plain through which flows the great transport artery of Colombia.

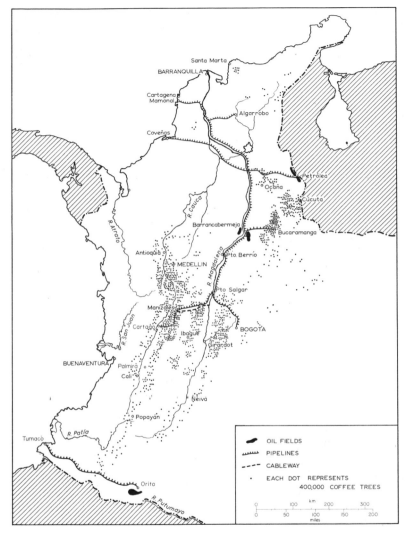

Fig. 47. *The distribution of coffee cultivation in Colombia*
The world's most important source of mild coffees. The map also shows the
oilfields and their pipelines to the ports

Above Neiva the continuity of the humid forest across the valley
from the Cordillera Oriental to the Cordillera Central masks the
structural separation of the two ranges, but below that town the
permeable Tertiary volcanic beds which floor the valley give rise to

a poorer covering of spiny scrub intermixed with irrigated river meadows and arable fields. Parallel with the cessation of the volcanic formations in the Cordillera Central, the volcanic floor of the valley gives way to alluvium and the forest re-appears, about 40 miles north of Honda. From the confluence with the Nare to Tamalameque, a distance of 150 miles, the flat-floored corridor contains an island-studded, braided river flowing through marshy and lake-fringed alluvial country until the Caribbean plains are reached.

The rift valley is approximately 40 miles wide until the Z-bend at Girardot, when it contracts to half that width. Here also a subsidiary rift valley, occupied by the Bogotá river, runs north-eastward towards the intermont basin drained by it.

The average gradient of the river is a gentle one, but it is most irregular, the Honda rapids being the greatest obstacle to navigation in this respect. Of more widespread significance is its irregular flow, for it is subject to sudden rises in level caused by local storms in its tributary valleys, and the seasonal level is so lowered by the winter dry season that navigation is difficult and irregular above Puerto Berrio until late April.

Settlements in the valley are not large in number or in population.

Plate 23. *Colombia's Magdalena River, despite its hazardous braided course, is still extensively used for goods traffic*

There is a fairly important concentration around Neiva (84,000) where the valley floor stretches into the tierra templada, and coffee and cocoa are the main produce. A number of old mining settlements, such as Mariquita, along the junction of the Tertiary valley strata with the crystalline rocks of the Central Cordillera, have now become important agricultural centres, particularly of coffee production, Ambalema on the mainstream being an important collecting point. These many western tributary valleys on the old Honda–Ibagué road provide a chain of forest clearings similar to those on the eastern slopes of the Magdalena basin.

The only other settlements of importance are the river ports, which serve as refuelling points and entrepôts for distribution of goods arriving by river for the Cordilleran settlements, and as collecting centres for export of their products. Barrancabermeja alone has another function, that of being Colombia's greatest developed oilfield. Although producing only some 5 per cent of Venezuela's enormous total, Colombia is surpassed in Latin America only by that country, Mexico, and Argentina as a source of petroleum. A pipe line links this oilfield with Mamonal, near Cartagena, following the Magdalena mainstream through most of this distance (Fig. 47). Others supply Bucaramanga and Manizales and Bogotá via Puerto Salgar.

The principal river ports with the areas they serve, going upstream from the Cauca–Magdalena confluence, are (Fig. 46):

1. Tamalameque, serving the lower César valley and the southern parts of the Sierra de Perija.
2. La Gloria, linking the Petrólea oilfield on the Venezuelan frontier to the Magdalena.
3. Gamarra, the terminus of the road to Ocaña and Cúcuta.
4. Puerto Wilches, joined by railway to Bucaramanga.
5. Barrancabermeja, linked by road to settlements in the upper Sogamosa valley and to the main intermont highway.
6. Puerto Berrío, providing the first link with the Cordillera Central and its Antioqueño region by railway to Medellín, and by road eastward to the Tunja region of the Cordillera Oriental.
7. La Dorada–Puerto Salgar, on opposite banks of the river, the former being the terminus of the railway to Neiva and to Medellín via Puerto Berrio, and the latter of the railway serving Bogotá, and of the oil pipelines supplying the capital

on the east and the Cartago, Pereira, Manizales areas on the west.

8. Honda, where rapids interrupt navigation of the Magdalena, and once of much greater importance, before the construction of the La Dorada–Neiva railway. It still controls an important road to Bogotá, a cable line over the Cordillera Central to Manizales, and a road which passes over the Quindío pass (11,099 feet) via Cali, Popayán, and Pasto to Quito in Ecuador.

9. Ambalema and several smaller ports, serving the coffee districts on the slopes on each side of the basin.

10. Girardot, where the Bogotá joins the Magdalena, providing another important rail and road link with the capital, and on the principal route linking it to the Pacific port of Buenaventura.

Upstream from Girardot to Neiva, the gradient of the Magdalena increases, and although navigable for shallow-draught boats during part of the year, the river is a much less important transport artery than downstream from Girardot. The Neiva–La Dorada railway and the main highway from the upper Magdalena basin to Girardot both follow the valley, and provide the only longitudinal land transport routes serving the valley.

THE CENTRAL CORDILLERA AND CAUCA–PATIA VALLEY

This great range, a continuation of the Cordillera Oriental of Ecuador, is the most magnificent of the Colombian Andes, and its volcanic peaks exceed 18,000 feet. Structurally, it is for the most part crystalline in composition, the granites, gneisses and schists containing the gold and silver veins which proved a stimulus to early immigration. For a better understanding of its geography it can be considered in two parts.

From the frontier with Ecuador northward to Sonsón it is a high narrow chain, with its peaks well above the line of permanent snow (15,000–15,500 feet), its slopes covered with ash and lava from several clusters of active volcanoes, and none of the passes through the range falling below 9,800 feet. North of Sonsón the Cordillera becomes lower (average height 8,600 feet) and spreads out to become the Antioquia plateau, a gently rolling tableland still largely of crystalline rocks. It is in fact a large batholith tilted from west to east, so that most of its drainage is to the Magdalena, the deep gorge of the Porce–Nechi dividing it into two almost equal parts.

The valley trough, aligned along the western flank of the Cordillera Central, is narrower and less continuous than the Magdalena valley. Progressing from south to north it is occupied firstly by the southward-flowing Patía which has eroded a narrow plain in the volcanic deposits within an inaccessible rift gorge. This is separated from the Cauca trough by the narrow Tambo sill south of Popayán. Between this latter town and Nechí, where the river of that name draining the Antioquia highland joins the mainstream, and the river enters on its Caribbean lowland course, the Cauca drainage basin can be divided into the following five parts:

(*a*) The Popayán basin, dissected by the Cauca's eastern tributaries into hills of volcanic ash which diminish in size northward.

(*b*) The Valle del Cauca, an almost level mountain-enclosed flood plain 125 miles long and 15 miles wide, between Calí and Cartago. Probably the site of a great Tertiary lake dammed by outpourings of volcanic material, the imperceptible slope of less than 1 in 5,000 means that the low central portions of the valley south of Calí frequently revert to their marshy character.

(*c*) The Cauca gorge between Cartago and Jericó, where the Cauca has cut its way through the flank of the Cordillera Central leaving a portion west of the river.

(*d*) The Antioquia valley, where once again, north of Jericó, the gradient becomes gentler and navigation is again possible, and the river flows through a plain much narrower (6–10 miles) than the Valle del Cauca, and bounded by cliff-like sides.

(*e*) The lower gorge which extends upstream from Cáceres, and which by its rapids again restricts navigation.

As in the Cordillera Oriental the dominant vegetation of the whole region is forest, varying considerably with elevation but rarely extending below 6,000 feet, where the drier rain shadow conditions of the deeply set valleys give rise to savana–steppe, except where, as in parts of the Cauca flood-plain, marsh conditions prevail and bamboo and forest reassert themselves, or where north of Puerto Valdivia the forest reaches the valley floor.

On the Cordillera the lower forested slopes are clothed with tropical species of which the cinchona has been the most important commercially, and above these, temperate forest of Colombian oak with bamboo undergrowth passes into páramos above 11,500 feet, which with the permanent snow fields above 13,000 feet form a narrow belt south of Sonsón to the frontier with Ecuador.

This complex region of the Central Cordillera and the Cauca–Patía trough shows great contrasts of landscape and many different patterns of land occupance. Only in the far south, in the Cordillera and in the Patía valley, is there a large Indian population, with Pasto as the centre. Agriculture is largely of a subsistence character, crops of maize and potatoes being grown on small holdings wherever slopes permit cultivation, and cattle being grazed on the páramos above. In many respects the region is very similar to the adjoining region of highland Ecuador.

Apart from this area, almost all the region has been peopled from the north, from the Medellín region; and the expansion of settlement southward from the Department of Antioquia is one of the most marked features of colonization in Latin America, accounting for more than 4 millions of the Colombian population. The basic economic characteristic of these Antioqueño people today is agricultural diversity, although in origin it was a migration drawn by the mineral wealth of the Cordillera. They have spread coffee cultivation until this region has become the most important one in Colombia, but they have not participated in the agricultural booms which have so often spelled disaster in other parts of the continent (Fig. 47).

Since the end of the 18th century, in a real frontier movement, the Antioqueños, a people largely of Spanish stock, but not unmixed with Indian and Negro elements, expanded their settlements from the core zone of Medellín southward in three main prongs through the tierra templada along both sides of the Cauca trough, and along the eastern slopes of the Cordillera Central. The introduction of coffee as a cash crop in the 1880s did much to provide a stimulus to the settlement of new lands by this rapidly growing mountain population. Throughout the zones of expansion, the Antioqueños have cleared the lower slopes of forest, but above, beyond the coffee zone, the forest is still untouched. With little capital and as a result of their own initiative and hard work the colonists have carved new homes and holdings from virgin territory.

Largely as a result of great changes in transport facilities, Medellín has become the leading industrial city of the North Andean republics, and an increasingly large number of Antioqueños are now swelling its number and so reducing the pace of the southward colonization.

Medellín, situated in the Antioqueño highland where the Porce valley widens out, throughout the colonial period and until this century, remained relatively isolated. It is now a city of 921,000, with textile factories and a thriving economic life, linked by road, rail and air to Bogotá, and to both Atlantic and Pacific ports.

The Antioquia tableland is nowhere above the limit of cultivation, and crops of maize, wheat and potatoes, dependent on elevation, form the staple crops of the area's food supply, the principal harvest occurring in January and a second but less reliable one in August.

South of Medellín, with Manizales (252,000) as its centre, is the great coffee region of the Department of Caldas, which with Antioquia accounts for half of Colombian coffee production. In fact the pattern of the distribution of coffee bears a striking resemblance to the spread of Antioqueño colonization (Fig. 47).

Conversely, the flood plain of the Valle del Cauca and the Popayán basin, which was peopled by Spaniards both from north and south, bears a completely different agricultural and ethnic correspondence. Never the scene of Antioqueño settlement, it bore from colonial times the characteristics of plantation agriculture so often associated with the tierra templada, large estates, extensive utilization, Negro labour and villages (because the Indian population was inadequate), and a major commercial crop, sugar cane. This pattern is still basically the same today, and although other crops such as cocoa around Cartago and tobacco around Palmira have been introduced, sugar is still dominant (supplying the country's needs), and the absentee plantation owners still reside in Popayán (65,000). In the southern extensions of the Valle del Cauca the low central zone, bordering the river and liable to flood, pastures thousands of cattle, while the arable fields spread from this zone on both sides to the alluvial fans of the tributary valleys.

The Cauca valley has never been the great transport artery which has been the role of the Magdalena, and both Medellín and Manizales are linked with the latter river by roads, and by railway to Puerto Berrío and by cable way to Honda respectively. Besides the longitudinal road following the Cauca for much of its course, a railway now links both cities with Buenaventura via Cali (767,000). This latter city has been transformed, as a result of the railway, from a small regional centre into Colombia's third city with a wide range of industries.

WESTERN COLOMBIA

There are few volcanic peaks in the third component of the Colombian Andes, and it is a great folded sedimentary and metamorphic chain with a huge batholith as its core. In only one place is this great barrier broken through, where the Patía river has carved its exit to the Pacific, and this is an inaccessible gorge of no use as a transport route. The passes over the range are, however, lower than those over the Cordillera Central, and two at 5,300 feet permit access from the Valle del Cauca to Buenaventura (97,000). In its northern extensions the Cordillera divides into three little-explored *serranias* which spread out on to the Caribbean plain.

Facing the moisture-laden Pacific air masses the western slopes are clothed with forest throughout, with páramos above the 11,000 feet elevation, whereas on the more sheltered eastern slopes forest rarely extends below 7,000 feet.

Although apparently well peopled before the Spanish conquest, except for a few areas it now has little settlement. In some sheltered valleys towards the north, Antioqueños have established the towns of Cañasgordas and Frontino, which are linked by road both to the Cauca trough and Medellín and to the Gulf of Darién, and once again coffee is the basic product of the area. Alluvial gold mining activity also continues along the slopes of the Cordillera in such old centres as Buriticá in the north-east and above Barbacoas and Timbiqui in the south-west.

From Buenaventura southward, in the region known as the Bajo Chocó, the Cordillera slopes down to a wide coastal plain made up of the deltas of the numerous rivers draining its western slopes. In the far south the deltas of the Patía and the Mira include a marshy zone some 30 miles wide.

North of Buenaventura a coastal range, the Serrania de Baudó, shuts off the Cordillera Occidental from the Pacific, and an almost continuous plain from the Gulf of Darién to the Bajo Chocó separates these two ranges. The headwaters of the Atrato and San Juan rivers drain the forested western slopes of the Cordillera Occidental, and on the plain a little north of 5°N., the main streams turn north and south respectively, one to flow to the Atlantic, the other to the Pacific.

The Serrania de Baudó extends into Panama but it is so low (460 feet) and narrow (5 miles) where the Bay of Cupica approaches the Napipi tributary of the Atrato that before the Panama canal was constructed this route was considered as the best site for an inter-oceanic canal. Farther south near the source of the Baudó river the range exceeds 6,000 feet, and the coastal plain is very narrow.

The population is at least 80 per cent negroid in composition. Introduced as slaves, their descendants, since the abolition of slavery, have penetrated into many parts of this region carrying on subsistence agriculture in forest clearings, and gold and platinum alluvial mining in the Atrato and San Juan basins. The heavy rain, for this is one of the wettest areas of the continent, and the dense forests make communications difficult, and only in the Buenaventura and Tumaco areas is the coast linked with the Cauca–Patía highway, the former with Cali, the latter with Pasto. Tumaco has also become the terminus of the pipeline from the new Putumayo oilfield at Orito. Quibdó (44,000), the mining centre in the upper Atrato valley, has a road connection with Medellín, but north of this the region is devoid of roads of any kind.

THE CARIBBEAN LOWLANDS

All the regions in Colombia so far considered merge on the north into the great plains drained and largely built up by the lower Magdalena system and the smaller Sinú river to the west.

The Magdalena has three great affluents, the Cauca, César and San Jorge, and the great network of rivers and streams meander in shifting courses over a lowland which in many parts is covered by swamps, marshes, and permanent lakes known as *ciénagas*, the largest of which, the Ciénaga de Zapatoza, receives the waters of the César before its confluence with the Magdalena. One of the greatest changes in the course of the Magdalena occurred in the middle of the 19th century, when it swung to the west at El Banco, rejoining its former course some 60 miles downstream. Another, of greater economic significance, was the silting up of El Dique, its former exit south of Cartagena.

Apart from the obvious structural and relief contrasts with Highland Colombia, this region shows great contrasts in climate, vegetation and land use. As a result of the pronounced dry season from October to March, which endows it with a typical Sudan climate, tropical grassland with scattered scrub forest is everywhere predominant. Cattle pastoralism has thus become the principal occupation of the rural population, which is for the most part negroid in race. This economy is also linked with movements of transhumance, from areas flooded in the summer, such as the Añegadizos which provide good dry-season pasture. Conversely, cattle from the lower Cauca move on to the savana for rainy season pasture. Arable farming takes place on the *bancos* or areas above flood level, and cotton, sugar, bananas, vegetables and fruit are important crops for the urban centres. The principal rural settlements occur on these raised parts or dry sites in the plains, and at levée stopping places on the Magdalena which have lost much of their importance with the coming of modern navigation.

The two coastal cities contain most of the population, and although the Pacific outlet, Buenaventura, has grown relatively in importance in this century, Barranquilla (568,000) is still overwhelmingly the great port of Colombia, as in spite of the river bar at the Magdalena mouth, it controls the exit and entrance of this great waterway into the most populated areas of the country. Vessels larger than 10,000 tons still must use Puerto Colombia, Barranquilla's outport, but good road and rail communications link this town with Barranquilla, and serve to increase its importance.

Until a century ago, however, Cartagena (279,000) was Colombia's chief port as it was a strategic harbour controlling the Magdalena entrance by El Dique channel. The silting of this channel led to its decline, but three factors have tended to increase its importance recently, the construction of a railway to Calamar on the Magdalena, its selection as the terminus of the oil pipeline from Barrancabermeja, and the increasing importance of the western part of the plain and the Atrato valley for gold and platinum production which is exported via Cartagena.

SIERRA NEVADA DE SANTA MARTA

The extreme north-east of Colombia, adjoining the Caribbean, is made up of two remnants of the old Antillean continent, having little structural relationship with the Andes. These two old blocks are the triangular-shaped Sierra Nevada de Santa Marta massif, rising to over 19,000 feet, and the relatively low (2,600 feet) Guajira peninsula. A third detached remnant is the Paraguaná peninsula of Venezuela on the opposite shore of the Maracaibo entrance.

The Sierra Nevada de Santa Marta rises so precipitously from the sea, that within 25 miles from the shore heights of 17,000 feet are reached, and the coast is rugged and unpopulated. Most of the drainage of this massif flows into the César which occupies a north-east–south-west trough parallel to the international frontier separating the granitic rocks of Santa Marta from the sedimentaries of the Sierra de Perija. A number of rivers hurtling down its steep western slopes empty direct into the tidal lagoon, Ciénaga de Santa Marta. Each valley has its village, its settlement or group of villages where the river reaches the plain and its water can be used for irrigation, and a south–north railway from Fundación links them with the port of Santa Marta. This zone has been famous for its cocoa and banana plantations cultivated by Negro labourers. After a temporary decline when disease hit banana production in the 1940s, the area is still an important supplier of the United States with this fruit. The largest city in this region, Santa Marta (104,000), which had a brief period of prosperity in the 19th and early 20th centuries, has a good harbour but a relatively restricted hinterland, and is being outpaced by its coastal rivals Barranquilla and Cartagena.

Some sugar is grown in the César valley and it is a reception area for cattle from the flooded pastures of the Magdalena plains in the wet season. The interior of the mountain zone is still largely Indian country with subsistence agriculture and pastoralism as its economic basis. There are great climatic variations, rainfall and the resultant forest being dependent on elevation, and the steep slopes of the north become too precipitous and devoid of soil for trees above 4,000 feet.

The lower relief of Guajira results in its being covered with forest, and extensive clearings on relatively fertile volcanic soils permit considerable subsistence agriculture, but rainfall amounts are small, Uribia being the driest station in Colombia (14 inches). The exploitation of the salt deposits at Bahía Honda on this peninsula promise to make it the world's greatest salt producing area.

THE ORINOCO–AMAZON PLAINS

This vast area known in Colombia as the Llanos Orientales comprises 60 per cent of the area of the country and contains less than 2 per cent of its people. In other words less than 400,000 people live in an area greater than England, Wales and France combined. Therefore for all practical purposes its present economic importance to Colombia is almost negligible (Fig. 45).

Seven important tributaries of the Orinoco and Amazon with hundreds of their affluents drain the region eastward. Of these, four rise in the Andes, the Meta and Guaviare flowing to the Orinoco, and the Caqueta and Putumayo to the Amazon. The Vichada, Inírida and Vaupés rise in the undulating plateau country to the east of the Cordillera. The Putumayo forms the international frontier with Peru for most of its length, but a small enclave of territory south of the river gives Colombia some 70 miles of frontage on the Amazon downstream from Iquitos, Leticia being the principal port.

Although geology and soils introduce considerable complexity there are two great vegetational zones, the Guaviare river forming an approximate boundary between them. To the north the marked October–March dry season gives rise to savana conditions, with gallery forests along many of the rivers, while to the south all-season equatorial rains produce dense forests.

Although the northern areas were the scene of some 18th-century Jesuit colonization, and the southern participated in the cinchona and rubber booms of last century, the most permanent utilization of these eastern plains has been for pastoral purposes. This is especially true of the piedmont zone, the Cordilleran settlements providing a good market for the cattle. Villavicencio (48,000) has become the great base for this movement to the Bogotá region.

The development of the Putumayo oilfield adjacent to the boundary with Ecuador, and the promise of a similar development in the Casanare department in the northern part of the plains will give an additional and more varied economic base to the region.

The easternmost areas of the llanos are more closely linked with Venezuela, and their outlet is by way of the Orinoco and Ciudad Bolívar. As with most of the Amazon basin the lack of transport facilities is one of the greatest hindrances to its fuller use, and while the country has to spend so much to link together the areas occupied by 98 per cent of the population, very little remains available for this vast and almost empty area. Indeed no country with a share of the great Amazon basin has done less to forward its development than Colombia.

PROSPECTS AND PROBLEMS

Second only to Brazil as a producer of coffee, Colombia is the world's greatest source of mild coffees, most of which is bought by the United States (Fig. 47). The dependence of Colombia's economy on coffee often meant that more than 70 per cent of all its exports were of this one commodity. There have been sustained efforts, therefore, to diversify the pattern, and 'minor exports', as they are termed, have been encouraged. These include products as varied as shrimps, cement, cotton, meat, petrochemicals and emeralds. Indications are that quite soon coffee will account for less than half of the country's exports. Low yield areas are being phased out in favour of the cultivation of other crops, and agricultural cooperatives have been established to service the 75,000 land holdings created in the 1960s decade from a re-distribution of 6 million acres under the republic's agrarian reform programme. Much, however, still remains to be done and wheat imports to supply domestic needs continue to increase.

Petroleum is next in importance in Colombia's export trade, but here again an increasing amount is being used internally. Moreover the long-established field of Barrancabermeja is declining in output. Fortunately the shortfall is being replaced by the new Putumayo field at Orito, and there appear to be good prospects of more petroleum reserves in the eastern Llanos.

Colombia is Latin America's greatest producer of gold, platinum and emeralds and these mineral products are significant components of the 'minor exports'.

Agricultural development and diversification and industrialization are also the solution to Colombia's other great problem, namely the provision of employment for its rapidly increasing population. Since 1950 population has more than doubled, and its growth rate of 3·3 per cent is one of the world's largest. Now it has the fourth largest population of all the Latin American states, but by 1975 Colombia's population will exceed that of Argentina, and only Brazil and Mexico will have more people than Colombia. The constant problem, therefore, is to provide jobs for the additional annual increment of some 200,000 workers, schools for the children, more and more houses and all the additional services for this growing population. Moreover, one quarter of the population is now in Colombia's six largest cities, and the growth rate in the urban areas is five times that of the rural districts. The emphasis, therefore, is on the encouragement of labour intensive manufacturing industries, but even the development of livestock production on the vast undeveloped areas suitable for pastoralism will help alleviate the problem. Cotton cultivation has almost eliminated the need for imports of this commodity, and increased sugar production has enabled Colombia to become an exporter of sugar. Decentralization of industry and the stimulation of employment opportunities in backward areas, it is hoped, will also reduce the flow of migrants to the cities. The establishment of free trade and industrial zones in cities such as Buenaventura and Palmira has also led to the setting up of industries as varied as electronics, cement, textiles, timber-processing and fishing.

International trade plays a relatively smaller role in the country's economic life than it does in Venezuela. Thus, although Colombia's population is almost twice that of its north-eastern neighbour, the value of its exports is less than one-fifth of Venezuela's. Colombia is in fact much more self-sufficient, and internal trade between the regions is very active. The physical make-up of the country is a strong influence in this respect for the contrasted crops produced at different altitudes are interchanged among the lowland and highland settlements. Thus plain dwellers exchange cocoa, sugar, molasses and cattle with the plateau and mountain folk for grains and potatoes. This traffic has its origin in the region's Indian past, but has been extended now to manufactured products, the textile mills of Medellín being supplied with cotton from the lower Magdalena plains, and the urban dwellers of Barranquilla with flour from Bogotá, while one of the principal cargoes of the Magdalena river boats is beef cattle from the northern plains en route to the centres of Bogotá and Medellín.

In view of the complex physical components of the country, both its export and internal trade have to overcome great transport difficulties (Fig. 46). These undoubtedly constitute the outstanding economic problems of Colombia, and the pressing needs have been to link its various regions together internally, and to provide links between them and the principal ports. For many centuries three means have been chosen to solve these problems, human porterage, animal transport and the Magdalena river route. All still survive in the mid-20th century. In the Chocó a dense network of tracks maintains communications by means of carriers in a region still devoid of roads. But the coming of motor, rail and air transport has accomplished great changes for Colombia. Bogotá is no longer at least eight days distant from Barranquilla but less than three hours. Medellín is not a day's arduous journey from Bogotá but a comfortable flight of one hour's duration. Buenaventura, from being relatively unimportant, has been linked by road and rail with the major settlement areas of the republic and has now become the principal exporting port of the country.

Much expenditure is being devoted to road and rail construction and improvement, and the Inter-American highway linking Colombia with Panama is now being completed. Road mileage has doubled since the end of the Second World War. This has meant lower transport costs, more efficient rationalization of industrial location and increased regional integration. There are, however, many backward areas, and economic and social reforms have not kept pace with population growth. There are strong political tensions, and it is problematical if Colombia can solve its socio-economic ills without a further eruption of violence, which has characterized many rural areas since 1948. Resistance to the status quo can now be more easily organized on a national basis, for increased transport facilities have also tended to weaken the strong regionalism which has always dominated Colombian life. The very different physical and human conditions underlying the many regions which make up the Colombian nation are, however, still potent factors in the moulding of separate regional identities. The Negro gold washer of the Chocó, the Motilone Indian agriculturalists of the Venezuelan Maracaibo border, the cattle men of the eastern plains, the Popayán Spanish plantation owner, the tri-ethnic Antioqueño industrialist, and the mestizo Bogotaño are but a few of the many diverse elements which still epitomize the geographical conditions of the contrasted regions they inhabit.

STATISTICAL SUMMARY — COLOMBIA

Area: 439,513 square miles

Population (1970): 22,106,000

Percentage of Land

(a)	Arable	4%
(b)	Pastoral	13%
(c)	Forest	61%
(d)	Other	22%

Animal numbers

(a)	Cattle	14·1	million
(b)	Pigs	2·3	,,
(c)	Sheep	1·2	,,
(d)	Goats	0·4	,,
(e)	Horses and Mules	1·4	,,

Communications

(a)	All-seasons road milleage	4,772
(b)	Railway mileage	2,134
(c)	Air routes	924 million passenger miles
		110 ,, ton ,,

Principal products

    (*a*) *Agricultural*

Maize	972,000 metric tons	
Bananas	965,000	,, ,,
Potatoes	800,000	,, ,,
Rice	662,000	,, ,,
Sugar	597,000	,, ,,
Coffee	474,000	,, ,,
Oilseeds	249,000	,, ,,
Beans	176,000	,, ,,
Wheat	93,000	,, ,,

    (*b*) *Mineral*

Petroleum	9,603,000 metric tons
Coal	3,100,000 ,, ,,
Gold	24,400 troy pounds

Exports

    (*a*) *Total:* $558,000,000

    (*b*) *Percentage share of principal commodities*

Coffee	63%
Petroleum	7%
Bananas	3%

CHAPTER TWELVE

Ecuador

ECUADOR has three clearly demarcated zones of Coastal plain, Andean highlands and Eastern plains (Fig. 48). These are always referred to as Costa, Sierra and Oriente, but as the latter area has been drastically reduced in recent years, and is in any case almost uninhabited, for all practical purposes the republic is made up of two contrasted zones of lowland and highland. Approximately 60 per cent of Ecuador's 6 million inhabitants occupy the Andean mountain basins, and the remainder live in the coastal region. This latter proportion is increasing steadily and it would seem that very soon it will be in every way the more important region of Ecuador. It has always produced the bulk of the country's exports, both agricultural and mineral.

THE COASTAL REGION

This zone, which is relatively narrow at both its north and south extremities, for most of its length is some 100 miles wide, and is not a simple coastal plain but a complex region of plain, hills and Andean piedmont, crossed by two important river systems, the Esmeraldas and Guayas.

Adjoining the Pacific is a low plateau known in the area north of the Gulf of Guayaquil as the Cordillera de Colonche, decreasing in height northward from approximately 2,500 feet to 750 feet. The recency of its uplift is indicated by its composition, in the north being mainly Quaternary sandstones deposited on folded Tertiary clays and sandstones, whereas further south Cretaceous limestones predominate. This plateau ends seaward in cliffs, and the rivers from the Andes have entrenched their torrent courses in it *en route* to the sea.

Behind this plateau zone is a flat alluvial plain built up by these rivers. Where the latter originate on the western slopes of the Andes the plain is generally flat and featureless as in the valley of the Catarama; where the rivers originate in the volcanic zone further east great masses of volcanic débris in huge coalesced fans spread out on

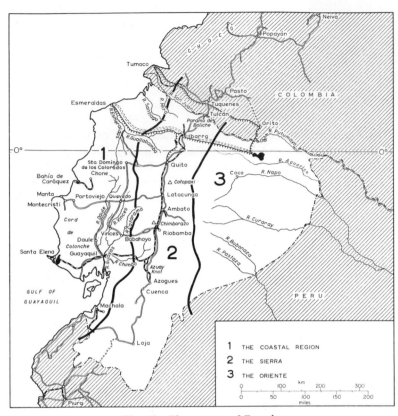

Fig. 48. *The regions of Ecuador*

to the plain, as in the case of the Mira Guaillabamba and Chimbo rivers. It is this piedmont zone which forms the third component of the coastal region throughout the northern two-thirds of its length.

The climatic transition which occurs in this coastal zone is one of the most rapid anywhere in the world. Adjoining the northern frontier, the constant rains characteristic of the Colombian Chocó give forest conditions in the Santiago and Esmeraldas basins. South of the latter river a dry season from June to November is a characteristic feature, and this season becomes longer and longer in duration, until at the Peruvian frontier desert conditions prevail.

The northernmost coastal province of Esmeraldas shares many features of the Colombian Chocó, with its Indian and Negro rural population occupied with shifting agriculture and alluvial gold washing. Many of the Negroes drifted into the forest after emancipation to avoid feudal labour on the Andean plateau, and the Indians have moved in a similar way to till the haciendas of the piedmont zone. Further south a much more densely peopled area has a more varied economy in the deciduous forest and coarse savana which there prevail. Cocoa and tagua nuts (for imitation ivory) are grown around Chone and are sent out to Bahía de Caráquez by rail. Manta (33,000) is likewise linked to Montecristi, and this area supports a thriving subsistence agriculture and the cultivation of the toquilla straw for the so-called 'Panama' hat industry.

Further south still, in the area north of the Gulf of Guayaquil, agriculture is restricted by the length of the dry season to a few crops of maize, beans and squash in the damper locations; and the dominant economic activities are pastoralism, the Panama hat industry and the exploitation of a relatively important oilfield in the Santa Elena peninsula.

It is the Guayas lowland east and north of the Gulf of Guayaquil which is the great productive zone of the coastal region. Here live a quarter of the people of Ecuador, and a network of navigable channels links together the cocoa, banana and rice plantations on the natural levées, the pastoral acres of the plain which are occupied in the dry season, and the undulating country of the upper basin used in the wet season. Here is Ecuador's greatest city and port, Guayaquil (739,000), situated at the meeting point of ocean and river navigation, where the Guayas affluents, Daule, Vinces, Cataraina, and Chimbo merge their waters into one course.

The northern areas of the Guayas basin between Quevedo and Santo Domingo de los Colorados appear to have the greatest potential for the future development of tropical agriculture. Relative to the good soil, terrain and hydrologic conditions prevailing there, population densities are low, and forestry in association with commercial agriculture offer opportunities for increased settlement. Santo Domingo de los Colorados (40,000) located where the road from Quito turns south into the Guayas basin and so to Guayaquil is a particularly important focal point for transport, trade and settlement in this new colonization area.

Cocoa was for long the dominant agricultural product, its high quality being world-famous. Since the First World War the ravages of witchbroom and other diseases so reduced production that during the Second World War exports fell to a third of the quantities produced earlier in the century. Increased prices in the post-war period encouraged large scale replanting and the industry is once more important, contributing a ninth of Ecuador's export income.

As cocoa declined so rice became an important crop, and in 1947 it was actually Ecuador's chief export. Production fluctuates greatly and its importance usually is greater in supplying increasing home demand than finding its way to the export market.

More steady in its expansion has been the development, particularly since 1955, of banana plantations, so that now Ecuador is the world's greatest exporter of bananas. Its total production is second only to that of Brazil. Unlike the Central American producers of this crop, cultivation is by small or medium-sized enterprises, but in spite of dry years, the competition of the Caribbean countries and the monopolistic nature of the banana trade, exports have been maintained at a steadily high level. The United States, continental Europe and Chile are the principal markets but Japan is also an increasingly important customer. Guayaquil is the chief port of shipment, but Puerto Bolívar on the southern shore of the Gulf of Guayaquil is rapidly expanding its share of the trade.

Coffee, grown in the piedmont zone, has also become much more important in Ecuadorean agriculture, and in most years yields a greater return than cocoa. Cotton, African palm oil, and sugar are other products of the coastal area.

The development of the country's fisheries now means that by value fish products rank fifth in Ecuador's export trade.

THE SIERRA

The Ecuadorean Andes are a relatively simple structural region, being like their counterpart further north mainly of crystalline formation of gneiss, diorites and micaschists. The Cordillera Central of Colombia is continued southward as the Cordillera Oriental or Real of Ecuador, and closely parallel to it the Cordillera Occidental of Colombia is continued under the same name. The plateaux enclosed between these two ranges form a narrow high corridor interrupted by volcanoes and volcanic outpourings which divide it into isolated compartments filled with débris from the adjoining cones and scarred by deep river troughs which have easily eroded these soft deposits. South of the Cuenca basin in the southern quarter of the Ecuadorean Andes, the volcanoes disappear, and the zone of highland becomes lower and wider reaching to the coast, but it has been so penetrated by the headstreams of the Amazon and coastal rivers that the watershed region is a narrow one.

The great volcanoes of Ecuador dominate the relief and greatly influence the distribution of population and transport routes. The present cones rise from an old basement of lava and nearly all are more or less active. Rarely do their lava flows reach the arable zone, but wind-blown ashes and disastrous mud flows, caused by sudden melting of snow on contact with lava, often cause damage. They are rapidly eroded, and such old areas as the Azuay knot which encloses the Cuenca basin on the north, are merely the roots of much more extensive masses. Glaciers crown the highest, Chimborazo, Cotopaxi, Sangay and Tungurahua all exceeding 16,000 feet, and the moraines on their lower slopes indicate that in the Pleistocene period these glaciers were much greater in area.

The intermont basins stand at elevations varying between 7,200 and 9,800 feet and are floored by a great variety of volcanic-derived deposits, one of which, *cancagua*, is believed to be a wind-blown product of the steppe conditions prevailing in the last interglacial period. It is a fine impermeable clayey soil which has been deeply dissected by stream action. Other deposits are flood-derived and carried down by rivers from the surrounding volcanic heights.

On the high páramos fine rain and misty conditions prevail throughout most of the year, but in the basins the dry season conditions of the coastal zone operate with a minor rainy period in October. More important, however, is the matter of exposure to Amazon influences. Where the Cordillera Ecuatoriana is less continuous and lower, the rainy season (May–August) conditions prevailing on the eastern slopes penetrate into the intermont basins.

The porosity of the soils has led to a relatively poor forest cover except on the outer slopes of both cordilleras, and the basins are covered by a scrub-bush maquis, from which pasture and arable areas have been won. In the higher areas this is replaced by *pajonal* or a zone of high tufty grass, and this type of páramo occupies half the Andean region, and is grazed by flocks belonging to Indian communities or those of the valley haciendas.

Within the volcanic area of Ecuador there are six distinct intermont basins, the three northern ones draining to the Pacific, the three southern to the Amazon. These together contain half the population of Ecuador.

The high basin of Tulcán (9,800 feet), which is merely a small remnant of the Colombian basin of Pasto and Túquerres, is almost in the páramo zone and is almost exclusively pastoral in its economy. South of the Páramo of Boliche, the Ibarra basin has a more diverse agricultural economy typical of tierras fria, templada and caliente, for sugar cane is grown in the deep plain of Chota 2,600 feet below the plateau. The same is true of the Quito basin and the Guaillabamba gorge and its irrigated terraces. The dense population typical of all the basins is here swelled by the urban concentration of the capital, Quito (496,000), on the site of an Indian village.

The Latacunga basin suffers both from aridity and the ravages of volcanic eruptions and mud avalanches,[1] but where irrigation is possible there is oasis-like cultivation, and near Ambato lucerne pastures at the lower end of the basin. The Riobamba basin is little better, and only where the water of the Chibenga is led to the plain and east of the Chimbo are there arable and pastoral areas. Porosity of soil and the high barrier of the Cordillera Ecuatoriana exacerbate the aridity.

The great basin of Cuenca with its 500,000 population is a much more prosperous land of large villages with a lively internal trade based on a flourishing agriculture and the Panama hat industry, and possessing the only urban nucleus of the Ecuadorean Andes outside Quito, that of Cuenca (71,000).

The deep basins of the rivers breaching the Cordillera south of Cuenca are not comparable with the intermont basins to the north. On the alluvial terraces of these narrow troughs, settlements such as Loja have been built, and the irrigated arable zones in this valley and in that of the Jubones form the last important areas of settlement before the aridity of the south produces the contrast between the desert of the western Cordilleran slopes and the forested eastern slopes which is typical of Peru. The Chaucha valley has some significant proved copper resources.

The principal products of the Sierra are maize, barley, wheat and potatoes, and the large clusters of population are supplied with foodstuffs either from their own small holdings or the haciendas of some 500 owners who control three-quarters of the Sierra lands.

In common with its southern neighbour, Peru, the Sierra has the problem of a centuries-old neglect of its Indian population. In addition to the social aspects of malnutrition, illiteracy and poor health, their economic poverty restricts even more the purchasing power of the small internal market for domestic manufacturing. *Minifundia*, absentee ownership of land, and a traditional reluctance to leave the Sierra further complicate the problems of the region.

---

[1] In 1949, Latacunga and Ambato were both largely destroyed.

THE ORIENTE

The Cordillera Ecuatoriana forms such a barrier to communication between the Eastern plain and the rest of Ecuador, even in the south where the transverse valleys are narrow and difficult of access, that no area of the trans-Andean plains has been less used than that belonging to Ecuador. Here 16th-century colonization was interrupted by the revolt of the warlike Jivaros which compelled evacuation of the settlements set up there, and the descendants of these Indians continue a hunting–cultivating existence not dissimilar to that practised for some thousands of years.

The loss, in 1941, to Peru of the major part of its Oriente region is still deeply resented by Ecuador, as the republic considers itself a victim of aggression from a larger and more powerful neighbour. For decades considerable efforts and much capital have been expended to discover oil in the region, and it was not until the late 1960s that the search proved successful. Now a major oil field in the Aguarico basin (a tributary of the Napo affluent of the Amazon) offers tremendous possibilities not only to satisfy Ecuadorean needs but to provide an important addition to the republic's export trade, and thereby to provide more capital for much needed development. A pipe-line paralleled by a new highway (Fig. 48) has been constructed to link the oilfield with the port of Esmeraldas, and to supply Quito *en route*. As a result, in 1973 petroleum replaced bananas as Ecuador's most important export commodity, and gave the country much needed financial resources for internal development. It is also possible that another pipe-line to Coca will provide an additional exit route for this Oriente oil, by barge, to Manáus.

PROSPECTS AND PROBLEMS

Few countries have two such clearly contrasted regions as Ecuador, and it is the antithesis between them which has largely prevented for so long a feeling of national unity. Apart from the obvious climatic differences, the Coast is relatively thinly peopled by Indians, Negroes and mestizos, yet produces all the exports, agricultural and mineral. The Sierra basins are densely peopled almost exclusively by Indians, or mestizos with very little European admixture, who survive by subsistence agriculture. There is pressure of population on limited land resources in the Sierra whereas on the Coast more land is available, especially on the forested low Andean slopes, which have recently been the scene of extensions of banana cultivation. On the

Plate 24. *Enormous expanses of almost impenetrable forest are still the home of Indian tribes; but oil prospecting and government-sponsored colonization are opening up many of these areas.* (Above) *in the* oriente *of Ecuador;* (below) *the interior of Zulia state, Venezuela*

Coast shortage of labour is endemic; in the Sierra the landless tenants always provide an abundance of cheap labour. The agricultural patterns of the Coast are constantly changing, adjusting themselves to world economic conditions. Cocoa is replaced by rice, rice by bananas. In the Sierra the traditionalism and primitive and inefficient method of grain production seem almost incapable of change. The Coast looks beyond Ecuador; the Sierra lives unto itself. Guayaquil is the thriving commercial seaport; Quito is the old colonial centre. Only in this century has Durán on the eastern bank of the Guayas been linked by rail with Quito. Contact between the two regions is now greater than at any time, and there is undoubtedly a slow but steady migration from Sierra to Coast, particularly to the Guayas lowland. As in Colombia, lack of transport facilities still hinders the development of many areas, and there are few good roads linking the northern basins with the Coast. With modernization of agriculture, careful land reform and re-settlement of population, quite apart from the development of the Oriente, Ecuador could not only feed itself better but be economically more prosperous from the sale of its surplus of tropical products.

Little progress has been made with agrarian reform, although some steps have been taken to set up peasant cooperatives, to rationalize domestic food supplies, to initiate modern sheep pastoralism, and to grow pyrethrum, maize, barley and potatoes for export. The fundamental problem, however, is that food production is growing by only 2 per cent annually, whereas population is increasing by 3·4 per cent per year. The cash crops of bananas, coffee and cocoa, accounting for 80 per cent of foreign exchange earnings are subject to considerable market fluctuations. Industrialization is very slow and the tourist trade relatively undeveloped. In total, therefore, economic growth barely keeps pace with population growth. Not only does this mean that there are chronic shortages in housing, water supply, drainage, education and other essential services, but that the country lacks the capital to utilize its considerable resources and so enable it to overcome its lack of development. Forest and mineral resources, potentially arable lands, hydro-electric power, and agricultural diversification all need capital investment and basic services such as roads to harness their potentialities, and pull the country from its economic paralysis. There are various possible steps to achieve this, such as the provision of foreign capital, a more equitable distribution of wealth, centralized planning and state-ownership of basic enterprises, but the perennial near-dictatorship from which Ecuador suffers scarcely provides the most stable political and economic climate in which such developments might occur.

STATISTICAL SUMMARY — ECUADOR

Area: 104,506 square miles

Population (1970): 6,180,000

Percentage of land

(a)	Arable	10%
(b)	Pastoral	8%
(c)	Forest	52%
(d)	Other	30%

Animal numbers

(a)	Cattle	2·0 million
(b)	Sheep	1·7 ,,
(c)	Pigs	1·3 ,,
(d)	Goats	0·2 ,,

Communications

(a)	All-seasons road mileage	7,380
(b)	Railway mileage	957

Principal products

(a) *Agriculture*

Bananas	3,300,000 metric tons
Root crops	639,000 ,, ,,
Sugar	294,000 ,, ,,
Maize	191,000 ,, ,,
Rice	182,000 ,, ,,

(b) *Mineral*

Petroleum	290,000 metric tons
Gold	1,048 troy pounds

Exports
   (*a*) *Total:* $206,000,000
   (*b*) *Percentage share of principal commodities*

Bananas	48%
Coffee	24%
Cocoa	11%
Sugar	5%

PART III

THE PACIFIC REPUBLICS

CHAPTER THIRTEEN

General Introduction to the Pacific Republics

MORE than half of the entire Pacific coastline of Latin America is shared by the two republics of Peru and Chile. For some 2,000 miles from the northern limits of Peru to Caldera in Chile conditions of extreme aridity are experienced. The desert slowly gives way southward to Mediterranean conditions and then to a rain-drenched wilderness of islands where precipitation amounts are the highest in Latin America. Contrasts in man's utilization of this 4,000 miles of ocean frontage will be obvious, yet they do not eliminate the fact that, in one way or another, the economic ties of all peoples dwelling in the coastal belt are with the Pacific and the inter-communications it affords. In the far south the primitive Indian tribes live most of their lives on its waters; throughout Chile maritime links from port to port have always been of significance, and in the past have often been easier than land connections; the nitrate and copper mines of northern Chile, the cotton and sugar oases of Peru and the petroleum fields of the north depend for their prosperity on the Pacific ports which send out their produce and cater to their needs.

Some suggest that trans-Pacific links were of importance even in prehistoric times. In this century the opening of the Panama Canal in 1914 greatly increased the economic significance of these Pacific republics and their oceanic links with the rest of the world. The growing importance of the independent nations of Asia, no longer so closely linked economically with their former colonial powers, is also leading to a development of trans-Pacific trade between Pacific Latin America and the Far East.

The combined barrier of the high Andean mountain backbone, Amazon forest and the thinly settled dry scrub lands of Patagonia tends to accentuate the orientation of the Pacific republics towards the western ocean. This physical 'no-man's-land' splits the continent longitudinally, and, until the coming of air transport, made the links between Peru, Bolivia and Chile and the republics of Atlantic Latin America tenuous ones. There is still no land communication between Peru and Brazil; only in the 1950s were road and rail links established eastward from Bolivia; and those between Chile and Argentina are few and far between (Figs. 11 and 12).

It is in this respect of relative isolation from the Atlantic that Bolivia, although since 1883 deprived of a Pacific coastline, is one of the Pacific republics. Although seeking remedies to overcome the disadvantages of its land-locked position by developing routes eastward through Argentina and Brazil, its economic outlets and ties are still with the Pacific republics of Chile and Peru, and the relative proximity of their ports will for long maintain these connections.

The maritime links are reinforced by the unity of the Andean mountain system which is common to all three states, and which for centuries has been a routeway of peoples moving southward through it. More than half of the region's people still dwell in this plateau area or the intermont basins strung out between the mighty ranges of the Cordillera. Throughout history to the present time the mineral wealth of 1 million square miles of mountainous country has attracted prospectors and mining companies from the Old and the New Worlds. The economies of Bolivia and Chile are still dependent on tin and copper respectively, and only the agricultural production of its desert valleys diminishes Peru's reliance on copper and mineral concentrates to a similar extent.

To Pacific frontage and Andean backbone should be added the historic unity of pre-Columbian civilizations which flourished over much of the area included within these three republics. Here for at least 2,000 years there developed the most advanced of South American cultures, culminating in the Inca Empire which extended from beyond the northern frontiers of Peru to the Maule river of Chile. From interior Bolivia to the Pacific a centralized administration with a good internal transport system supported a self-sufficient economy on irrigated and terraced agriculture, adapting methods and crops to the physical qualities of the land at various altitudes. Superimposed on this indigenous cultural foundation came Spanish power and people, and finding adequate mineral wealth to support both, the region became in due course the heart of the Spanish Empire in the New World. It is this dual Indian basis and Spanish invasion which characterizes the human endowment of the Pacific republics today. The impact varies from state to state and the differentiation is in large measure both the cause and effect of their separate political identities. In Bolivia the Indian element has remained dominant numerically in the high plateaux mining camps and farming plots; in Peru the 'coast' and 'sierra' split the nation into two ethnic

Plate 25. *Ruins of the Inca Empire, stretching from Quito to the Maule river of Chile, indicate a civilization characterized by massive stone fortresses and an extensive transport system*

halves of European and Indian worlds respectively; while in Chile, except for the small Araucanian minority of the Middle South, a European-Indian fusion has produced the homogeneous mestizo population which characterizes that republic. These contrasts in the assimilation of Indian peoples and European colonists are reflected in many aspects of their social and political geography, and account in no small measure for the contrasted political development of Chile on the one hand and Peru and Bolivia on the other. In Chile a relatively uninterrupted evolution towards democratic institutions stands out in sharp relief to a long succession of Peruvian authoritarian régimes.

When Independence came to the region there was a distinct possibility that two states only (Chile and Peru) would result from the overthrow of Spanish power. The similarities of Peru and Bolivia were sufficiently strong to justify a federation on more than one occasion. The 19th century saw, however, the increasing dominance of Chile on the Pacific coast, a dominance based largely on sea power. It was not difficult, therefore, for Chile to sever political links between her two northern neighbours, and in the War of the Pacific 1879–83, to deprive Bolivia of a coastline.

One of the more interesting and significant steps towards co-operation between the Pacific republics has been the establishment in 1969 of the Andean Pact, a sub-group of the Latin American Free Trade Area (LAFTA). Devised as a transitional form of economic integration, its purpose is to reduce the existing unevenness of development in the republics of Peru, Bolivia, Colombia, Ecuador and Chile, and ultimately to accelerate development within LAFTA as a whole.

The quality and characteristics of this uneven development can be partly gauged from these comparative statistics for the Andean Group countries:

ANDEAN GROUP COMPARATIVE FIGURES, 1967

Item	Unit	Bolivia	Chile	Colombia	Ecuador	Peru
Area	'000 sq. km.	1,098	742	1,179	290	1,331
Population	m.	4·35	9·20	19·20	5·50	12·40
Urban population	per cent	35	68	52	36	47
Gross product	U.S. $m.	700	5,040	5,715	1,320	3,700
Product per head	U.S. $	162	563	297	243	333
Industrial product	U.S. $m.	76	1,300	1,040	222	714
Steel production	'000 tons	—	638	256	—	79
Cement production	U.S. $m.	60	1,236	2,112	342	1,115

Exports (f.o.b.)	U.S. $m.	148	898	500	215	757
Imports (c.i.f.)	U.S. $m.	152	800	510	200	819

SOURCE: *Revista Progreso* and *Sociedad Nacional de Industrias*, Peru.

To promote a more balanced development, the pact aims to unify their economic and social policies, progressively to remove trade barriers until a customs union is brought about, and in the meantime to facilitate more rapid development in Bolivia and Ecuador by preferential tariffs. As with all similar schemes of economic integration the obstacles are enormous, but there is no doubt that if they can be overcome, the opportunities for economic expansion in a much larger market of healthier, more contented and more affluent populations would be almost unlimited.

CHAPTER FOURTEEN

Peru

OF ALL the Latin American states only Brazil, Argentina and Mexico exceed Peru in size, and it is often not realized that this republic is as large as the Union of South Africa, with a coastline of 1,500 miles, the greatest extent of desert shores of any of the nations of the world.

Within its bounds there arose one of the greatest Indian civilizations of the Americas, and for three centuries it was the core of Spanish power in the New World. Since political independence was achieved in the 19th century the balance of economic power and population has swung from the Andean states centred on Peru to the Atlantic republics of Brazil and Argentina. The loss of its southern extensions to Chile, and its defeat by that republic further reduced Peru's prestige, and its sharp division into Indian and European culture worlds, which show little sign of fusing, weaken its political, social and economic framework. It has in many respects never shaken off its colonial traditions, and few Latin American economies have been quite so controlled by foreign investments over such a wide field of production and transport. Nor is it surprising that, with half the nation politically unrepresented, democracy has not flourished for long on Peruvian soil.

Three units aligned parallel to its coast, the Coastal Oases, the Sierra or Andean mountains, and the Montaña or Amazon forest, each unit progressively larger in area as one moves inland, dominate the physical and human geography of Peru (Fig. 49).

THE COASTAL OASES

But for the some forty rivers which flow from the Andes towards the Pacific, the 30-mile-wide coastal belt of Peru would have little economic significance. Its shifting sand dunes and bleak cliffs would offer no inducement for man to settle, and no means for him to survive. The streams on their way to the sea provide, however, the valuable supplies of water which convert this desert into 'little Egypts' and enable Peru to be an important producer of cotton and sugar, which together account for one-seventh of her total exports.

There are, however, considerable differences in these oases dependent on various factors, such as the quantity of water carried by each stream, the nature of the coastal strip on to which it flows,

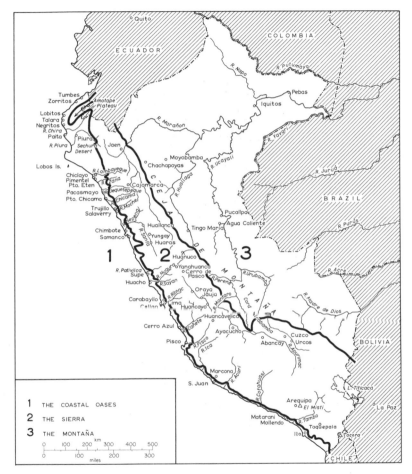

Fig. 49. *The regions of Peru*

the latitudinal location influencing the season of flood, the methods of agriculture and water utilization, and the demand for the products grown. Indeed each oasis valley is a study in itself with its own peculiarities, and any summarized treatment must contain generalizations which in some instances are only partially true.

Plate 26. *For 1,400 miles the only breaks in the monotonous sand and rock desert of coastal Peru are the rivers from the Sierra. From their oasis-like valleys come the two chief crops of sugar and cotton*

Generally, however, the demand for water is so great that little is permitted to reach the sea; all experience floods in the southern summer, with the period from August to October being the most arid; the upper oasis valleys have the coarser soils and earliest and most water available, the lower valleys the finer and water-retentive soils and the most precarious water supply; and commercial agriculture is everywhere more important than subsistence farming.

The regional differences modify this plan considerably. In the far north in the Departments of Tumbes and Piura, the land decreases in altitude from the Paita (Amotape) plateau southward to the Sechura desert (Fig. 50). Nowhere else is the coastal zone so wide, in parts being over 100 miles from west to east. The region is in every way transitional from the Ecuadorean coastlands to the true Peruvian desert. In fact, the Chira of all the west Peruvian rivers alone maintains its flow throughout the year. A small summer rainfall throughout the area gives rise to a scrub vegetation with xerophytic plants, and cattle are kept over wide areas. Cultivation is restricted for the most part to the Chira and Piura valleys, Egyptian cotton being grown in the former, and the finest Peruvian cotton and rice in the latter. A great diversion scheme to abstract water from the upper Chira and divert it into the Piura has now been completed and should materially increase the agricultural area of the Piura pampa. Piura City (55,000) is in the heart of the main cotton-producing area of the country, and is the oldest colonial settlement of Peru. Paita (37,000) although small in size, is the third port of the republic, achieving this importance by its exports of cotton, and of Panama hats, the material for which is obtained across the frontier in Ecuador.

Even more important than its agriculture are the petroleum resources of this broad plain. In the area between the Ecuadorean frontier and Paita are three producing fields, of which the La Brea and Pariñas field near Negritos is most important. Originally operated by a United States company, this field was nationalized in 1970. It accounts for 80 per cent of Peruvian production and refines nearly all the oil produced in the country at the nearby port of Talara (41,000). The second field is 14 miles to the north at Lobitos, some of this oil being piped to Talara for refining. The third and oldest field is at Zorritos south-west of Tumbes which refines the oil on the field for domestic consumption. The 3,600 wells in these north Peruvian fields have increased their output less rapidly than most Latin American oilfields, so that no longer is Peru self-sufficient in petroleum production. Until recently a significant oil exporter, the country now imports 20 per cent of its requirements. There are, however, large reserves both on the continental shelf and in the Amazon basin, and many foreign companies have invested large amounts of capital in exploration and development in these two areas. Already off-shore output from over 100 wells yields one-fifth of Peru's oil.

As the plain narrows to a width of 20–30 miles, and the summer rains cease except in the Sierra, six rivers provide the oases which produce 90 per cent of Peru's sugar cane. Of these, the Chicama valley north of Trujillo is by far the most important, both from the points of view of total production and the size and intensive nature of the plantation system established in the valley. So dominant did sugar become in the Chicama valley that the monocultural system had to import food from the other valleys, and the growth of the large estates drove subsistence farming into the foothills. In 1970, however, under a radical agrarian reform programme, the latifundia system

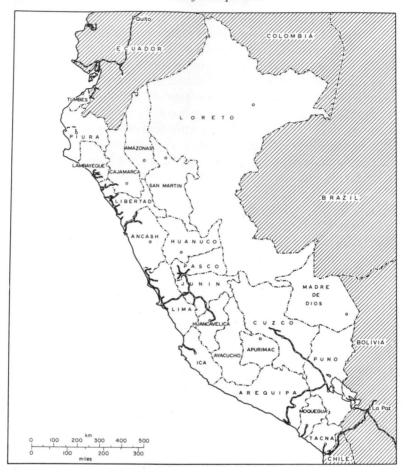

Fig. 50. *The departments of Peru*
The limited railway pattern has been developed primarily for export of
mineral and agricultural produce

disappeared, and more attention is now given to domestic food
production. The productivity of these sugar lands, always high, has
even increased since agrarian reform came into operation, and the
controlled use of relatively plentiful supplies of irrigation water taken
from higher up the valley enables the cane to grow throughout the
year. Harvesting and crushing is therefore not a seasonal occupation
as in the West Indies. The estates have a self-contained transport and
export system. Nearly half of the republic's sugar crop comes from

this area, and is mainly exported by Puerto Chicama and Salaverry (5,000), open roadsteads typical of most ports of this Pacific coast. The Lambayeque valley centred on Chiclayo is next in importance, and the irrigation water from the distributaries of its great alluvial fan is used on areas which until recently were vast haciendas which were both well organized and financed. The diversion of water from the upper Marañón headstreams into this area has considerably increased the area under cultivation, and a further 45,000 acres will soon benefit from irrigation waters from the Chancay valley's Tinajones dam. Less exclusively devoted to the one crop, considerable quantities of rice and cotton are also grown. Chiclayo (134,000) is the important collecting and distributing, manufacturing and marketing city, the sugar, cotton and rice being exported by Pimentel and Eten, the latter also serving the important Zana valley to the east.

The third most important sugar area is the Santa Catalina or Moche valley, also served by Salaverry; and in the heart of this oasis is situated Trujillo (149,000), an old colonial city which is increasingly becoming a manufacturing centre with textile, leather and cocaine factories. In population it now ranks as Peru's fourth city.

The Jequetepeque valley inland from Pacasmayo between the great producing oases of Chicama and Lambayeque also grows sugar, but on a less capitalized scale. Small primitive mills here grind the cane to produce *chancaca*, a form of raw sugar, for local needs. Similarly, rice is grown to supply the oasis.

Even this second group of oases produces a region not entirely dependent on agriculture for in its southern extension has been developed the Santa Corporation's great industrial scheme, the largest state-organized development in Peru. Plans are in hand to use the water of the Santa river to irrigate 350,000 acres, and a considerable hydro-electric plant has been established at Huallanca, 86 miles upstream. This provides power for electric furnaces of an iron and steel plant at Chimbote near the mouth of the Santa river. Later it is hoped to establish other heavy industries, including a zinc refinery, and fertilizer and cement plants. Thirty miles inland in the upper Santa valley south of Cabana are the anthracite fields, the coal being exported via Chimbote, which has all the facilities of a modern port. It receives iron ore from Marcona in southern Peru, via the port of San Juan; and exports iron ore pellets and sinter feed to Japan. In a devastating earthquake in 1970 much of Chimbote was destroyed, and one-third of the old city will be re-sited 12 miles south to form a nucleus of the new Chimbote, the previously destroyed areas being given over to new industrial developments.

South of the Santa, the coastal lowland is so restricted by the proximity of the Sierra that, although a little agriculture is carried on in three or four very narrow valleys, of which the Nepena sugar area exporting through Samanco south of Chimbote is probably the most important, it is not until the Pativilca river is reached that the third group of important oases occurs. Centred on Lima, these extend along more than 100 miles of coast north and south of the capital, as far south as Pisco. The coastal lowland is largely the coalescence of the alluvial fans of the rivers, and the soils vary considerably, most needing much fertilizer to yield adequately. Probably they would not be so extensively used were it not for the influence of the needs of the 2 million population congregated in the Lima–Callao urban nuclei.

Although cloudier conditions prevail than in the north, sugar is very important particularly in the oases north of Lima, Carabayllo on the Lima–Ancón railway being the most important. Considerable production comes also from the Huaura and Sayán valleys, exported through Huacho, the Pativilca and Supe valleys, through Supe, and the Rimac valley itself in which Lima stands. The only important sugar oasis south of Lima is that of the Cañete, where the plain is 10 miles wide and where the irrigation schemes of the Pampas Imperial behind its port Cerro Azul are especially noteworthy in having reclaimed 20,000 acres from the desert.

Cotton is more widespread, and is of the Tanguis variety, and although of less fine quality than that from the Piura valley these oases account for a large proportion of the Peruvian crop.

Considerable vegetable and fruit supplies for the Lima market are produced in these valleys, and cattle from the Sierra are also fattened on the temporary pastures created in mid-winter by the *garuas* (or Scottish mist) typical of this part of the coastal region, and later on the irrigated river meadows.

Towards the south, especially in the Chincha and Pisco valleys, vineyards are more important, the latter oasis giving its name to a brandy famous throughout the continent.

Lima and its port Callao with a combined population of 2,700,000 account for the greatest urban concentration in Peru, and provide the market for much of the produce from these oases. Callao is the great importing port of the country, and Lima, apart from its administrative functions as the capital, is a great distributing centre for these imports. The development of Lima's international airport on the coastal plain north of the Rimac is increasingly converting the city into the major hub of South America's air traffic.

South of Pisco the coastal plain disappears, and behind a narrow coastal range which in a few points exceeds 5,000 feet occurs a relatively flat or gently sloping transitional zone fringing the Andean sierra, increasing in elevation southward from 600 to 3,000 feet. Although overlain throughout most of its length by sand dunes, the white Tertiary clays beneath preserve a subterranean water supply, and where the coastal rivers have incised themselves sufficiently to reach this, basins of fertile agriculture occur. Subsistence crops, maize, vines and olives are the chief products. The Tambo valley grows some sugar for export to Bolivia, while the Ica valley is important for its vineyards and cotton fields, and an increasing supply of water is now being diverted from lakes in the upper Mantaro basin to this valley.

Mollendo (14,000) once served as an outlet for Bolivia and the South Peruvian sierra, but Matarani, a new port 9 miles to the north, now performs this function, and exports iron ore and copper from the Chapi mines near Arequipa.

Like the two northern groups of oases, the economic position of agriculture is now being supplemented by mineral developments. Between the mouths of the Ica and the Acarí occurs a great iron ore reserve estimated to contain 100 million tons of ore of 60 per cent content, known as the Marcona field. Mining operations are carried out here by a United States company for the dual purpose of export and supplying the Chimbote iron and steel plant. A new port, San Juan, 40 miles south of the Ica mouth, handles these exports, which now exceed 5 million tons annually, and are expected to double in the 1970s.

Together these series of oases give rise to a million acres of cultivated land, and this region also provides the fertilizer to maintain their productivity. Off the coast, from the Chincha to the Lobos islands (west of Lambayeque), nest millions of sea birds, such as the cormorant, pelican, lancer and guanay. Their manure, deposited around their nests and preserved by the coastal aridity, is rich in nitrogen, and in the 19th century was an important Peruvian export. Now it is collected for use in the oases, and its mining and distribution are controlled by the Government to avoid excessive exploitation.

The attraction for the birds is the wealth of marine life living in the low salinity and steady temperature waters of the Peru current.

Fishing in these seas was, however, an economic resource largely neglected by Peru until 1940. No other industry has expanded its activities so phenomenally in recent years, both for home consumption and for export to the United States, and it is estimated that it now supports directly and indirectly at least 100,000 workers. Tuna, bonito and swordfish are important products, but fish meal derived from anchovies and used primarily as the basis for livestock feed is the principal concern, accounting for 70 per cent of fish exports. The total annual catch of some 10½ million tons of fish makes Peru the greatest fishing nation in the world. Apart from the 150 plants producing fish meal there are a number of ancillary industries manufacturing fishing nets and constructing fishing vessels and their equipment.

The mixed economy of agriculture, mining, fishing and industry which is characteristic of the Peruvian coastal region is a striking example of the utilization of a desert area. Here occur most of the republic's cities and approximately half its population. With foundations laid in early colonial times, its rapid increase in economic prosperity is largely the result of 20th-century growth. Commercial agriculture, oil exploitation, iron and steel plants, and fish canneries have within fifty years transformed an arid belt into a unique area of all-round development. In this, foreign capital has played a large share, and the European and mestizo sections of the population control these developments. While considerable numbers of seasonal migrant labour move in from the Sierra, they are transitory residents, and the whole social, cultural and political life of the republic is concentrated in the old colonial cities and new towns of coastal Peru.

THE SIERRA

The great mountain belt aligned on a north-west–south-east axis becomes progressively wider southward from the Ecuadorean to the Bolivian frontier, varying from 60 miles to three times that width. Outstanding is the uniformity of the plateau surfaces throughout the 1,500 miles of its length. This great tableland between 10,000 and 14,000 feet high, known as the *puna*, has been attacked on its western flanks by the headstreams of the forty rivers which plunge towards the coastal strip. Much more destructive, however, has been the erosion of its eastern side, fed by the copious summer rains (October–April) of the Amazonian slope. The deep longitudinal gorges of these headstreams, such as the Marañón, Huallaga, Apurimac and Urubamba, form one of the most significant relief elements of the

Sierran zone. They have been responsible for the attempt to subdivide the Sierra into eastern, central and western ranges, the gorges dividing the mountain blocks. It is more correct, however, to see the cordilleras not in this way, but as great jagged glacially-torn mountain lines standing some 3,000 to 6,000 feet above the puna surface, and far more often, therefore, bearing local names such as the Cordillera Vilcabamba, Cordillera Blanca, etc.

Inevitably, the superior cutting power of the Amazon tributaries has captured most of the drainage of the Sierra, and pushed the watershed far to the west. Likewise the steady ascent from the coastal zone presents relatively few problems to communication compared with the dissection of the east, and it is probably no exaggeration to say that nowhere else in Latin America does physical geography impose problems comparable to this transition from Sierra to Montaña.

Structurally, the western zone of intrusive diorites succeeded eastward by Mesozoic and Palaeozoic sedimentaries in great folds overturned to the east reflects the familiar pattern of Andean structures throughout the continent. While the diorites reappear in the heart of many of the Cordilleran ridges and often compose their crest peaks, extrusive volcanic rocks only appear in the far south adjoining the Bolivian and Chilean frontiers.

As aridity increases southward in the coastal zone (except for the restricted and local influence of the garua), so it does in the Sierra, the main effect here, however, being progressively to raise the snowline and the limits of cultivable crops as one proceeds towards Bolivia. Throughout most of the region the sharply defined rainy season restricts agriculture to an annual crop.

The Sierra, the home of Inca and pre-Inca civilizations, rests throughout on the economy of difficult subsistence agriculture, pastoralism and the winning of its mineral wealth. The latter alone has brought the European, from Spanish pioneer to American mining company, but otherwise it is still an Indian world, as it has been for thousands of years.

Just as there is a uniformity of economy and culture in the coastal zone, so there is an entirely different one in the Sierra, but likewise there is local differentiation throughout its length. In its northern extensions it is a relatively narrow plateau with the joint erosion of Pacific and Amazon tributaries lowering the region and providing an area of cols and interlocking valleys which permit easier communication between coast and Montaña than anywhere else in the

Plate 27. *Agriculture in the Andean republics is limited by mountain terrain, elevation, transport facilities and primitive techniques. Two scenes in Cuzco province, Peru*

Sierra. This area, throughout recent geological history, has offered a transverse relatively weak relief zone, as is evidenced by the spread of sedimentary rocks westward over the intrusives, some of the former containing anthracite beds.

Cajamarca (48,000) and Jaen (3,500), both in the Marañón basin are the principal centres of the northern Sierra. Both have links with the coast and Montaña. Jaen, a centre of pastoralism and irrigated cotton, cocoa, rice and tobacco estates on the river margins, exports its products eastward on rafts via the Marañón to Iquitos, and sends its cattle convoys to the Piura and Lambayeque valleys of the coast. Cajamarca's links are via Chachapoyas and Moyobamba to the Huallaga, and westward to Trujillo. The higher altitudes around Cajamarca permit cultivation of maize and alfalfa.

To the south the general elevation is still higher, and the great relief features of high ridges and deep valleys are here developed to their fullest extent. Greatest of the ridges are the glacial cordilleras Blanca, Negra and Huayhuash; greatest of the gorges those of the Santa, Marañón, and the Huallaga tributaries. Here a coastal river, the Santa, high in its upper course provides the most favourable environment for settlement. Flowing north-westward parallel to the Cordillera Blanca and the general mountain axis, it passes through a series of basins of fluvio-glacial deposition, where deposits torn from the moraines of the cordillera provide good sites for agriculture (and in the past, alluvial mining activity). Huarás (51,000) at 10,000 feet above sea-level and Yanahuara are two such settlements, the latter being in an old lake basin. Silver, cinnabar and coal are mined and a variety of agricultural products grown, including sugar in a few areas. This area, and the settlements of Huarás and Yungay in particular, suffered enormous damage in the disastrous 1970 earthquake.

The Marañón offers few possibilities because of its incision, but the upper Huallaga centred on Huánuco (35,000) is more open, well-settled, and a key area in the developing communications pattern being established east of Lima to the Montaña. Likewise the upper Mantaro offers closer opportunities of linking with the Montaña, and produces a similar settlement pattern to that of the Santa on the east of the continental divide. Through a series of plains interspersed with limiting gorges the river plunges eastward to join the Apurimac. Jauja and Huancayo (89,000) are the principal centres, the latter being linked with Lima by a daily non-stop express service, indicative of its centrality in the Sierra zone. Huancavelica (8,000) and

Plate 28. *Huancayo in central Peru, a typical street market*

Ayacucho (24,000) are similar centres linked to the Mantaro incised basin (Fig. 49).

Four thousand feet above in the Cordillera of Huarochiri stands Cerro de Pasco (29,000) the highest city of its size in the world, which for four centuries, punctuated by recessions and booms, has been the mineral centre of Peru. Its modern period of U.S. capitalized mining dates from early in the 20th century and most of the copper, lead, zinc, bismuth, vanadium, silver and many other metals produced in Peru originate in this area. At Goyllarisquisga is produced nearly 90 per cent of the country's bituminous coal, half of which is used to make coke for the smelter at Oroya.

Many of the mines stretch to 16,000 feet above sea-level, and are at the foot of the glaciers. Cerro de Pasco itself is on the high puna and above cultivation level, the Indian communal pastures being the only other scene of activity. This is the region *par excellence* of the Sierra. The mining communities which produce its principal exportable wealth are fed from the lower valleys of Junín department, particularly the Mantaro's tributaries, where maize and barley are leading crops and where dairy farming is being developed. The scores of small Indian farms supply themselves by an agricultural system

Plate 29. *Nucleated basin settlements from the principal pattern of human occupance in the Peruvian sierra. Near Ayacucho*

which often produces a crop only in alternate years, ploughing in March, after the rains have ceased and the ground is soft, sowing in October when the rains start, and harvesting in the mid-dry season in June, when their inadequate ploughs are unable then to plough the soil. Supplying labour both to sierran mines and coastal farms, it is a zone of constant emigration. The nineteen farms, or 600,000 acres of agricultural holdings previously owned by the Cerro de Pasco Corporation were expropriated under the country's new agrarian reform legislation, and the land distributed to local communities.

South of this dissected area, especially south of Abancay, a greater unity prevails in the Sierra. The incised river systems of the east have not penetrated so devastatingly into the Cordillera. Two great cities dominate the settlement pattern in contrast to the scattered small towns further north. These are Cuzco (105,000) and Arequipa (187,000). The former is a nucleus with commercial and cultural ties over a considerable area of the Urubamba basin, dating from its metropolitan functions in the days of the Inca empire. The Urubamba alluvial floor is an almost continuous zone of arable and pastoral farming, and, with the other favourable areas of the plain of Anta and the Cuzco and Sicuani valleys, which grow crops of maize and barley, it provides one of the densest population clusters of the Sierra.

To the south-west, the Sierra becomes a great zone of pastoralism, with sheep, llamas and alpaca in the west and cattle and horses in the northern and damper margins. The puna is here so high that only the tierra fria crops of potatoes and quinoa and barley grow in the more humid areas. The surface is more monotonous, the product of the deposition plains of Titicaca in the south and of the volcanic covering outpoured on its western flanks. The sedimentaries are buried beneath vast accumulations of lava and ashes, which have been eroded by a few streams, as in the Cotahuasi gorge. The porosity of the soils increases the effect of the climatic aridity and entrenches the pastoral economy, settlement being limited to a few wet points where a glacier supplies some water.

Fringing the Sierra are the volcanic cones, and that of Misti provides the background for the Arequipa plain where, if there were adequate water, the fertile soils would yield an abundant harvest. A major irrigation project designed to irrigate some 150,000 acres by means of 75 miles of tunnels and canals, bringing water from the Andes, is planned for the area. Wherever irrigation is possible there is careful agriculture, yielding two harvests a year. The crops of alfalfa, maize, potatoes, beans and wheat help to supply the large population of Arequipa from its limited area before the Chili gorge makes agriculture impossible.

Arequipa is the exchange city serving the southern Sierra and coastlands, the market for the wool products of the pastoral Sierra, and the great linking urban centre between the Pacific and Bolivia. Its semi-metropolitan character has added to its important administrative functions, and its industries include woollen and nylon textiles, leather, glass, metals, and those connected with food processing. Moquegua department, south-east of Arequipa, has become

Plate 30. *Volcanic peaks crown the Cordillera of the Andes in many areas from Ecuador to Chile. El Misti overlooking the Arequipa oasis of southern Peru*

increasingly important for its copper production, notably at Toquepala and Cuajone, Peru's output of this metal having more than quadrupled in the 1960s. Ilo (2,000) is the exporting port for Moquegua's copper, some of which will be refined there.

The increasingly high prices obtained for Peru's commercial crops of sugar and cotton have tended in recent years to diminish relatively the importance of the Sierra in providing a large proportion of Peruvian exports from the Oroya smelters of the Cerro de Pasco Corporation. The contribution of the Sierra to metalliferous production is not only large but extremely diverse. The ores are complex and contain a variety of minerals, many being obtained as by-products of smelting. Copper accounts for 44 per cent of total mineral output, silver 10 per cent and lead and zinc 8 per cent each.

Nor must be omitted the importance of the pastoral production, the quality of its alpaca and merino wool tending to be improved by more scientific attention to this industry, there being a Government model farm at Chuquibambilla near Puno.

THE MONTAÑA

The third and largest region of Peru, occupying more than half the country, is the Montaña or Amazon forest, separated from the Sierra by the broad transitional zone often known as the Ceja de Montaña. The latter belt, 50 to 100 miles wide, is a complicated zone of intensive river erosion and of great variations in vegetation dependent upon aspect, rainfall, relief and soils. The plain or true Montaña is a forested plain with relatively gentle undulating interfluves, and movement is restricted to the river network. All the settlements are riverside in location, and all the communal life of the area is dependent on the river communications linking these settlements.

There is no sharply defined dry season as in the Sierra but the maximum rainfall throughout most of the region occurs in the summer half year. On the northern margins adjoining Ecuador and Colombia the reverse is true. Thus tributaries from the south and north have different rainfall régimes, and the Marañón–Amazon mainstream receives floods at all seasons.

Over most of this vast area the fundamental economy of the indigenous Indian tribes has remained unaltered. This consists of fishing and subsistence agriculture based on cassava and bananas in the forest clearings. Early Spanish colonists penetrated the Urubamba from Urcos, but their most successful colonization of this zone occurred further north in Loreto department, in the Moyobamba area, where sugar and tobacco estates supplemented by pastoralism provided an economy which maintained these settlements. Two booms of the 19th century, that of cinchona bark for quinine and that of rubber, increased the knowledge of the region, although the former left little permanent result. The search for rubber displaced the principal centre of the Montaña from the Loreto fringe towards Iquitos. Navigation eastward by the Huallaga and Amazon to this city and beyond to Manáus and Belém was relatively easy and contrasted with the hindrances to river transport on the Madre de Dios system by the Beni and Madeira falls.

Developments in this century, especially in recent decades, have increased the tempo of colonization in the Peruvian Montaña, and no other Andean country has devoted so much effort and capital to utilizing its Amazon component. Between Ciudad Bolívar in Venezuela and Santa Cruz in Bolivia, the Peruvian settlements stand out in sharp contrast to the areas adjacent on north and south (Fig. 52).

Agriculture, mineral development and communications are the three-pronged attack being made to incorporate this potentially rich region into the nation's economic life.

In agricultural development two areas predominate, that of the Perené valley (a tributary of the Apurimac) east of Cerro de Pasco, and the upper Huallaga valley centred on Tingo María (7,000). The principal products grown in increasing quantities are tea, cocoa, coffee, jute and tobacco. The main centre of coffee production is in the Perené valley, but cocoa is grown as far east as Pebas on the Amazon. Coffee production is increasing rapidly, and it provides Peru with its third most important agricultural export. The Perené colony is a British venture connected to Oroya by road, and the Tingo María–Pucallpa project is a State sponsored scheme to settle 12½ million acres in the Huallaga–Ucayali region, linked by road to Lima.

The principal mineral development is that of petroleum exploitation centred on the Ganso Azul field on the Pachitea river, the oil being refined at Agua Caliente, near Pucallpa. A vast area has been granted in concessions, and if drilling is successful, the oil will either have to be exported down the Amazon to Brazil, or be piped over the Andes to the Peruvian consuming centres (Fig. 51).

Interesting developments such as the production of hardwood veneers, the establishment of small industrial plants for the Indian communities, and the construction of short airstrips for cargo planes are other indications of Peru's continuing involvement in the opening up of the Montaña.

Realizing, however, that without communications to export produce and to facilitate settlement, the region can never be adequately developed, a coordinated system of transverse roads is being constructed eastward from the coastal region, the most important of which now links the navigable river system, and thereby Iquitos (66,000), with Lima (Fig. 52). Work is also in process to link the railway system from Lima via Tambo del Sol to Pucallpa, and if this is completed, there will be through rail connection between the Montaña, Sierra and Coast. Nor is the longitudinal pattern being

Plate 31. *Inca terraced farm-land of Machu Picchu, above the Urubamba valley in the Peruvian Sierra, indicates man's long struggle with a difficult terrain. Within this defensive settlement there is ample evidence of the indigenous people's knowledge of soil and water conservation*

neglected. Most of the 1,500 miles from Tumbes to Arequipa, forming part of the Pan American Highway, is now a wide asphalted
surface, playing an increasingly important part in linking the country
together. Most imaginative, however, is the marginal highway of the
Montaña (*carretera marginal de la selva*) along the eastern slopes of
the Andes, a vast project designed not only to encourage colonization

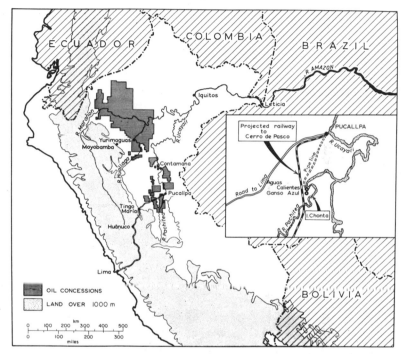

Fig. 51. *Petroleum exploration in Peru's Montaña*
Post-war development of this region has led to the exploitation of the
Ganso Azul oilfield

programmes but link the Peruvian Montaña with that of Ecuador
and Bolivia (Fig. 52).

PROSPECTS AND PROBLEMS

In spite of its physical background of three sharply contrasted regions
which offer a variety of formidable obstacles to economic development, the export products of Peru reflect a much more balanced
picture than those of most Latin American countries. No one single
commodity involves the country in all the problems of excessive

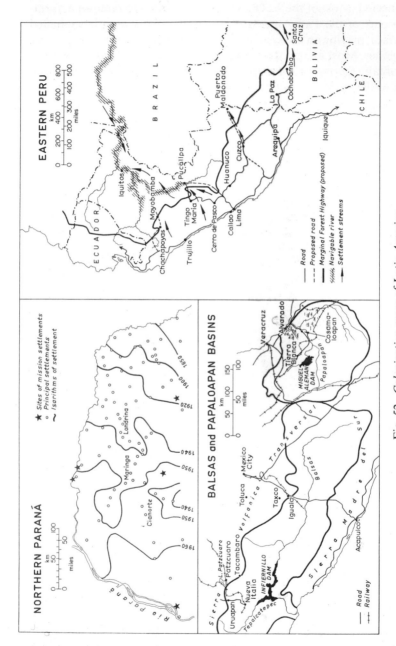

Fig. 52. *Colonization areas of Latin America*

Three areas where there have been important population movements to previously empty lands

dependence on that product. There is also a fairly even balance between agriculture, mining, pastoralism and fishing, and more recently, a growth of industry. A growing population with rising living standards inevitably affects the position, and domestic consumption of sugar has cut exports from 80 per cent to 60 per cent of the crop grown, but increased acreage by intensive efforts at irrigation and the development of more Montaña land are compensating factors. Likewise, increasing exhaustion of mineral resources is being balanced by further exploration and by the codification of mining law which has permitted considerable fresh foreign interest and investment. Peru is thus still the world's fourth producer of silver and fifth in output of lead and zinc. Since 1960 the expansion of its copper production has been so marked that exports of this metal now yield as much foreign exchange as do exports of fishmeal.

The major difficulties facing the country are the scarcity of cultivated land, which amounts to less than half an acre *per capita*, the inequitable distribution of land ownership, the low yields of much of the land, reflecting inadequate agricultural techniques, and the lack of roads which restricts marketing possibilities. Much is now being done in the way of agrarian reform, extension services, agricultural credits and improved communications.

A new agrarian reform programme begun in 1969 has already made a radical attack on Peru's long-established latifundia system in which 1,200 landowners controlled 60 per cent of the total cultivated land of Peru. Within three years 14 million acres have been allocated to over 200,000 families; and there is increasing emphasis on the growing of food for the domestic market. There are parallel measures to consolidate fragmented farm holdings and to develop agricultural co-operatives.

Population is undoubtedly growing faster than the increase in food production, and almost one-quarter of the country's import bill is made up of food imports, principally wheat and meat, costing Peru some 150 million dollars annually. This deficit also explains efforts to divert more of its enormous catch of fish to domestic consumption. This will be possible only by a considerable expansion of refrigerated units for storing, distributing and marketing. Long distances and poor roads, however, hamper such developments, and the processing of salted and dried fish may be a more practicable proposition.

Much of the economic production of Peru has been for a long time controlled by foreign investment, particularly of United States interests. More recently steps have been taken to ensure that such investment, while welcomed in the interests of national development, does not control the direction of the nation's economic policies. In this respect the state has formulated plans to develop Peruvian industry to the point where it can compete with that of other members of the Andean Group of LAFTA, by massive national investment in basic industries such as chemicals, paper, steel and engineering. Similarly steps are being taken to ensure that most raw material exports are processed before export, particularly the refining of lead, zinc and copper and the manufacture of cotton into yarn.

There is undoubtedly a great need for industrial growth to provide employment opportunities at the rate of some 100,000 new jobs annually. Most of this increase will occur in Lima, where already 60 per cent of manufacturing industry is located. The Sierra contributes only 1·3 per cent of total industrial production, and this underlines Peru's continuing problem of integrating its Indian world into the nation. The development of hydro-electric power, the extension of the country's road system, linking together the contrasting regions and strengthening the unity of each, and the land reform programme together with its social provision are component parts of a gradual process which, in time, will fuse the dissimilar European and Indian sections into the Peruvian nation.

STATISTICAL SUMMARY — PERU

Area: 496,223 square miles

Population (1970): 13,672,000

Percentage of land

(a) Arable	2%
(b) Pastoral	21%
(c) Forest	68%
(d) Other	9%

Animal numbers

(a) Cattle	3·6 million
(b) Sheep	14·5 ,,
(c) Pigs	2·0 ,,
(d) Goats	4·0 ,,

Communications

   (*a*) All-seasons road mileage   13,940
   (*b*) Railway mileage   2,512
   (*c*) Air routes   387 million passenger miles
                                  4   ,,   ton   miles

Principal products

   (*a*) *Agricultural*

Root Crops	2,250,000	metric tons
Sugar	731,000	,, ,,
Maize	630,000	,, ,,
Rice	458,000	,, ,,
Wheat	140,000	,, ,,
Oilseeds	129,000	,, ,,
Cotton	89,000	,, ,,

   (*b*) *Mineral*

Iron	5,426,000	metric tons
Petroleum	3,453,000	,, ,,
Zinc	303,000	,, ,,
Copper	216,000	,, ,,
Lead	165,000	,, ,,
Silver	1,094	,, ,,
Tungsten	437	,, ,,
Gold	8,700	troy pounds

   (*c*) *Marine*

      Fish products   10,110,000 metric tons

Exports

   (*a*) *Total:* $866,000,000
   (*b*) *Percentage share of principal commodities*

Fish products	27%
Copper	27%
Silver, iron, lead and zinc	23%
Sugar	7%
Cotton	6%
Coffee	4%

CHAPTER FIFTEEN

Bolivia

ALTHOUGH a very large country, greater in size than France, Spain and Portugal together, the economic importance of Bolivia compares more with the smaller countries of Ecuador and Paraguay than with Peru and Colombia which resemble Bolivia in area.

Once the long sought-for goal of those seeking the fabulous mineral wealth of Latin America, when the silver mines of Potosí poured their treasure into the coffers of Madrid, it has declined to be one of the poorest and least developed countries of the continent. Once the great highway of Spanish colonial times linking the Plata estuary lands with the Viceroyalty of Peru and so to Spain, it has become the most isolated state, harassed and handicapped by the problem of communications with its neighbours. Few countries in the world have been so greatly thwarted by both natural and historical forces, and it is perhaps amazing that it has survived at all as an independent political unit.

One-third of the republic is over a mile high, literally the roof of South America; the remainder is periodically flooded jungle and semi-desert. Chile, Brazil and Paraguay have all detached peripheral parts of its territories within the last century, and it finds itself landlocked behind the barriers of Andes, Atacama desert, Amazon forest and empty Chaco lands.

Its $4\frac{3}{4}$ million people are fragmented both by natural environments into scores of clusters of population, and by language and race into distinct groups of very different cultural and economic bases, the only unity being the Indian strain which most possess in varying proportions. No Latin American nation has so large a proportion of Indians, almost two-thirds of the people speaking indigenous languages (Fig. 2).

The fundamental division into Highland and Lowland Bolivia is the only realistic approach to a study of its geography, but this in itself conceals the many differences which both these major areas contain (Fig. 53).

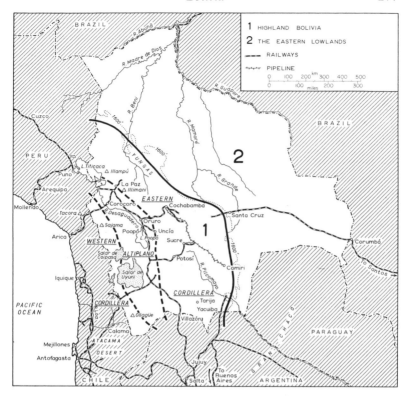

Fig. 53. *The regions of Bolivia*

HIGHLAND BOLIVIA

As the great Andean mountain system leaves Peru and swings into a north–south alignment, it reaches its maximum width. This great bend of the Andes, some 500 miles wide, forms Western Bolivia, and within it three structural and physiographic units may be delineated. These are the Western Cordillera, a central depressed plateau or Altiplano, and the Eastern Cordillera.

(a) *The Western Cordillera*

This great mountain mass, aligned parallel to the Chilean frontier, is for the most part an igneous plateau littered with volcanic cones and solfataras, of which Tacora, Sajama and Ollagüe are examples. Most of the region exceeds 13,000 feet in height, and several perpetually snow-capped peaks rise over 16,500 feet above sea-level. Eastward branching spurs penetrate on to the Altiplano throughout its length.

It is naturally a great watershed region, and drainage is either into the many streams which head towards the Pacific or into the central Altiplano. Of the former only the Loa maintains its course throughout the year to the sea.

Aridity increases southward, which has meant that less volcanic débris has been carried into the southern Altiplano than into its northern areas, and scrub vegetation in the north disappears into barren rock wastes in the south.

Pastoralism is the chief occupation, the shepherds supplementing natural pasture with crops of quinoa and barley raised under irrigation in the valleys, and more often than not harvested green and unripe. Some potatoes also help the food supply. Llamas, alpacas, sheep and donkeys wander over extensive areas and some transhumance is also practised. Salt is 'harvested' from the Coipasa lagoon and sulphur from the slopes of Tacora and Ollagüe. There are no important population centres, and the southern areas are almost uninhabited.

(b) The Central Altiplano

The great central basin to the east of the Western Cordillera is the largest basin of inland drainage in South America, containing the continent's greatest lake, Titicaca, which is as big as Puerto Rico. A vast structurally depressed area, it has received enormous quantities of alluvial material and glacial débris carried into it by glaciers and rivers of melt-water throughout recent geological time. The platforms, terraces.and old shore lines on the Altiplano now reveal the former greater extents of 'Lake Minchin', in a similar way to those of Lakes Bonneville and Lahontan in the Great Basin of North America. The basin slopes upwards to both bounding cordilleras, but there is also a gradual descent from its northern limits in southern Peru to the Salar de Uyuni (east of Iquique) in the south.

Lake Titicaca therefore drains southward by the Desaguadero river (which literally means 'a drain') into Lake Poopo, which occasionally overflows into the Salar de Coipasa, but which more often loses the water received by evaporation. As a consequence Titicaca is fresh water, and Poopo very saline, its saltiness being increased by dissolved salts carried into it from the Desaguadero valley.

The contrast in climatic and vegetational conditions between the north and south of the basin is most marked, as a result of two principal factors, increasing aridity southward, and the contrasted influence of lakes Titicaca and Poopo. The former, a large and deep mass of water, exerts a 'maritime' influence on the surrounding region, the temperature of its water remaining about 51°F. throughout the year, thus reducing diurnal and seasonal temperature ranges of the adjacent lands. The very shallow Lake Poopo (10 feet) on the other hand has no such influence. Grassland thus deteriorates southward until even dry scrub disappears and merges into the red clay and salt flats of Uyuni.

A similar decline in economic importance and population densities therefore results, and the northern lands of the Altiplano adjacent to the Titicaca shores are some of the most important parts of Bolivia.

Subsistence agriculture, growing crops of maize, wheat, barley and potatoes maintains a relatively dense population, whose origins go back to pre-Inca times, the former city of Tiahuanaco giving its name to a great cultural period in which communal agriculture, not very different from the present pattern, was established.

The lands are terraced where necessary but irrigation is not needed in this favoured corner of Bolivia. It is another of the few areas of Latin America where a political frontier passes through an area of close settlement, but the villages and farmers of Bolivian and Peruvian Titicaca are so self-contained that such a division means little to them.

Southward, pastoralism of sheep and llamas occupies an increasingly important part, but on the slopes of the Eastern Cordillera to the east of Poopo, where water is more plentiful, some irrigated agriculture is carried on.

Corocoro (4,500) in the centre of the basin is an important copper mining settlement and once its product, pure natural copper, was shipped up the Desaguadero to Lake Titicaca. Most of Bolivia's small copper output still comes from this area.

The eastern portion of the central Altiplano offers a relatively easy longitudinal transport route between northern and southern Bolivia, now followed by a railway, but in colonial times this was the principal link between the Plata estuary lands and the Viceroyalty of Peru. Oruro (91,000) is an important junction on this railway, where lines branch off to the valleys of the Eastern Cordillera. It is also the greatest mining centre of Bolivia, and tin has replaced the silver for which it was once famous. In spite of a tendency to declining output, the country is still the world's third producer of tin and antimony.

South-east of Lake Titicaca, close to the mountain wall of the Eastern Cordillera, is situated the principal city of the republic, La Paz (525,000). Wedged in a deep valley 1,500 feet below the general surface of the Altiplano, yet still over 12,400 feet above sea-level, it is sheltered from the coldest extremes of the great plateau and is yet still accessible to the north–south routeway from Guaqui on Lake Titicaca to Oruro and the south. The city is the chief political and commercial city of the country and is linked by rail not only to Lake Titicaca but with the shortest route to the sea by the line to Arica in Chile.

(c) The Eastern Cordillera

Continuing the Corabaya cordillera of Peru, the Eastern, or Cordillera Real of Bolivia is one of the most magnificent of all the Andean ranges. A relatively simple range structurally, it consists of a granitic core flanked with sedimentary rocks. Many of these granite peaks exceed 20,000 feet, and the largest glaciers of tropical Latin America descend from the sides of Illimani and Illampú.

Hinged on a point east of Cochabamba the Cordillera is best considered in two halves, the northern hinge trending north-west–south-east, the southern hinge north–south.

The northern section drops precipitously in the north-east to the plains of Beni, by means of a ravined surface of forested interfluves and deep fertile valleys where coffee and sugar cane are grown in clearings. This zone of the Yungas was the scene of the 19th-century quinine boom, and of considerable workings for alluvial gold, especially in the Tipuani river basin, but population clusters are few and far between, and no centre is of any great importance.

Not only does this region suffer from isolation caused by the great mountain barrier separating it from central Bolivia, but its outlet towards the Amazon is obstructed by jungle, river rapids and an absence of transport links. Dissection of the mountain wall by river action has been so great that the headstreams of the rivers have cut through the Cordillera to the Altiplano by some of the greatest gorges in the continent. Their Altiplano courses permit some irrigated farming, and one of them, the River La Paz, has carved the valley where the city of that name is situated. Not only does all the drainage of this part of the Cordillera therefore flow to the Amazon, but also many plateau streams which previously went to Lake Titicaca.

The southern portion of the Cordillera differs considerably in relief and drainage, and in utilization. The western face of the Cordillera in this case is the sharper, rising by a series of escarpments above the Altiplano and creating a marked watershed between the westward-flowing drainage of streams heading towards Lake Poopo and those contributing to the Amazon–Paraguay drainage systems. These western hills and faces of the Eastern Cordillera are the scene of the major mineral workings of present-day Bolivia, particularly the tin mines of Uncia, which are linked by railway with Oruro. Silver, lead, bismuth, antimony, wolfram and zinc also occur in small mining centres scattered through this region, and partly account for the importance of Oruro as a great collecting centre for their export. Nearby, at the town of Vinto, has been constructed Bolivia's first tin smelter, with an annual output capacity of 7,500 tons of electrolytic tin.

The more gradual eastern slope of the Cordillera is known as the *puna*, an unfortunate term not to be confused with the similar one used in a vegetational sense elsewhere in the Andes. Dissected by tributaries of the Mamoré and Pilcomayo, long narrow valleys and some larger basins provide favourable areas for settlement and cultivation. Some are the floors of entrenched meanders, others of rift basins. The increasing width and cutting power of the rivers eastward have reduced the puna to a series of narrow interfluves.

The valleys of Cochabamba and Sucre are the most important, and the former supports the second largest cluster of Bolivia, Cochabamba city being the second city of the republic (157,000). On the rich alluvial lands maize, potatoes, barley, wheat, alfalfa, vines and many fruits are grown. In some cases irrigation is necessary, especially towards the south, and even in the Cochabamba valley lack of water restricts cultivation in most parts to the rainy season. The area was once farmed in large estates but the chief problem now is too great a fragmentation of the farms.

The milder climate and lower altitude have encouraged settlement, and in spite of isolation and transport difficulties, this region is becoming of increasing importance in Bolivia's economy, supplying the Altiplano with some food supplies. Sucre (58,000) is the town chosen to be the country's capital. Tarija (22,000) in another rich basin is more isolated from the rest of Bolivia, and its main link is outward to Villazón on the Argentine frontier. Potosí (64,000), higher in the Eastern Cordillera, is the old centre of Spanish America's mineral exploitation, and still a source of tin and silver.

(d) The Eastern Lowlands

The vast area lying to the east of the Andes is the largest of the Bolivian regions, and yet like the similar areas in Colombia, Ecuador and Peru, contains only a sparse population and plays an almost insignificant role in Bolivia's economy.

The northern portion drained mainly by the Beni and Mamoré tributaries is really Amazonian Bolivia. Drenched by heavy rainfall with mid-summer maximum, equatorial forests cover much of it, and from these in two world wars a quantity of rubber was extracted. The Llanos de Mojos is a great clay plain flooded for four or five months of the year when the Mamoré overflows. The possibility of this part of the lowlands being developed in the near future seems very doubtful.

The central section, however, has been the area which recently has received much attention. Considerably drier, more accessible to the rest of Bolivia and to Argentina and Brazil, it grows a wide variety of crops, especially sugar cane, rice and coffee. Cotton is also of increasing importance. Santa Cruz (109,000) is the great regional centre, and a new road linking it with Cochabamba has been built. This will enable the foodstuffs and cotton to be sent to the populated centres of the republic further west. In 1954 a railway joining it with Corumbá in Brazil was completed, and another from Yacuiba on the Argentine frontier will enable a further development of this region's resources (Figs. 11, 12 and 53). The exploitation of the petroleum and natural gas fields in the Camiri, Monteagudo, La Peña and Río Grande districts is also making this part of eastern Bolivia increasingly significant in the nation's economy.

The south-eastern or Chaco section of the Lowlands is alternatively a semi-desert for nine months of the year and a swamp for the other three rainy months. Pastoralism is its principal wealth, cattle being marketed in Argentina. A recent discovery of iron and manganese at Mutún, north of where the boundaries of Bolivia, Brazil and Paraguay meet, promises to be among the richest of the continent.

PROSPECTS AND PROBLEMS

Bolivia has not yet succeeded in shaking off its complete dependence on mineral production and exports which has dominated its economy for over four centuries. At least 80 per cent of its exports are metals, principally tin, silver, antimony, lead, zinc and wolfram, and most of its imports are food, fuel and manufactured goods. La Paz has a few cotton and woollen mills, but otherwise industry scarcely exists in Bolivia, the country lacking coal and iron. Hydro-electric power and petroleum occur in appreciable quantities, and with increased transport facilities, will be of great value in developing the country's industrial fabric.

The national plan for industrialization includes the location of non-ferrous metal industries at Oruro, steel and petrochemicals at Santa Cruz, construction materials, such as asbestos and cement plants, at Cochabamba and engineering at La Paz. The country's large resources of natural gas provide a source of energy, and liquefied natural gas is the fuel for thermal electricity plants at Santa Cruz and Sucre.

A gas pipeline from Santa Cruz to Yacuíba on the Argentine frontier is under construction, and several internal lines link the gasfields with major urban centres. An oil pipeline, 350 miles long, has been completed from the oilfield of Camiri to Cochabamba, the railhead for the Altiplano. This makes Bolivia self-sufficient in petroleum, and some is now exported by a pipeline from Sica-Sica to Arica in Chile. Previous to oil nationalization in 1969, these exports went to California for refining. Alternative markets for this production may not be easy to find, and the short-term effects of Bolivia's expropriation of its major oilfield will not help the country's economy.

Sugar, cattle, wheat, flour, rice and fruit are all imported to help feed its 4¾ million people, yet the country is capable of producing all these crops in abundance. The great problem is inaccessibility and isolation of one region from another, and especially of the eastern valleys of the Eastern Cordillera from the Altiplano. Some progress is being made in building the transport links which are so necessary. A new highway now links Oruro with the Chilean port of Iquique, and several roads have been driven north-east from the La Paz–Cochabamba–Santa Cruz axis to settlements on the Amazon basin tributaries. The country's landlocked position is, however, its continuing and major problem. Dependent on its neighbours for all its external trading facilities, Bolivia has endeavoured to spread this dependence, the most recent arrangement being the provision of free port facilities in Rosario.

The 1952 social revolution profoundly changed the socio-economic structure of Bolivia, and went a long way to overcoming problems which it had inherited from its colonial past. The tin mines

were taken over by the state, an extensive agrarian reform programme was carried out, and the Indian majority is increasingly
being integrated into the national life. Nevertheless its economic
problems are so severe and its financial resources are so limited that
it is one of Latin America's most underdeveloped nations and hence
has been the recipient of an increasing amount of technical aid.

STATISTICAL SUMMARY — BOLIVIA

Area: 424,163 square miles

Population (1970): 4,780,000

Percentage of land

(*a*)	Arable	3%
(*b*)	Pastoral	10%
(*c*)	Forest	43%
(*d*)	Other	44%

Animal numbers

(*a*)	Cattle	1·5	million
(*b*)	Sheep	6·1	,,
(*c*)	Pigs	0·7	,,
(*d*)	Goats	1·3	,,

Communications

(*a*)	All-seasons road mileage	5,200
(*b*)	Railway mileage	2,328
(*c*)	Air routes	38 million passenger miles

Principal products

(*a*) *Agricultural*

Root Crops	784,000	metric tons
Maize	239,000	,, ,,
Sugar	102,000	,, ,,
Wheat	70,000	,, ,,
Rice	42,000	,, ,,

(*b*) *Mineral*

Petroleum	1,838,000 metric tons	
Tin	27,700	,, ,,
Lead	20,000	,, ,,
Tungsten	1,950	,, ,,
Silver	138	,, ,,
Gold	5,000 troy pounds	

Exports

(*a*) *Total:* $176,000,000

(*b*) *Percentage share of principal commodities*

Tin	53%
Silver	6%
Tungsten	6%
Lead	3%
Antimony	˙3%
Zinc	2%

CHAPTER SIXTEEN

Chile

ALTHOUGH the remarkable shape of Chile has been in large measure determined by structural features which run in a long narrow north–south pattern, it is not structure but climate which plays the major rôle in distinguishing one region from another, within the country.

This is not to say that the three relief components of high Andes, central depressions and coastal plateaux, which are all represented throughout its 2,600 miles of length, do not profoundly affect the natural and cultural landscape. The changes occasioned by relief are, however, variations within the climatic pattern which stamp a four-fold division upon the nation, transitional as must be the borderlands between these divisions (Fig. 54). The pattern is as follows:

(*a*) The Northern Desert.
(*b*) The Mediterranean Provinces.
(*c*) The Central and Southern Forests.
(*d*) Atlantic Chile.

THE NORTHERN DESERT

Over the desert which comprises the three large northern provinces of Tarapacá, Antofagasta and Atacama, the climate is markedly arid throughout its 600 miles. Only in very exceptional years is any rainfall experienced west of the Andes, although coastal mists do produce a little moisture. The mountains in the north, above 6,000 feet in height, receive a few showers in summer, and in the south this changes to a régime of winter snow.

Temperatures of the coast are relatively uniform but low for their latitude owing to the cooling influence of the Humboldt current and the upwelling of cold ocean water off the coast. Inland, seasonal and diurnal ranges are greater, a product of the cloudless skies and consequent maximum insolation and radiation.

Vegetation, therefore, is restricted to a few areas tapping underground water, where mimosa thickets occur, to the higher slopes of

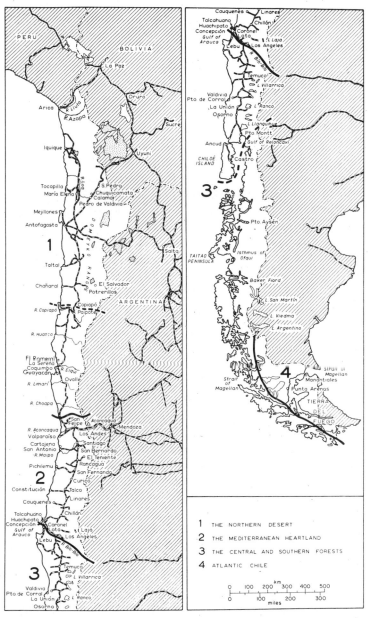

Fig. 54. *The regions of Chile*

the Andes with a xerophytic scrub, and to the watered groves of the coastal towns.

The structural pattern upon which this widespread aridity is superimposed is that of the Andean Cordillera, a central belt of high basins, and a precipitous coastal plateau block.

The Andean cordillera fringing the Bolivian Altiplano and north-west Argentine provinces is more dissected in its southern extensions, where greater precipitation has produced ephemeral streams with storm erosion. Further north the western slopes are more gradual, enabling relatively easy communication across the mountains. The Domeyko range stands out as a horst block west of the main structural line of the mountains, and numerous volcanic cones provide considerable supplies of sulphur. The principal economic value of the Cordillera is that of water supply for the arid western areas. Only the River Loa maintains itself in an incised trench westward to reach the sea, but the Lluta and Azapa in the far north carry adequate water to provide irrigation facilities in the Arica district. Elsewhere the small mountain torrents peter out in the piedmont zone fringing the central depressions, but underground water in the Andes is tapped to supply mining camps east of Taltal and the town of Iquique.

Structurally, the rich copper deposits mined at Chuquicamata, Potrerillos, and El Salvador mines, which account for 65 per cent of Chile's copper exports and 45 per cent of all her exports also belong to the Cordilleran edge, but from the point of view of relief they appear more as economic manifestations of the central depression.

The central zone of high plateaux basins is not a continuous depression, but a series of tectonic basins partially filled with alluvial rock débris carried into them in past geologic ages by the Andean streams. Sands, clays and crystalline salt deposits are the chief components of this material, all cemented into a *caliche*, the name given to the saline 'ores' from which sodium nitrate especially is extracted.

The relatively gentle but barren slopes of these basins give rise to a landscape which characteristically is described by the Spanish term *pampa*, and it is there that the great nitrate *oficinas* or plants refine the saline rock material torn from the *salares*, which were once probably extensive salt lakes.

Until 1932 the mining activities were located in some 150 sites scattered throughout this central series of basins, but rationalization of the industry has resulted in most of the activity being centred in the two great plants of Pedro de Valdivia and María Elena, east of Tocopilla, and in the Pampa of Tamarugal east of Iquique.

The coastal plateau, usually some hundreds of feet above the central depressions, varies between 2,000 and 3,000 feet above sea-level, and plunges into the Pacific in a series of abrupt cliffs and steep barren hill sides. In a few areas piedmont marine terraces provide sites for coastal settlements, those sheltered by coastal promontories such as Tocopilla, Mejillones and Antofagasta having an additional advantage in this respect.

The great nitrate and copper mining camps are the principal utilization of Chile's desert lands, and the coastal ports are mainly supply bases, export outlets of the copper, nitrate and their by-products, and termini of the transit routes across Chile into Bolivia and Argentina. These railways up and over the coastal plateau from the ports are only possible by means of zig-zag routes, and in addition to linking the mining camps with their Pacific ports, they provide the principal means of access to Bolivia.

Arica, Antofagasta and Mejillones are the ports connected with this international trade, while Iquique and Tocopilla are more exclusively concerned with copper and nitrate exports and imports for the mining camps. Antofagasta (127,000) and Iquique (50,000) are the largest settlements with the most extensive railway network in their hinterlands, and they are the only ports with pier facilities on this inhospitable coast. Tocopilla, however, because of its proximity to the principal nitrate plants, and Chañaral, as the outlet of the Potrerillos copper mine, are important exporting ports. Flamenco, near Chañaral, also exports $2\frac{1}{2}$ million tons of concentrated iron ore from a Japanese capitalized iron field at Santa Clara. Calama and San Pedro on the Loa are the only oasis settlements of any significance, their importance having been increased by their location on the route to Bolivia.

Arica, Chile's northernmost port, has become an important centre of manufacturing industry, particularly of motor vehicle assembly. Subsidiaries of Leyland and Citroën have established factories there for this purpose. This development was stimulated by a period during which the city was a free port. The 30 million tons of sulphur in the Tacora range provide the raw material for the establishment of a sulphuric acid plant in Arica. Manufacturing industries and copper processing are increasingly significant aspects of the economic framework of many of the larger desert ports such as Iquique and Antofagasta.

Plate 32. *The Chilean desert produces the republic's principal exports, copper and nitrate; Chuquicamata is Latin America's greatest copper plant*

Chile's participation in the enormous fish resources of the Humboldt current waters, although producing only 10 per cent of Peru's output, still makes the country Latin America's second fishing nation. The pattern of industrialization of the anchovy catch for fishmeal, in factories located in the desert coastal towns, is identical with that of Peru. Similarly, with adequate marketing and distribution facilities, the contribution of the fishing industry to the food supply could be much greater.

The southern half of Atacama province and the province of Coquimbo form a transitional semi-desert region known to Chileans as the Norte Chico, or Desert fringe. In no part of this region are rainfall amounts large. Copiapó, at its northern limit, receives less than 1 inch annually, but absolute drought rarely extends south of the Huasco river. Both the Copiapó and Huasco rivers, fed by Andean melt water and heavily loaded with rock débris, persist to the Pacific, but forests do not occur until the Limarí valley at Ovalle is reached.

Mining, agriculture and pastoralism form a trio of economic activity in the Norte Chico. La Serena was once famous for copper, but more important today are Guayacán and Huasco, the outlets for iron ore from El Romeral and Algarrobo respectively. These ports supply both United States steel mills at Sparrows Point and the Chilean iron and steel centre of Huachipato, 600 miles to the south. Output of iron ore, some 12 million tons per year, has tripled since 1960. Paipote, south-east of Copiapó, is the site of a smelting plant refining copper, gold and silver from smaller mines of the region.

Sheep pastoralism is linked with mid-summer transhumance to the Andean valleys, and the alfalfa, barley, wheat and fruit farms of the Elqui, Huasco, Choapa and Limarí valleys provide the arable component. Construction has begun of a canal 40 miles in length which will irrigate over 100,000 acres of fertile land in the Choapa valley. The dried peaches, raisins, figs and brandy of the Norte Chico are famous throughout Chile.

Ovalle (62,000), La Serena (56,000) and Coquimbo (65,000) are the principal settlements of this transition zone, the latter town having a relatively good harbour and a growing industrial structure based on water power from the Limarí.

THE MEDITERRANEAN HEARTLAND

From the valley of the Aconcagua to the valley of the Bío-Bío, the persistence of a Mediterranean rainfall régime has stamped a unity on the area. This is Chile's heartland, which until a century ago was the only effective part of the nation and even today is the home of 65 per cent of its people. This is the only region of Latin America with a régime of a marked winter rainfall maximum, and it is by far the most favoured zone of Chile which Inca and later Spanish invaders recognized as having outstanding economic potentialities. In addition, the central longitudinal depression is here best developed, becoming progressively wider towards the Bío-Bío. Built up by alluvial deposition and the outpourings of volcanic ash from the Andes to the east, its rivers still flow on the apexes of great fertile fans, and in some cases the depositional areas have been likened to inland deltas, that of the Maipó being called the Isle of Maipó.

The Andes, decreasing in height southward from the highest peak, Aconcagua, 23,003 feet, a snow-covered and majestic range, form a

Plate 33. *Mediterranean Chile has two principal components, the hill slopes of the coastal range* (above) *and the flat acres of the central plain* (below). *In both, agricultural practices are slow to change, and only recently has agrarian reform penetrated the* hacienda *system*

great back-drop to this Central valley and provide it with a continuous supply of silt-laden melt-water to irrigate the sun-drenched crops of the summer-drought period.

Scattered over the northern limits of the plain are outlying hills of the Andes, and north of Santiago these extend in a great westward spur linking the Andes to the coastal plateau. The northernmost part of the valley is therefore an isolated basin, drained by the Aconcagua river, and to this fertile oasis-like area the Incas gave the name Vale of Chile. Calera, San Felipe (30,000) and Los Andes (33,000) are the principal centres of this agricultural province which produces most of Chile's tobacco and hemp; and the Aconcagua river is the line followed by the trans-Andean railway from Valparaíso to Buenos Aires via the Uspallata Pass through the Andes, west of Mendoza. San Felipe and Los Andes have also become centres of motor vehicle assembly.

The coastal plateau is broken into separate blocks by the rivers flowing westward from the central plain, and they resume their erosive character in this structural unit of Mediterranean Chile. Although near Valparaíso these plateau units exceed 3,000 feet in height, for the most part they are rarely over 1,500 feet and are characterized by monotonous surfaces (which in some cases contain marshes), and steep marginal slopes to the coast, to the transverse river valleys, and to the central plain.

Good harbours are therefore rare, the best being Talcahuano (109,000) at the extreme south-west of the zone. This is an important base for the Chilean navy, and shipbuilding is a new development there. Valparaíso (286,000), at the northern margin, is less protected but is the country's greatest port for imports. San Antonio (65,000), nearer to Santiago, has been developed more recently, and is the outlet for the copper exports from El Teniente, high in the Andes east of Rancagua. Quintero, north of Valparaíso, has been developed both as the reception port for petroleum from Atlantic Chile (whence it is piped to the Concón refinery at the mouth of the Aconcagua river) and as the smelting centre (Las Ventanas) for the products of the smaller copper mines of the Mediterranean region.

None of the rivers is navigable and the only other large settlements of the coastal plateau are tourist resorts such as Pichilemu, Cartagena and Constitución. South of the latter town a new port, Maguellín, has been developed to export products from a large cellulose plant at Constitución. Using insignis pine from the provinces to the east, especially in the Maule basin between Curicó and Linares, this new industry, besides supplying internal needs, contributes 2 per cent of Chile's exports.

Agriculture in the intervening valleys, pastoralism on the hills and increasing attention to afforestation with eucalyptus (especially in the Bío-Bío basin) are the principal economic activities, but population densities are low compared with the central plain.

The great central valley is a zone of economic activity, of thriving industrial cities and market towns, and, until recently, of the large Chilean haciendas which dominated the country's agricultural pattern. Santiago (2,448,000) is the northern terminus of this Mediterranean vale and Los Angeles the southern. Between are the important urban centres (usually provincial capitals) of Chillán (97,000), Linares (51,000), Talca (100,000), Curicó (96,000), San Fernando (42,000), Rancagua (74,000) and San Bernardo (37,000). These are linked by the country's longitudinal road and rail spine from which subsidiary lines branch off to the coastal and piedmont settlements.

Until the introduction of agrarian reform measures in 1965 most of the land was held in a relatively few large estates, with pastoralism as the dominant land use. Although much land is still devoted to fodder crops and pastures, thousands of acres previously idle are now cultivated. Barley, wheat, beans, peas, lentils and grapes, with increasing attention to vegetable oil seeds such as sunflowers, are the principal commercial crops, but no longer is Chile a wheat exporter as it once was. Maize, vegetables and fruit for home consumption are also grown largely by irrigation.

Many of the principal industries of the towns of this region are based on these crops and the pastoral basis of the zone. Examples are the shoe and tobacco factories of Talca, the wine warehouses of Linares and Cauquenes, and the flour mills of Curicó, in addition to the multiple food industries of the capital.

Fringing the Mediterranean zone in the south-west is the Arauco–Bío-Bío coalfield and industrial region, with Concepción at its centre. Rainfall here is still mainly winter seasonal in type but much heavier than in the Mediterranean zone proper, frequently exceeding 50 inches annually.

This zone promises to become one of the most important economic areas of Chile, having many advantages, of which the chief are:

(*a*) A favourable relief situation where the broad valley of the Bío-Bío permits easy access to the interior central valley.

(b) Equable well-watered agricultural possibilities.

(c) One of the largest coalfields in South America on the shores of and under Arauco Bay, with centres at Lota, Lebu and Coronel.

(d) An excellent harbour in Talcahuano, and sheltered tidewater sites such as San Vicente Bay.

(e) Abundant supplies of hydro-electric power from the Laja river in the Andean piedmont.

(f) Central location with respect to populated markets of Mediterranean and Forest Chile.

Concepción (187,000) has become, therefore, in spite of disastrous earthquakes, the third city of Chile; and in 1950 the location of the country's principal iron and steel centre at Huachipato, as the starting point of a host of subsidiary industries, has further enhanced the importance of this new industrial region.

The local coal mixed with United States imports provides the coke; iron ore from El Romeral and limestone from Guarello Island in the archipelago to the south provide the raw materials; and water from the Bío-Bío, and power from the Abanico hydro-electric power station are utilized. The iron and steel products are consumed mainly within Chile, but some are exported to its neighbours. Gas from the coking plant is used in the cities of Concepción and Chillán, and many industries, such as the ceramic factories of Penco, are completely dependent upon this supply.

The growing significance of the Concepción area has been further enhanced by the completion there of Chile's second major oil refinery (Fig. 57). The by-products of the refinery and of a new ethylene plant also form the basis of a petrochemical complex on the shores of San Vicente bay.

The Lota coalfield produces some $1\frac{1}{2}$ million tons annually, which is a significant contribution to the fuel supplies of the country. The seams are irregular and mechanization is difficult; and since 1956 output has tended to decline. The electrification of the railways, now virtually complete in Mediterranean Chile, has also reduced the demand for coal for locomotive fuel.

THE CENTRAL AND SOUTHERN FORESTS

The Bío-Bío is the oustanding geographical frontier in Chile, for it not only separates two great physical regions, but marks the boundary between the old settled heartland and the new pioneer lands of Araucania.

While the basic structural pattern remains the same, there are distinct differences. The Andes are lower; the volcanic peaks, more or less coincident with the Cordillera in the heartland, now lie to the west and sprawl towards the central valley; the latter is therefore less continuous and is fringed by lakes such as Villarrica, Ranco and Llanquihue; glacial débris has been spread upon its surface, and the southern margins descend by a series of terraces to the Gulf of Reloncaví. The coastal plateau is lower and submergence of its coastal fringes has produced a more indented shoreline, the good harbour of Corral and the lower Valdivia river being a product of this.

The heavier rainfall, however, and the disappearance of summer drought (although winter maxima are still preserved) lead to a forest cover, mainly of deciduous beech. This became the refuge of the Araucanian Indians driven south by the Spanish conquest of the heartland, and for three centuries it remained outside the economic and social unity of Chile.

In the last hundred years, by dint of slow peripheral colonization and immigration, by Chileans from the north and by Germans, the area has been incorporated into national life. The cultural geography is therefore distinct. The hacienda is relatively rare; cut-over land is the predominant landscape; forestry is of some importance; population densities are lower, and many settlements bear the impress of imported foreign styles. The arable crops are typical of those of cool temperate regions, and include wheat, oats, hay, apples, flax and potatoes, and considerable quantities of peas. Pastoralism on luscious meadows is important, but no longer is transhumance of any significance.

The communications pattern is similar to that of Mediterranean Chile, the central trunk system linking together the principal market towns of the valley, Temuco, La Unión and Osorno, and terminating in Puerto Montt (80,000), a fishing, tourist and communications base for the far south.

Temuco (117,000) is the centre of the last nucleus of Araucanian Indian occupance in Chile, and their principal market. Osorno (93,000) is an important centre for the tourist industry built up on the scenic value of the lake- and volcano-strewn countryside. Valdivia (73,000) is the largest manufacturing centre south of Concepción, and its industries, which include breweries, tanneries and woodworking plants, are based principally on local raw materials. The city, however, suffered severely from the 1960 earthquake and tidal wave, and an iron and steel plant at Corral at the mouth of the Valdivia ria was completely destroyed in this disaster.

A detached portion of the coastal plateau is represented in the large island of Chiloé, which suffers economically from its isolation from mainland Chile. Only the eastern half of the island is utilized, the west consisting of almost impenetrable forest consequent upon the heavy rainfall experienced. The economy is reminiscent of parts of coastal Brittany, being based on fishing and agriculture in which potatoes and wheat and hay are important crops. A railway links the only two settlements of any size, Castro (22,000) and Ancud (14,000). Considerable numbers of Chilotes work in the shearing sheds and meat-freezing works of the far south on a seasonal basis.

For 700 miles to the south of Chiloé the coastal plateau consists of thousands of island remnants, uninhabited save for less than 100 primitive Alacaluf Indians. Deciduous forest changes into evergreen forest, and in the more exposed areas to stunted and gnarled bush and bare rock surfaces. The steep slopes and poor or non-existent soils offer little scope for settlement or economic use.

The central valley is drowned by the sea except in the narrow isthmus of Ofqui, and the inland channel so created is utilized for sea communication between mainland Chile and the far south. Although the Ofqui isthmus forces ships around the Taitao peninsula, the economic importance of the route scarcely justifies the cutting of a canal through the isthmus.

The transverse fault lines which split the coastal plateau into islands are continued eastwards in fiords which penetrate the southern Andes. At the head of one of these, north of Taitao, is Aysén (11,000) the port serving the sheep farms of the Simpson valley and the western outlet of the only important trans-Andean road south of Lake Llanquihue. South of Aysén the considerable ice fields north and south of Baker fiord, the largest in Latin America, blanket the Andean relief, pour their glaciers into the western fiords and the eastern lakes San Martín, Viedma and Argentino, and effectively isolate Archipelagic Chile from any contact with Argentine Patagonia.

ATLANTIC CHILE

The lands on both sides of Magellan's Strait are Chilean, and the Strait gives the first sea-level penetration of the Western Cordillera in all Latin America. It is the region to the east of the mountains which is of economic importance. Occupied by Chile for more than a century it is only since 1880 that its value as a great pastoral region was realized. Rearing 2½ million sheep of high quality on extensive farms on the New Zealand model, it yields important quantities of cross-bred wool. Punta Arenas (48,000) is the collecting centre for export of this product and the commercial and industrial capital of the far south. Since 1946 the bringing into production of Chile's only

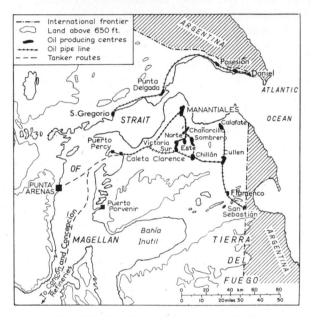

Fig. 55. *The Tierra del Fuegian oilfield*
Discovered in 1946, Chile's only oilfield is supplying the country with three-quarters of its oil requirements

oilfield on Tierra del Fuego has added another important economic prop to this region (Figs 55 and 56). In 1960 an extension of this field on the mainland north of Magellan's Strait went into production and now yields 45 per cent of the total output. The field is becoming increasingly industrialized (Fig. 56) and a liquefied gas plant produces 400,000 tons of this product for export to Argentina and Brazil. Chile still needs to import petroleum, but the Magallanes field produces most of the nation's requirements.

Agrarian reform involving the sub-division of some of the large sheep estancias is leading to closer settlement of the region, and the expansion of cattle numbers will lessen its dependence on wool.

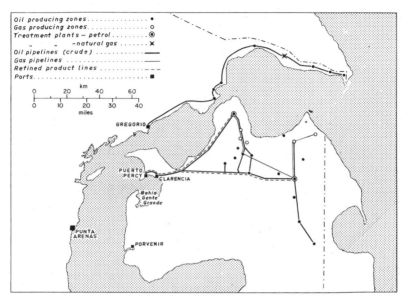

Fig. 56. *Chile. Magallanes field industrialization*
The field supplies Atlantic Chile's power requirements, most of Central Chile's petroleum, and liquid gas for export

PROSPECTS AND PROBLEMS

The economic importance of Chile is greater than the population would seem to indicate. Approximately equal with the Rhodesian copper belt as the second most important source of copper in the world, for long the only producer of nitrate, and now as one of the most industrialized of the Latin American nations, it compares favourably with larger yet less developed republics. In spite of its long areal sprawl it has welded a strong centralized nation from its diverse and frequently difficult terrain. Lacking enormous supplies of coal and oil it has developed its rich heritage of water power into an electric grid to supply farms, factories and homes. Faced with great physical difficulties it has united by rail, road, sea and air routes the far-flung corners of its national territory. Its principal problem

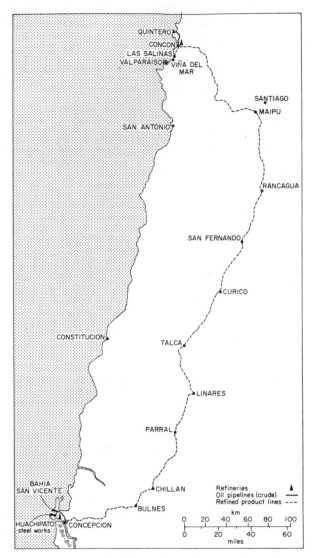

Fig. 57. *Central Chile. Industrialization of petroleum*
Chile's core population area is supplied with petroleum products from the
Concón and San Vicente refineries

now is to adapt its agriculture to modern conditions and so increase production to feed its rapidly growing cities.

Once a considerable exporter of wheat, even to California, Chile since 1941 has had to buy supplies from Argentina. Similarly, large numbers of cattle are imported from the same source to provide the country with a sufficient meat supply. Yet the central valley is one of the richest areas agriculturally in the continent. The principal need is to use it more intensively, and it is estimated that, with the extension of irrigation and mechanization, another 2 million acres could be brought into cultivation. The out-dated hacienda system with its lack of interest in maximum output has been for so long a further brake on increased productivity, but already the new agrarian reform measures have led to considerably increased wheat yields, a growth in meat production and the cultivation of previously unused land.

Having no humid tropical regions, the republic is also, inevitably, an importer of such products as cotton, bananas, cocoa, coffee, tea and jute. The same was true of sugar until the 1950s, but a determined effort to overcome this deficiency by growing sufficient sugar beet in the cooler parts of the central valley is meeting with much success, and factories to process the sugar have been built at Curicó, Los Angeles, Valdivia, Linares and in Llanquihue province (Fig. 58). With a total annual output of more than a quarter of a million tons of sugar these factories now supply 60 per cent of the national consumption of this commodity. In a similar manner the flatter areas of Mediterranean Chile, especially in the provinces of Talca and Linares, now grow sufficient rice in most years to avoid the need for imports.

The efforts of the Chilean Development Corporation have been instrumental, since 1939, in increasing the diversification of Chile's economic basis. By means of international loans, mainly from the United States, and by internal investment, an electricity grid based on the republic's rich water-power resources has been constructed, the southern oilfield has been developed, the integrated iron and steel plant at Huachipato has been set up, and a wide variety of industries have been brought into being, especially noteworthy being those making cement, paper, copper wire and chemicals. The Corporation's work is probably the most successful example of State-sponsored economic planning in Latin America, and several other republics have established similar institutions for the same purpose.

Chile, however, has some difficult problems to overcome. Industrial growth has been relatively slow in recent years; inflation is

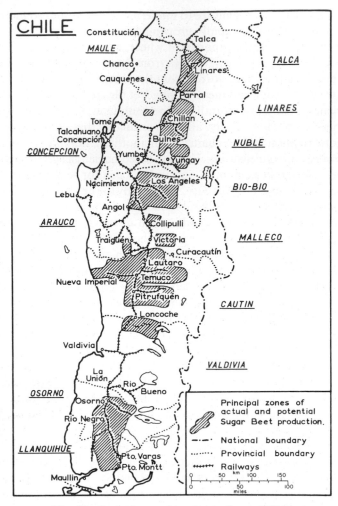

Fig. 58. *Sugar beet cultivation in Central Chile*
The Chilean Development Corporation's efforts to create a
sugar-growing and refining industry have made great headway
since 1952

persistent; urbanization has outstripped the provision of housing,
education and social services for the city populations which now
represent 65 per cent of the republic's people; and about one-fifth of
its imports are agricultural produce.

After several attempts to overcome these fundamental problems,

Chile decided, in 1970, by the democratic process, to attack its difficulties by the development of a socialist-oriented economy. This has involved the nationalization of the large mining companies, and of the large production and distribution monopolies, such as textiles and cement, state control over external trade, and a radical programme of agrarian reform. The latter requires the expropriation of all estates with over 170 acres of irrigable land, and the provision of technical aid, loans, and guaranteed markets for the produce of the new farms. The agricultural population of some 3 million Chileans is being drawn into a major reform of the country's food production on a national level for the first time. An imaginative project to take water from Forest Chile to the arid north by means of a 3,000 mile long irrigation system will take forty years to complete, but is indicative of long-term planning to feed the country's growing population.

Forty per cent of manufacturing employment is provided by Santiago and Valparaíso, but by means of regional planning agencies, industry is being increasingly decentralized in Chile's many smaller cities on the basis of providing employment and using local raw materials. There are considerable opportunities for industrial expansion in the production of steel, petrochemicals, cellulose and metal manufactures, all of which have real export potential in Latin America. They already represent 10 per cent of Chile's total exports. There is also a much greater processing of raw materials before export. As an example, 78 per cent of Chilean copper is now refined within the country, compared with 28 per cent in 1964.

Trade is much less exclusively with the United States than is the case of the republics to the north of Chile. In some years West Germany has been the principal export market and the growth of trans-Pacific trade, especially with Japan, and more recently with Australia, has been a marked change in commercial patterns. The development of trading links with China, Russia, Eastern Europe and Cuba will further diversify these patterns.

In late 1973 a violent *coup d'état* completely reversed the economic, social and political directions followed in the previous three years. The principal results have been a considerable concentration of economic resources into sectors controlled by multi-national and local industrialists and the landed aristocracy, and an increase in the proportion of the Chilean population afflicted by malnutrition and poverty.

STATISTICAL SUMMARY — CHILE

Area: 286,397 square miles

Population (1970): 10,183,000

Percentage of land
    (*a*) Arable   6%
    (*b*) Pastoral 13%
    (*c*) Forest   27%
    (*d*) Other   54%

Animal numbers
    (*a*) Cattle   3·1 million
    (*b*) Sheep   6·6 ,,
    (*c*) Pigs   1·1 ,,
    (*d*) Goats   1·5 ,,

Communications
    (*a*) All-seasons road mileage   31,120
    (*b*) Railway mileage   6,252
    (*c*) Air routes   413 million passenger miles
                           17 ,,   ton miles

Principal products
    (*a*) *Agricultural*
        Wheat   1,174,000 metric tons
        Potatoes   739,000 ,,   ,,
        Maize   362,000 ,,   ,,
        Sugar   270,000 ,,   ,,
        Barley   141,000 ,,   ,,
        Oats   123,000 ,,   ,,
        Beans and lentils   111,000 ,,   ,,
        Oilseeds   109,000 ,,   ,,
        Rice   89,000 ,,   ,,

(*b*) *Mineral*

Iron	12,246,000 metric tons
Coal	1,357,000 ,, ,,
Nitrate	679,000 ,, ,,
Copper	664,000 ,, ,,
Molybdenum	3,900 ,, ,,
Gold	5,200 troy pounds

Exports

(*a*) *Total:* $893,000,000

(*b*) *Percentage share of principal commodities*

Copper	76%
Industrial products	10%
Iron Ore	8%
Fish products	4%
Nitrate	2%

PART IV

THE PLATA REPUBLICS

CHAPTER SEVENTEEN

General Introduction to La Plata Republics

THE three republics of Argentina, Paraguay and Uruguay form one major region of Latin America, orientated to the estuary of La Plata. Through this great gateway pass their exports to the outside world and the fuel and manufactured goods which they buy in exchange. Their common interest in this trading artery is so striking that it would not have been surprising if they had emerged as one nation. Indeed their historical, physical and economic unity gave them a better opportunity of successful co-operation than is the case in any other collection of Latin American states. The history of the early years of independence, however, is largely the story of their political breakup, a fragmentation with its roots in history, ethnic composition, politics and strategy.

HISTORICAL UNITY

Except for the early colonization of Asunción and the north-western Andean areas of present-day Argentina, the whole region was relatively neglected in the 16th and 17th centuries. Spanish interest and attention focused on the western coasts and plateaux of South America, the source of labour and minerals to bolster up their colonial system. The apparently limitless expanses of Chaco and Pampa were the home of hunting Indian tribes, devoid of mineral wealth, and the cul-de-sac of a transport system which was hinged on Panamá and turned its back on the estuary which was to become so important at a later date. Not until 1776 was the Viceroyalty of La Plata established, 232 years later than its neighbour Peru (Fig. 1). Throughout most of that period a traveller visiting Buenos Aires from Seville journeyed via Portobelo, Panamá, Lima and Salta, taking a year to complete the trip. Although difficult to enforce, Spanish law forbade Buenos Aires to carry on trade with other colonial ports until the mid-18th century. It was thus an historical unity of neglect, of relative emptiness, and later of administrative control. There were exceptional areas such as the thriving settlements of the Andean Northwest, linked more to the fortunes of Chile than to the Plata lands, the long-established (1537) capital of Asunción and the *misiones* converting the more numerous Indian population of the Paraguay valley, and the strategic Brazilian outpost on the Banda Oriental (or eastern shore) of La Plata estuary. It was the increasing significance of their separation from the rest of Spanish America, and their orientation eastward which offered a basis of later political unity. The 19th and 20th centuries' process of immigration to develop these previously neglected areas resulted in a common ethnic addition of many millions of Spanish and Italians, and more recently of Central and East Europeans, which changed completely the population of the republics of Argentina and Uruguay, and to very much less extent that of Paraguay. This European and non-Indian population is one of the most characteristic features which differentiates the region from the rest of Latin America, and is further evidence of the historical unity of its development.

PHYSICAL UNITY

The great plains stretching eastward from the Andean piedmont, monotonous and boundless in their horizons, and drained for the most part by one great river system, the Paraná–Paraguay–Uruguay, into La Plata provided the physical basis on which the historical Viceroyalty was created. Except for relatively limited areas, climate and vegetation combined to emphasize the physical unity (Fig. 4). Grassland in one form or another was the principal cover over most of the region, and adequacy and uniformity of seasonal rainfall and (for South America) a marked temperature rhythm providing in its heart almost continental conditions, gave its inhabitants an environment sufficiently common to prevent regional break-up on physical grounds. The apparently barren and semi-arid plateaux of Patagonia were peripheral to the unity of the grassland basin but were then, and now, of marginal significance.

ECONOMIC UNITY

On this relatively uniform physical basis has developed a strikingly uniform economic utilization, based on livestock-rearing and extensive agriculture. The natural grasslands (later improved in some areas by imported grasses) became the home of millions of cattle and sheep, the traditional scene on which the *gaucho* lived his life, and the economic wealth of each of the three national states which shared these lands. In spite of considerable diversification recently, the importance of meat, wool and hides production is still vital to the fortunes of all the Plata republics.

Over considerable areas arable farming is integrated with the basic pastoralism, and the physical advantages of climate, soil and landscape have permitted the region to become one of the world's main sources of wheat, maize and linseed. Of all Latin America no other major region offers such opportunities for large-scale mechanized agriculture, and it will continue to be the continent's principal producer of temperate cereals. Even in its peripheral regions the economic emphasis is on agricultural and extractive production of commodities such as cotton, tobacco, fruit and quebracho.

This economic concentration on products of the grasslands, farms and peripheral woodlands is even more emphasized by the region's mineral poverty. Its lack of fuel and metallic minerals has thus imposed an additional similarity on its $1\frac{1}{4}$ million square miles. No other comparable area of Latin America is so deficient in minerals, and this places a continuous strain on the development of industry both from the shortage of raw material metals to process and the lack of fuels to provide manufacturing power. It explains Argentina's dependence on imported coal and Paraguay's costly military efforts to gain control of the Chaco in the hope of finding oil. The contrast of agricultural wealth and mineral poverty is best epitomized by the use of maize and grains soaked in linseed oil for railway fuel during crises in coal importation at the time of the Second World War. It may indeed be argued that the economic similarity of the whole region, while providing a unity of common economic interests, has provided no impetus for its political unity. Economic diversity, the basis of interdependence, may have been a more powerful means of welding the region together.

POLITICAL DISUNITY

In spite of the basic historical, physical and economic unity of the region, and the efforts of Buenos Aires to control it, and thus to produce one nation when independence was achieved, the result has been its political fragmentation. Various reasons account for this, but the settlement pattern of population clusters, separated either by great distances or physical obstacles, played an important part.

Uruguay, separated from the Buenos Aires nucleus by La Plata estuary and the deltaic lands of the Paraná, was claimed by both Argentina and Brazil. It is in essentials a natural continuation of both Brazil's Río Grande do Sul and Argentina's pampa, and as a transitional area between two powerful neighbours, the solution of its creation as a buffer state between Portuguese and Spanish America was not an illogical one. Inevitably, by ties of language and peopling, and its location on La Plata estuary, it has more in common with Argentina than with Brazil, but its differing political and economic evolution since Independence, and especially in the 20th century, has led to a marked individuality in the human geography of Uruguay.

Paraguay, separated by the shifting course of the Paraná–Paraguay river system and vast thinly populated areas from the Argentine capital, had greater reasons for separation from its control. Not only was it an area transitional in character between the grasslands of La Plata and the forests of Amazonia, but the indigenous Indian population made up a much larger share of its total human stock than anywhere else in the lands claimed by Argentina. To these basic physical and human endowments can be added the impetus of an early historical regionalism when Asunción was the only significant settlement of the lowland. Although successful in maintaining its political independence, and defending it in aggressive fierceness against all its neighbours, its economic well-being must be largely at the mercy of the states which lock it in the interior of the continent. Persistent military dictatorship and the aftermath of its unequal struggles have left it a weakened peripheral fragment, in considerable contrast to the other states of La Plata.

The population clusters of the Northwest, Córdoba, Tucumán, Mendoza and Salta, for long resisted the centralized authority of Buenos Aires. Their long historical traditions and their differing economic interests and associations with the Andean regions were strong forces for the maintenance of their autonomy. Only by the slow process of political evolution and compromise and the increasing strength of economic ties to the east has the Northwest been effectively incorporated into modern Argentina.

The remaining peripheral areas of the Northeast, the Chaco, and Patagonia by post-independence settlement and economic utilization have become part of Argentina in a natural process of occupation and extension into the limiting areas of this great natural region. In the far south a military clash with Chile over rival claims was only narrowly avoided, and led to the partition of Tierra del Fuego, the demilitarization of the Strait of Magellan, and the confirmation of its status as an international waterway.

CHAPTER EIGHTEEN

Argentina

THE vast republic of Argentina, the largest of the Spanish American states, presents many features of human geography sharply in contrast to those typical of the other countries of the continent. Unless these are borne in mind at the outset, the details of its regional geography are difficult to relate to the whole national pattern.

First there are the implications of its size and extent. Stretching through 2,000 miles from the tropics to latitudes comparable (in the Northern hemisphere) with the Scottish Hebrides, and from the South Atlantic to areas 1,000 miles within the continent and high in the Andes, the climatic variety is greater than that presented by any other country of Latin America. Likewise, the direct distances involved in journeys from Jujuy in the north-western Andes to Posadas on the fringe of the Brazilian plateau or to Bahía Blanca on the Atlantic coast are comparable with those from Paris to Rome and Salonika respectively (Fig. 59).

The second distinctive feature is the welding into one nation of regions experiencing contrasting historical evolutions (Fig. 1). The Andean settlements originating from colonization via Bolivia and Chile, the northern settlements, offshoots of Paraguayan developments, and the largely 19th-century colonization of the Pampa lands of the east by overseas immigration present a much more complex amalgam than the relatively simple development of the one or two-nuclei type of nations like Chile, Uruguay or the Central American states. Nor is it usual in Latin America to find a newly settled region dominating the older historical centres, as Buenos Aires outshines the cities of the north-west.

Thirdly, there has been Argentina's amazing growth in population, economic importance and the characteristics of a modern state. In the late 18th century it was still a neglected and unimportant wilderness of the Spanish empire (except for its north Andean fringes which looked towards Lima), and even less than a century ago it was a thinly inhabited land of some $1\frac{1}{2}$ million people. During the 20th century it has grown into a nation of some 23 millions and the source

313

Fig. 59. *The regions of Argentina*

of at least one-tenth of all Latin America's exports. With the second
city in the world south of the equator, the most extensive railway
network in the continent, and the greatest degree of urbanization,
its growth is comparable with the rapid opening-up of the interior
lowlands of North America in the same century. Similarly, the
contribution of overseas immigrants to this process is greater than

elsewhere in Latin America. Uruguay's development and peopling is in many ways a similar story on a miniature scale.

Only in recent years, Brazil, with its much greater population and three times Argentina's area, has been forging ahead to wrest the economic leadership of Latin America from its neighbour. For the first half of the 20th century Argentina was the undisputed economic colossus of the South.

On the basis of relief alone the country falls into two contrasting regions of a western mountain-plateau and an eastern lowland, but the climatic contrasts and the variations in economic development dependent on historical evolution and trends differentiate the country into at least four well-marked geographical regions (Fig. 59):

1. The North-western Andes.
2. The Chaco and the Northeast.
3. The Pampa and Entre Rios.
4. Patagonia.

THE NORTH-WESTERN ANDES

This broad mountain and plateau zone, averaging 300 miles in width, stretches from the southern boundary of Bolivia, parallel with the Chilean frontier following the high crest line of the Cordillera, to the southern boundary of Mendoza province. Its basic elements are high plateaux (often referred to as *punas*), fringing mountain ranges, deep rift troughs aligned in a north–south direction and described as *valles*, erosion valleys or *quebradas* cut back westward into the ranges, and outlying piedmont blocks of hills fronting the Pampa to the east (Figs. 60 and 61).

Not all these features occur throughout the region, and on the basis of relief and even more of climatic differentiation, four sub-regions can be distinguished approximately corresponding to the provinces of

(*a*) Jujuy, Salta and Tucumán,
(*b*) Catamarca and La Rioja,
(*c*) San Juan and Mendoza (once the province of Cuyo), and
(*d*) Córdoba and San Luis.

JUJUY, SALTA AND TUCUMAN

Eastward from the Chilean Cordillera Domeyko the Altiplano of north-west Argentina resembles that of Bolivia, being some 19,000

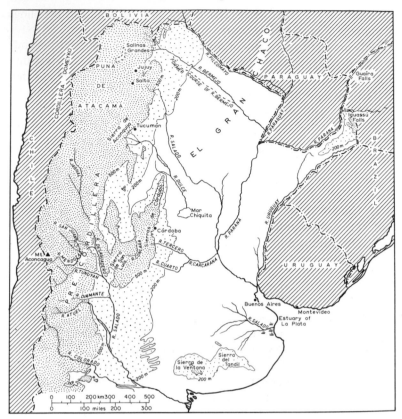

Fig. 60. *Relief units of Northern and Central Argentina*

feet above sea-level and containing dry intermont sandy and clay-filled *salares* or salt basins, residual ranges occasionally exceeding 10,000 feet in altitude, and volcanic cones and débris, the latter occurring especially on the Chilean margins. This puna or altiplano is bounded on the east by a range some 2,000 feet higher than the average surface of the plateau. Torn by mountain streams flowing towards the lowlands, its eastern face shows a marked contrast with the depositional features capping its western flanks.

Eastward, long north–south ranges, of which the Sierra de Aconquija, more than 17,000 feet high, is the most spectacular, spread towards the Chaco. Separating these peneplained hog's-back hills are rift valleys in which are preserved the younger sedimentary rocks long since eroded from the ridges. Salta is in such a trough, the valle

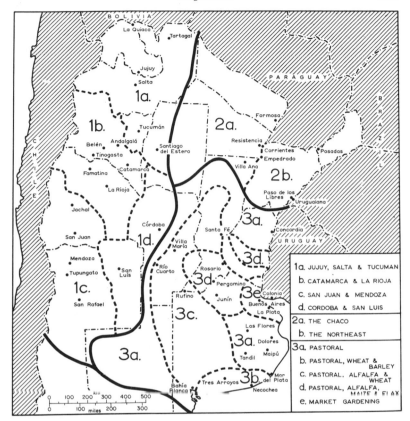

Fig. 61. *Sub-regions of Northern and Central Argentina*

of Lerma, and the railway north of Tucumán follows a valle to Jujuy.

Rainfall decreases westward throughout this sub-region, until on the puna arid landscapes prevail. Tucumán, exposed to eastern humid winds receives as much as 38 inches, and is thus one of the rainiest parts of Argentina's Northwest. Jujuy (29 inches) and Salta (28 inches) are more sheltered by the piedmont hills, whereas La Quiaca (11 inches) close to Bolivia indicates conditions on the puna. Vegetation is closely related to this rainfall pattern. The desert scrub of the plateau gives way eastward to mixed scrub forest in the valles and to semi-tropical humid forest on the slopes of the Sierra de Aconquija in the Tucumán district.

This extensive mountain zone separating the altiplano from the Chaco was one of the earliest scenes of colonization in Argentina, and the north-western metropolis of Tucumán (290,000) and the smaller towns of Jujuy (52,000) and Salta (240,000) were all founded before 1600. Even before the Spanish spread into this region *en route* from Peru to Chile, the Inca Empire had realized its value and absorbed Tucumán as its south-eastern outpost.

These early settlements were linked to the heart of Spanish power in Lima, and their importance in the colonial economy of Peru and Bolivia lay in their supplying mules for the mining camps of the high Andes, Salta's annual mule fair being the largest in the continent.

Both before and especially since Independence, the increasing realization of the other economic potentialities led to the development of both subsistence and commercial agriculture and pastoralism. In this Tucumán was especially favoured. Streams rising in the Sierra de Aconquija provide abundant water; cloudy conditions in the mountain area prevent frost; and the open exposure of the zone to the warm damp winds from the east prevents air stagnation and consequent frost.

Always an important route centre in colonial times, it had acquired much capital from this function, and aided by immigrant capital and labour from adjoining areas, human conditions combined with the physical advantages to convert the zone into the greatest sugar-producing region of Argentina. Most of this crop is grown in large plantations under irrigation, but on the lower slopes of the Sierra de Aconquija the rainfall is sufficient to make irrigation unnecessary, and a large number of producers grow the crop on farms of less than 20 acres each. The intensive cultivation of sugar has not only drawn many people into the Tucumán area, so that the small province has more than three-quarters of a million population, but the rural densities are the greatest in the country. This growth of population has been largely dependent on the growth of the sugar industry, which in turn was made a profitable economic industry by the linking of the area to the consuming centres of the Pampa by railway.

The flourishing agriculture of this so-called *falda de Tucumán* is in many ways unique, especially in respect of the extensive area it covers. Some sugar is also grown in Jujuy and Salta, but alfalfa, maize and wheat and cattle ranching on the hill slopes in winter and in the valles in summer dominate the economic life of these provinces. Even a third of the Tucumán falda is devoted to maize, and an increasing acreage to rice production. Tucumán city, however, has an increasingly industrial component, notably that of textiles and motor vehicles, in its development.

On the puna Jujuy produces the wool and skins of sheep and llamas, and salt from the Salinas Grandes salar, while Salta's volcanic areas yield sulphur from mines located at elevations exceeding 17,000 feet. Potatoes, quinoa and beans are grown to feed the Indians and mestizos, but maize will not ripen and is obtained by bartering puna products in the valles.

The oil from the Campo Durán refinery is piped to San Lorenzo on the Paraná river and natural gas is similarly exported to Buenos Aires. There have also been recent further discoveries of petroleum in this province and at Caimancito in Jujuy. Tupungato in Mendoza province is another piedmont field where output is on the increase, and the products of the Luján de Cuyo refinery there are sent by a multi-channel pipe-line to both Córdoba and Buenos Aires.

The Salta–Guimes–Jujuy urban triangle is one of the country's selected 'growth centres' where it is planned to undertake coordinated development to promote rapid economic growth.

CATAMARCA AND LA RIOJA

South of Tucumán, in the provinces of Catamarca and La Rioja, the Argentine Andes form a disordered complex of ranges and basins, revealing the past geological history of mountain building in the area. Intense metamorphism, with granites and gneisses containing the rich silver and copper ores of Famatina and Tinogasta, is evident in the high ranges, some of which reach 20,000 feet. In others, sedimentaries of all ages cap these crystalline foundations. Troughs, known as *bolsones* or *campos*, reveal the tectonic collapse of large areas, some mountain-enclosed, others opening on to the plains eastward. All are partially filled with detritus of all shapes and sizes from the adjoining hills.

Rainfall decreases considerably in this zone, La Rioja having less than 14 inches annually, and a poor scrub vegetation clothes most of the area. Nor have human conditions favoured the utilization of this part of the Northwest. Located midway between routes which led via Tucumán to the north-west and via Mendoza to the west it has never been stimulated by much through traffic. It has remained somewhat of a backwater, in the past linked more to Chile than to Argentina by reason of their common mineral inheritance and exploitation, and often supported by the same capital and labour on both sides of the Andes.

Pastoralism of sheep and goats is the principal economic activity, and transhumance is an integral part of this system. In favoured areas of the bolsones (Tinogasta, Jachal, Belén, Andalgala, La Rioja) where ground water is available in finer dumps of clayey material or natural underground barrages, crops of alfalfa, cotton, wheat, figs, olives and grapes are grown, largely on a subsistence basis and to supply the larger population of the Tucumán region, which also receives the cattle fattened in Catamarca. In the past these were driven over mountain trails to the mining camps of northern Chile; and Tinogasta is linked by road to Copiapó.

Only the capitals of the two provinces, each with some 30,000 population, rank as urban centres and the sub-region contains only one-fifteenth of the population of north-western Argentina.

SAN JUAN AND MENDOZA

The structure of the southernmost part of the Andes of the Argentine Northwest is comparatively simple in the provinces of San Juan and

Plate 34. *North-western Argentina is a semi-arid land. The Andean fringe of Catamarca province*

Mendoza. It consists of three major units, the high boundary Cordillera dominated by the soaring peak of Aconcagua, highest point of the Americas; a north–south trough 250 miles long occupied in part by the courses of the rivers San Juan, Jachal and Mendoza; and the easternmost range, nowhere exceeding 13,000 feet, usually known as the Pre-Cordillera, which spreads out its detritus towards the eastern plains and the great saddle linking the sub-region with the Sierras de Córdoba.

The glaciers and snowfields of the high Andes feed the rivers, the largest of which flow through the great depression and tear their way eastward through the Pre-Cordillera to peter out in sloughs or *playas* in the western areas of the state of San Luis. The most important are the San Juan, the Mendoza, the Tunuyán, the Diamante and the Atuel. Without these streams the sub-region would have little economic significance, for rainfall is almost negligible (San Juan 3·3 inches, Mendoza 7·7 inches) and agriculture is dependent on irrigation from the rivers. There are thus three principal oases, those of San Juan (142,000), Mendoza (180,000) and San Rafael (46,000) growing crops of alfalfa for cattle and a wide variety of fruits including grapes, olives, peaches, apples, plums, pears, cherries, quinces and apricots. Water has in fact converted the area into the 'Garden of the Andes'. This is also the premier wine-producing region of Argentina, almost all the wine being consumed in the country. The vineyards are for the most part small, farmed on a basis of peasant proprietorship, and selling their grapes to the large *bodegas* or warehouse factories for conversion into wine.

The two principal towns Mendoza and San Juan are 16th-century Spanish settlements. The former, founded from Chile, has always been important in linking the districts of the central Chilean valley with Tucumán and so avoiding the desert country of the north. The sub-region has shown greatest economic growth since the coming of the railway. This has linked it with the markets of the east and has made possible the extensive use of irrigation, which is unrivalled throughout Argentina. The summer floods with the melting of the snows swelling the rivers with sand and volcanic ash are often difficult to control, but they have their advantages in renewing the productive soils in this dry and dusty land. Its productivity has encouraged rapid population growth by immigration, over 1 million people being supported in this otherwise relatively difficult region. No other Argentine region has suffered so severely from earthquakes. Mendoza was practically destroyed in 1861 and San Juan in 1944.

These are evidence of the great instability of the longitudinal depression, which in small scale reproduces the Great Vale of Chile to the west of the Andes. So recent geologically has been its formation that Andean-derived sediments, once spreading continuously eastward, have been faulted down and their eastern continuations remain on the slopes of the Pre-Cordillera.

CORDOBA AND SAN LUIS

Standing as a great outpost zone, both from the physical and human viewpoints, the Sierras de Córdoba and San Luis form a unit of the Pre-Cordilleran Andes. They stretch for some 300 miles from north to south, aligned as a physical barrier between the Mendoza–San Juan area and the Pampa. There are considerable areas over 5,000 feet in height, with 8,000 feet in the highest area, and they are by no means a simple single range. They reproduce many of the structural characteristics of the ranges further west, with peneplained plateau surfaces called *pampas*, the steep and abrupt fractured edges of which face westward, and tectonic troughs and bolsones, while on their eastern margins the Pampa sediments lap around their base.

The Sierra of San Luis is separated from the three longitudinal Sierras of Córdoba by the Conlara trough, but all reveal the threefold structural basis of the Andes, of ancient crystalline rocks, vast sedimentation and more recent volcanic activity. Their present trend is largely determined by the great north–south fractures which divide them. Of the Sierra's five eastward-flowing rivers most peter out, or like the Río Dulce from the Tucumán district, manage to reach the salt depression of Mar Chiquita in the north-east. In the south, two streams, the Ríos Tercero and Cuarto combining to form the Carcarañá, reach the Paraná.

Vegetation is largely dependent upon aspect, the massif of San Luis being scrub-covered, as are also the Sierra slopes facing north, but those exposed to humid influences from the east support almost dense forests of carob bean, quebracho and tala trees. The level plateaux surfaces are scrub and grass covered. Córdoba with 28 inches and San Luis with 22 inches of rain per annum indicate the wetter conditions which prevail and partially account for the flocking of population to the margins of this zone. Córdoba city (846,000) has grown into the third city of Argentina, which is in many ways the result of its locational functions at the junction of Andes and Pampa and its centrality with regard to the country as a whole. It, too, was a Spanish colonial foundation of the 16th century with a university,

Argentina's first, as early as 1613. Indeed long before the wealth of the enveloping Pampa was realized, the Córdoban hills were populated with wheat farmers, gold washers and pastoralists. Today, livestock ranching and irrigated agriculture supply the urban nucleus of Córdoba, and many tourist resorts, offering relief to the Pampa dwellers from the monotony of the plains, provide the basis of livelihood. There is still considerable mining activity, tungsten and beryllium being important products. Córdoba has become a great industrial city, and most important among its 15,000 factories are those producing Kaiser and Fiat motor cars and the State mechanical industries turning out aircraft parts, trucks, tractors and armaments. Other plants manufacture a great variety of consumer goods such as glass, ceramics, plastics, fertilizers, leather and foodstuffs.

The south-eastern half of Córdoba state forms an integral part of the Pampa region and will be considered in that connection.

All four parts of the northern Argentine Andes have a unity, both physical and human. Their structural association with the continental mountain system, in spite of its variety, is obvious; and as a natural corollary they contain the reserves of Argentina's only important metalliferous wealth. Their increasing aridity as one progresses southward, and the concentration of rainfall in the summer season provide a climatic unity. Their colonization and settlement from the north-west and west, and their historical and economic links with Chile and Bolivia form the basis of their human geography. Likewise their re-orientation south-eastward with the establishment of Argentine nationhood and railway links with Buenos Aires form a common characteristic of all parts of the region. The unifying features of their common economic geography are the oasis-like nuclei of settlement, giving rise to relatively large urban centres, surrounded by unproductive lands or domains of the pastoralist; the importance of irrigation, with the increasing significance of cash crops of sugar, wine and fruits; and the resultant recent rapid growth in population by which the nine provinces now account for one-fifth of Argentina's population.

Yet it would be a mistake to over-stress this unity. The divergences among the sub-regions are of extraordinary significance, such as the productivity of Tucumán and Mendoza contrasted with the thirsty expanses of La Rioja and Catamarca; the basically colonial population of Tucumán contrasted with the new immigrants to the vineyards of Mendoza; the primitive Indian people of the puna contrasted with the culture of Córdoba. Local variations dependent on aspect, water-supply and facilities for transport routes are frequently dominant in influencing urban location and economic developments. Perhaps nowhere is this more evident than in respect of the Sierra de Aconquija and the *falda de Tucumán*, but throughout the region the map of population distribution is largely a reflection of the economic potentialities offered by favourable combinations of local physical conditions.

Apart from the more widely based industrialization of Córdoba, industrial development in the region is largely the processing of the local agricultural and mineral products. The refining of sugar and manufacture of industrial alcohol at Tucumán, and the wine industry at Mendoza and San Juan are most important. A charcoal iron industry at Zapla in Jujuy province utilizes Argentina's principal iron-ore deposits, and mines of lead and zinc in Jujuy, Catamarca and San Juan provinces, and of sulphur in Salta and Mendoza provinces, produce most of the country's output of these minerals.

More recently petroleum developments have taken place at Tartagal (Salta province) where the Madre Jones field is a southern extension of Bolivia's petroleum zone.

THE CHACO AND THE NORTHEAST

The great diagonal north-west–south-east boundary of northern Argentina follows the course of the river Pilcomayo, and is in no sense a natural frontier (Figs. 60 and 61). The interior expanse of El Gran Chaco is divided by it into the Bolivian and Paraguayan and Argentine portions of this vast region. Within Argentina most of the provinces of Formosa, Chaco, Santiago del Estero and northern Santa Fé fall within its bounds, and its southern boundary is the Río Dulce and the 30°S. parallel of latitude. On the west it merges almost imperceptibly into the mountain provinces of Salta and Tucumán; in the east the Paraná river forms a distinct limit.

Formed of sands, clays and débris swept eastward from the Andean foothills, this extensive plain, 200 miles in width, slopes gradually from a height of some 1,000 feet above sea-level towards the Ríos Paraná and Paraguay, where it is less than 150 feet in altitude. Although there are several seasonal water-courses, especially in the north-east, only four permanent rivers, three of which are tributaries of the Paraguay–Paraná, flow in parallel formation across it, the Pilcomayo, Bermejo, Salado and Dulce. The latter, fed by the rains of the Sierra de Aconquija, only reaches the Mar Chiquita inland drainage basin. All suffer from the principal disabilities of river drainage in a zone of unconsolidated material, namely shifting courses, sandbanks, shallow reaches, seasonal floods, braided courses and marshes.

Climatically, the region experiences the highest summer temperatures in Latin America, that of Santiago del Estero exceeding an average of 83°F. in January; and seasonal ranges are frequently in the thirties. Rainfall decreases fairly steadily westward, from averages of approximately 50 inches along the Paraná to 20 inches in the west. The vegetation pattern is, however, not a simple one, being dependent on the distribution of ground water in the diverse subsoils, and the presence or absence of salt. Stands of semi-deciduous trees occur in the river valleys and especially along the Paraguay–Paraná; red quebracho forest in the drier western areas; white quebracho forest in the salty soils of the southern and eastern margins; groves of palm trees amid stretches of grass in clay-filled depressions; and mixtures of spiny scrub and trees in the piedmont, dependent again on local deposits of water-bearing soils (Fig. 6).

The exploitation of its forests has been one of the principal economic activities of the Chaco, white quebracho being cut for fencing, telegraph poles, charcoal, railway sleepers, and fuel for locomotives, and red quebracho for tannin. The extraction of tannin needs a plentiful supply of water, so the factories must be near the few rivers. As this frequently involves a long haul for the logs, it is often more advisable to move the siting of the factories nearer to the cutting zones. *La Forestal Argentina*, one such company, abandoned its mills at Villa Ana and Fontana in 1956 for this reason, moving their processing plants nearer the sources of quebracho cutting. The railway system north of Santa Fé is largely the result of logging operations in this industry.

It was however in the south-west of the region that the first settlers arrived, Santiago del Estero being Argentina's oldest town. Founded in 1553 from Peru it shares many features of the Northwest, and large pastoral estates were established in the district, using the scrub forest north of the Río Dulce for cattle grazing. Like the northwestern oases, there is irrigated agriculture in the flood-plains of the Dulce and Salado, maize, linseed, wheat and cotton being grown.

The land is replenished both in soil and water by the summer floods, and the arable hollows are known as *bañados*. They vary in location often from year to year depending on the vagaries of flood water and the shifting courses of the braided rivers. Tenants till the bañados, the *hacendados* being more interested in the pastoral activities of the estate, in spite of the fact that cattle tick is an endemic problem. The forest settlements are the principal market for the meat. In recent decades the Chaco has witnessed another form of colonization, of immigrants from overseas especially from south-eastern Europe, who have either cleared forest or utilized areas already cutover for quebracho logs. In this case the penetration has been mainly in the north-east in a two-pronged drive westward from the towns of Formosa and Resistencia, using the railways which run into the Chaco from those two towns.

Basing their economy on a certain amount of subsistence agriculture and cattle pastoralism with maize as the chief fodder crop, they have concentrated on cotton production to supply Argentina's textile mills, and largely made the country self-sufficient in this respect. Some sugar and tobacco are also grown. The farms are medium-sized, being occupied on the basis of squatting rights on State territory. In the period 1947–57 the population increased by 50 per cent. In 1924 the two territories of Chaco and Formosa supported 84,000 people; forty years later this had been multiplied by eleven. Resistencia (94,000) and Formosa (40,000) are the principal towns of the Chaco, serving as outlets for their respective provinces and bases for the agricultural and forestry activities. Resistencia has also some cotton-ginning plants and cotton-seed oil factories.

The Paraná forms a formidable barrier east of the Argentine Chaco. Unbridged, difficult to navigate because of its shallow nature, sandbanks, shifting channels and strong floods, it fairly effectively isolates the Chaco from north-east Argentina which stretches as a salient between Paraguay and Brazil.

This sub-region consists of two provinces, Misiones and Corrientes, unlike in their physical basis, but both settled from the north and still bearing the stamp of their historical origins.

The plateau of Misiones forms a continuation of the Brazilian massif and thus declines in height south-westward from the boundary with Brazil, where it reaches 2,500 feet above sea-level. It stands out as a great spur, 150 miles long, above the flanking Paraná and Uruguay rivers, and tributary valleys have torn into its surface which is covered in large part by basalt flows. Over and through this lava capping the tributaries hurl themselves to the Paraná. The Iguazú is the most famous of these and the Guaíra falls on the Paraná mainstream is another, tantalizingly situated in Argentina's north-east extremity and so remote from the industries of Buenos Aires.

These lavas weather to deep fertile red soils which in places may be as much as 30 feet thick. Favoured with a plentiful rainfall of 60 to 80 inches annually, with little semblance of a dry season, the province is one of the most densely forested areas of Argentina. The level expanses of the plateau carry stands of the Paraná pine, the slopes a dense broad-leaved jungle of trees, lianes, bamboos and undergrowth, thinning westward as the plain of Corrientes is reached. This is a land rich in wild bird and animal life and totally unlike any other part of Argentina.

The area was settled by the Jesuit missionaries and their Indian converts who had fled from their previous settlements in the Brazilian state of Paraná to escape the slave-raiding *bandeirantes* of São Paulo, in the mid-17th century. By the early 18th century there were many mission stations, San Ignacio being an important centre. The communities practised agriculture and pastoralism, supplied most of their own needs and had a surplus to barter. After the expulsion of the Jesuits by Spanish royal decree in 1767 the settlements were abandoned and their remains alone witness to the past.

The recovery was slow until the 20th century as the more accessible parts of Argentina received attention, but in recent decades the tempo of economic growth and population expansion has increased considerably, the latter helped by foreign immigrants, which constitute 18 per cent of the population. Otherwise the province still suffers considerably from poor communications with the other parts of Argentina which are the market for its many products. Forestry, plantations of yerba maté, tea and tobacco, citrus orchards and the extraction of tung oil all provide employment, the agricultural activities being especially concentrated in the lower areas east of Posadas (82,000), the only town of significance. This is where the international Asunción–Buenos Aires railway is ferried across the Río Paraná.

The plain of Corrientes to the west is a great quadrilateral of riverine lowland surrounded on three sides by the Ríos Paraná, Aguapey and Uruguay, and merging southward into the alluvial province of Entre Ríos which is much more linked economically with the Pampa.

The surface of the lowland is undulating, which is partly the result of past erosional and depositional history of the Paraná system, and drainage is poor. Marshes, some temporary, like the bañados of the southern Chaco, others permanent esteros, as on the Bermejo in the northern Chaco, have accumulated where surface deposits of clay have prevented run-off. Few are open expanses of water but rather swampy depressions scattered among the sandy rises which appear to be fossil dunes. These latter are frequently covered with yatai palm groves in a vegetational cover made up mainly of coarse grassland and park-like expanses, which towards the south were once predominantly of timbo and red quebracho. This was the first area of quebracho cutting and the forest has long been removed on this eastern side of the Paraná.

Pastoralism with criollo cattle (for this area is still susceptible to tick) is the basic economic occupation, and sheep-raising is not unimportant. There are some aspects of the landscape and its utilization which remind one of the Venezuelan llanos, such as the high-grass interfluves, the depressions, the reliance on cattle, and its relative isolation. Along the Paraná river numerous small farms raise manioc, maize, oranges and fruit, for rainfall amounts are relatively large. Although there is a summer maximum, winter rainfall is not insignificant, but drought is also a danger. Increasing quantities of rice are being grown in the wetter marshy areas. Empedrado (24,000) being an important centre, and also along the northern river margins between Corrientes and Posadas. Cotton is also of some significance.

The Uruguay river is bridged at Paso de los Libres and so affords road and rail communication with Brazil, via Uruguayana to Porto Alegre; and numerous small ports on both Ríos Uruguay and Paraná serve as collecting and distributing centres for the plain. Corrientes (104,000), the capital, is the limit of important navigation on the Paraná, and Concordia (60,000) on the Uruguay.

Diverse as are these three portions, Chaco, Misiones and Corrientes, of Argentina's northlands they too have a unity in their physical and human resemblances with the neighbouring regions of Brazil and Paraguay from which they were originally settled. They were remote peripheral lands inhabited by people with an important Indian strain, but in this century they are being converted into pioneer regions of increased development. The basic economies of forestry and pastoralism still survive, and as a result the percentage of urban population is much less than elsewhere in Argentina. The significance of the whole region, now containing 12 per cent of all Argentinians, continues to increase in the national economy, and the Corrientes–Resistencia and Posadas–Oberá–Santo Tomé urban areas are two other zones designated as economic 'growth centres'.

THE PAMPA AND ENTRE RÍOS

South of the Chaco and Corrientes lowland, east of the Andes, and north of the Río Colorado stretches the great economic region of the Pampa and Entre Ríos (Figs. 60 and 61), from which are derived 80 per cent of the nation's exports, and where two out of every three Argentinians live.

The dominant characteristic of its relief is the monotony of its great lowland surface, which impelled its Spanish settlers to stress this unique and extensively plain in the term La Pampa. It is a great accumulation of sedimentary deposits, clays, loess and sands filling an enormous basin of uneven depth (and throughout most of its area of unknown depth). The surface of this foundation basin is, in all probability, of most irregular relief not unlike the exposed Brazilian plateau to the north, and it protrudes through and around the margins of this great sea of deposits in several areas, which in part relieve the monotony of the plain. The north-west–south-east ridges of the Sierras del Tandil and de la Ventana in Buenos Aires province are two such conspicuous features, the latter exceeding 4,000 feet in height. Composed of granites, gneisses and quartzites they may be regarded as southern fragments of the old Brazilian massif. In the west the Sierras de Córdoba are often referred to as Pampean hills in that they rise from its outer margins. The rolling, undulating country of Entre Ríos, 'between the rivers' Paraná and Uruguay, and not unlike the landscape of Uruguay, also rises from a crystalline foundation, the continuation of the adjacent Brazilian shield.

Except for the alluvial flood plain of the Paraná between Santa Fé and Buenos Aires and some areas of the eastern Pampa, the shell-derived limestones of which reveal a marine origin, all the deposits of the great plain appear to be continental in origin and derived from the west. It is indeed one of the most conspicuous areas of æolian deposition, the size of the particles carried by the winds decreasing eastward, especially as humidity also increases in that direction. This has meant that vegetation has stabilized the sands, only the loess dust being moved onward as in the dust storms of the eastern Pampa today. This fine-grained permeable Pampa loess may almost be considered as extensive cappings of fossil soils of fine tilth. On the hilly margins of the west, where river erosion and deposition play a more important part, pebbles occur, but otherwise the plain lacks all stones and gravel. The value of the rocks of the sierras of

Buenos Aires province for road making in such a stone-less land is obvious.

Over large areas the surface of the Pampa is so flat that rain in heavy downpours remains on the ground as sheets of water until it percolates through the loess. In other parts it accumulates in *cañadas* or *esteros* as slight depressions are called. The sierras provide a series of streams but these either peter out on the flatness of the plain, or by means of erratic channels reach marshy hollows where their flood waters are absorbed or evaporated. Only the Carcarañá, with its affluents the Ríos Tercero and Cuarto, reaches the Paraná. A series of small streams flow to the Paraná flood plain between Rosario and Buenos Aires, breaching the *barranca* or steep bank which fringes the flood plain on the south-west. Further south, the Río Salado, a line of marshy and sluggish swampy watercourses, gives the semblance of a river valley some 250 miles long and is often referred to as the Salado slough. In the first place it was partially caused by coastal uplift, but a subsequent rise of sea-level has meant the infilling of its tributary valleys.

The only other surface variations of significance are lines of dry valleys orientated from north-east to south-west, particularly in the central Pampa, some as much as 150 feet deep, some invaded by sand dunes and some marsh-filled, which reveal the power of wind erosion. On the western margins circular sand dunes appear wherever vegetation removal has permitted their formation. Further east these are gentler grass-covered undulations often with sandier soils than the surrounding plain, and on the Atlantic edge coastal dunes are features of extensive stretches of the coast. In the southern extensions of the Pampa, and particularly surrounding the Sierras del Tandil and de la Ventana, there occurs a *tosca* layer of a hard calcareous pan beneath the surface soil. Probably formed by the re-deposition of lime salts dissolved from the upper layers under the more arid conditions of the south, it is a thick and fairly continuous layer which on the sierra margins has been eroded in ravine-like formations.

The rainfall régime of this region has considerable differences from that prevailing in the regions to the north and west already considered, where a summer maximum is the common characteristic. Indeed it is the combination of relief and soils with climatic advantages which has provided the favourable physical environment on which the economic pattern of the region has developed. Rainfall decreases fairly steadily across the region from the north-east to the south-west. In Entre Ríos 45 inches is an average figure; Buenos

Aires has 38 inches; Mar del Plata 30 inches; Bahía Blanca 22 inches; thus most of the region receives at least 25 inches. More important is its distribution throughout the year, with the absence of any marked dry season. In Entre Ríos and the Plata estuary lands the maxima occur in spring and autumn. Similar trends appear as far south as Bahía Blanca, but as one progresses westward the dominant summer maximum increasingly reasserts itself.

Under natural conditions at the time of the coming of the European the greater part of the area was covered with tall bunch grass with intervening spaces between the tufts, the *pasto duro*, which has now been replaced in the grazing areas by imported European grasses or *pasto tierno* giving a good sward. Where water was present at ground level, stretches of tough reeds and rushes covered the swamps, sloughs, marshes and esteros as the various depressions were termed. In the Entre Ríos portion of the region the more plentiful rainfall gave rise to a park-land of trees and grass; while to the west as more arid conditions prevailed the grass cover gave way to a scrub forest usually referred to as *monte*. This consists of xerophytic deciduous trees and bushes and fringes most of the piedmont border of the Pampa.

This great region impressed the colonizing Spaniards but little. Although Santa Fé and Buenos Aires were founded in the last quarter of the 16th century from the nucleus of Spanish power at Asunción, they languished as unimportant settlements for quite 200 years, literally in the cul-de-sac of routes which led northwestward to Lima and thence via Panamá to Spain. They were useful as bases, either to assert Spanish sovereignty in view of the Portuguese penetration as far south as Colonia across the Plata estuary, or to check by means of forts along the Salado valley the northward attacks of the more hostile Indians to the south. They were also provisioning points for the river journey northward to Asunción. In the belt of territory between the Paraná–Plata and the Salado, pastoral estates raising cattle, horses and mules were established for local needs and to supply the Salta market far to the west. This area is known as the Pampa rim and from it has spread in progressive stages the utilization of the region in its present form.

The transformation from these simple and primitive beginnings to the modern economic structure of one of the world's greatest food and raw-material producing areas inhabited by 15 million people and with a considerable industrial and urban basis is not the result of one event but a combination of factors. Some of the more important were the coming of political stability in the new Argentina after the overthrow of the dictator Rosas in 1852; the expanding markets offered in the industrialized nations of Western Europe; the elimination of the nomadic Indian hunters to the south-west; the introduction of agricultural and pastoral techniques such as barbed wire fences, windmills and machinery; the influx of capital from a prosperous and expanding British economy; the immigration of Italian labour on both a permanent and a temporary basis to till and harvest the new lands; the spread of a railway network over the region; and last but not least, speedy trans-oceanic transport with refrigerated facilities to bridge the gap of 6,000 miles between producer and consumer.

In no other part of Latin America has there been such a comparable transformation of an apparently valueless region to one of the premier economically developed zones of the continent within much less than a century. It is a story more reminiscent of the settlement of the interior lowlands of North America where much of the development followed similar lines and for broadly comparable reasons.

The progressive development and changes in land use which have ensued now present a picture of several sub-regions where the prevalence of particular types of arable and pastoral farming differentiates one area from another. Yet there is still fundamentally the basic dominance of pastoralism in almost all the regions. The raising of beef cattle is the central theme of rural life, to which all other activities are more or less subsidiary. Second in importance comes the commercial growing of wheat, maize and linseed. It is within this double pattern that the activities of the separate zones must be viewed (Fig. 61).

(a) The Pastoral Zones

The whole of the Pampa is set in a background of pastoralism in which little attention is paid to arable farming of a commercial kind, except in very specialized areas. The flood plain of the Paraná east of Rosario, the pastoral lands of northern Entre Ríos (a continuation of the Corrientes lowland), and the great crescent of dry grazing lands swinging from northern Santa Fé around the Mar Chiquita and the Sierras de Córdoba to the Colorado valley south of Bahía Blanca form a pastoral rim to the whole region. Conditions vary considerably from the northern lands subject to cattle tick to those of the south largely devoted to sheep. Physical factors of aridity and of water meadows only suitable for animals, and human factors of relative isolation, tradition, and conditions within the rest of the Pampa all influence the utilization of these rim lands, which are marginal and transitional areas closely associated with the surrounding regions of the Northeast, the Northwest and Patagonia.

Within the eastern Pampa itself, however, some 20 per cent of the area is solely concerned with livestock raising. An approximately circular region with a radius of 80 miles, west of Cape San Antonio, in the province of Buenos Aires and including the Sierras del Tandil and de la Ventana is the principal breeding zone for beef cattle. Much attention is also given to sheep raising and increasingly to dairy cattle. It is an area of rich pasture grasses, and less than 20 per cent of the land is devoted to arable farming of any kind. Las Flores, Dolores, Maipú and Tandil are important centres in this zone, but population densities associated with such pastoral activities are obviously light and the area is the most thinly peopled part of the Pampa proper.

(b) The Pastoral, Wheat and Barley Zone

This is a fairly well-defined area stretching between Mar del Plata and Bahía Blanca and extending up to 50 miles inland from the Atlantic shore, and approximately bisected laterally by the railway connecting those two towns. Still predominantly pastoral, the animals' feed is supplemented by rye and oats as hay, but considerable land is devoted to growing wheat and barley as commercial crops, and in some years more than half the area is under these two grains. This is part of the tosca zone and is thus unsuitable to the long-rooted alfalfa. Tres Arroyos (40,000) and Necochea (30,000) are the principal urban centres, the latter exporting some wheat, and like Mar del Plata it is an important tourist holiday centre.

(c) The Pastoral, Alfalfa and Wheat Zone

Extending in a broad 300-mile wide zone towards the north-west interior, behind zones (a) and (b) and swinging northward to include eastern Córdoba province and northern Santa Fé province this is by far the largest area of the region, accounting for half the expanse of the Pampa. This is therefore the most widespread and typical economic structure prevailing, although there are obviously variations within such an extensive zone.

In few places is less than half the area of the farm devoted to pasture land, and towards the drier western margins this proportion

Plate 35. *Harvesting wheat on the Argentine pampa*

may rise to more than 80 per cent. Of the arable land, most is devoted
to the cultivation of alfalfa, and especially is this true in the western
areas of the province of Buenos Aires. The growing of this forage
crop is intimately linked with the whole economic history of Argentina, for its introduction marked the change-over from an industry
based on natural grasses to one relying on cultivated alfalfa. This
involved, however, the introduction of immigrant labour to plant and
cut the crop for the animals. A system of preparing the land for
alfalfa by growing several crops of wheat became the common rule,
the immigrants being tenants of the areas involved in this system.
The landowning pastoralists then became aware of the value of a
commercial crop as an additional product of their ranches, and thus
wheat became an integral part of this widespread economic system.
Throughout this zone it is the most important commercial crop, and
although acreages devoted to it vary considerably with world
demand, its subsidiary position within the pastoral economy enables
it to adjust itself to such fluctuations without serious dislocation of
the farming unit. A north–south line drawn through Córdoba and
Río Cuarto forms the western limit of wheat and alfalfa cultivation,
where both rainfall and ground-water supplies become inadequate.

Bahía Blanca (150,000), the port of outlet for all the southern reaches of the Pampa, is well situated for this zone, its three trunk railway lines to Buenos Aires, Rosario and Mendoza and their numerous feeders serving to export the wheat via this port and its several satellite ports situated on the north bank of the Naposta river. Puerto Ingeniero White with its great grain elevators is a typical member of this group. The construction of a natural gas pipe-line from the Neuquén field to Bahía Blanca and the establishment of a petrochemicals industry there have broadened its economic base. The flour milling and cereal industries of Santa Fé (204,000) on the northern limits of this zone are of considerable importance; and Río Cuarto (70,000), Rufino (11,000) and Villa María are other urban centres of some significance.

(d) The Pastoral, Alfalfa, Maize and Flax Zone

Occupying a belt 200 miles long and 100 miles wide aligned parallel to the barranca overlooking the Paraná flood plain, this zone stretches from the outskirts of Buenos Aires beyond Rosario and includes the important urban settlements of Pergamino (31,000) and Junín (60,000). A similar but distinct area lies across the flood plain of the Paraná in the province of Entre Ríos.

Fundamentally this is the richest agricultural region, and of the areas devoted to pastoralism it supports the heaviest density of rural population. The basis is essentially the same as in the pastoral-alfalfa-wheat zone, but here the favourable factors of rich soils, plentiful rainfall, high temperatures and the relatively rare occurrence of seasons of drought combine to permit the substitution of maize and flax for wheat, with consequently higher yields and greater profits for the farmers. There is in fact a close relationship between local climatic conditions and the areas devoted to commercial crops within the region. Entre Ríos is by far the most important area for flax, which withstands the higher temperatures experienced there, but maize and wheat are not unimportant. The Rosario district is the area *par excellence* for high yields of maize, but much flax is also grown. As soils become sandier, temperatures lower and droughts more frequent to the south-west, so wheat increasingly replaces maize in the farm economy.

More land has been extracted from the pastoral system and devoted to commercial agriculture in this zone than elsewhere, another indi-cation of the favourable environment prevailing for arable farming. In some areas the landowner has leased the whole of his estate to several tenants, but the prevailing system is still the basic one of intensive cattle production and alfalfa leys.

The maize exported from this zone accounts for three-quarters of this grain, and most leaves via the central collecting point and great port of Rosario (620,000), Argentina's second city. A monument on one of the city's skyscrapers contains two figures holding aloft a stalk of wheat and a cob of maize, symbols of the basis of its commercial prosperity.

San Lorenzo, upstream from Rosario, the terminus of the oil pipeline from Campo Durán has one of the largest petrochemical complexes in Latin America; and with the completion in 1977 of the harnessing of the hydro-electric resources of the Salto Grande on the Uruguay river, a vast addition of power will be available for the industrial development of the province of Entre Ríos.

(e) The Market-Gardening Zone

The enormous market provided by the $5\frac{1}{2}$ million people of the city of Buenos Aires and its immediate surroundings, the largest urban market in Latin America, has almost inevitably given rise to the growth of a zone surrounding it, from the mouth of the Río Uruguay almost to the mouth of the Río Salado. Well favoured with deep, fertile loess soils, adequate rainfall, few temperature hazards, and a network of transport facilities leading inward to the city, large areas of land are farmed on an intensive horticultural basis, and support a large rural population. Dairying has become specialized along the Plata fringe where water meadows support a rich growth of grass; fruit orchards have been developed in the Paraná delta where the fertile alluvial soils yield not only abundant crops of tree fruits and melons but willow material and poplar wood for the containers in which they are marketed; and the vegetable gardens are concentrated as near to the city or its transport routes as possible.

This five-fold gradation from a farming economy solely devoted to livestock through increasingly intense arable farming of alfalfa, wheat, barley, maize, flax, dairying, fruit growing and horticulture is not only distributed in space in the form shown on Figure 61, it is also an evolutionary pattern through time from complete dependence on pastoralism to increasing spread of activities into other farming types consonant with local physical and human conditions. The whole process began in the early 1890s and was instrumental in peopling this major Argentine region. Perhaps when one realizes its recent nature, it is less surprising that the pattern of extensive latifundia should still remain the prevalent type of land tenure. Indeed with such rapid changes and their inevitable impetus to increased land values, there was every inducement to maintain ownership of large estates. Especially was this possible when the immigrant tenants were satisfied with the opportunities which tenancy offered, for compared with their homeland this was 'a land flowing with milk and honey'.

Apart from their contribution to the economic development of Argentina, it is important to stress that, as in the case of Uruguay, no other region of Latin America has been such a large recipient of overseas immigrants. The great surge of immigration corresponds with a similar movement by similar people in North America, and dates from the 1880s with peak years in 1913 and 1929. In the last half of the 19th and the first half of the 20th century, some 7 million people entered the country. It is true that many of these were temporary seasonal workers, and many thousands of others also returned whence they came, but the contribution of Europeans to the ethnic composition of Argentina is overwhelming. In 1914 30 per cent of its people were foreign born, and although the proportion is now smaller (13 per cent) it still represents a total of 2,800,000 people. Some 45 per cent of the immigrants were Italians and 30 per cent Spanish, the remainder being of all nationalities of Europe and the Middle East. Their assimilation has been extraordinarily rapid, and minority problems scarcely exist. The main mass of the Argentine people is a homogeneous European unity, with little admixture of Indian ethnic strains. Only on the periphery, especially in the northwest and north-east, are there significant numbers of Indians and mestizos.

The region of the Pampa contains the best railway network in the continent (Fig. 62). Its construction on the thinly occupied landscape of last century was as easy as anywhere in the world. Indeed railways involved less difficulties than roads in the soft stone-less expanses. As their lay-out indicates, the principal objective was to secure direct and rapid transport of the economic riches of the region to the ports, and especially to Buenos Aires, for export. There were few settlements to attract a particular line to serve them; many towns grew up at convenient railway junctions where feeder lines linked into the system. Roads now lead off at right angles from the lines, forming a draught-board pattern of road and rail communication, varying in its intensity according to the developments of the area.

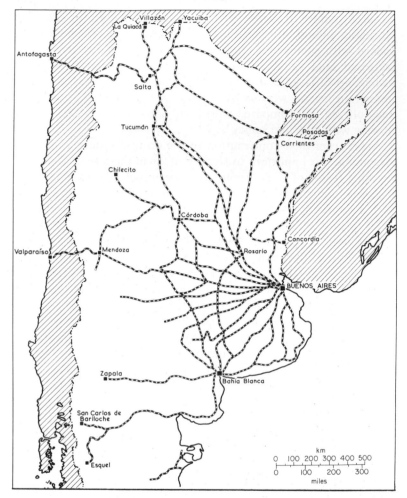

Fig. 62. *The railways of Argentina*
These provide the best national communications network in South America,
but they were designed primarily for the export market

Bahía Blanca, Córdoba, Santa Fé and Buenos Aires function as the
four nodal points linking the network with the peripheral regions.
With increased development of road transport and the modernization of the railway system, it is planned to eliminate 5,000 miles of
the least efficient parts of the rail network.

BUENOS AIRES

In this century, and particularly since 1914, when Argentina found itself deprived of its normal imports of manufactured goods which its primary products purchased, there has been an increasing tempo of industrialization, and almost all the country's factories occur in the Pampa cities. Apart from its dozen meat-refrigerating plants and the numerous plants processing raw material products such as cotton, wool, tobacco, sugar, fruits, flax and vegetable oils, strenuous efforts have been made to establish metallurgical, chemical and consumer-goods industries. Over a quarter of a million people are employed in mechanical and electrical types of industry including vehicle and machinery parts; and nearly all the textile needs of the nation, in wool, cotton and rayon, are met by home industries.

The industrial structure of Buenos Aires is only equalled by that of São Paulo (Fig. 63). There are at least 50,000 plants employing in greater Buenos Aires more than half a million workers. From the port of La Plata to the Paraná delta and in some dozen industrial suburbs of the capital, factories, large and small, manufacture an enormous variety of goods ranging from cement and heavy steel products through electrical goods and motor car assembly to rubber, cellulose, plastics, paper, leather, food and pharmaceutical goods, in addition to the service industries associated with electricity, communications, printing and many others. The development of a new steel plant and a deep water port at Ensenada, near La Plata, will further increase the economic significance of this industrial belt.

This industrial structure has been built upon tariff protection, an abundance of urban labour, the accessibility of the port to world suppliers of raw materials and capital goods, the very considerable areally-concentrated local market and the network of roads and railways to distribute the products of the industries.

In other parts of the Pampa too, industrialization accounts for much employment, the province of Santa Fé having some 19,000 plants and 140,000 workers. Petrochemical, tractor, truck, railway and agricultural machinery works feature largely in this structure, many of these being based on the Duperial chemical plant at San Lorenzo or the iron and steel plants of Villa Constitución, Rosario, Ramallo and San Nicolás.

The great drawback is lack of accessible power resources. With little coal and distant hydro-electric power sources, the country has had to rely on oil and natural gas from Patagonia and the Northeast

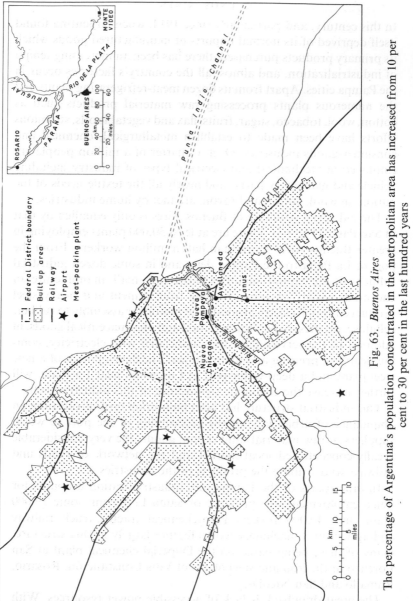

Fig. 63. *Buenos Aires*

The percentage of Argentina's population concentrated in the metropolitan area has increased from 10 per cent to 30 per cent in the last hundred years

and imported supplies of coal. In spite of efforts at decentralization of industry in peripheral cities like Córdoba, Salta, Jujuy, Tucumán and Mendoza, most of the factories occur in the suburbs of Buenos Aires and its satellite towns, La Boca, Avellaneda and Quilmes, and the city has spread especially southward at an amazing rate (Fig. 63).

The dominance of the city of Buenos Aires (5,574,000) is of great importance in the human geography of the region and of Argentina as a whole. Although not easy of access as a port, in view of the sand-banks of the Plata estuary, the inertia of its historical location, the convergence of land communications, and the capital invested in it will enable the city to overcome its disadvantages. Most of the import and export trade of the country is still funnelled through it and its outport La Plata (340,000). Its growth is as phenomenal as that of any city in the world, its inhabitants having increased fifty-fold in the course of a century. The commercial, financial, industrial, cultural and administrative nucleus of the whole nation, it represents in many respects a separate human region of its own, almost unique in a continent with more than its share of large cities.

Plate 36. *Buenos Aires is the hub of all rail and road transport, and the economic heart of Argentina. The obelisk commemorates the country's political independence*

PATAGONIA

Argentine Patagonia (Fig. 64) stretches through 1,000 miles of latitude from the Cólorado river to the shores of Beagle Channel, south
of Tierra del Fuego. It consists predominantly of a great plateau

Fig. 64. *Patagonia*
A land of sheep-farming, irrigated agriculture and oil drilling

sloping eastward from the Andes to the bays and headlands of the Atlantic coast, where it is truncated by the coastline, giving cliffs which range from some 200 feet high in the north and south to over 1,800 feet north of Comodoro Rivadavia. In parts a narrow coastal plain fringes these cliffs or a river valley pierces them from the west.

Although over extensive areas the surface is monotonously undulating or flat, it is by no means uniform in elevation. Considerable areas north and north-east of the Chubut river exceed 5,000 feet above sea-level, and most of the region is over 2,000 feet in altitude. Over large expanses there appears to be a peneplained surface at about the 2,200 feet level.

Into this surface has been incised a series of rivers draining eastward from the Andes. They flow, however, as misfit streams in wide canyons which at the time of melting of the great Andean ice sheets must have contained many thousands of times the volume of water which their present rivers hold. These great overflow channels have gouged out high-cliffed corridors with a poor development of lateral stream valleys, and they have the typical cross-section of rivers in arid country, with the more resistant rocks in their sides standing out as ledges above the less resistant, a feature which has been emphasized by wind erosion.

Structurally, the region probably rests on the same ancient crystalline foundation as that of the Pampa region, and it is sometimes referred to as the Patagonian Shield. In places, especially in the highest parts, this foundation of granite outcrops on the surface, as in the Añecón Grande, east of Lake Nahuel Huapí. Over most of the surface, however, there is a thick accumulation of predominantly continental deposits of a very long geological period, principally sandstones, but towards the coastal areas large expanses of clay and marls. This surface has suffered warping and faulting in the Andean period of mountain building, and over great stretches fissure flows of basalt have enveloped the landscape. On the Chilean frontier in the far south even small post-glacial volcanic cones give variety to the surface.

Along the western margin of the region the Andes with ice-fields, glaciers and moraine-dammed lakes, most of them draining to the Pacific, give a very different set of physical and human conditions to those prevailing over most of Patagonia.

Except for these Andean fringes the region suffers from aridity. Choele Choel in the north has less than 9 inches annually, Santa Cruz in the south less than 6 inches, and with such small amounts seasonal distribution is not of vital significance. Where the mountain locations still reap advantages from the Pacific cyclones precipitation may be as much as 40 inches as at Bariloche. Likewise, on the southern archipelagic margin polar maritime air masses raise Ushuaia's total to almost 20 inches.

The region is much colder in winter than similar latitudes on the Pacific coast, and correspondingly warmer in summer, yet nowhere are conditions extreme, temperature ranges varying between 20 and 30 degrees, increasing northward. Absence of pleasantly warm summer conditions plus prevalence of wind are the main climatic difficulties of the southern half of the region, but the relatively mild winters and warm summers of the north give a favourable basis where water exists for agriculture.

The Andean margins contain similar vegetational zones as on the Chilean side, with deciduous and evergreen beech forest and stretches of Chilean pines in the northern fringes. The national park of Nahuel Huapí contains a wealth of forest vegetation of this luxuriant mountain zone, and the combination of winter sports, fishing and unspoilt landscapes of mountains, glaciers, lakes and forests has made this zone a popular holiday area for the Pampa dweller.

Just as the transition of relief from the southern Pampa to northern Patagonia is a gradual one, so the deterioration of grassland into tussock bunch grass interspersed with low bush, which is the prevalent cover of the plateau, takes place slowly south of the Río Colorado. In some of the more exposed areas, especially in the coastal fringes, wind erosion and sand dune deposition are common features.

It is the shelter provided by the canyons which makes them the most favoured zones economically in the Patagonian region, and there, in the last quarter of the 19th century, the sheep pastoralists established their headquarters. Until that time Patagonia was an almost unknown land offering little inducement to settlement, and inhabited by hunting Indians living as their ancestors had done for many thousands of years. Just as the military campaign of 1879–83, which eliminated these indigenous people, opened the way to the colonization of the Pampa, so did it permit English, Welsh, Scottish and Spanish shepherds and capital to stock this thirsty land with sheep.

The colonization of Patagonia with its extensive sheep ranches (*estancias*) may be regarded as an appendix to the great events which were occurring in the Pampa to the north, offering different oppor-

Plate 37. *Patagonia is Argentina's greatest area of sheep pastoralism*

tunities to different people, but all part of a great and sudden transformation in which unknown lands became of value and the economic history of the nation was set on another course. In the Pampa it had been beef and hides; in Patagonia it was mutton and wool; the Lincoln, the Romney Marsh and Corriedale were substituted for the Shorthorn, the Hereford and the Aberdeen Angus.

The northern valleys of the Colorado, Negro and Chubut, however, offered arable potentialities. Protected from winds and sufficiently warm, the flat irrigated lands of the valley floors, early in this century, were brought under cultivation. Alfalfa is the principal crop, again as in the Pampa, to support the cattle and sheep pastoralism which is the basic economy. In the Negro valley, however, extensive irrigation has converted the area into a zone of pear orchards and vineyards of considerable importance.

Simultaneously came the development of Argentina's principal oilfield at Comodoro Rivadavia (50,000) which supplies the nation with 40 per cent of its needs, and is now connected by 1,100 miles of natural gas pipeline with Buenos Aires. Additional oil and natural gas fields have been developed during the 1960s and have considerably enhanced the contribution of Patagonia to Argentina's energy resources. An oil pipe-line from the Neuquén and Río Negro fields links Medanito and Allen with Puerto Rosales; natural gas is piped to Bahía Blanca from the Neuquén field; and another gas pipe-line feeds supplies from the Condor and Cerro Redondo deposits in Santa Cruz province into the Comodoro Rivadavia terminal. The Argentine extension of Chile's Tierra del Fuego oilfield in the north-east of the island exports its production from San Sebastián bay.

Considerable iron ore resources have been discovered at Sierra Grande, and a railway is being constructed to Punta Colorada on the Gulf of San Matías for shipment of the ore (after reduction and pelletizing) to the Plata estuary steel mills.

In its desperate search for power supplies, since the Second World War, the small and poor lignitic coal supplies of Río Turbio in the far south-west of the region (an extension of the Magallanes coalfield of Chile) have been linked by rail to the small port of Río Gallegos (16,000). This railway is typical of the transport system of the region, of long east–west arteries tapping the interior and bringing the products to the ports, which are little more than open roadsteads. In most cases their value is a seasonal one to take the wool clip away, but the coming of the motor lorry has reduced their importance considerably. The northern parts of the region are more favoured in that they are linked with the southern Pampa metropolis of Bahía Blanca. Choele Choel (1,500) and Villa Regina (2,000) are two important centres of the Río Negro irrigated belt. Neuquén (18,000) is near the dam which makes this zone possible. More than half the population of the whole region is found in these northern territories of Río Negro and Neuquén, and only Comodoro Rivadavia can be called an urban settlement of any size in the southern half of the region.

The economic contribution of Patagonia, although the region contains only $2\frac{1}{2}$ per cent of the population of Argentina, has more than doubled in recent decades, and its potentialities are by no means exhausted. Recognition of this is seen in the selection of three new 'growth centres' in the region, Zapala–Neuquén in the northern interior, and Puerto Madryn–Sierra Grande–Trelew–Rawson, and Río Gallegos–Río Turbio in the central and southern coastal areas respectively. Particularly significant is the increased attention being given to the great hydro-electric resources of the Southern Andes. The El Chocón–Cerros Colorados development in Neuquén province, involving an expenditure of U.S. $500 million, is one of the most ambitious ever undertaken in Latin America; and besides the provision of increased irrigation, will supply Buenos Aires with an additional electricity capacity of $1\frac{1}{2}$ million kW of power. The har-

Plate 38. *Raw material production still forms the economic basis of Latin America. Argentine wool (right) and Peruvian cotton (below) are but two examples from the semiarid lands of the southern and northern Andes*

nessing of the Futaleufú river in Chubut province will soon provide the power to enable a new aluminium plant at Puerto Madryn to produce 140,000 tons of this metal annually.

PROSPECTS AND PROBLEMS

The economic transformation of Argentina within less than a century from a thinly peopled region of little significance to the second commercial nation of Latin America is almost entirely the result of the utilization of the Pampa. This is not to under-rate the growing contribution of the North, Northwest and Patagonia to the nation's economic structure. Without, however, the pastoral and agricultural exports of the great plain the transformation could not have taken place.

Today these products account for 85 per cent of the total export trade, being mainly meat and its by-products, hides, wool and dairy products on the pastoral side, and wheat, maize, other cereals, flour and linseed on the agricultural side. There are obviously fluctuations from year to year, dependent on seasons and world conditions but the financial contribution from each side is not greatly dissimilar.

This raw material producing economy is, however, by no means static. It is one of the great advantages of the pastoral-agricultural system as practised in Argentina that it is resilient and adaptable to changing conditions. It is relatively easy, depending on price relationships between crops and livestock products, to convert quickly large areas usually used for crops into pastures, and vice versa. This has been, and will continue to be, a feature of the Argentine landscape. There are, however, some long-term tendencies which, in spite of these fluctuations, have been marked for a considerable period.

One of these is an increasing emphasis on the pastoral aspect. With more than 40 million head of cattle, numbers are 50 per cent higher than in the 1930s. This involves not only an increase in pastures, but increased attention to the cultivation of forage crops, and alfalfa in particular. It has also meant a contraction in acreage devoted to commercial crops, and the increasing concentration of these crops on the land most suitable for them. Linseed especially has fallen both in acreage and output to about half of its former significance, whereas the importance of sunflower seed continues to grow.

The increase in meat products has been very largely absorbed within the country, because one of the greatest changes in the economy has been the swing in the percentages from the export market to home needs as these statistics indicate:

	Percentage exported	Percentage consumed within Argentina
1925	43	57
1935	32	68
1942	37	63
1945	22	78
1947	31	69
1953	12	88
1962	20	80
1967	14	86

Until 1969 high wool prices similarly stimulated the maintenance of large flocks, and the figure of 46 million head, while lower than at the end of last century, is concentrated on a much smaller area, for in those years the Pampa reared far more sheep than cattle.

This increasing reliance on pastoralism is probably an inevitable tendency with increased demand at home and overseas. There is little to suggest that it has reached its maximum potentialities on the Pampa alone. The up-grading of cattle in the grasslands of the North, especially in the more favourable parts of the Chaco and the Corrientes plain, the elimination of cattle tick which would make this possible, the eradication of foot and mouth disease, and the fuller utilization of the lands of northern Patagonia as a rearing area integrated with the fattening lands of the Pampa offer immense additional possibilities.

On the other hand, the importance of Argentina as a supplier of beef to the United Kingdom market continues to decline. Not only does Britain now import 25 per cent of its consumption of beef, compared with 50 per cent in pre-war years, but Argentina's contribution to those reduced British beef imports fell in the 1960s from 60 to 17 per cent. The character of this Anglo-Argentine trade in meat has also changed, pre-packed special beef cuts replacing the once dominant sales of carcass beef.

The enlargement of the European Economic Community could have important repercussions on Argentina's meat exports, and already increased living standards in many European countries have provided enlarged markets in this respect.

In common with other large primary producers of wool and wheat, such as Australia, Argentina in the early 1970s has also felt the adverse effects of world surplus of wheat and of greatly reduced returns from wool sales.

The second major long-term tendency has been the increased attention paid to industrial crops and to grains other than wheat and maize, a movement in which all regions have played some part. The country's new self-sufficiency in rice is one example; the growth of production in sugar, wine, edible oils and fruits is another; but perhaps most outstanding is Argentina's rise as a cotton producer for its own textile industry, the area devoted to this crop being sixty times what it was before the First World War.

It is, therefore, in some ways surprising to realize that less than 20 per cent of the country's labour force is engaged in this pastoral and agricultural production, a smaller percentage than that of any other Latin American country except Uruguay (which shares similar conditions). It is in some way a measure of the efficiency of the industry and its high productivity. It also stresses the importance of the rise of industry in the republic's economy. An equally large labour force is now employed in the industrial sector, and while some 40 per cent of these are concerned with handicraft and domestic industry, at least 1 million men and women are in modern industry. As indicated previously, the scope of the products manufactured is very wide and the rise of increasingly elaborate industries is much faster than those of the simple processing kind. Capital goods to increase the country's industrial potential are, therefore, a high priority.

This spread of industry, typical of all Latin America, and in part the result of two World Wars and a great economic depression, appears almost contradictory in Argentina. Many of the industries are eminently suitable and related to its raw material production. The cotton and woollen textile factories are good examples. Less economically based is the attempt to establish heavy industry with mineral resources lacking in almost every respect. Few South American countries are less concerned with mining activities and only half of one per cent of its workers are miners.

The poverty of the nation in respect of fuel and power supplies needs no emphasis, and the increased use of its petroleum and natural gas resources (together these provide 90 per cent of the energy produced in Argentina), the development of its hydro-electric power resources, and the construction of a nuclear power plant at Atucha in Buenos Aires province all emphasize the country's concern to meet this deficiency of energy supplies.

In spite of these difficulties, however, the republic plans to expand its iron and steel production to an annual total of some 4 million tons by 1974 and so make itself self-sufficient in most products of this kind.

Another great change of a permanent nature and of real significance has been the growth of the country's economic independence. Until 1939 few politically independent states were so clearly 'colonial' in their economy as Argentina. Dependent on overseas sources, and Great Britain in particular, for supplies of consumer goods, for markets for its produce, for capital, for fuel for its railways, for technicians, and for shipping, no part of Latin America was so linked with Europe. It was largely by this means that its economic prosperity was established. With increasing nationalism and economic maturity, a great effort at emancipation resulted in the purchase of its railways, in the establishment of a merchant navy and in its conversion from an importer to an exporter of many manufactured products. At the same time changing world conditions have orientated a much larger share of its trade toward the United States.

Another feature of modern Argentina is the urban nature of its population. Again only in Uruguay does a smaller proportion of the population live in rural conditions. The distribution of Argentinians in this respect is as follows:

	Percentage
In cities over 100,000 population	39
In towns 10,000–100,000 population	14
In towns below 10,000 population	12
Rural population	35

This latter figure contrasts with 60 per cent for Latin America as a whole. The dominance and share of Argentine population represented by Buenos Aires has already been stressed, and the numbers of those in the larger cities (over 100,000) has tripled since the First World War. It is also an advanced degree of urbanization, for a much larger percentage of the urban population is engaged in industry than the Latin American average.

Considerable efforts are being made to encourage industrial development in cities other than the metropolis. Special tax and import duty concessions and public works programmes operate in all areas except within a 25-mile radius of the centre of Buenos Aires; and the designated growth centres in the Northeast, the Northwest and Patagonia are further steps to facilitate decentralized industrialization. Most foreign investment in the 1960s occurred in the metal using industries, in chemicals and petrochemicals and in the motor vehicle industry, which expanded six-fold during that decade.

All these striking economic changes have taken place on a general background which in fundamentals has remained remarkably stable. As in many other parts of Latin America, the basic land system of the large estate has withstood the vicissitudes of many financial and political stresses. That this should have been possible in Argentina where a transformation of much of the human geography has been carried out in some 90 years is largely due to the adaptations which the large estate permitted, particularly in respect of immigrant tenants. This was feasible because all parties, owners, tenants and the nation benefited from the adaptation. Yet most of the economic progress was achieved before 1930. Since then its remarkable economic growth based on the export of agricultural and pastoral products has slowed down almost to the point of stagnation. More products have been consumed internally, poor world prices have further curtailed its export earnings, and, as a result, imports have been reduced. Its urge for self-sufficiency has almost resulted in economic isolation.

Considerable political disharmony within the country plus persistent inflation have also contributed to the nation's erratic economic growth. If a more widespread stability and social progress could be established, few countries of Latin America have such inherent advantages for tremendous economic development. There are no cultural or racial cleavages, very limited population growth, very few shortages of skills, and no impossibly difficult terrain to cope with.

Traditions, however, take long to change. Military intervention in politics has so often interrupted the peaceful evolution of Argentina into a strong, economically viable, state. If this could be replaced by greater social and political maturity, no other nation of Latin America has greater possibilities to pass from the ranks of the under-developed to become a part of the developed world.

STATISTICAL SUMMARY — ARGENTINA

Area: 1,072,748 square miles

Population (1970): 23,360,000

Percentage of land

    (*a*) Arable   7%
    (*b*) Pastoral   43%
    (*c*) Forest   25%
    (*d*) Other   25%

Animal numbers

    (*a*) Cattle   46·7 million
    (*b*) Sheep   46·1 ,,
    (*c*) Pigs   3·5 ,,
    (*d*) Goats   5·1 ,,
    (*e*) Horses   3·8 ,,

Communications

    (*a*) All-seasons road mileage   47,388
    (*b*) Railway mileage   24,971
    (*c*) Air routes   960 million passenger miles
                                 13   ,,   ton miles

Principal products

    (*a*) *Agricultural*

Maize	9,360,000	metric tons
Wheat	7,020,000	,, ,,
Sorghum	3,820,000	,, ,,
Root Crops	2,398,000	,, ,,
Oilseeds	1,731,000	,, ,,
Sugar	1,100,000	,, ,,
Barley	570,000	,, ,,
Oats	425,000	,, ,,
Cotton	400,000	,, ,,
Rye	377,000	,, ,,
Rice	217,000	,, ,,

    (*b*) *Mineral*

Petroleum	15,953,000	metric tons
Coal	411,000	,, ,,
Iron	154,000	,, ,,
Lead	32,000	,, ,,
Zinc	27,000	,, ,,

Exports

    (*a*) *Total:* $1,610,000,000
    (*b*) *Percentage share of principal commodities*

Cereals and Linseed	27%
Meats	25%
Manufactures	13%
Oilseeds	6%

CHAPTER NINETEEN

Paraguay

ALTHOUGH larger than Uruguay or Ecuador, Paraguay has the smallest population of any of the Spanish-speaking South American countries; and in all Latin America only the much smaller Central American states of Panama, Costa Rica and Nicaragua have fewer people. This is largely the result of Paraguay's unfortunate history in the last hundred years and its resulting poverty and lack of development. Dragged into war and ruin by one of its dictators in a hopeless struggle against Brazil, Argentina and Uruguay in 1865, the country is a sad example of the disastrous folly of man and the misuse of a generally favourable natural environment.

It was the first of the Plata lowlands to be occupied. Asunción, founded as early as 1537, was the only major base of the Spanish Empire in the heart of this great river basin, and it formed an important link on the route from the rich silver mines of Potosí to the Atlantic. In pre-Spanish days the Guaraní Indians who occupied the region were aware of the agricultural wealth of the land they lived in, and in the 17th century the Jesuit missions established flourishing settlements, self-sufficient in foodstuffs, and exporting cotton, tobacco, yerba maté, meat, hides and wood.

All this was swept away by the avarice of Spanish landholders (who secured the expulsion of the Jesuits) and the succession of Indian revolts which followed. War and *coups d'état* made the nation an easy prey to the great economic strength of its neighbour, Argentina, and Paraguay's isolation and dependence on tenuous transport links completes its heritage of difficulties.

The north–south line of the Río Paraguay most effectively divides the country into two contrasting regions (Fig. 65):

(a) The Eastern Plateau, Hills and River Plain.
(b) The Western Paraguayan Chaco.

THE EASTERN PLATEAU, HILLS AND RIVER PLAIN

As its name implies the physical landscape of this region is far from homogeneous. Bounded on the west by the Río Paraguay, on the

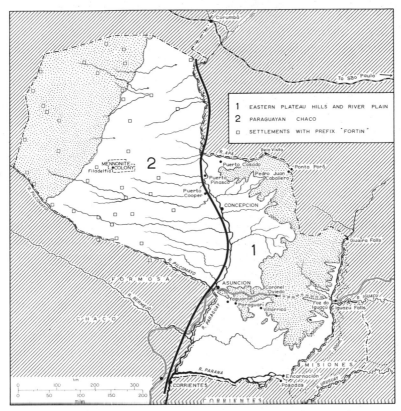

Fig. 65. *Paraguay, oriental and occidental*
The strategic nature of the settlement of the Chaco is indicated by its place
names

north by its tributary the Río Apá, on the south and south-east by
the Paraná and on the north-east by the Paraguay–Paraná watershed,
its geological structure for the most part is a continuation of the
Brazilian plateau. The old crystalline rocks underlie almost all the
region, but they are covered in many areas by sedimentaries, especially red sandstones; and the lavas and basalts of South Brazil
also extend into the eastern part of the region. Nearer the Paraguay
river the old plateau is masked by extensive alluvial deposits of the
river's flood-plain, especially in the south-west of the region. East
of Asunción the red sandstone hills interrupt this plain, and the
country's principal roads and railways use this higher and drier land

in linking the capital with the other main settlements and with the Paraná crossing in the south-east.

Rainfall is highest in the east, decreasing from 60 inches on the Brazilian border to 52 inches in Asunción, and there is little seasonal variation. Temperatures rarely fall below 60°F., but summer heat is often the greatest in the continent. This abundance of sunshine and rain has given a land of extensive forests and grasslands, offering considerable scope for agriculture, pastoralism and forestry.

Shortage of labour and of capital, political instability, and lack of security of tenure have all contributed to the relative neglect of development which is the fate of most of the region. Only in the zone around Asunción is there an efficient agricultural system. Elsewhere the burn-and-slash technique of shifting agriculture holds sway. In recent years much has been done by means of expropriation of unused lands, credit to farmers and control of prices to encourage farmers to utilize these eastern Paraguayan lands more efficiently. Many now own their farms and have a direct interest in increasing production, manioc, maize and beans occupying the greatest area. Both yield and quality are high, clear indications of Paraguay's agricultural potentialities. Pedro Juan Caballero in the far north-east of the region has become a small thriving centre of coffee production in a sound mixed-farming economy. Most of the arable land of the country is devoted to supporting the 1 million people in the Asunción area, where nearly half the people of Paraguay live; but yerba maté (gathered from the eastern forests), cotton, tobacco and vegetable oils are exported.

In the Paraguay flood-plain, on both sides of the river, but especially on the western margins, extensive stands of quebracho forest provide the country with a product which has long been important in the economic history of Paraguay. This is tannin, an extract obtained from the tree and used in tanning hides into leather. The principal factories are at Puerto Casado, Puerto Pinasco and Puerto Cooper all located on the Río Paraguay. The flood-plain also supplies the hides which still provide 2 per cent of the nation's exports. Cattle, however, need up-grading, both to make Paraguay a more important exporter of meat and to provide better quality hides which could then form the basis of an excellent leather industry. Petitgrain oil, distilled from bitter oranges, and used in perfume manufacture, is a specialist product of which Paraguay has almost a world monopoly, the Yaguarón district, south-east of Asunción, producing most of this essence. Production of citrus crops, especially grapefruit, appears to have a promising future potential. Cotton is one of the principal commercial crops grown and provides some 4 per cent of total exports.

There is very little development of industry, a fact again related to lack of capital, coal and oil. There is a considerable reserve of undeveloped water power but Paraguay has few funds for the high cost of constructing barrages to use this energy. The construction, however, of the Acaray hydroelectric plant to supply Asunción with power results in a large saving on fuel imports; and, in co-operation with Argentina, plans have been drawn up to utilize the Yaciretá–Apipé falls on the Paraná river. The only factories which exist produce cement and cotton textiles to supply the home market, or are concerned with the processing industries already mentioned. There is increasing emphasis on the production of finished wood products in preference to the export of sawn timber and logs.

Asunción (437,000), the capital and the only large city in the country, contains 18 per cent of the people. Situated opposite the confluence of the Pilcomayo with the Paraguay, where the eastern hills most closely approach the river, it is the goal of all routes, river, road and rail. Coronel Oviedo (45,000) and Villarrica (34,000) to the east are the next most important centres and serve as collecting and distributing centres for the agricultural, pastoral and forest products of plateau, hills and plain. They also are junctions on the road and rail routes to Encarnación (46,000) which is linked via Posadas on the Argentine side of the Paraná with Buenos Aires. The construction of bridges across the Pilcomayo, near Asunción, the Paraná at Foz do Iguaçú and the Apá at Bella Vista is a major development linking the country by road with Argentina and Brazil.

THE PARAGUAYAN CHACO

Although half as big again as the eastern region, the Chaco lands of Paraguay are almost uninhabited and they play an insignificant role in the country's limited economy. The scene of another disastrous war (1929–35), against Bolivia, which increased the area of this wilderness belonging to Paraguay, this region is far less favoured naturally to contribute to national prosperity.

Sloping very gradually and uniformly eastward from an altitude of some 900 feet to 200 feet above sea-level along the course of the Río Paraguay, this vast plain, as large as Great Britain, consists of unconsolidated deposits of sediments, largely sands and gravels, with clay-based hollows giving rise to water campos or shallow depressions, marshy in character and somewhat relieving the monotony of the bleak surface. Old channels and meander scars, flooded in rain storms, litter the landscape, but the Pilcomayo which forms the southern boundary is the only permanent river of any importance, and its marshy course is useless for navigation or water power. A bridge recently constructed across the river provides the only road link between Paraguay and Argentina.

Temperatures increase and precipitation decreases westward, the Bolivian margins being bleak arid areas of little promise. The vegetation of the wetter areas is quebracho forest, especially along the Río Paraguay, and mixed thorn scrub and coarse savana.

A few scattered Indian settlements and a Mennonite colony (of 13,000 people derived from Germany and Canada) west of Puerto Casado, based on subsistence activities, represent the principal population nuclei of this vast region. Quebracho is the great economic product, formerly for logs for export especially to Argentina and now for tannin, but otherwise the region produces very little of significance for the country's export trade.

Some 40 per cent of the nation's cattle population is located in the Chaco, but livestock development is hampered by the long dry season. An exploration programme in the central and north-western parts of the region seeking underground water for irrigation and drinking purposes is probably of greater long-term importance for the region than the persistent but fruitless efforts to find petroleum. The completion of the trans-Chaco road from Asunción to Filadelfia will provide all-weather communication with the region's most populous area and probably stimulate further development of a better road network.

PROSPECTS AND PROBLEMS

Apart from the inherent disadvantages from which Paraguay suffers as a result of its history, the great drawback of the country is its isolation in the heart of the continent. Until recently the only routes out were via the Paraná river, a winding course with shifting sand banks, or by a railway involving two long river ferry crossings of the Paraná at Encarnación–Posadas and Zárate–Ibicuy. The difficulty and length of these exits greatly increased the cost of freight, and while air travel has made a profound difference to passenger traffic, it has not yet contributed greatly to easing international trade. The completion of the Santa Cruz–Corumbá highway and railway and the road from Asunción into Brazil via Coronel Oviedo and the new bridge across the Paraná (Fig. 53) may drain some of Paraguay's trade eastward, and so provide alternative outlets for its products, via Brazilian ports. Similarly the construction of bridges across the Pilcomayo near Asunción and the Apá at Bella Vista will facilitate road transport into Argentina and Brazil respectively; and road transport is rapidly becoming as important as river transport. The establishment of free port facilities in both Paraguaná and Antofagasta, in addition to the traditional exit ports of Rosario and Buenos Aires reflect these changes in the country's transport links. However, the considerable economic influence which Argentina can exert on Paraguay in such matters as capital investment (especially in the quebracho and pastoral industries) and communications is still strong. Argentina buys 27 per cent of Paraguay's exports and sells to the landlocked state 17 per cent of its imports.

Paraguay also suffers in full measure from the price fluctuations on world markets for the agricultural, livestock and forest products which constitute all her exports; and for many years the country has had an adverse balance of trade. This situation is made worse by the need to import food such as wheat, which could be produced within Paraguay. Increased industrialization of raw materials before export, expansion of domestic production of materials such as cement, and the growth and diversification of exports, are steps being taken to overcome the deficit.

Endemic dictatorship, political repression and slow social change add to the republic's problems.

Many Paraguayans, overwhelmed at the difficulties inherited by their country, have sought their livelihood in their richer neighbours' lands, and unlike most Latin American states, emigration to Brazil and Argentina of professional people, workers and peasants, has been a powerful influence which has further handicapped Paraguay's recovery and development.

STATISTICAL SUMMARY — PARAGUAY

Area: 157,047 square miles

Population (1970): 2,396,000

Percentage of land

    (*a*) Arable   2%
    (*b*) Pastoral   25%
    (*c*) Forest   51%
    (*d*) Other   22%

Animal numbers

    (*a*) Cattle   6·0 million
    (*b*) Sheep   0·4   ,,
    (*c*) Pigs   0·8   ,,

Communications

    (*a*) All-seasons road mileage   1,859
    (*b*) Railway mileage   274

Principal products

    Agricultural
        Root Crops   1,620,000 metric tons
        Maize   225,000   ,,   ,,
        Sugar   39,000   ,,   ,,
        Beans   27,000   ,,   ,,
        Oilseeds   26,000   ,,   ,,

Exports

    (*a*) Total: $48,000,000
    (*b*) *Percentage share of principal commodities*
        Meat products   28%
        Timber   17%
        Oilseeds   10%
        Tobacco   9%
        Quebracho extracts   4%

CHAPTER TWENTY

Uruguay

THE smallest of the South American republics, created as a buffer state between its two powerful neighbours Argentina and Brazil, shows a remarkable homogeneity of physical and human geography. Forming the southern flank of the Brazilian plateau, it is an area of gentle relief, no part exceeding 2,000 feet in height, and only a relatively small area being over 650 feet. The principal granite ridges known as *cuchillas* occur in the eastern part of the country, while to the west fertile limons, wind-blown soils, cover considerable areas giving way in the Uruguay river lowland to alluvial plains. Most of the drainage is to the Uruguay river (which is the boundary with Argentina) and its tributary the Negro which bisects the country along an east-north-east–west-south-west axis.

Submergence of the Plata–Atlantic shorelands is seen in such features as the ria of Santa Lucía and Montevideo harbour, but coastal deposition is slowly making the coastline more uniform, Lagoa Mirim being shut off by deposits swept along the shore, and dunes being a feature of the coast.

Although it is the only Latin American state completely outside the tropics, it experiences no great range of temperature, and rainfall amounts, although irregular, are rarely inadequate and are all-seasonal in character.

Soils and climate have given rise to a prairie cover, except along the river margins, and this grassland is the basis of Uruguay's economy.

Occupied effectively relatively late, due principally to the clash of Portuguese–Spanish interests in the region and its lack of mineral wealth, it was developed by *gauchos* for the sake of the hides of wild cattle introduced earlier. By the early 19th century a more settled pastoral system had evolved with cattle *estancias* as the principal feature of the cultural landscape. The introduction of sheep, and the immigration of two-thirds of a million Spanish and Italian immigrants, many via Buenos Aires, completed the occupation of the country and the entrenching of the pastoral pattern as the dominant

361

form of land use. In no other Latin American country is pastoralism so important in the national economy. There are 22 million sheep and 8 million cattle, eight times as many sheep as people, and nearly three times as many cattle as the total population. Forty per cent of the country's exports by value are wool, and another 40 per cent are meat products, hides and skins. More than 7 out of every 10 acres in the country consist of natural grassland on which are raised large flocks of Merino, Lincoln and Romney Marsh sheep and herds of Hereford and Shorthorn cattle, often grazing together. Although there are some seventy estancias each exceeding 25,000 acres in extent and more than half the nation's land is in estates of more than 2,000 acres, there are many small and moderate-sized farms, and *latifundia* in Uruguay is not the economic problem it was in Chile or in Mexico. There is increasing emphasis on sheep farming, until recently stimulated by high wool prices, but also a continuing process of the last three-quarters of a century. The quality of the animals raised is very high, and the intensity of the pastoral economy is seen in the fact that the natural pastures support almost one animal per acre, and very little additional feeding stuff is used.

The country is so homogeneous that any regional division must to some extent be an arbitrary one. Based principally on differing economic utilization the two principal areas are (Fig. 66):

(*a*) The Plata–Uruguay Agricultural Lowland.

(*b*) The Pastoral Plateau Interior.

THE PLATA–URUGUAY AGRICULTURAL LOWLAND

This zone, stretching from Salto on the River Uruguay to Maldonado where the south coast of Uruguay swings north-eastwards, and extending inland for an average width of some 50 miles, is by no means all lowland. North of the Río Negro hilly uplands stretch down to the Uruguay river and the region also includes the east–west trending extension of the Cuchilla Grande. Land rarely rises above 600 feet, however, and nowhere does altitude or slope prevent economic land use. The lower Uruguay coastlands are for the most part an alluvial flood-plain of that river. Although granite and marble outcrops in many localities, and is quarried north of Maldonado at Minas, most of the region is underlain by sands, grits, clays and æolian-formed limons. There is a good network of drainage westward to the Río Uruguay and southward to the Plata. The area is influenced by the proximity of the estuary and the Atlantic, so that temperature ranges usually do not exceed 20°F. (50–70°F.), and on the whole there is less likelihood of the periodic droughts being so pronounced in their effect compared with the interior.

Relief, soils and vegetation vary so considerably within the region that there is a great diversity of land use. Agriculture, however, is the principal occupation of the rural dwellers and has become of

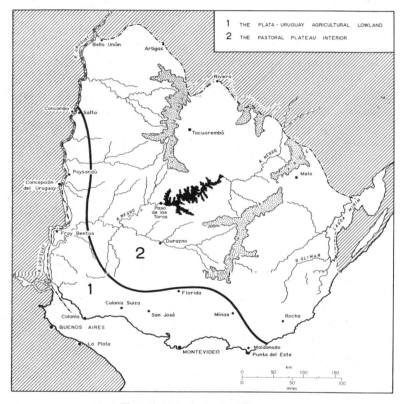

1 THE PLATA - URUGUAY AGRICULTURAL LOWLAND

2 THE PASTORAL PLATEAU INTERIOR

Fig. 66. *The regions of Uruguay*

much greater importance in the post-war years. As a result of three bad seasons for wheat cultivation which led to the purchase of grain from Argentina, wheat-growing was subsidized. The acreage under this crop more than doubled compared with pre-war years to nearly 2 million acres, and surplus production, much of it in the form of flour, is now exported to Brazil. Maize, rice, oats and barley are also grown for domestic consumption and animal feeding-stuffs,

and this cereal production, plus vegetable oil seeds, especially sunflower, forms the basic foundation of most of this agricultural
region. Flax is second only to wheat in the acreage occupied, and
provides a useful source of vegetable oil both for home needs and
export. Malting barley and rice are also significant exports. Output
of all agricultural commodities, however, fluctuates considerably in
response to quite variable weather conditions, especially in respect
of drought and frosts. Nevertheless the country is self-sufficient in
most foodstuffs which, climatically, can be grown within the republic.

There are specializations in some areas of the zone, the most
important of which are vines for wine production in the zone tributary to Montevideo, sugar cane, oranges and tangerines in the Salto
district, and sugar beet north of Maldonado. Similarly the proximity
of the principal centres of urban population throughout this region
has led to increasing concentration on dairying and fruit growing
especially in the portion of the belt facing the Plata. Exports of dairy
produce and citrus fruits have also been developed. There is obviously also no lack of pastoral farming, and less than half of the
total area of this region is under crops. San José to the north-west
of the capital is an important mixed farming centre, and Colonia
Suiza to the west is a settlement owing its origins to Swiss agricultural
pioneering and a reminder of the immigrant character of most of the
Uruguayan people.

Fishing is of some importance, especially where the Plata estuary
merges into the open Atlantic, but far more employment is given to
those catering for the large tourist industry provided by the extensive
beaches east of Montevideo, which attract as many as 150,000 foreign
tourists, mostly from Argentina, in addition to the considerable
internal supply of holiday-makers. Punta del Este, near Maldonado,
is the principal centre.

Industrial activity is also at its greatest in this zone. Apart from
the important meat-freezing plants at Montevideo and Fray Bentos
with their wide range of meat products and by-products, there are
dairy product industries making butter and cheese, woollen spinning
and weaving mills, leather factories, breweries and industries processing products like wine, flour, vegetable oils and cement. All these
are based on local raw materials; but in spite of small power resources, high costs and a limited domestic market, other industrial
efforts such as cotton textiles and electrical and chemical establishments, using imported raw materials, have also taken root.

The concentration of agricultural, industrial, tourist and fishing activities within this region, and the historical development of the state northward from the Plata estuary shore has resulted in this zone having considerably more than half of the 3 million people of the country. Forty per cent of all Uruguayans live in Montevideo (1,200,000), the capital and chief industrial, commercial and route centre, and this has led to a rather sharp antithesis between the capital and the rest of the nation which is not in the best interests of the country. No other Latin American country has such a large proportion of its population in one city, and this is even more emphasized by the fact that no other town in Uruguay is one-twentieth of Montevideo's size.

The region also contains the next two largest towns, Paysandú (65,000) and Salto (65,000), both on the navigable Río Uruguay and both drawing considerable importance from the pastoral zone eastward, beyond the agricultural zone. Fray Bentos, too, is a meat-canning centre, and Colonia serves as a ferry port to Buenos Aires. This latter town is a reminder of the clash of the claims of Brazil and Argentina to Uruguayan territory, for it represents the southernmost strategic claim by occupation in 1680 by Brazilian settlers, and it changed hands many times during the 18th century. Montevideo was not founded until 1726, and it was during the 19th century that it grew into the national metropolis, being the port through which the great immigrant stream of Italians and Spanish entered to develop the economic resources of the country. Having a more accessible harbour than Colonia higher up the estuary, and occupying a central coastal position, it has become one of the great exporting ports of Latin America to which all roads and railways in the nation lead, and its significance as an international airport is considerable.

THE PASTORAL PLATEAU INTERIOR

The remainder of the country, accounting for three-quarters of its total area, is an area of rolling relief bounded by the Brazilian frontier, the Atlantic, the Río Uruguay and the agricultural zone. The most conspicuous relief features are the two major cuchillas, or ranges of hills, Cuchilla Grande and Cuchilla de Haedo, which spread southward from the Brazilian plateau pointing in the direction of Montevideo. The Río Negro flowing westward towards the Río Uruguay from its source in Brazil forms a broad valley basin feature between these two cuchillas.

The foundation of most of this region is composed of granites, gneiss and red sandstones with an extension of the basaltic plateau of Brazil in a broad band for some 70 miles east of the Río Uruguay. The broad swells and corridors which separate the major and minor cuchillas are floored with clay and re-sorted sedimentary deposits, above which the more resistant tor-like rocks stand out as cuesta formations and rocky slopes. The latter are frequently bracken-covered, and in the north-eastern valleys stretches of mixed forest link the region with its Brazilian counterpart. Throughout most of the area, however, natural grassland is the dominant vegetational cover.

This is the Uruguayan pastoral region *par excellence*; a land of cattle and sheep estancias with paddocks or' *potreros* fenced and managed to secure the best seasonal use of the grass, wide driveways for the animals, the estancia headquarters with wool barns, shearing sheds, stables, the shepherds' and herders' houses, and the *estanciero's* residence set in a delightful garden of fruit, vegetables and flowers.

On this pastoral basis, as monocultural as any in Latin America, Uruguay has prospered as a major producer of meat and wool for Western Europe. The picture of flourishing prosperity has, however, some dark patches. Animal diseases, especially foot-and-mouth disease and tick fever, are a recurrent problem, although less so south of the Río Negro in the cooler part of the plateau. Locusts and droughts are other difficulties which have to be met, and soil erosion dangers increase wherever there is a tendency to over-stocking.

Several *saladeros* or factories preparing salted beef or *charqui* still survive as relics of the days when this was the principal utilization of the animals raised on the Uruguayan pastures, and their products are exported to Brazil and Cuba, one at Artigas being adjacent to the international boundary. The better-quality animals are sent by rail and road to the freezing works and canning factories at Montevideo, Salto, Paysandú and Fray Bentos. The two latter towns are now linked by new modern bridges across the Uruguay river with the Argentine road network.

The meat exporting industry, however, has contracted in the post-war years owing to the competition of agricultural extensions and high wool prices and the increasing domestic consumption of meat. Cattle are relatively more numerous north of the Río Negro, except in the agricultural zone where they form an integral part of the mixed farming economy practised there, and where much land is also devoted to fattening the animals.

Plate 39. *Pastoralism dominates the economy of Uruguay, prize Hereford cattle*

Dairying and some agriculture is carried on near the principal centres like Melo, Rivera, Artigas, Bella Unión and Durazno, and large quantities of rice (half of which is exported) are grown in the area west of Lagoa Mirim and east and west of Tacuarembó. These small centres have grown up at junctions on the principal roads, which for the most part follow the cuchillas and avoid the wooded valley bottoms. Railways, built by British capital, tend to follow a similar pattern. The harnessing of the Olimar river for irrigation and hydro-electric power will permit a significant expansion of rice cultivation in the Lagoa Mirim area.

The south-eastern extension of the region reaches the Atlantic shore where a succession of largely undeveloped beaches offers great scope for the extension of Uruguay's Riviera. This dune coast is backed by plantations of pine and eucalyptus and fields of sunflower.

A large hydro-electric power station has been built, almost in the geometric centre of the country at Paso de los Toros, where subsidiary spurs of the Cuchilla Grande and Cuchilla de Haedo approach each other and constrict the Río Negro valley. A second dam at El Palmar will further increase the power output of this river. Most of this electricity is consumed in Montevideo's homes, offices and industries.

There is a good network of road and rail communications south-ward towards Montevideo and northward into Brazil, but east–west travel is less easy.

PROSPECTS AND PROBLEMS

With the possible exception of El Salvador no Latin American nation has so fully utilized all its national territory as Uruguay. There are no undeveloped areas awaiting pioneer settlement. This does not mean that all the country's area is used to the best advantage, and there is considerable scope for more intensive development and conservation. The pastoral industry is an extractive one, and in-sufficient attention is paid to the use of fertilizers, the growth of leguminous plants for subsidiary feeding of animals (especially as a reserve for drought periods), the improvement of pastures, and other aspects of scientific farming. The extension of agricultural land is a welcome step from the overwhelming dependence on pastoralism, and the diversification into a mixed farming economy offers many possibilities.

The lack of important supplies of minerals and fuel resources and the small size of the internal market prevent the development of an elaborate industrial structure, although the stimulus of shortages caused by two world wars has led to the growth of several industries lacking a sound economic basis which are protected by subsidies. Three-fifths of its industries, however, are those of textiles and food-processing. Indeed the principal industrial function of Uruguay would seem to be increased processing of its natural products, wool, meat, skins, oil-seeds and wheat; and there are several additional sources of hydro-electric energy which could be harnessed to supply the necessary power.

In no other Latin American country are so many activities and industries under state control. Rail transport, banking, insurance, telephones, electricity, water supply, oil refining, fisheries and the capital's meat supply are merely some of the aspects of the economic life of the nation which have been nationalized. Similarly, the country has the reputation for advanced social legislation which makes its standard of living, especially of the citizens of Montevideo, amongst the highest in the continent.

Considering the proximity of its two neighbours Brazil and Argentina, it has maintained its own individuality to a remarkable

Plate 40. *The Plata estuary is Latin America's greatest waterway, the capital cities of Buenos Aires and Montevideo dominating its commerce. Montevideo harbour*

degree, and has pursued an independent foreign policy with especially close ties with Great Britain, to whose mediation in the Brazilian–Argentine struggle it largely owes its independence. The development of more road transport links with Argentina by the new bridges over the Uruguay river at Fray Bentos and Paysandú, and growing economic integration on a complementary basis in some industries, such as that of motor vehicle components, presage much closer collaboration between these two Plata estuary nations.

No nation of Latin America, however, has experienced such economic deterioration relative to its former prosperity as Uruguay in recent years. There is a high incidence of unemployment and inflation, and there has been in the last decade a decline of real income *per capita* of not less than 10 per cent. Much of this situation can be attributed to Uruguay's dependence both on exports of primary products and fluctuating world prices and on increasingly high-priced imports, but there are also many serious defects in the internal structure of the republic. Among these are the lack of new capital investment, increasing obsolence of its industrial plants (which led to the United Kingdom suspending meat imports from Uruguay in 1968 on grounds of hygiene and sanitary controls in the frigorificos) and the need for widespread financial, social and economic reform. (Although its population growth rate is the lowest in Latin America, one-third of its work force of 900,000 is employed in the services sector of the economy.)

Uruguay has, therefore, been subject recently to an unusual amount of political and social tension; and there are few apparent easy solutions for its many economic difficulties. Its dependence on overseas markets for its food exports must inevitably continue, and, in this respect, there are increased opportunities for sales of meat to southern and south-eastern Europe. The location of the country is also propitious for exporting to the two largest urban markets of Latin America, Buenos Aires and São Paulo; and at least part of the remedy for its present situation would seem to be more attention to crop production by more intensive methods and a modernization of its industrial structure, including transport.

STATISTICAL SUMMARY — URUGUAY

Area: 72,172 square miles

Population (1970): 2,897,000

Percentage of land
(a)	Arable	12%
(b)	Pastoral	74%
(c)	Forest	3%
(d)	Other	11%

Animal numbers
(a)	Cattle	8·1 million
(b)	Sheep	21·9 ,,
(c)	Pigs	0·4 ,,

Communications
(a)	All-seasons road mileage	5,489
(b)	Railway mileage	1,872
(c)	Air routes	45 million passenger miles

Principal products

    Agricultural

Root Crops	158,000
Wheat	147,000
Maize	117,000
Rice	116,000
Oilseeds	83,000
Sugar	70,000

Exports

    (*a*) Total: $179,000,000

    (*b*) *Percentage share of principal commodities*

Wool	44%
Meat products	34%
Hides	9%

CHAPTER TWENTY-ONE

The Falkland Islands

THE Falkland Islands, known to Latin Americans as the Malvinas, lie some 300 miles to the east of Magellan's Strait and may be regarded as a detached fragment of the Patagonian region. They consist of two main islands, East and West Falkland, together with many smaller islets, with a total area of some 4,600 square miles. The surface is undulating moorland plateau of an average height of 1–2,000 feet, covered with tussock grass and in some areas 'runs' of angular boulders.

The climate is cool and windy with rain at all seasons, absence of summer conditions being a marked characteristic. The bleak and inhospitable character of the weather, however, provides a good environment for sheep-rearing which is the islands' only occupation. Some 2,000 tons of wool and skins are exported annually from 600,000 sheep which graze on over 3 million acres of land. More than one-third of the sheep and farm land is owned by one company. There are no other exports as attempts to introduce a frozen mutton industry in the period 1953–5 failed.

Population has remained at a total of 2,200 since the 1930s, half of whom are concentrated in the one settlement of Stanley which serves as the collecting and distributing centre for the islands. Internal communications are poor, although a seaplane service links the capital with outlying farms. External maritime links are maintained via Montevideo.

The islands were first settled in 1764 by the French, but in the early 19th century they were uninhabited. From this period stems the rivalry between Britain and Argentina for their possession; but it was not until the decade 1870–80 that the present economic pattern became established. This is now completely dominated by commercial ties with the United Kingdom, the population being wholly Anglophile in every respect.

The Falkland Islands' dependencies include South Georgia with its important whaling stations, and a sector of the Antarctic continent south of Drake Strait. Since 1940 conflicting Argentine and

Chilean claims to this latter area and the establishment of bases there by both these republics have made Graham Land a zone into which Latin Americans have penetrated for both strategic and scientific objectives.

STATISTICAL SUMMARY — FALKLAND ISLANDS

Area: 4,618 square miles

Population (1970): 2,200

Animal numbers
    Sheep   0·6 million'

Exports
    (*a*) Total: $3,000,000
    (*b*) *Percentage share of principal commodities*
        Wool   97%
        Hides   3%

PART V

PORTUGUESE AMERICA

CHAPTER TWENTY-TWO

Brazil

BRAZIL is so immense that it is difficult to convey an impression of its area. Only Russia, China and Canada extend over a greater area. As only a relatively small proportion is north of the equator, it is the greatest nation of the southern hemisphere, both in extent and in population. Stretching for some 2,300 miles from east to west and the same distance from north to south its territory is in a relatively compact form, with only 7 per cent of its area outside the tropics. Its boundaries are adjacent to every state in South America except Chile and Ecuador, and its Atlantic coastline exceeds 4,500 miles in length.

Nor is it only in size that Brazil is the Latin-American giant, for, although vast areas are uninhabited or thinly peopled, no other country of Latin America has half as many people (Fig. 8). There are, in fact, approximately four Brazilians for every Argentinian, and two Brazilians for every Mexican. Growing at the rate of over 2 millions each year, and with an expanding economy, it is clear that Brazil's significance in the Americas of the future is and will be increasingly far-reaching.

Although for most of its colonial history consisting of a series of coastal settlements with limited hinterlands, the nation absorbed, largely by default of Spanish interest in forested lands, this huge expanse of territory right up to the slopes of the Andes in the west and those of the Guiana plateau in the north. Only in the extreme south, as increasing interest developed in the lands tributary to the Plata estuary, was there a serious clash of rivalries with Spanish America, and from this was born the state of Uruguay.

In spite of its huge area, the relatively simple structural basis of an old shield area covering 60 per cent of Brazil, a great lowland river basin and the fringes of the Guiana massif, is indeed striking. The units are on the same enormous scale as the country they form. The Brazilian plateau is one of the largest old tableland areas of the globe, and if the Guiana block be considered as merely a detached portion, its size is all the more impressive. Similarly, the enormous

377

drainage basin of the Amazon extends its network over 60 per cent
of the country and completes the galaxy of superlatives in being the
world's greatest hot forest.

Fig. 67. *The sections of Brazil*
A regional division based on state boundaries

Within this fundamental basis there are literally dozens of major
regions which could be differentiated on grounds of physical and
human geography. To do so would present a picture of such complexity as to be almost valueless. It is proposed, therefore, to treat
the regional geography on the basis of the territorial division of the
country as recognized by most Brazilian geographers. Within each
of these five major human regions, the principal sub-regions of
which they are composed will be indicated, and the various influences,

physical and human, which have created the many facets of the whole will be analysed.

The division has also some historical basis in relation to the growth of the Brazilian nation, and therefore it will be useful to treat each region in the broad chronological order in which their main significance was established. The pattern, controlled by state boundary lines for statistical convenience, is, as indicated in Fig. 67:

1. The Northeast.
2. The Southeast.
3. The South.
4. The Central States.
5. The Amazon.

THE NORTHEAST

Although this is a vast territory covering almost one-fifth of the area of the country and containing about one-third of its people, the unity of its regional geography is remarkable (Figs. 68 and 69). Whether looked at from the physical or human viewpoint, certain regional characteristics can be delineated which set it apart from the rest of the nation. The more significant of these will appear as the constituents of the region are analysed.

It contains the two basic components of the structure of the Brazilian plateau. These are the crystalline granitic and gneissic foundation and the relatively horizontal sheets of sedimentary rocks which cover considerable areas of the foundation. In the Northeast approximately half the region is formed of each of these formations. The eastern half, east of a line joining Parnaíba on the coast to Barra on the São Francisco, consists of the old complex of crystalline rocks peneplained into extensive level surfaces, from which rise residual serras, mainly of granite, aligned on both north–south and east–west axes. The eastern part of this peneplain is called the Borborema plateau. Little of this exceeds 3,000 feet in height but slopes to the east coast are abrupt, while those to the north coast are much more gradual. The western half of the region still retains the sandstone covering, which presents a cuesta scarp facing east, as the layers dip towards the Amazon basin. This scarp is called the Serra Grande and follows closely the western boundary of the state of Ceará, the basin of the Parnaíba being almost exclusively on the sandstone surface. Other remnants of this sedimentary covering exist on the eastern crystalline base, the largest, some 100 miles long and 40 miles wide, being the Serra do Araripe (where the boundaries of the states of Piaui, Ceará and Pernambuco meet). Their extensive level highland scarp-bounded surfaces are so different from the ridge-like crystalline serra that *chapada* or tableland is a much more suitable term, corresponding to the Spanish *mesa*.

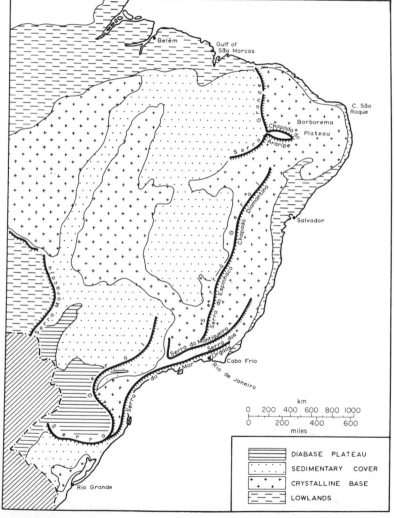

Fig. 68. *The Serras and structural elements of Eastern Brazil*

Younger sedimentary rocks fringe the east coast from Cape São Roque southward and provide a coastal plain, varying in width throughout most of its length from 20 to 40 miles. In some areas, however, the crystalline core reaches the coast and pinches out the coastal plain into relatively isolated units. South of the mouth of the São Francisco these sediments extend much further inland, encircling Salvador bay. This coastal fringe has been subject to both uplift and depression. The former has created low mesas as the rivers have cut through the sandy sediments; the latter has permitted the drowning of the Paraguacú mouth creating Bahia bay, and the silting of the coastline with long beaches and lagoons and the formation of coastal reefs for 200 miles to the north and to the south of Recife. These dunes, lagoons and reefs and the coconut palm stands remind one of the South Sea islands.

The northern coastal plain is much more extensive, and a gradual transition and widening takes place westward from Cape São Roque until it merges into the deltaic lands of the Amazon mouth. Subject also to depression, the coastal sand deposits have been flooded by the Atlantic, and the Gulf of São Marcos in Maranhão state is another product of submergence.

With the one great exception of the Rio São Francisco, all the rivers of the region are self-contained within the region. On the north they consist of the large basin of the Parnaíba system, draining the sandstones west of the Serra Grande, and numerous smaller rivers draining the northern slopes of the plateau. In the east a similar series of rivers has entrenched itself in the crystalline surface, and one of these (the São Francisco) has been sufficiently powerful to cut back and capture a great expanse of southern plateau drainage. All these rivers are good examples of superimposed drainage, of a river system evolved on an earlier landscape of the sedimentary cover. Their courses now continue irrespective of whether that cover has been removed or not and largely irrespective of the crystalline base they have revealed. The rivers of the western half of the region have a more regular flow, largely the result of the sedimentary surface and higher rainfall. Those of the east flood rapidly during storms when run-off from the crystalline rocks is rapid.

The relief contrasts between coastal and plateau zones are conspicuous, but even more so are the sharp differences in rainfall amounts experienced in the region. South of Cape São Roque the coastal strip, following the broad sweep of this north-eastern bulge, 15 miles wide in the north broadening to a width over 50 miles in

Fig. 69. *Brazil's Northeast*
The states of plantation settlement and of the *sertão*

Alagoas state, receives more than 50 inches of rain annually. South of the São Francisco mouth the belt again narrows to some 25 miles width. A small strip centred on Recife has more than 60 inches. West of the Serra Grande there is also fairly adequate rainfall, São Luis having over 80 inches. Between these two zones of sufficiency there stands a vast area, comprising all the crystalline plateau of the east, where rainfall is both small in total amount and very irregular and unreliable from year to year. In a few limited areas of high relief such as the Chapada do Araripe the amount may rise to 50 inches, but on westward-facing slopes of the Borborema plateau in the north-east, average amounts are half that quantity. With temperatures in the eighties throughout most of the year it is clear that these are conditions of aridity even if the rainfall were reliable. It is mainly of the summer convectional type, and heavy down-pours often cause serious flooding.

The rains of the western areas are more regular being associated with the southward migration of the inter-tropical front during the autumn months. The eastern coastal fringe receives its rain mainly in winter from southerly and south-westerly winds associated with northward-moving depressions.

The sharp contrast between rainy east coast and dry plateau interior is emphasized vividly in the vegetational pattern (Fig. 5). Although the coastal rain forest has largely disappeared, the green agricultural zone which has replaced it provides a striking change of landscape from the aridity of the plateau interior, especially in the winter months when the drought has had its full sway and the grasses have been burnt to browns. The vegetation of this interior zone is unique in Latin America. Termed *caatinga* it consists not only of plants able to withstand aridity, but those able to take advantage of seasonal rains. Mimosas are especially abundant and a wide variety of giant cacti, with carnauba wax palm in the wetter areas.

It is obvious that such a sharp differentiation of physical land-scapes, dependent on relief, structure, climate and vegetation, should give rise to considerable divergence in land use and economic devel opment. This however, is an under-statement, for two human regions of sharply separated modes of life have evolved. It would be difficult to find two other inhabited contiguous areas of Latin America which display so dramatically the cleavage of economies, races, customs and ways of life as those of the north-east coast and the north-east interior.

Although Portuguese settlements were made at several points along the Brazilian coast, even south of the Tropic, in the first half of the 16th century, it was the success of those of the Northeast which laid the foundations of their American Empire; and Salvador, founded as early as 1502, and Recife, not until 60 years later, were the corner stones of that success. It was a prosperity built on sugar cane, the coastal plantations, financed by Portuguese *hacendados* and worked by imported Negro slaves, providing most of the world's supply of this commodity.

It is on this early basis that a regional consciousness exists still in the Northeast. Not only did the planters provide the leaders of the Brazilian nation (as did the Southern plantation states of the United States in a similar way) but they built beautiful towns and churches with their surplus wealth, and established the beginnings of a cultural heritage. São Luis was regarded as the Athens of Brazil. So flourishing was the region that it stimulated the Dutch to seize it in order to control the sugar trade. From 1630 to 1654 most of the coastline of the Northeast was under their control, as some of the houses of Recife still clearly show today. The fact that their expulsion demanded the united effort of the Brazilian colonists further entrenched a regional spirit in the inhabitants of the Northeast.

Considerable areas of the coastal belt still grow sugar, and the fact that for 400 years these deep red soils have maintained this arable system is clear evidence of their fertility, especially as very little fertilizer is used. In parts the old colonial plantation system of an *engenho* or sugar mill near a small source of water power, with its supplying estate adjoining, still survives. No less than 50,000 of these primitive establishments produce *rapadura*, brown cakes of sugar for local consumption. Elsewhere there has been consolidation of several estates to supply a modern *usina* or sugar-refining factory, which produces centrifugal sugar. The sugar surplus to requirements goes to make industrial alcohol which is added to motor fuel to reduce Brazil's petroleum imports. From the southern boundary of the state of Rio Grande do Norte to the southern margins of Salvador bay, sugar is still the dominant crop in a belt varying from 20 to 50 miles in width. In the hinterland of Salvador, in the bowl-shaped district tributary to the bay, known as the *Recôncavo*, the zone attains a width of over 100 miles.

No longer, however, is the Northeast a sugar producer for the world market, less primitive and more economic suppliers having displaced it. Indeed it grows now only about one-third of Brazilian needs in a tariff-protected market, but the growing demand of this increasing domestic market promises to sustain sugar cultivation in the Northeast for a long time. Brazil is in fact still second only to Cuba in total sugar production, and in some years exceeds the latter country's output.

On the landward side of the sugar belt stretching up to 100 miles into the interior, into lands of much lower rainfall, where 35 inches may be taken as an average figure, cotton replaces sugar. In the Recôncavo it is one of many crops utilizing the area. Cotton in the Northeast has also suffered many vicissitudes. It experienced a boom during the United States Civil War, and expanding world markets and Brazilian industrialization have maintained its significance. Droughts, however, leading to abandonment of some cotton producing areas have resulted in big fluctuations of output. The arable system of its production is much less stable than that on the sugar lands further east. It compares closely with the alfalfa-commercial crop system of the Argentine Pampa. Most of the cotton lands occur on the pastoral estates of the interior plateau fringes. The owners' primary interest and concern is that of cattle raising. To improve pastures or to produce additional income they allow tenants to cultivate cotton (often for a share of the crop) on a temporary basis. Such a system is obviously quickly adaptable to changing physical and economic conditions, of which drought and the relation between supply and demand are the principal factors. Nearly all the production (the largest in Latin America) is consumed in Brazilian industry in the south.

The cotton lands, therefore, are in the nature of a transitional belt between the arable coastal zone and the pastoral interior. In fact they have made the cleavage between the coast and the interior less sharp than it was in former centuries. The way of life on the plateau is essentially pastoral. This is the _sertão_, the pioneer, thinly-occupied lands which form an important element in many of the Brazilian regions. Occupied for centuries by Portuguese who have moved inland from the coastal zones and by its original Indian inhabitants, the sertão of the Northeast consists of a vast region devoted to raising cattle, goats, sheep and donkeys, principally for a meat supply for the coastal settlements, and for the export of hides and skins. Although the agricultural lands of the east have slowly encroached on the sertão, three-quarters of the area of this great north-eastern region is still devoted to ranching. Pockets of agriculture in clearings or *roças*, mainly of a subsistence variety, but in some cases of commercial crops, exist in the more favoured areas of higher and more reliable rainfall or where irrigation water is available. The use of the word *jardim* in place names is a significant indication of their oasis-like quality in the midst of the semi-arid plateau, such as Jardim de Seridó. The Cariri zone north of the Chapada do Araripe is another such arable area. Maize, beans, manioc, sweet potatoes, a little coffee and some sugar for rapadura are the chief food crops grown. Goat's milk, cheese and beef complete the pastoralist's diet.

Upon this fundamental basis of cattle pastoralism and subsistence farming have come other activities of a cash-cropping nature. Demand for fibres, essential oils and other vegetable products has enabled the people of the sertão to utilize the few advantages of climate and vegetation which the region possesses. Some long-stapled cotton is grown in the drier irrigated areas or where springs occur at the foot of the Chapada do Araripe cuesta. Known as 'tree-cotton' it supplements the imports of Egyptian cotton that the tyre industry of the South uses.

Sisal, the product of the agave, is grown in extensive plantations in the state of Paraíba, with an important centre at Campina Grande. Output is increasing fast, sufficient to leave a considerable surplus for export. Caroa fibre derived from a similar plant to the agave is now produced from the sertão of Bahia, Ceará, and Pernambuco, and is used in canvas and rope manufacture. Piassava fibre, similarly, being salt-water resistant is in much demand for hawsers. Paineira from a xerophytic cotton-like bush yields a kind of kapok.

Of even greater significance than all these fibres is the output of carnauba and ouricouri wax extracted from the palms growing over large areas of Ceará and Piauí. In these waxes Brazil has almost a world monopoly; their value is high in relation to bulk and they are of increasing importance in the exports of the country. The uses of these waxes are so multiple that a recital of them seems like a catalogue. Floor, furniture, shoe and motor-car polishes, insulation, binding base for carbon black in carbon paper, gramophone records, electric batteries and waterproof paper are some of the ways in which the product is utilized.

Babassú nuts collected in the states of Maranhão and Piauí provide one of the majòr sources of vegetable oil in the country. Oiticaca oil, one of the best substitutes for tung oil, used in paints and varnishes, is also derived from a tree in the same area. Nor must there be forgotten the considerable production of copra from the thousands of miles of coastal areas, especially in Bahia state.

At present, as a general rule, nearly all these fibres and oils, which are of increasing significance in industrial communities, are gathered from vegetation in its wild state. The growth of the agave plantations, however, clearly indicates the possibilities of the Northeast in respect of organized cultivation. The planned utilization of these xerophytic and semi-xerophytic trees and palms would do much to absorb surplus labour from the sugar areas and give a much greater degree of stability to the sertão. Similarly the industrial processing of the products offers diversification in the urban settlements, and

Plate 41. *The interior of Brazil's Northeast is a land of uncertain rainfall.
One of its chief economic assets is the production of fibres and waxes. Carnauba
wax trees in Ceará State*

Recife and Natal have textile and vegetable oil factories of this kind.

Except for several oasis-like valleys and areas with better rainfall amounts, the sertão extends to the north coast all the way from Cape São Roque to approximately longitude 43°W. The valleys of the Parnaíba and the rivers draining to the Gulf of São Marcos at São Luis, and the Fortaleza region where relief rains provide a better water supply are the most conspicuous exceptions to this pastoral economy, although numerous small coastal enclaves support considerable nuclei of population. Cotton, sugar, rice, beans, bananas, coffee, manioc and many other subsistence foodstuffs are grown, for the most part under irrigation of a primitive kind. These supply the needs of the coastal settlements and the pastoralists of the interior.

The importance of the salt industry along the coast of this northeastern bulge from Ceará into the state of Espírito Santo in supplying the needs of Brazil, by evaporation of sea water, is relatively recent. Natal is an important centre, and Areia Branca, in Rio Grande do Norte, is an important salt terminal. The fishing industry is also relatively well developed; swordfish are a product of the corner states of Rio Grande do Norte and Paraíba, and shrimps, crabs, lobsters and turtles occur along most of the coast. Considerable quantities of fish are dried and despatched to the sertão.

The area south of the Rio São Francisco, while sharing in many respects the basic physical and human conditions of the Northeast, has developed along rather different lines from that north of the river. The agricultural belt of the Recôncavo is not only much more extensive in area than that of the arable zone further north, but there is far less dependence on one crop. A relatively flourishing system of tropical mixed farming, with tenants growing crops of sugar, tobacco, cotton, rice, maize, manioc, coffee, castor-oil seed and many subsistence foodstuffs, extends for over 100 miles on all sides of the city of Salvador. There is also a slightly larger concentration of Negro and mulatto population, although throughout the coastal areas of the Northeast these ethnic elements rarely fall below two-thirds of the total population. This is one of the most distinctive contrasts with the sertão throughout the region, for the interior is dominantly peopled by Portuguese with some Indian admixture. As agricultural land extends into the sertão so the distinction is being blurred.

The persistent efforts of Petrobrás, the state oil company, to find oil have recently been partially rewarded in the Northeast, with the discovery of off-shore oil resources near the coast of Sergipe and Alagoas. As a result Aracajú will probably become the most significant petroleum centre in the country. In view of the fact that the state of Bahia, adjacent to Sergipe on the south, has 90 per cent of Brazil's proven natural gas resources, the significance of these sources of energy in the development of the Northeast can scarcely be exaggerated.

In the south of Bahia state another agricultural zone is best considered as a part of this north-eastern region, for in some essential basic characteristics it shares the physical and cultural environment of the area to the north. This is the cacao belt of Ilhéus (80,000), near the mouth of the Cachoeira. Grown in favourable areas in the basin of that river and of the Rio Pardo to the south, and in the zone west of Caravellas further south, and with small enclaves in the adjoining state of Espírito Santo, this cocoa zone is the most important in the world outside the famous cocoa plantations of Ghana. Nearly all Brazil's cocoa is grown here on the deep red soils derived from the crystalline rocks which here reach the sea, or on alluvial soils of the river valley terraces. Shelter and plentiful rainfall are the principal physical assets in addition to the fertile soils, but the region is fortunate in having escaped the swollen shoot disease which has played havoc with the African plantations.

The zone is, however, not well farmed and exhibits many of the most serious defects of Brazilian agriculture generally. These include absentee ownership, the planting of trees without adequate protection from other trees, lack of attention to cultivation methods, and abandonment of exhausted estates, all of which show an attitude of careless land use with little respect for the consequences of such destructive exploitation. Although there are some 23,000 planters, 1,400 of these produce 60 per cent of the output. Some of these estates are efficiently farmed and yields have been maintained, but in the area as a whole yield per tree has fallen by 50 per cent since the First World War. The size of the beans is smaller and many are deformed. Although world demand is now high and inefficient production continues as a result, under less favourable conditions Brazil's cocoa plantations could scarcely survive competition. There is increasing home consumption, and cocoa forms the region's second export, mostly consigned to the United States. Brazil is in fact the third producer of cocoa in the world, its output being exceeded only by those of Ghana and Nigeria. There are two crops a year, the main harvest being from October to February. In this season much temporary labour enters the district and the sertão supplies a large proportion. Two-thirds of the crop passes through Ilhéus, being collected from the estates by motor lorries. That exported from Caravellas uses a railway running west through the zone.

The sharp differentiation of this region of north-east Brazil into the sertão and the peripheral agricultural lands of the coastal margins is one of the most pervasive features in every aspect of its human geography. As has been indicated, the differentiation is more blurred in some parts today than it has been since the first days of its colonization. Yet they still remain two human regions, separated by the law of the *travessão*, by which the pastoralist of the agricultural zone must fence his lands to prevent animals gaining access to cultivated lands, and the agriculturalist of the pastoral zone must fence his cultivated fields against the depredations of animals. This is a shifting boundary that throughout history has been steadily but slowly pushing inwards into the sertão.

Yet the two regions have not lived in isolation from each other. Apart from the colonization of the sertão from the coast and the rather exceptional migrant labour from the sertão to the cocoa estates, the principal contact has been at the fairs where the products of the two zones are exchanged. Feira de Sant'Anna, Itabaiana, Campina Grande and Baturité are but a few of the more important linking the Bahia, Paraíba and Ceará parts of the sertão and coast. The penetration of railways contributed in some measure to more contacts and aided particularly the distribution of coastal food supplies to sertão settlements which lived on the margins of self-sufficiency, but most of these rail links were far between and built mainly to transport the products of the arable zone to the ports (Fig. 75). North of Salvador there is no continuous rail network, even in the coastal zone, and the longest penetrations into the sertão are those from Camocim along the Serra Grande scarp, from Fortaleza to the Cariri country at the foot of the Chapada do Araripe, and the line from Salvador to Juazeiro on the São Francisco, each tapping areas of some agricultural importance or linking oases together. The Juazeiro–Salvador line also provides an outlet for the middle São Francisco valley, for the river is navigable for some 700 miles south of Juazeiro.

This is also the region where energetic efforts have been made to improve the system of roads (Fig. 76), and by this means to provide not only a regional network but an integration of the region into the national economy. A great trunk highway now links Fortaleza with Rio de Janeiro via Salvador and the other coastal cities, and connects with those penetrating into the sertão.

As with so much of Brazil, the distribution of population within the region is very uneven. Regarded as *average* figures, many of the states of the Northeast have high average densities, Alagoas with 132 per square mile, Pernambuco with 127, Paraíba with 106, and even Ceará and Rio Grande do Norte with 67 and 63 respectively. With a total population exceeding 40 millions the Northeast can in no sense be called a depopulated region. But the great majority of these people live in the coastal belt and its cities between Paraíba and Salvador. Many *municipios* of Pernambuco state have more than 250 persons per square mile; others have less than 20. The Recôncavo area's density exceeds 200, the sertão units rarely average more than 15 persons to the square mile.

The sertão of the Northeast has become increasingly an area of emigration, both to the coastal towns and to other parts of Brazil. Under present economic conditions it can maintain its population only so long as rainfall is both sufficient and reliable. Yet this has always been one of the great physical hazards of the area. Droughts, and often floods, have so dislocated the economy that mass emigration has taken place. In the past the coastal cities were the nearest and most obvious destinations, sometimes on a temporary basis until conditions in the sertão improved, more often to swell permanently the over-large populations of these cities. Thus Recife (1,100,000) and Salvador (892,000) together contain 2 million people, and in all Brazil only São Paulo, Rio de Janeiro, Belo Horizonte and Pôrto Alegre are larger, while Fortaleza (846,000), Natal (239,000), Maceio (221,000), São Luis (219,000) and João Pessoa (189,000) are all major cities.

As other economic attractions offered, the periodic movements spread to other parts of the country. Over 50,000 went into the Amazon region in the early years of the rubber boom; the industrial labour market of Rio de Janeiro and São Paulo has become the magnet of recent years, and attracted 200,000 in the drought year of 1952. The droughts of 1957 and 1969–71 were probably the worst this century and revealed all the classic features of these periodic disasters. Huge influxes of drought-stricken peasants seeking food, water and work invaded the towns, and in 1971 all roads out of Ceará to other states were closed to prevent these mass migrations.

The penetration of a more effective road system has released outward currents of people who were previously dissuaded by difficulties of transport from moving far afield. But the emigration of people to other regions of Brazil is not confined to the sertão. The zone of dense population in the sugar lands also supplies many emigrants, and Bahia is one of the main sources, especially since it has been linked by road and rail with Rio de Janeiro. Others go by rail to Juazeiro, thence by river steamer to Pirapora and by rail, lorry or on foot to São Paulo. These movements from the coastal regions are related to soil exhaustion under present farming systems, the persistence of old colonial traditions and rigid social groupings, the poor development of industry and above all, the exceptionally high birth rate. Natural increase in the states of Rio Grande do Norte, Maranhão, Piauí and Ceará exceeds the national average of 3 per cent per annum, and this is especially true of the sertão areas. At the last census, 55 per cent of Ceará's population was under twenty years of age; and this disproportion of dependent population increases the economic difficulties of the Northeast.

Of five priority areas selected by the Brazilian government for agrarian reform, two are in the Northeast, the states of Pernambuco and Ceará, where conditions of land tenure are almost feudal in character. It is not unusual for peasants to be required to allocate half their crops to the landlords, and with the money return from the other half to buy their food needs from landlords' shops at exorbitant prices. A radical agrarian reform programme, designed to end these abuses, is now being put into operation. It includes the expropriation of badly worked estates, redistribution of the land to the peasants, and the creation of co-operatives.

Continuous efforts have been made to lessen the effect of the climatic hazards, especially by the construction of dams and irrigation works. This has led to some local improvement of conditions, but frequently favourable years lead to neglect of these schemes, and the individualism of the sertão dweller does not take kindly to anything of a co-operative nature, which is the essence of water conservation.

The costly development of hydro-electric power at the Paulo Afonso falls of the São Francisco is a significant effort to bring modern facilities of cheap electricity and industrial power to a larger area of the Northeast (Fig. 70). As capital becomes available it is hoped that this is but the beginning of a scheme to rehabilitate the region, and to provide for integrated development of mining, irrigated agriculture and industry. Two such developments have been the establishment of alumina, and oil refining and petrochemical plants in the state of Bahia. Without such modern development to stabilize the population and improve the basis of the whole economic fabric of the Northeast, it is inevitable that it will continue to decline relatively in significance, as the South and Southeast grow.

THE SOUTHEAST

The states of Minas Gerais, Espírito Santo, São Paulo, Rio de Janeiro and Guanabara included within this region (Figs. 68 and 71) occupy less than 11 per cent of the area of Brazil, but they contain 44 per cent of the population of the country. The two large states of Minas Gerais and São Paulo, with some 12 and 17 million people respectively, account for nearly one-third of all Brazilians.

Like the Northeast the region contains a great variety of zones which could be differentiated on physical, economic and human grounds, but also like the Northeast it has passed through somewhat common historical experiences which have welded the vast area into a territory with a considerable regional consciousness which stands

Fig. 70. *The Paulo Afonso hydro-electric power plant*
An example of the increasing use being made of water
power in Latin America

out from the three adjacent regions of the South, the Centre and the
Northeast.

From the viewpoint of structure and relief the complexities may be
simplified into three zones:

(a) The coastal belt.
(b) The plateau escarpment.
(c) The interior plateau.

These show considerable differences throughout the length of the
region, and only their principal and most significant characteristics
can be indicated.

The coastal area throughout most of its length has a width of
150 miles, but is somewhat narrower in its southern extensions. In
essentials of structure it is part of the old crystalline foundation of
the continent. At many points the resistant granites and gneisses
form the coastal cliffs, which under tropical humid conditions
weather into the famous sugar-loaf peaks like that at the entrance to
Rio de Janeiro harbour. Elsewhere low swampy deltaic fringes like

those of the mouths of the Paraíba and Doce rivers, and coastal terraces, the product of recent uplift, like those of southern Bahia, form
a marginal belt of relatively narrow width. Throughout most of its
length this old peneplained crystalline massif as exposed in the coastal belt consists of a series of plateau surfaces rising progressively
westward, and dissected into mesas, many of which exceed 3,000 feet
in height. The principal agents in this dissection have been eastward-
flowing rivers, the Paraguacú, das Contas, Pardo, Jequitinhonha and
Doce being the most important ones. Rising some 250 miles west in
the plateau escarpment, their main streams are for the most part a
continuation of the series of superimposed drainage channels already
indicated in the Northeast. Their tributaries, however, frequently
reveal the old fault trends of north-north-east–south-south-west and
east-north-east–west-south-west direction which have had considerable influence on the grain of this part of the country. This is especially evident towards the south of the region where even the coastline at Cabo Frio changes its trend from south-south-west direction
to the west-south-west. This also leads to a complete squeezing out
of the coastal zone, so that south of the Doce delta it is extremely
narrow, and from Rio de Janeiro to Santos, for all practical purposes, it ceases to exist, the plateau escarpment forming the shoreline.

From the Rio São Francisco at Juazeiro the watershed between
the coastal rivers and the plateau drainage systems of the São
Francisco and Paraná consists of an escarpment called progressively
from north to south the Chapada Diamantina, Serra do Espinhaço
and Serra da Mantiqueira. With a crystalline base, this zone for
most of its length is composed of sedimentary strata of a wide range
of geological age, the most extensive and thickest layers being in the
north. Warping of some of these rocks and differential erosion of
limestones and sandstones have produced in some areas a series of
ridges which frequently define the drainage lines of some of the headstreams of both the coastal and plateau systems. The Serra do Espinhaço in Minas Gerais exceeds 5,500 feet, while the Mantiqueira
range has peaks of 8,500 feet. In the sedimentaries of this escarpment
occur the diamond-bearing deposits and the *itabirite* which provides
the great iron-ore wealth of Brazil.

Just as the Serra da Mantiqueira follows the west-south-west–
east-north-east trend as distinct from the Serra do Espinhaço's
south-south-west–north-north-east trend, so is it duplicated further
south by a parallel almost detached region of the escarpment running
from Santos to the Paraíba delta, with isolated portions beyond.

This is the Serra do Mar fronting the ocean between Santos and Rio de Janeiro, and continued as the Serra dos Orgaos north of the capital and as a broken coastal serra through the Rio de Janeiro area and the coastal section to Cabo Frio. The great rift valley between these block mountains of the escarpment is occupied by the Rio Paraíba, running, therefore, parallel to the coast, between Rio de Janeiro and São Paulo city.

The third element in the structural relief of the Southeast is the plateau itself. In the north this is predominantly the crystalline peneplain lying between the plateau escarpment (as represented by the Chapada Diamantina) and other sedimentary chapadas of Goias to the west, and drained by the main stream and tributaries of the São Francisco in its plateau course. Considerable areas are less than 1,800 feet above sea-level and the broad undulating surfaces are perhaps best realized from the fact that for some 700 miles the São Francisco falls less than 2 feet per mile. This is its navigable portion between Pirapora and Juazeiro. Broad interfluves, some rising to over 2,500 feet, spread from the surrounding chapadas east, north and west into the basin, forming watersheds between its major tributaries. Some of these are capped with sedimentary rocks and present scarped edges above the valleys. The southern portion of the plateau in the state of São Paulo, and in the southern extensions of Minas Gerais, is more complex in its structure and relief. Considerable areas of the east, extending from the Serra da Mantiqueira and the block mountains overlooking the Paraíba rift, are undulating granitic tablelands, approximately 2,600 feet in height. Further west the crystalline rocks pass under sedimentary rocks which dip westward at a greater angle than the plateau surface. This has the effect of producing

(i) a surface where more and more recent rocks outcrop on the surface as one goes westward, and
(ii) a series of cuestas concave to the crystalline plateau in the east, and outward facing from the Paraná drainage system.

Into and on this sedimentary cover have been intruded great thicknesses of diabase stretching beyond this region into Brazil's southland, and forming the most prominent cuesta.

The consequent drainage system developed on this crystalline-sedimentary-diabase surface is a series of tributaries of the Paraná, notably the Paranapanema, Tieté, Rio Grande and Paranaíba. The differential erosion of these contrasting rocks has produced falls at the crystalline-sedimentary junction and where the more resistant diabase occurs. In the lower and middle parts of their valleys the rivers have eroded the cover of sedimentary rocks and flow in diabase-floored valleys for a considerable distance, including the main stream of the Paraná itself.

The proximity of the plateau escarpment to the ocean, south-west of Rio de Janeiro, obviously means that this Paraná drainage system has extended the affluents of its tributaries to within a few miles of the Atlantic. This is notably so in the case of the Tieté, the source of which is 10 miles 'as the crow flies' from Santos, in contrast to the watershed in the north of this region which lies some 250 miles to the west.

The relatively complex relief background of the region is compensated for by fairly broad patterns of climatic regularity, a marked contrast to the Northeast. Except in the northern margins of Bahia, where Juazeiro has only 10 inches of rain, the plateau escarpment receives usually between 50 and 60 inches of rain annually, 80 per cent of which falls in the summer months. East of the escarpment, high humidity and plentiful rainfall give rise to a forest zone throughout the coastal area (Figs. 5 and 6). The Brazilians termed this *matta* but it was far from a homogeneous cover, deteriorating westward from true *selva* to semi-deciduous stands of timber, and in places to scrub forest. Most of this has now been removed by timber-cutters and charcoal burners, and in the uncultivated areas secondary forest of poor quality has replaced it. The escarpment's sandy soils form a fairly sharp vegetational boundary, for to the west savana country, *campo limpo*, predominates, The higher rainfall conditions of the southern extensions of the region are limited to parts of the coast (Santos receives 85 inches) and the high areas of the Serra do Mar with averages exceeding 100 inches annually. Over most of the plateau of São Paulo at least 50 inches is a fairly dependable quantity, and this is reflected in semi-deciduous forest covering large areas. Towards the extreme south this gives way to Araucaria pine forest, a fairly clear indication of frost in some years.

Temperature ranges throughout the whole of the Southeast are very small. Santos in the far south has a range of 12°F. (66–78°F.); Belo Horizonte in the heart of the region, on the western side of the escarpment, has a range of 10°F. (62–72°F.); São Paulo one of 11°F. (58–69°F.) and Rio de Janeiro of 10°F. (69–79° F.). Elevation obviously has its effect in reducing temperatures, as is evident from these statistics, but a broad tropical pattern of hot summers and warm winters with summer maximum of adequate rainfall prevails throughout the vast extent of this region to a remarkable degree. Often soils have greater influence on vegetational distributions than climate, and in any case the impact of man over great areas has considerably modified the original plant cover. There is a generally close association between the diabase areas and forest, and between the sandstones of the east and grassland, whereas the crystalline plateau rim is heavily forested. The southern boundary of the region, the Paraná–São Paulo frontier, is in many ways a zone of considerable climatic transition from tropical to warm temperate conditions.

Except from the viewpoint of adequate rainfall the Southeast offered far less attraction to the Portuguese colonists than did the Northeast, and for almost two centuries, the 16th and the 17th, this was a relatively neglected portion of Brazil, providing little to compare with the wealth of the sugar plantations of Bahia and the Northeast. Those who ventured into it were relatively poor adventurers contrasted with the wealthy planters further north. The mountainous country, for this was the highest and most rugged part of the east of the continent, and the dissected landscape repelled settlement. Where this was less of a hindrance all-pervasive forest blocked the way to the interior, and the Portuguese loathed the hazards of forest travel as much as the Spanish. To add to their difficulties hostile Indian tribes in parts gave them no welcome. Yet in spite of these difficulties and its relatively late start, the region has been transformed into the wealthiest and most developed part of Brazil, with two of the greatest cities of the continent and the broadest-based industrial structure in Latin America.

Five major phases in this transformation can be delineated:

(*a*) The phase of the *bandeirantes*.
(*b*) The gold and diamond phase of Minas Gerais.
(*c*) The coffee phase in the Paraíba valley.
(*d*) The agricultural utilization of São Paulo.
(*e*) The growth of the industrial Southeast.

The early 16th-century colonists who pushed inland from Santos Bay by the quickest and most direct route on to the plateau and established themselves in the lands of the present state of São Paulo found little on which to base a secure livelihood. They formed themselves into adventurous groups known as *bandeirantes* who as roaming pastoralists pressed south, west and north into the unknown to seek riches. Herding cattle, growing a little subsistence food, enslaving Indians and seeking precious metals and stones, they ventured into lands where no Europeans had been before. Their exploration and occupation of the interior of Brazil was instrumental at the time of Independence in securing the lion's share of the continent for their nation. São Paulo became the base for their operations, and as a result of their activities a vast area of the plateau and the interior had a thin scatter of settlements of *mameluco* (Portuguese-Indian) population.

In the closing years of the 17th century their wanderings and searchings produced the biggest prize yet won, and ushered in the second phase of settlement. In the area which is now central Minas Gerais and in the southern parts of the Serra do Espinhaço alluvial gold was discovered in considerable quantity. Thirty years later, in 1729, the discovery of diamonds near Diamantina proved a secondary magnet. Thousands flocked in a gold and diamond rush to this new Eldorado, and as elsewhere in the world, the inward movement of people proved a mighty colonizing force. Early settlers in the São Paulo region moved northward, planters from the Northeast streamed southward, and emigrants from Portugal poured westward across the ocean. Ouro Preto became the metropolis of the gold fields, and other centres such as Sabará and São Jõa del Rei grew into towns flaunting the wealth the region produced. The phase lasted a hundred years and during that time Brazil was the world's greatest source of gold. Perhaps more important than the basic settlement pattern and colonization of Minas Gerais which resulted from the immigration was the fact that it established Rio de Janeiro as the country's greatest port and capital. This outlet for the mineral wealth of the interior was chosen for its easily defended site and for its proximity to the scene of operations. Longer and easier routes via the Doce valley to Vitória had the double hazards of forests and Indians. Rio de Janeiro was the geometrically direct exit for the gold, and roads were constructed over the difficult relief linking it with the wealth-producing centres.

The exhaustion of the stream gravels was inevitable. The marvel was they had lasted so long. By the early 19th century the phase was over. The surplus population of Minas Gerais reversed the immigrant flow. Emigrants trickled westward into the interior, others occupied the sertão of the São Francisco, but more important in its effect was the current of settlers who moved south and south-east into the district of Ribeirão Preto of São Paulo and especially into the Paraíba

Plate 42. *Ouro Preto, in Minas Gerais State, founded in the days of the gold rush, is typical of the old Colonial Settlements of the interior of Brazil*

valley inland from Rio de Janeiro, to become the first coffee-planters of Brazil. This was a new crop becoming popular in Britain at that time, and profits from the expanding market were high. Grown on the terraces of the long valley trough, accessible to the new and flourishing port, the pattern of settlement became much fuller. A third phase in the colonization of the Southeast had been enacted.

The settlers on the fringe of the crystalline plateau in São Paulo practised a pastoral-arable economy of cattle herding and sugar and maize cultivation at this time. As coffee became of increasing importance in the Paraíba valley, its cultivation spread westward into this area near Campinas, Sorocaba and São Paulo. Simultaneously the demand both in Europe and in North America continued to expand. Gradually the planters of the new areas realized the fertility of the *terra roxa* soils developed on the diabase. The establishment of coffee estates (*fazendas*) involved the clearing of lands, the planting of trees and all the tasks of new agricultural settlement. To fill the demand for labour which this involved came a great overseas immigrant stream, second only to that which peopled the Argentine Pampa. Like the latter, the Italians formed the largest group, accounting for one-third of those who entered São Paulo state, but

Portuguese, Spaniards, Japanese and those from other parts of Brazil (especially Bahia and Minas Gerais) contributed large numbers. Since 1880 probably some 2 million immigrants is not an exaggerated estimate of the people who arrived and stayed in this new agricultural zone. Thus the south-west of the region was peopled in this fourth stage of colonization.

The fifth and current period is the rapid transformation of the cities of the Southeast into the great industrial centres of Brazil. The same stimuli of world wars and an economic depression were operative here as in Argentina and elsewhere in Latin America. Deprived of imports, but with the great advantage of water power as a source of energy, the region was better endowed than the Pampa to industrialize. Especially noteworthy was the fantastic utilization of the waters of the Tieté by causing them to plunge *eastward* more than 2,000 feet down the slope of the Serra do Mar. The production of such an abundance of hydro-electric power was a basic economic foundation on which much else has been built. Tariff protection, the powerful influence which São Paulo state wields in national policy, the pool of labour created by coffee crises of the 1930s, the accumu- lated wealth and profits of agricultural prosperity, the abundant confidence and initiative of the Paulistas and even the snowball effect of its rapid expansion have all contributed to make São Paulo city the metropolis of Brazilian industry, producing some 40 per cent of the country's output. Sorocaba, Campinas and Ribeirão Preto also share in this industrial growth in the state; and the development at Volta Redonda (89,000), in the Paraíba valley, of Latin America's greatest steel industry is another aspect of this latest phase which still makes the Southeast, and now its cities in particular, the goal of Brazilians from far and near.

The net results of these successive periods of colonization are now reflected in the economic pattern, pastoral, agricultural, mineral and industrial, which the Southeast displays.

The mining exploitation which initiated the sweep of colonization still survives in its parent area Minas Gerais, but in a very different form. Gold is still produced, but from the Morro Velho mine south of Belo Horizonte, where the deepest shafts in the world penetrate the Serra da Espinhaço; and diamonds, mainly for industrial use, are still derived from Diamantina. Of much greater importance, however, are the vast deposits of iron and manganese which the Serra contains. The rich and easily worked iron ore reserves are the greatest in the world. High in metal content and free from impurities, the potential wealth is incalculable, but conservative estimates of the reserves exceed 2,000 million tons. Two centres are the main points of production: Lafaiete for the Volta Redonda mills to the south, and Itabira for export via the Doce valley railway to Vitória. In the same area the fantastic variety of ferro-alloys, of which tungsten is the most important one exported, offers enormous scope for future developments of these important metals.

These operations, however, concern but relatively few people and the basic economic foundation, not only of Minas Gerais but of considerable areas of the rest of the Southeast, is still that of pastoralism. It is the only stable rural pursuit which has been maintained for centuries, and it controls the settlement pattern of large pastoral fazendas and scattered villages throughout Minas Gerais. Tracks link these settlements to centres where cattle fairs are the most important economic and social event. The state has a quarter of Brazil's cattle, and acts as a great supply area for the large populations of Rio de Janeiro and São Paulo states, where the cattle are driven for fattening. In river valleys and more favoured areas, agriculture is carried on largely with a view to supplying the subsistence needs of the population. Sugar, maize, manioc, rice and beans are the principal crops, although some cotton and coffee are also grown. The general poverty of the distant sertão still prevails. Far from markets, the area still lacks a good communication system, yet as soon as routes are driven into it, this only aids the process of depopulation and migration to the more prosperous areas of the southern part of the Southeast.

The second most extensive system to pastoralism, taking into account the area involved and the people concerned in it, is subsistence agriculture. Over very large areas of the east of the region, from the Paraíba delta northward and extending some 100 miles from the coast, this takes the form of almost primitive shifting cultivation of the burn-and-slash technique of forest clearing to provide sufficient space to grow a little maize, beans, rice, bananas and manioc and to rear a few animals. South of the Doce delta, lumbering and charcoal burning still persist, but some coffee cultivation has been added more recently.

A more satisfactory agricultural landscape has developed east of Rio de Janeiro, where clearing of forest and mangrove swamps and the drainage of swamps have provided small holdings for the cultivation of a wide variety of fruits and vegetables for the nearby urban market.

The Paraíba valley today is largely a scene of subsistence agriculture, although the pastoral activities of Minas Gerais have spread over much of the northern half of the depression, and now dairy cattle graze over many hundreds of acres of agriculturally impoverished lands. In many cases these lands have actually been invaded by pastoralists from Minas Gerais. The dairy products naturally find their markets in the two great cities of São Paulo and Rio de Janeiro. Yet this valley has been the scene in the past of many agricultural booms which have supported and affected Brazilian agriculture. The sugar economy of the Northeast spread into it at an early date, and there are still survivals of these estates growing sugar and producing rapadura in the upper part of the valley. It was the introduction of coffee as a major crop which brought a greatly increased population to the valley (and a few isolated remnants survive), but soil exhaustion, the abolition of slavery, economic crises, the competition of lands further west, and the attraction of other crops led to its collapse. For a few years a boom in orange growing held sway, and then rice fields on the flood plain became the means of providing quick financial returns. These paddy fields still provide the most significant cash crop of the area, but methods are still largely exploitative, and yields are only one-eighth of those obtained in the Po valley of Italy.

The planting of eucalyptus over large areas of abandoned estates is now a common practice, in some areas as a soil-protection measure, but more often in a continuation of the boom crop activities. It has in fact been termed 'firewood agriculture' for the demand for charcoal in the homes and industries of the city is almost insatiable. The forest has been largely cleared from the Serra da Mantiqueira, and inroads are now being made on those of the Serra do Mar. Afforestation in the Doce valley is designed to supply a cellulose plant.

It is, however, in São Paulo that the typically Brazilian boom agriculture has held sway unchecked for three-quarters of a century. In actual percentage of arable land, coffee is almost as important as the rest of the crops combined. In fact the growth of São Paulo can be directly attributed to the spread of this crop across the state. A map of the diabase outcrops shows clearly how it has been increasingly realized that this is the most productive land for coffee, and the principal railways have been constructed like the fingers of a hand into these lands to transport the beans south-eastward to Santos (314,000). The system of coffee cultivation on the fazendas of São Paulo is for the most part on a large scale, with managers, overseers and tenants, but for owners and tenants it is still an exploitative materialistic system to derive as much profit as possible, and then if greater opportunities exist elsewhere to move to them, whether in city or pioneer lands of the west. Much arable làmd, even on the fazendas, is still devoted to maize, beans and rice, and a great area of the 'corner lowland' (where the older soft sedimentaries adjoin the crystalline plateau) is still pastoral country.

Cotton has become a most important product of the estates further west, particularly in the area between the lower Tieté and the Paranapanema, but older areas south of the Rio Grande in northern São Paulo yield significant amounts. The Japanese take an active part in cotton cultivation, which is rarely combined with coffee growing, as their demands on labour at harvest time are too coincident and heavy. Sugar, especially in the Piracicaba district, is offered a nearby market in São Paulo city, and the state produces a quarter of the Brazilian crop. Bananas, oranges and market gardening with vineyards on the cooler hilly regions add variety to the arable activities of this productive region.

Yet even in the abundance which São Paulo produces, accounting for 40 per cent of Brazil's coffee exports and more than half of its cotton production, there is little permanent linking of the colonists with the land they own or work. The raising of crops is a means to an end, that of greater wealth. There is no traditional attachment to the land, to improve it, to utilize it in as broad a way as possible, to conserve its value and make it a permanent heritage for their descendants. Thus even in this rich region, the features of the 'hollow frontier', of abandoned lands, of declining yields (in coffee they are half those of Paraná) and the absence of stable rural communities are disquieting portents for the future when all the land to the Paraná has been 'developed' in this way.

Just as the agricultural booms epitomize the rural landscape of the Southeast, so has the rise of industry accompanied and stimulated amazing urban growth. The region has become not only the foremost industrialized zone of Brazil, but of all Latin America. In addition to the advantages of abundant labour, hydro-electric power and raw materials, the constantly expanding home market for the products made has been a great incentive to industrialization. Textiles and foodstuffs account for some 40 per cent of Brazil's manufacturing production, and some textiles are even exported. In many other branches the output is not yet sufficient to meet home demand, in such commodities as paper, cement and iron and steel goods. The most impressive creation of the post-war years has been the heavy industry of Volta Redonda in the central Paraíba valley, where it is accessible to the two great urban markets. Coal from Tubarão in Santa Catarina is imported via Rio de Janeiro and Angra dos Reis and mixed with imported coal from the United States. Output is expanding steadily and accounts for almost half of Latin American iron and steel production. Subsidiary industries are springing up nearby to use its products, and over 400,000 motor vehicles of all types are now made in Brazil. Another steel mill is being constructed between São Paulo and Santos at Piassaguera, and several smaller charcoal iron works are still operating in Minas Gerais.

Chemical, metallurgical, mechanical and electrical supplies industries are now slowly filling in gaps in the industrial pattern, and the industrialization of São Paulo especially is reaching a very complex stage. As one Brazilian succinctly puts it, the aim is 'to supply the home market with every possible manufactured article. It is only the comparative difficulty of getting hold of certain raw materials and developing skilled techniques that stands in the way of a greater diversification of the industrial output.'

There are, however, other hindrances than those of technical skill and raw materials. The enormous expansion is inevitably making severe strains on the capital resources of the country, and foreign capital must be persuaded to participate without dominating the industry. The rail network, while second in extent to that of Argentina, is not a good one. Built under completely different economic conditions with little direct relationship to present trends, it is for the most part an antiquated high-cost transport system, lacking adequate supplies of coal and faced with the maintenance of track in difficult relief conditions. It has for a long while proved a brake on the economic progress of the Southeast, and to a certain extent prevented the growth of medium-sized industrial cities. What other industrial centres exist are small-scale, selling to a limited local market, because of transport costs and difficulties. Much has already been done to extend, modernize and electrify the most essential lines. This in itself has facilitated iron ore exports and the growth of Volta Redonda. The major concentration, however, has been on road building to supply an alternative transport network, but the country's shortage of petroleum, involving overseas purchases which make up 20 per cent of its imports, is another serious drawback to efficient intercommunication within the region. It is not surprising, therefore, that the rich bituminous schists of the Paraíba valley are being exploited for the production of gas to help meet this energy deficit; and plans for the establishment at Angra dos Reis of the nation's first nuclear energy plant are well advanced.

The pattern of population distribution in the Southeast is dominated by the two great cities which together account for almost one-quarter of the region's people. São Paulo, with a population of nearly 6 millions, is now the largest city in all Latin America, its growth rate exceeding 100,000 annually. It has become not only the focus of the Southeast but the goal of thousands beyond the region. A spate of statistics show the rapidity of its growth from a town of 25,000 in 1874, and the dominance of its industrial output, which is more than that produced in the whole nation outside the city. It is difficult to summarize the causes of this great urban sprawl. They include good communications with Rio de Janeiro via the natural route of the Paraíba valley, a direct link with the nearby port of Santos, almost unlimited electric power in the Cubatão plant, the profits of the coffee boom, the initiative of the cosmopolitan Paulista immigrants, and a boundless confidence in the destiny of São Paulo.

The conurbation on the shores of Guanabara bay is a slower and steadier growth, to a city of $4\frac{1}{4}$ million population. It is now linked by a road bridge with Niterói (304,000), the capital of Rio de Janeiro state, on the eastern shore. Its advantageous position with respect to one of the world's finest harbours, as a seaport, as capital and as the outlet since the early 18th century of much of Brazil's agricultural, pastoral and mineral produce are all pointers to the economic significance of its site. The focus of ocean routes to Brazil from overseas, the focus of land routes from all parts of the Southeast, it has maintained its pre-eminence in the commercial life of Brazil, in spite of the proximity of Santos to São Paulo. With increasing use of its adjacent lands to supply it with perishable foodstuffs, and with the growth of a more efficient transport network it cannot but maintain its supremacy.

The Duque de Caxias oil refinery at Rio de Janeiro has facilitated the establishment there of a synthetic rubber plant; and the shipbuilding yards of Camu are the only significant such industry in Latin America.

Belo Horizonte (1,167,000) the capital of Minas Gerais, founded in the closing years of the 19th century to replace colonial Ouro Preto, ranks as the only other major city of the Southeast. Located in the Serra do Espinhaço and planned as a modern well laid-out city, it has become an important administrative and industrial nucleus, standing as an urban outpost between the more densely peopled

Plate 43. *The growth of Brazil's Southeast into the premier region of the country has produced a mixture of the colonial past and modern skyscrapers. A scene in Rio de Janeiro*

south of the state and the sertão óf the north. Cotton mills, food industries and diamond cutting are its principal occupations.

The development of hydro-electric power at Volta Grande on the Rio Grande of Minas Gerais will facilitate the rapid industrialization of that state, which is growing steadily in importance as Brazil's centre of gravity moves westward.

Campinas (252,000), Ribeirão Preto (170,000) and Sorocaba (143,000) are growing industrial centres of São Paulo state, important clearing points for coffee, cotton and other agricultural produce, and distributing centres on the fan-like railway system to the interior and west of São Paulo state. At Cubatão, near Santos, Brazil has its largest oil refinery, and ancillary industries of asphalt and fertilizers have grown up nearby.

In addition to these major cities, smaller urban units have tended to grow up at railway junctions and points serving particular industrial and agricultural needs and supplying their markets. The pattern of distribution in the rural areas of São Paulo is closely related to the interfluves between the major westward-flowing consequents of the Paraná, where railways have pierced the interior of the state to serve the agricultural estates. In the rest of the Southeast, a boundary swinging from Vitória to Belo Horizonte and thence to the termini of the São Paulo railway network separates the northern sertão and thinly occupied lands of Espírito Santo from the more fully occupied south. Yet even in this latter area, settlements are not thickly distributed. Villages are few in number, and the prevalent estate with tenant employees accounts for the majority of the rural population. The Paraíba valley, the area of so much economic history and so much transit of peoples, is the most densely populated zone. It shows within its limits, in many ways, the restless movement of the peoples of the Southeast through four centuries, the agricultural adventures they have undertaken, the pastoral basis which is their only stable feature, and finally the growth of modern industry as the current stage in the Southeast's evolution.

THE SOUTH

Representing only one-fourteenth of the area and more than one-sixth of the population of Brazil, the three southern states of Paraná, Santa Catarina and Rio Grande do Sul (Figs. 68 and 71) form a fairly compact and relatively homogeneous region, but with characteristics which strikingly differentiate it from both the Southeast and the Northeast.

Structurally the region is very different from most of the Brazilian plateau, for the old crystalline basis of that massif is exposed in only limited areas. Most of the region is covered with the continuation of the great diabase flows, the beginnings of which were indicated in São Paulo state. The crystalline outcrops of the plateau and the Serra do Mar escarpment have a width of some 80 miles from the coast in the Paranaguá–Curitiba area and in the Itajaí valley, but south of Tubarão they narrow to some 20 miles and end at latitude 30°S. West of the coastal lagoons which fringe the southern part of the state of Rio Grande do Sul the crystalline foundation reappears and extends over 100 miles westward in a mass of rounded hills drained eastward by the Rio Camaqua. Although for the most part.

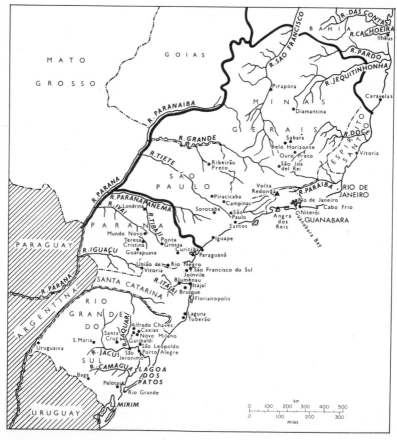

Fig. 71. *The Southeast and South of Brazil*

only 1,000 feet high, they still retain the characteristic of an abrupt slope to the east so typical in more majestic form in the great escarpment of the Southeast region.

The Serra do Mar's extension into the Curitiba region is again a sharp ascent from the coast, but further south it is more complex, being broken by faults into block ridges which give rise to cliffs, intervening valleys and the fairly broad and uneven salient of the Itajai basin, before again resuming its relatively simple form west of Tubarão. The coast throughout this region of southern Brazil reveals increasing submergence as it winds to the south. The drowned harbours of Rio de Janeiro and Santos are continued in those of Paranaguá and island-protected Florianopolis. Further south 300 feet of sands and clays blanket the seaward edge of the crystallines, and the lagoon-fringed coast with low expanses of sand and dunes is seen in Lagoas Dos Patos and Mirím. This, like its continuation in the Uruguayan coast, is the combined effect of currents and alluvial deposition to regularize the indentations of drowned estuaries like that of the Jacuí, in the post-submergence period.

As in the state of São Paulo, the crystalline areas adjoin the tilted sedimentary and diabase formations. These latter cover two-thirds of the region but are relatively more simple than in São Paulo. They form the typical outward-facing cuestas, which in the northern part of the region are partly a continuation of those further north, facing eastward. The first cuesta of sandstone, some 20 miles west of Curitiba, and in a more broken form in the Blumenau area, varies in height from 150 to 600 feet, but does not extend south of 28°S. There it is replaced by the diabase cuesta which as it swings to the northwest rises to an elevation of 2,700 feet overlooking the inner lowland of the sandstones. The general name given to the contact cuesta (whether of sandstone or diabase) where it overlooks the crystalline zone of the east is the Serra Geral.

The inner lowland and great lava plateau dipping westward are drained by the rivers Uruguay and Iguacú, two more consequent tributaries of the Paraná. The limited extent of the crystalline zone restricts drainage towards the Atlantic, and only in the faulted zone of the Itajai basin is a river valley of some significance possible.

The westward extension of the crystalline basis in the extreme south of the region results in the cuesta formations and geological boundaries running east and west instead of north and south. Thus north of Porto Alegre the diabase plateau rises to over 2,400 feet but declines in height westward in conformity with its westward tilt.

The lowland between the lava tableland and the crystalline rocks is drained by the eastward-flowing Jacui, and its sandstone ridges and terraces correspond to the inner lowland of Paraná state.

Two outstanding climatic transitions differentiate the South from the São Paulo area adjoining it on the north. The changes on either side of the Paranapanema are not abrupt but they are none the less significant. The first is the transition as one passes to the south from a rainfall régime with a marked summer maximum to one in which rain is increasingly well distributed throughout the year. The second is the increasing likelihood of frost, especially in the higher parts of the plateau towards the south. The influence of these factors on crop distributions is naturally of vital importance. Summer temperatures in the South do not differ critically from those experienced in much of the Southeast. Porto Alegre's hottest month records 76°F., that of Rio de Janeiro 79°F., but winter temperatures decrease considerably, especially under the influence of cold southwest winds from the interior, known as the *minuano*. The corresponding winter temperatures for Porto Alegre and Rio de Janeiro are 53°F and 69°F. respectively. Parts of the plateau of Santa Catarina and Rio Grande do Sul above 3,000 feet in height frequently are snow covered in winter.

Rainfall amounts received on the Atlantic margins backed by the plateau escarpment are relatively high, such as the 73 inches of Paranaguá, but they decrease southward, Porto Alegre's 50 inches being typical. Amounts on the plateau are also fairly uniform, varying between 50 and 60 inches.

As in the state of São Paulo, geology plays a greater influence than climate in influencing the distribution of natural vegetation in this region, although there are some aspects of the pattern which are probably due to human influences, for it must be remembered that this land has been occupied by Indians for some thousands of years. Broadly, the region is bisected by a line some 50 miles south of and parallel to the Uruguay river. North of that line the predominant vegetation is forest, especially Araucaria pine forest which clothes the diabase lands extensively (Fig. 6). To the south, prairie or campo limpo covers the region, extending across the Uruguayan boundary to give the typical vegetational features of that country.

Within this broad pattern there are variations. The edge of the diabase highlands overlooking the Jacui basin has a semi-deciduous forest cover, and this links up on the east with similar stands of trees and the humid forest of the coastal crystalline plateau rim of the northern half of the region. On the other hand, within the general forest cover of the north, there are large areas of prairie, as suggested by the name *campos geraes* given to the eastern margins of the plateau, especially on the sandstone-based inner lowland. In the deep western valley of the Paraná semi-deciduous forest again replaces the Araucaria pines.

The colonization of this region, by which it has been incorporated into the Brazilian nation, is related to three fairly distinct movements, those of

(*a*) the bandeirantes of the 17th and 18th centuries,
(*b*) European immigrants of the 19th century, and
(*c*) a Paulista movement across the Paranapanema of the 20th century,

and the impress of these movements on the economic life of the South dominates population, crops, land tenure systems, settlements and their whole way of life.

The bandeirantes, avoiding forest wherever possible, spread south from São Paulo (as they had done northward into Minas Gerais), utilizing the *campos* of the eastern areas, and descending from the plateau into the rolling grasslands of Rio Grande do Sul and beyond. Reaching the Plata they established Colonia as a strategic southern outpost of Brazil. Their efforts were supplemented by direct government intervention with the purpose of occupying these distant lands, especially once the Empire had been established and it was necessary to stake claims to prevent Spanish occupation. The basic pastoral economy so established still persists over most of the state of Rio Grande do Sul south of the Jacui river, and a considerable part of the southern third of the diabase plateau, with smaller prairie enclaves in central Santa Catarina and central Paraná. This is the zone of the gaucho, herding criollo cattle for their hides and salt beef, and shepherding almost as many sheep for their wool and tallow. This is the principal area in Brazil for production of cross-bred wools, two-thirds of which are used in Brazilian textile mills and the rest exported. Bagé (48,000) is in the heart of this pastoral country, and Pelotas (209,000) and Rio Grande (118,000) are its chief ports. Both are concerned with industries processing the raw materials, such as woollen mills, tanneries, leather factories, frigorificos and dried meat works. Rio Grande is also one of the major ports of Brazil, serving the whole region in addition to its local significance.

Except for the urban centres, the pattern of life has changed little over the centuries in these pastoral lands. The area, in the past, was a southern sertão providing mules for the great fairs of Sorocaba, on a similar pattern to the pastoral lands of Argentina supplying the markets of Salta. Today latifundia still prevails, although first steps have been taken towards agrarian reform; examples of scientific pastoralism are few and far between. One or two forested areas on the crystalline rocks support mixed farming communities, but these are oases in a sea of pastoralism, and in this characteristic the South differs little from the basic pattern of the other regions of Brazil.

Contemporaneous with bandeirante expansion southward, Brazilian colonists spread in the same direction along the coastal margins with similar objectives of strategic occupation and a search for gold. In the process they established the settlements of Iguape, Paraguaná, São Francisco, Florianopolis and Porto Alegre. Choosing strategically defensible sites, such as islands, to protect their new colonies from Indian attack from the forests, they established a series of footholds along the coast unconnected with the colonizing work of the bandeirantes in the interior.

From these coastal bases the region was penetrated westward by the second great colonizing phase, that undertaken by foreign immigrants, mainly Germans, Italians, Poles, Russians and other Slav peoples. Like the southern movement of the bandeirantes this involved all three states of the region, but it is in Rio Grande do Sul and Santa Catarina that the greatest effects are seen.

The motives of these immigrants from overseas were mixed. They were another aspect of the movement by Brazil to colonize their southern lands in order to reinforce their claim to them. In addition there were both individual and state efforts to open up undeveloped lands, and the pioneer urge of the immigrants to seek new homes, freedom and independence away from the oppressed parts of Europe. The movement lasted for more than a century from the 1820s to the 1930s. It first reached Rio Grande do Sul and was felt later in Santa Catarina and finally in Paraná; and it accounts for the major agricultural developments which have taken place in all except northern and western Paraná.

From their base at São Leopoldo north of Porto Alegre, a great current of German immigration has penetrated the northern terraces of the Jacuí basin and the slopes of the cuesta fringe of the plateau in a wide belt of settlement stretching east and west to beyond Santa Maria, up the valleys of the southward-flowing tributaries of the Jacuí, especially the largest, the Taquarí, and beyond to the north and the north-west in the high basin of the Uruguay. The economy has a sound mixed-farming basis of cultivation of maize, rye and potatoes, and the rearing of pigs fattened (principally for lard) on the maize. This is unlike anything anywhere else in the whole of Brazil, and is more typical of North American agriculture, and in some respects, of the practices of their German homeland. The large estates have been bought and subdivided into permanent farms, to which the owners are strongly attached. There is a stability having no relationship to the boom agriculture of the Southeast. Near Santa Cruz a zone has been developed for tobacco cultivation for cigarette manufacture (unlike the cigar tobacco of Bahia), and this is the most important area of Brazil for this crop.

Towards the end of the 19th century a second wave of immigrants, this time of Italians, entered Rio Grande do Sul, passed through the German settlements and established themselves high on the diabase cuesta on the periphery of the Jacuí basin. Clearing forest like the Germans, and partitioning big estates into small farms, they set up vineyards as their principal land use, and from this zone, centred around Alfredo Chaves and Caxias, come most of the grapes and wines produced in Brazil. This is not an export trade, but there is a large domestic market to be supplied. The area is littered with Italian place-names like Garibaldi and Novo Milano; and in styles of rural and urban architecture and in the speech of the people the recency and national characteristics of these settlements, both German and Italian, are outstandingly clear

The last major penetration of the state of Rio Grande do Sul has been Brazilian colonization of the Jacuí flood plain for the purpose of rice cultivation, and here is grown one-quarter of the Brazilian crop. The Jacuí floods in winter when rains are heaviest, which is not the most suitable season for rice. Some attempt is made to conserve water for the summer, but many features of the arable system here remind one of the Southeast, with tenant farmers on large estates, and the cultivation of a profitable crop as the keynote of the economy.

The varied basis of agricultural development in Rio Grande do Sul has contributed considerably to the growth of Porto Alegre (933,000) into Brazil's fourth industrial city. It is in reality an inland port, linked by ocean-going shipping with overseas markets, and by good road, rail and river communications with the interior. Its chief exports are rice, timber, tobacco, cattle products and wine, which indicate the extent of its hinterland. Its industries have the great advantage of proximity to the coal mines south of São Jerônimo, a short distance up the Jacuí, and the establishment of a steel mill at Charqueadas will aid industrial expansion.

Another prong of this overseas-immigrant penetration of the south entered the state of Santa Catarina in the 1850s. This, too, was by Germans in the first place, and was similar to their simultaneous colonization of Forest Chile on the other side of the continent. Basing themselves on Itajaí, Blumenau and Brusque they settled the broken forested country of the Itajaí basin where the crystalline zone has been revealed by river erosion and block faulting. Austrians, Swiss and Italians also entered the area and the colonies spread northward to Joinville, Rio Negro, and the Curitiba district, and west as far as União da Vitória. Wherever they went a sound mixed-farming economy transformed the countryside, and small industries using its products were established in the towns. Each ethnic element contributes a speciality product which they enjoy cultivating; and poultry farming, dairy farming, market-gardening and the cultivation of rice, manioc, tobacco and grapes characterize these zones of eastern Santa Catarina. Itajaí (40,000), Florianopolis (130,000) and São Francisco do Sul (80,000) are all ports exporting not only the output of these farms but of a much wider area including the timber of the Paraná pine, and yerba maté collected in the forests of the west. Laguna (9,000) and Imbituba export the coal mined at Tubarão, 40 miles inland, to the steel mills of Volta Redonda.

In addition to the Germans who penetrated into eastern Paraná from Santa Catarina, a great variety of European immigrants, including Russians, Dutch, Germans, Italians and Poles, have settled in the state in the period 1876–1939. The contribution of those from Eastern Europe has been the largest in this area, and both individual and state pioneer schemes have produced a very similar economic pattern to that already described in the two southern states. Ponta Grossa, Mundo Novo, Teresa Cristina and Guarapuava are focal points in this penetration, Ponta Grossa being a supply base for the movement westward. Increasing use of lorry transport to link these new areas with Curitiba and Paranaguá is a reflection of how roads are taking over the function of railways in many parts of Brazil (Fig. 76). The accessibility of the pioneer mixed-farming communities to such transport is a vital factor in their success. In a few areas where farms have failed the neglect of transport has been a contributary cause of their abandonment. Curitiba (617,000) is the commercial, administrative and cultural centre of the state, and its function as a route centre linking the south with São Paulo is of considerable importance. Paranaguá's role as the outlet of an expanding hinterland has grown in significance, its coffee exports having increased considerably in recent years.

The third, and very different, colonizing force which has affected the south is so recent that almost anything written concerning it is out of date within a year or so (Figs. 52 and 72). It is probably the greatest pioneer movement taking place in Latin America today. This is the sweep of the agricultural frontier across the Paranapanema from São Paulo state into northern and western Paraná. Attracted by the fertile terra roxa soils on the diabase plateau, and the broad swells of the *espigões*, or interfluves, and valleys of the Ivaí and Tibaji which offered almost unlimited arable land, the frontier crossed the Paranapanema in the 1930s. Aided by the foresight of a British company which purchased the land of many estates in the region, the settlement of the colonists has gone forward in a planned manner. Farms were allocated to give the holders land in valleys and on slopes with access to roads, and there is conservation of forest areas to prevent soil erosion. In addition, urban settlements to serve the new area were planned, built rapidly, and linked with new trunk roads and railways. Londrina's growth from a town of 15,000 inhabitants in 1935 to a city of 230,000 thirty-five years later is symbolic of the peopling movement which is in process. Over 90 per cent of the immigrants involved come from other parts of Brazil, and in this respect it is different from the foreign penetration from the east. Seventy per cent of these Brazilians are Paulistas, the remainder being predominantly from Minas Gerais. Japanese and Italians are the largest foreign elements.

Being in the transitional area where frosts sometimes occur, the farmers dare not rely exclusively on coffee, so a great variety of crops is grown, their location on the slopes of the espigões being dependent largely on aspect. On the north-facing lands, cotton, pineapples and oranges share the area with coffee; on the south-facing, there are wheat, maize, barley and potatoes. In the valley bottoms cattle pastures are frequent. In limited areas where sandy soils occur potatoes are an important crop; and pigs are raised on maize as in the United States corn belt. Soya bean production likewise is of increasing importance. In yields the coffee crop is outstanding, being more than twice that produced per acre in São Paulo, and already Paraná's output accounts for nearly 45 per cent of Brazil's enormous production. Thus even in this northern zone, which in many aspects

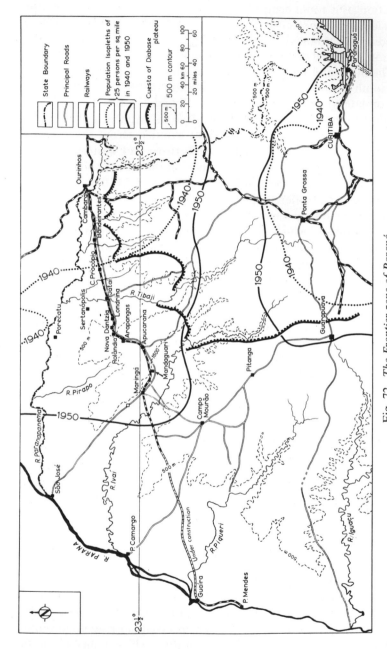

Fig. 72. *The Frontier zone of Paraná*

A region of rapid expansion, with a fast developing communications system

is more tributary to São Paulo than to Curitiba and Paranaguá, the characteristics of the South prevail. In spite of the importance of a cash crop and the Paulista traditions which have brought it into northern Paraná, the prospect of a greater stability in agricultural patterns seems bright.

The fortunes of the coffee industry are, of course, fundamental to the prosperity or otherwise of the commercial agricultural sector of the economy, and much depends upon supplies of coffee available from other producers on the world market, and international agreements between those producers. There are also considerable fluctuations in production from year to year. For example, Brazil's 1970–1 crop was 9 million bags, but the 1971–2 crop was at least twice that quantity. The small output of the earlier year reflected the effect of severe frosts in 1969, among the worst ever known; and considerable re-planting is now taking place. This creates much rural employment, attracts population from depressed areas, and also raises agricultural production generally for there is considerable inter-planting of cereals and other staple crops for many years until the coffee trees come into production.

In the far west of Paraná and Santa Catarina, and in many areas of the southern extensions of those states, forest products are still of great significance. In a land where so much forest has been cut, stands of timber accessible to road or rail yield good profits, and charcoal burning and collection of yerba maté are important occupations.

The need for energy supplies in these areas of expanding settlement is now leading to the harnessing of the Iguaçú and Paraná rivers. One of the largest such schemes, the Urubupunga complex on the Paraná, has been initiated by the construction of the Jupiá hydroelectric plant.

The distribution of population in the South closely conforms with this pattern of colonization, the most densely peopled areas being the Jacuí and Itajaí basins, the zones served by the railways, the important ports, and the expanding settlement of north-western Paraná. The significance of the South in the national pattern is increasing year by year, now not only by immigration but by big natural increase of the population. This in itself is filling in previously unoccupied areas, and Preston James stresses that this is another of Latin America's areas of expanding settlement without decrease in the original areas of colonization. The state of Paraná continues to grow in population at a faster rate than that of any other part of Brazil, the increase in the decade 1960–70 being from 4¼ millions to 8 millions. Very soon it will have more people than both Santa Catarina and Rio Grande do Sul combined, the population of which grew by 2 millions in the same decade.

Thus the future of the South seems assured, because of the variety of its economic wealth, the stability of its agricultural systems, the relatively favourable physical environment it offers and the heritage of pioneering peoples it has received.

THE CENTRAL STATES

The vast area of the two states of Goiás and Mato Grosso (Fig. 73), covering together some three-quarter million square miles, one-fifth of all Brazil, and as large as the whole of Mexico, contains less than 5 million people, and is one of the least-known areas of all Latin America.

Considering the huge area involved, the structural framework of the region is remarkably similar over enormous extents of territory. This is the region of tabular mesa-like plateaux *par excellence*, composed of great sheets of gently inclined or almost horizontal sandstones. These chapadas are bounded by high cliff-like cuestas, and where surface erosion has started to destroy them more vigorously, detached fragments of these mesa block surfaces stand out isolated from each other by intervening stream valleys. The term *serras da rapadura* (sugar block plateaux) adequately and picturesquely describes them. In parts, especially southern and eastern Goiás and the upper Paraguay basin, areas of the old crystalline floor or older folded sedimentary rocks outcrop, but viewed as a whole, there is a remarkably similar and uniform appearance in the plateaux, regardless of underlying surface rocks. The drainage systems which are eating into the chapadas on all sides have divided the plateaux into great lobes. Most of these run from north to south, as the powerful Amazon tributaries, and the Tocantins and Araguaia in particular, have gouged out deep valleys to a much greater extent than those of the Paranaíba and Paraguay. In the south-west of the region, the chapada edge, eaten into by the Paraguay and its tributaries, and approximating to the 1,000-feet contour line, swings in a great semicircle concave to the west, to enclose the alluvial plain of the Pantanal. The encircling chapada in the south-east, south-west of the Araguaia source, is a continuation of the diabase plateau. At the foot of the chapada the crystalline base of the Brazilian massif is exposed and is known as the *Pé de Serra*, a zone some 500 feet above

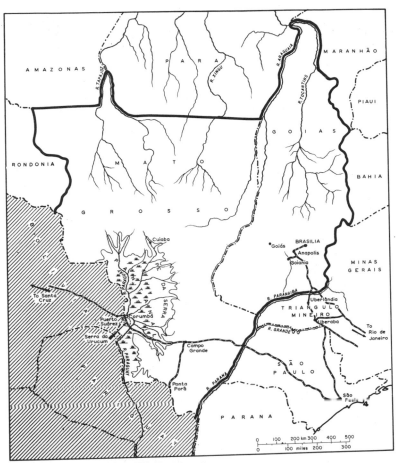

Fig. 73. *Brazil's Central States*
A new frontier zone being settled via the Triángulo Mineiro. Brazil's new
federal capital, Brasilia, is being built in southern Goiás

sea-level, and above the level of the Pantanal floods. The Paraguay
main stream winds its way around isolated blocks of old folded
sedimentary limestone remnants scattered on the Pantanal, the
massif south of Corumbá, the Urucum block, being one of the
world's greatest reserves of manganese.

The general level of this great central plateau is about 2,000 feet
above sea-level, except in the east where in parts it exceeds 3,000 feet.
Over most of the area the slope is a gradual descent towards the

north, with the exception of the Pantanal zone and the Paraná basin.

The outstanding characteristics of the region's climate are the pronounced nature of the summer maximum of rainfall, which in parts accounts for 80 per cent of the annual amount, and the high diurnal ranges of temperature consequent upon the clear skies of the dry winter months, giving maximum insolation by day and maximum radiation by night. This range may be as much as 40°F.

Total rainfall varies between 50 and 70 inches annually. Corumbá has 49 inches, Goiás 67 inches. In each case, June, July and August are almost rainless. Seasonal temperature ranges are almost negligible, that of Corumbá being 11°F. (69–80°F), and Goiás 3°F. (72–75°F.). As one descends to the Amazon northward, so rainfall distribution becomes all-seasonal, and diurnal temperatures more equable.

The distribution of vegetation in this vast area is only known in general, and knowledge of local and sub-regional differences is very imperfect (Fig. 5). Over most of the area, probably some three-quarters of the whole, the prevalent cover is the tree-savana which is so typical of large areas of Brazil, and is usually known as *campo cerrado*. It is predominantly the grassland of the normal African savana, but unlike the latter, the trees are much more thickly distributed over it. The semi-deciduous trees rarely grow tall, nor do they prevent sunshine reaching the grassy areas which surround them. It is neither an easy landscape through which to build roads nor to clear, yet it forms good cattle country so long as water is available for the animals. One such area is the Pé da Serra east of the Pantanal, crossed by the Paraguay's tributaries. When the Pantanal is flooded, at the end of the period of summer rains, cattle can be driven on to the higher campo cerrado of the Pé da Serra, whereas when the floods subside, the Pantanal is a rich grazing ground of tender grasses.

Deep valley troughs have gallery forests, and the diabase areas are also tree-covered. Other zones are those of campo limpo, for the most part treeless grassland, such as near Campo Grande on the Paraná–Paraguay watershed, above the chapada cuesta. Boundaries between vegetational zones in the region are often remarkably sharp, that, for example, between the forested east bank of the Paraná and the campo cerrado of the west being typical of these often unexplained abrupt changes.

More than half the population of the region is concentrated in two areas, and two-thirds of this is distributed over south-eastern

Goiás, the other third in the upper Paraguay basin of Mato Grosso. Into both areas railways have been extended from the São Paulo network, and these, together with improved roads and the expansion of air routes, are overcoming the greatest single obstacle to the region's economic progress, that of isolation. In no area is this more evident than in the Pantanal zone served through Campo Grande and Corumbá which is now linked with the Bolivian railways via Puerto Suárez and Santa Cruz. Corumbá (39,000), once a cul-de-sac, is now developing as a central focus of routes east and west between La Paz and São Paulo and north and south between Cuiabá and the river system to Buenos Aires, for it stands at the head of navigation. Hides and skins and dried and salted beef are exported by rail and river, and it may soon be economic to exploit the manganese reserves of Urucum and the nickel resources recently discovered near Goiania. Campo Grande (111,000) and Cuiabá (100,000) are both centres of the ranching country around them, where huge estates raise criollo cattle on the campo limpo and campos of the Pantanal and Pé da Serra respectively. Campo Grande has become important from its position on the railway, Cuiabá from its significance as an old bandeirante centre of the sertão where both gold and diamonds were discovered. In the future it will probably become a significant base for the penetration of southern Amazonia. The highway linking Cuiabá with Pôrto Velho is already complete; another is being constructed northwards to Santarém.

Much more economically developed is south eastern Goiás, a region also reached by the bandeirantes in their drives north and west from São Paulo. Their routes led through the Triángulo Mineiro, the broad westward-facing salient of the state of Minas Gerais which separates Goiás from São Paulo, and which is really a part of this great central region. Located between the rivers Grande and Paranaíba, it shares some characteristics of São Paulo to the south, the diabase forested areas with their terra roxa soils offering a good basis for agriculture. Crops of coffee, maize, beans, sugar and rice are grown, and in semi-deciduous forest areas, cattle pastoralism with subsistence agriculture is predominant. This savana-scrub forest cover continues northward into Goiás. Through it, from the Triángulo Mineiro, have moved not only the bandeirantes but the pioneers planting coffee and sugar cane and subsistence maize and beans with some rice. This is another, and the most recent, of the new pioneer areas of Brazil, developing fast and even since the movement into north-western Paraná. It already produces more than

Plate 44. *The new capital of Brazil, Brasília, is located on the great interior plateau, with unlimited area for its expansion*

10 per cent of Brazil's coffee crop, and land is increasing in value rapidly. Urban centres, like those of western Paraná, are being planned in consonance with this economic development, Goiania (345,000) being laid out with a view to its population becoming 500,000. Anapolis (60,000) to the north-east, also on the railway linking the area to the south, is the second most important centre at present. The new capital of Brazil, Brasilia (380,000), is being built nearby (Fig. 73), and the new source of power developed at Cachoeira Dourada for these urban centres is one of the largest hydro-electric plants in Brazil. Both are indications of the nation's determination to open up and people the interior.

Much will depend on how far it is possible to utilize the campo cerrado beyond the pioneer zone and whether expansion of settlement will continue in Goiás. Its population increased by nearly 80 per cent between 1950 and 1960 and by 50 per cent between 1960 and 1970, largely by settlers from São Paulo and Minas Gerais. Thus, on an ethnic basis which was predominantly mameluco, have come the European-derived immigrants from the south-east. In the pastoral area of Cuiabá negroid elements, carried there as slaves by the early pastoralists, add an anomalous facet to the pattern of the Central States (Fig. 3).

THE AMAZON

The remaining region of Brazil (Fig. 74), its vast almost empty northlands, north of the central and north-eastern regions, has twice the area of the central states, yet less than 3½ million people. Half of this population lives in the lower Amazonian state of Pará, and more than half a million in Belém city alone.

Unlike most great lowland river basins of the world, the Amazon does not flow in a great plain which becomes progressively wider towards the river's mouth. It is shaped like the cross-section of a bulbous flask, more than 800 miles wide from north to south where Bolivia is separated from Venezuela, narrowing to less than 100 miles in the Obidos area, and then widening east of its confluence with the Xingú tributary from the south into a region of islands and coastal lowlands which stretch away north and south to the Guianas and the Maranhão section of the Northeast. It is not unlikely that in previous geological eras, before the Andes emerged as a continuous mountain system, the drainage of the old Brazilian-Guiana massifs by an earlier Amazon was to the west through the zone of the Peruvian-Ecuadorean boundary, rather than to the east.

This great lowland rises fairly abruptly but progressively on the west and the south-west in the area of the Andean tributaries, where sweeping interfluves separate the valleys, but where it merges into the Guiana and Brazilian plateaux the junction between the plain and the crystalline rocks of the tabular uplands is often a line of chapada cuestas, some of which may be as much as 1,000 feet above the lowland. These are visible from the river itself in the narrowest part of its plain course.

Composed over nearly the whole of its area of sands, river clays, silts and alluvial débris, the plain is not extending its surface seaward. This is the result of steady submergence which prevents the formation of a delta in spite of the enormous load the river carries to the ocean. Instead, what appears to be an old deltaic region has suffered depression, and arms of the sea flood inland along its distributaries amidst a medley of islands, the largest of which is Marajó. Not only does the delta not grow, but the mangrove-matted shores act as a defensive sea wall preventing further erosion from wave and tidal attack. In this coastal mouth zone the Pará river enters from the south, flowing to the ocean south of Marajó island.

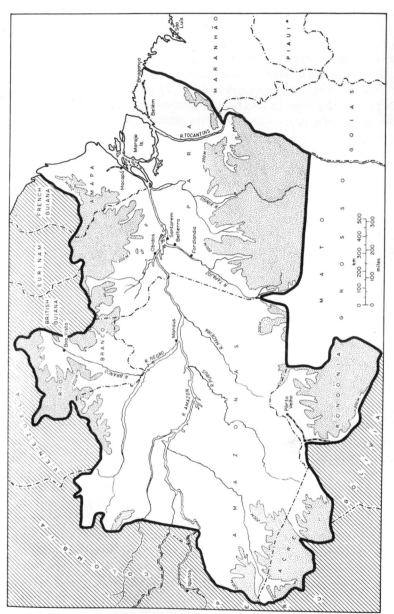

Fig. 74. *Brazilian Amazonia*
Latin America's largest undeveloped area

Although sometimes considered as a tributary of the Amazon, its mouth is almost independent with little interconnection with the Amazon mouths. It brings far less sediment, having almost entirely a highland basin, and its flood-plain is narrower and less swampy. There is in fact a considerable difference in the Amazon's tributaries between the *rios brancos* heavy with silt and the *rios negros* with their more stable courses coloured by vegetable débris rather than mud. The difference is obviously dependent upon the relative extent of their lowland and highland courses. Where the tributaries pass from the crystalline basement to the lowland, falls and cataracts occur, those on the Madeira being the farthest to the west. Thus the rivers of the west, especially in Acre territory, are relatively unobstructed for navigation; and the falls on the Negro and Branco on the north are in their higher courses.

The Amazon main stream is impressive in its great length, enabling ocean vessels of 14 feet draught to reach Iquitos in Peru; in its depth which reaches 300 feet in the Obidos section and is rarely less than 75 feet in its lower course; and in its imperceptible gradient, which really means that it flows by the weight and volume of water rather than because of any slope. It is tidal as far upstream as the Xingú confluence.

The river flows in a flood-plain some 50 miles wide, bounded by bluffs which fairly sharply define it on either side. Within this flood-plain occur all the features associated with such a feature, such as braided channels, temporarily abandoned meanders, lakes, swamps and cut-offs. It is obvious, therefore, that the flood régimes of its upper tributaries, such as the contrasting seasonal floods of northern and southern Peru, are to a great extent equalized out in the enormous flood-plain of the main stream where water is absorbed in the lateral swamps and lakes. Thus its flood volume rarely exceeds three times its normal flow, and its persistently huge volume is relatively unaffected by seasonal variations. Only in exceptional years is the whole of the flood-plain covered with flood water, and much depends on local conditions as to the area which is available to accommodate the surplus flow.

The monotony of high temperatures and high humidity is the double characteristic which is typical of climatic régimes in the region. Belém has a range of only $2\frac{1}{2}$°F. between the hottest and coldest months (77·4–79·9°F.). Relatively little of the region experiences average temperatures below 80°F. in any month of the year, but the diurnal range may be five times the seasonal range. Humidity is relieved somewhat in the eastern part of the lowland by the breezes from the ocean, but in the almost stagnant air conditions of the interior it is particularly oppressive. Rainfall amounts are also high; Belém has 86 inches annually and most of this falls in the period January to June (76 inches), when westward-moving air from the Atlantic is heavily saturated with water vapour. This is the region of convectional downpours almost on a daily pattern, and in the heart of the broad basin there is no dry season, and in many years the total rainfall exceeds 100 inches.

Such conditions naturally give rise to the vast extent of selva which distinguishes the Amazon basin from that of any other region of the world (Figs. 5 and 6). This is a forest, predominantly of hardwood evergreens or trees which are deciduous at different seasons of the year, a forest of thousands of varieties of trees growing at random distributions which may or may not be related to local ground or water conditions. It is a canopy forest of high-foliaged trees, where nearly all the animal and land life is concentrated, and movement within it on the *terra firme* away from the flood-plain is less obstructed by vegetation than in the *matta de varzea* or dense jungle which clothes the river banks and flood-plain. In some of the more permanently swamp areas a wet savana undergrowth prevails, and in sandy areas patchy grass openings occur, the northern zones above Obidos having relatively large expanses of more continuous campos.

Some livestock rearing takes place in these savanas, and more particularly in the higher country of the Rio Branco basin near Boa Vista, and on Marajó island. The area north of the river, having a smaller Indian population than south of it, was less attractive for slave raiders, and we thus have the paradox that it is now better supplied with labour. The persistence of a pastoral basis even in this region is a fantastic aspect of the stability of this occupation, for it is almost incredible how the cattle survive the pest-infested swamp environment of some of the areas in which they are kept.

Over most of the inhabited area the primitive system of shifting cultivation prevails. This involves the slashing and burning of a portion of forest to reveal a patch where the poor soils will yield subsistence crops for a few years, and the repetition of the process elsewhere when soil exhaustion sets in. This economy is supplemented by fishing, gathering of roots and nuts, and the commercial exploitation of rare skins, expensive cabinet woods, gums and medicinal plants, such as rotenone obtained from timbo vines and of special value as an insecticide. From this same collecting economy comes the principal export 'crop' of the region today, namely Brazil nuts, which are gathered especially in the Tocantins river basin. Output often reaches 30,000 tons annually for it is still virtually a Brazilian monopoly. Some 25,000 tons of rubber are also gathered annually to help supply the Brazilian rubber industry. This is a survival of the rubber boom which collapsed in 1910, when the value of Brazil's rubber exports almost equalled that of her coffee.

There are a few very limited areas of arable farming, producing crops of cocoa, sugar, tobacco, cotton and food crops such as maize, bananas and manioc. These are near the larger centres of Manáus (250,000), Santarém (112,000) and Obidos (4,000), but the most important zone of the whole basin for cultivation is on both sides of the Belém–Braganca railway, where in addition to the crops indicated, Japanese settlers have succeeded in raising sufficient amounts of jute and pepper to supply the home market.

The region is deficient in minerals, but where the Guiana shield area approaches the Amazon mouth extensive deposits of manganese have been discovered in Amapá territory. This area is now connected by a railway, 125 miles long, to the port of Macapá (33,000), thus offering a much more accessible source of this mineral than the other parts of Brazil where it occurs. Exports now total some half a million tons annually. There is also the great hope of Brazil that in the Andean margins of the basin there will one day be found supplies of oil to make the country self-sufficient in this source of power. There appear to be large areas of sedimentary formations favourable for this development, but all efforts to date have been unremunerative, and the needs of the region are supplied via Iquitos from Peru's Ganso Azul field, and refined at Manáus (Fig. 51). The other principal industrial activities of the latter city are connected with jute, plywood and food-processing.

Much of the settlement pattern evolved during the period of rubber exploitation when small nuclei were established in collecting areas especially in the headwater zones of Acre territory, at the heads of navigation and particularly at river junctions. Many of these have now been abandoned; others maintain a languishing existence. The river junction sites are the most important still, for all communication is by water, and now where two tributaries join, or at a confluence with the main stream, cargoes of wild rubber, balatá gum, nuts, medicinal roots, wild animal and reptile skins, and rafts of fancy woods are still bartered and collected for transport downstream. These confluence sites often owe their origin to Jesuit missions or slave-raiding collecting points, where Indians were transported down river to the sugar plantations of Belém and São Luis. They became of immensely greater importance during the rubber boom, and Manáus in particular was an exotic urban community in the heart of the forest. The only railway, from Pôrto Velho on the Madeira to the Bolivian border, is another reminder of the days of that period. Even more recent and scientific efforts in the Tapajoz valley at Belterra and Fordlandia to grow rubber on a plantation scale have largely failed to overcome the difficulties of this region.

The principal hindrance to the development of this enormous zone is scarcity of labour. Gone are the days when thousands of drought-stricken folk from Ceará sought an economic livelihood from rubber collecting. There are so many other areas of promise in Brazil, now relatively easily accessible, and offering far greater opportunities than does Amazonia. Nor does Brazil favour large-scale Asiatic immigration which would lead to unassimilated foreign colonies having few contacts with other Brazilians. In a country developing so rapidly throughout its 3 million square miles capital obviously cannot be found for all regions equally. Considerable effort, thought and money have already been expended, but the full utilization of this region awaits greater pressure of population on land resources, greater quantities of capital and full scientific exploration of the best means of tackling its problems. It may be much better that this area should be a reserve of land for development in next century, rather than it should be pillaged and wastefully exploited today.

Meanwhile its population increases steadily, a growth of 30 per cent being recorded in the 1960–70 decade. Yet, with a density of less than 3 persons per square mile, this is still the empty heart of Latin America, and its extent spreads far beyond Brazil's political boundaries into the Guianas, Venezuela, Colombia, Peru and Bolivia. Unless oil is discovered its significance in the Brazilian economy for decades to come is likely to be minimal, and when it is welded by settlement into the nation, the process is more likely to take place from the Southeast through the pioneer lands of Goiás and Matto Grosso than from any other direction.

The most important steps taken in recent years to develop the region have been firstly, the construction of roads to link together the principal centres, and secondly, the establishment of Manáus as a free zone. Highways linking the latter city with Boa Vista in the north and Pôrto Velho in the south are the first important surface connections in western Amazonia other than the rivers; whereas the

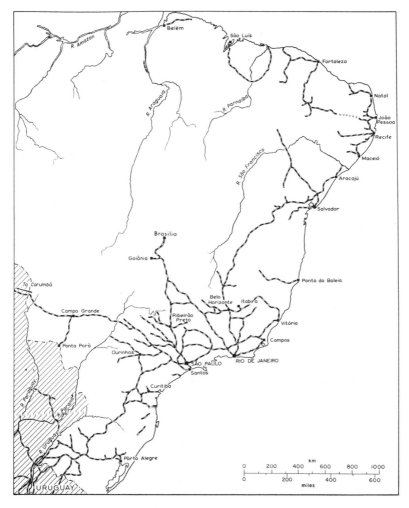

Fig. 75. *The railway systems of Brazil*
Only in the Southeast is there a relatively good network

tariff concessions for Manáus have as their object the creation around the city of a commercial, industrial and agricultural area endowed with sufficient economic resources to permit its development in the face of adverse factors, such as the small size of the local market and the wide dispersal of the population.

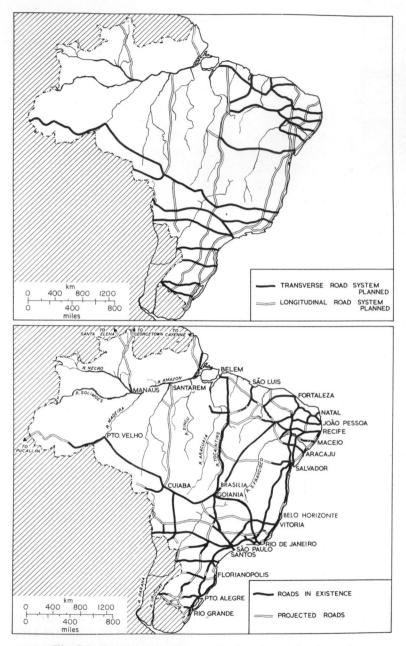

Fig. 76. *Transverse and longitudinal road systems of Brazil*

An arterial road pattern is being developed to aid the opening up of under-developed areas, and to facilitate internal trade in Latin America's largest potential market

PROSPECTS AND PROBLEMS

Like Argentina, Brazil's whole economic structure is maintained on the export of pastoral and agricultural products. In spite of its vast reserves of minerals, they are really barely touched. An increasing amount of iron ore is exported, but the competition of more accessible Venezuelan ore is likely to reduce the pace of such expansion. Much of its other mineral potential is isolated in the interior, and except for domestic needs, it is unlikely to be developed in the near future. As in all South America, coal supplies are meagre, of relatively poor quality, and inadequate for its growing industrial fabric.

Three export crops, coffee, cotton and sugar, dominate the position in respect of Brazil's international trade. Coffee in recent years has often represented half of the value of its exports and frequently two-thirds. Together with timber, mainly Paraná pine, the three crops usually account for over 60 per cent of all exports. To these must be added other commodities of agricultural and pastoral origin which are prominent trading assets, such as wool, cocoa, tobacco, hides and skins, carnauba wax, edible oils and other fibres.

This predominance of foodstuffs and primary raw materials in this way is especially remarkable when one considers the enormous areas which are either untouched or poorly utilized. In all Brazil only 3 per cent of the area is cultivated. It is in some respects an index of the potential production which could be won from this vast nation. It also needs to be stressed that the major part of the country's rural production is not recorded statistically, the part which is feeding the rural dweller and his family. If one tries to estimate this amount and add it to the statistically recorded output, there is little doubt that today, even with Brazilian industrialization, some two-thirds of the national income is derived from the agricultural, pastoral and forest industries.

This accounts for the fact that 60 per cent of the population is still rural, in sharp contrast to Argentina, and in spite of the rapid process of urbanization that is taking place, especially to the cities of São Paulo and Rio de Janeiro.

More than 90 per cent of the cultivated area is devoted to maize, coffee, cotton, rice, beans, manioc, sugar and wheat, in that order. Maize occupies a quarter of the land used, and the three other staples of Brazilian diet, rice, beans and manioc, another quarter. In most foodstuffs the country is therefore self-sufficient, most remarkable

Plate 45. *Brasilia. The residential blocks form neighbourhood units with church, cinema, shops, schools and parking space, all isolated from the highways*

progress having been made in converting rice from an import crop to an export earner. Much has also been done in the post-war period to meet the deficiency in wheat, the country's principal imported foodstuff, and both area and output have quadrupled since 1946. A similar effort is needed to provide the population with home-produced dairy products, many of which are still purchased from overseas, an objective easily within reach of such a pastorally minded people.

This concentration upon a rural way of life, and its achievements in the output of products of the soil, are all the more remarkable when the components of the rural scene are analysed. The defects are glaring, even in a continent where examples of efficient agriculture are limited. Over large areas shifting cultivation still prevails; rotation of crops is unknown over most of the cultivated area; mixed farming is limited for the most part to the South; and the hoe is almost everywhere the pivot of agricultural equipment. Although some parts of the South practise a long fallow, and some coffee planters plough in cover crops and use fertilizers, the plough is rarely used outside these regions. Problems of land tenure, inadequate and careless methods of farming complete the main aspects of the picture.

But the situation is not static. Techniques are changing, and machines, fertilizers, scientific methods and new crops are all being introduced. Brazil's industrialization is aiding the evolution, and the products of her chemical industry supply some fertilizers. Others are imported in growing quantities; and local reserves are being quarried. Hybrid maize is gaining ground; pedigree cattle are being imported; soil conservation methods are being used, especially in parts of São Paulo; and the number of tractors grows steadily. Agrarian reform is taking place in the areas most needing such attention. As a result the indices of agricultural production show Brazil as registering the greatest all-round advances in all Latin America.

Such progress, however, involves a vast amount of capital, and much of it in agricultural credits to maintain the stability of the farming community in the modernization process. It is the familiar problem of Latin America on a large scale, for the tasks Brazil has in hand are staggering in their immensity. The programme includes the re-equipment of its agriculture, the establishment of an industrial basis, the rationalization of the communications system and the education of its population. When seen against a background of a physical landscape of bewildering variety, it is a programme that might well daunt more developed nations. Meanwhile the growth in population by over 2 million annually increases the burden temporarily, in view of the large percentage of young people to be maintained by the producers. With increasing life expectancy, this burden will later be converted to an asset, to give the nation the man-power to tame the sertões, to fill in the lacunae of the settlement pattern, and to increase the country's economic output commensurate with its size and physical endowment.

In the meantime there is considerable emphasis upon the encouragement of labour-intensive exports (and coffee itself is a highly labour-intensive crop and one of the most profitable commercially) and labour-intensive developmental projects. Included in the latter are the development plans being carried out for the Northeast and for Amazonia; and the role of road construction and energy production is fundamental not only in providing employment but in the winning of Brazil's huge potential, particularly by co-ordinating the resources of the various regions of this vast country.

The size of the enormous internal market, in the long run, will, of course, prove one of Brazil's greatest assets. Steel consumption, for example, is already growing at a rate of half a million tons annually; and a programme of expansion of steel output to a yearly figure of 20 million tons by 1980 has been undertaken (Fig. 16). The integration of this kind of development with other industries will generally assist the total expansion of the economy. It is, however, only part of an ambitious growth policy embracing the production particularly of motor vehicles, cement, chemicals, petrochemicals, synthetic rubber, pulp and paper, and expanding investment in transport, power, mining, agriculture, education and health. As a result, for several years now Brazil has had the highest economic growth rate (approaching 10 per cent annually) in all Latin America.

STATISTICAL SUMMARY — BRAZIL

Area: 3,287,204 square miles

Population (1970): 93,317,000

Percentage of land
   (a) Arable   3%
   (b) Pastoral   29%

(*c*) Forest   42%
(*d*) Other   26%

Animal numbers

    (*a*) Cattle   84·0 million
    (*b*) Sheep   21·9   ,,
    (*c*) Pigs   59·0   ,,
    (*d*) Goats   13·8   ,,
    (*e*) Horses and Mules   14·0   ,,

Communications

    (*a*) All-seasons road mileage   23,990
    (*b*) Railway mileage   19,860
    (*c*) Air routes   1,995 million passenger miles
                        54   ,,   ton miles

Principal products

    (*a*) *Agricultural*

Root Crops	28,178,000	metric tons
Maize	12,824,000	,, ,,
Rice	6,792,000	,, ,,
Bananas	4,531,000	,, ,,
Sugar	4,275,000	,, ,,
Beans	2,470,000	,, ,,
Oilseeds	1,800,000	,, ,,
Coffee	1,398,000	,, ,,
Wheat	629,000	,, ,,
Cotton	444,000	,, ,,
Tobacco	243,000	,, ,,
Cocoa	195,000	,, ,,

    (*b*) *Mineral*

Iron	21,000,000	metric tons
Petroleum	6,994,000	,, ,,
Coal	1,957,000	,, ,,
Manganese	598,000	,, ,,
Bauxite	303,000	,, ,,
Gold	15,700	troy pounds

Exports

    (*a*) *Total:* $1,881,000,000
    (*b*) *Percentage share of principal commodities*

Coffee	41%
Cotton	7%
Iron Ore	6%
Sugar	6%
Cocoa	2%

LATIN AMERICA

TOTAL TRADE OF EACH COUNTRY, 1965–1968
(million U.S. dollars)

	Exports (f.o.b.)				Imports (c.i.f.)			
	1965	1966	1967	1968†	1965	1966	1967	1968†
Argentina	1,493	1,593	1,464	1,368	1,199	1,124	1,096	1,169
Bolivia	110	126	145	153	126	138	151	152
Brazil	1,595	1,741	1,654	1,881	1,096	1,496	1,667	2,132
Chile	685	877	910	933	604	755	868	—
Colombia	537	510	510	558	454	674	497	—
Costa Rica	112	156	144	172	178	178	191	214
Dominican Republic	126	137	156	164	100	185	201	226
Ecuador	180	185	200	—	168	164	191	—
El Salvador	189	192	207	212	201	220	224	216
Guatemala	187	228	199	222	229	207	247	247
Haiti	37	35	34	36	34	38	36	38
Honduras	127	143	156	186	122	149	164	186
Mexico	1,120	1,199	1,145	1,254	1,560	1,605	1,746	1,960
Nicaragua	144	138	146	157	160	182	202	185
Panama	79	89	93	95	208	235	251	266
Paraguay	57	49	48	48	55	59	71	73
Peru	666	763	774	865	745	817	833	630
Uruguay	191	186	159	179	150	164	170	165
Venezuela	2,744	2,713	2,886	2,857	1,454	1,331	1,464	1,697
TOTAL*	10,380	11,040	11,030	11,560	8,860	9,740	10,290	11,100

† Provisional. * Excluding Cuba. Totals include estimates for listed countries for which data are not available.
SOURCE: IMF: *International Financial Statistics.*

UNITED STATES TRADE WITH LATIN AMERICA, 1965–68
(million U.S. dollars)

Country	Exports (f.o.b.)			
	1965	1966	1967	1968
Argentina	268	244	230	281
Bolivia	42	47	59	55
Brazil	348	575	547	709
Chile	237	256	248	307
Colombia	198	287	218	319
Costa Rica	61	62	64	74
Cuba†	0	0	0	0
Dominican Republic	76	88	97	115
Ecuador	80	83	99	98
El Salvador	61	70	60	61
Guatemala	96	90	91	93
Haiti	21	22	22	24
Honduras	54	68	71	75
Mexico	1,106	1,180	1,222	1,365
Nicaragua	69	71	70	62
Panama	125	138	139	136
Paraguay	16	19	19	25
Peru	282	308	258	196
Uruguay	20	25	22	38
Venezuela	626	598	587	655
TOTAL	3,788	4,231	4,124	4,689
Latin America as % of all countries	*13·8*	*14·0*	*13·1*	*13·6*

† Less than U.S. $0·5 m.
SOURCE: *Statistical Abstract of the United States.*

UNITED STATES TRADE WITH LATIN AMERICA, 1965–68

(*million U.S. dollars*)

Country	Imports (f.o.b.)			
	1965	**1966**	**1967**	**1968**
Argentina	122	149	140	207
Bolivia	31	28	43	30
Brazil	512	600	559	670
Chile	209	229	175	203
Colombia	277	245	240	264
Costa Rica	57	60	70	88
Cuba†	0	0	0	0
Dominican Republic	111	128	134	156
Ecuador	106	94	101	90
El Salvador	48	44	54	45
Guatemala	67	82	64	71
Haiti	20	19	21	26
Honduras	72	85	70	83
Mexico	638	750	749	893
Nicaragua	36	31	42	50
Panama	60	68	76	78
Paraguay	13	13	11	12
Peru	241	311	310	328
Uruguay	36	30	13	22
Venezuela	1,018	1,002	980	950
TOTAL	3,675	3,970	3,851	4,266
Latin America as % of all countries	*17·2*	*15·5*	*14·4*	*12·9*

† Less than U.S. $0·5 m.

SOURCE: *Statistical Abstract of the United States.*

JAPANESE TRADE WITH LATIN AMERICA, 1965–68
(*million U.S. dollars*)

Country	Exports (f.o.b.)			
	1965	1966	1967	1968
Argentina	44·1	30·5	39·3	42·4
Bolivia	12·8	15·5	16·5	22·7
Brazil	26·8	44·0	54·6	102·1
Chile	26·0	22·9	11·9	12·3
Colombia	12·9	23·9	15·6	27·5
Costa Rica	14·2	14·4	12·8	13·4
Cuba	3·5	6·5	7·4	2·4
Dominican Republic	5·0	14·3	11·9	13·1
Ecuador	8·9	11·2	13·6	15·9
El Salvador	16·3	13·8	13·9	14·8
Guatemala	13·9	15·9	18·5	18·6
Haiti	1·2	2·0	2·4	2·6
Honduras	5·6	4·6	6·6	9·1
Mexico	40·7	50·3	91·8	106·3
Nicaragua	11·1	8·4	11·6	12·1
Panama	56·3	63·5	52·4	77·4
Paraguay	3·9	3·7	4·4	4·4
Peru	47·7	57·1	50·6	31·0
Uruguay	0·9	0·9	0·8	1·2
Venezuela	56·4	62·7	63·0	74·3
TOTAL	408·2	466·1	499·6	603·6
Latin America as % of all countries	*4·8*	*4·8*	*4·8*	*4·7*

SOURCE: IMF/IBRD: *Direction of Trade.*

JAPANESE TRADE WITH LATIN AMERICA, 1965–68
(million U.S. dollars)

	Imports (c.i.f.)			
Country	**1965**	**1966**	**1967**	**1968**
Argentina	47·8	53·6	52·3	41·1
Bolivia	6·4	5·4	10·7	8·9
Brazil	49·7	60·7	85·6	87·1
Chile	131·7	149·3	166·9	187·1
Colombia	4·4	8·4	9·9	11·0
Costa Rica	1·0	1·4	1·8	2·3
Cuba	29·3	22·5	26·1	33·3
Dominican Republic	0·1	0·3	0·2	1·7
Ecuador	6·4	11·9	12·9	41·5
El Salvador	33·9	22·4	16·3	15·9
Guatemala	24·0	22·8	18·8	27·9
Haiti	2·6	3·5	2·5	2·1
Honduras	5·5	4·5	5·1	10·6
Mexico	144·8	177·8	171·8	172·9
Nicaragua	54·5	47·3	51·3	47·3
Panama	6·0	9·0	4·0	2·5
Paraguay	0·5	0·2	0·7	1·4
Peru	111·2	124·1	154·6	194·8
Uruguay	0·9	4·0	2·6	1·6
Venezuela	29·5	25·0	29·2	26·9
TOTAL	690·2	754·1	823·3	917·9
Latin America as % of all countries	*8·5*	*7·9*	*7·1*	*7·1*

SOURCE: IMF/IBRD: *Direction of Trade*.

JAPANESE INVESTMENTS IN LATIN AMERICA, APRIL 1951–MARCH 1966
(CUMULATIVE TOTALS)
(*million U.S. dollars*)

Economic Sector	Equity Investments	Loans	Total	Per cent of Total
Agriculture and forestry	0·3	0·3	0·7	0·2
Fishery	2·9	1·5	4·4	1·3
Mining	2·3	29·5	31·8	9·6
Construction	—	27·8	27·8	8·4
Manufacturing	154·5	24·4	178·9	54·3
Food	*4·0*	*0·5*	*4·4*	*1·3*
Textiles	*24·7*	*7·5*	*32·1*	*9·7*
Chemicals	*2·3*	—	*2·3*	*7·1*
Iron and other metals	*43·7*	*6·8*	*50·5*	*15·3*
Machinery (non-electric)	*72·6*	*7·7*	*80·3*	*24·3*
Electrical machinery	*5·0*	*1·2*	*6·2*	*1·9*
Total production industries	160·0	83·4	243·5	73·9
Trade and other	11·4	71·1	86·0*	26·1
TOTAL	171·4	154·5	329·5	100·0

* Includes U.S. $3·1 m. investments in overseas branches.
Figures in italics are estimated.
SOURCE: Ministry of International Trade & Industry: *White Paper on Trade and Commerce*, Tokyo, 1968.

THE PRINCIPAL INDUSTRIAL STATES OF LATIN AMERICA

	Electricity Installed capacity in thousands of kW	Crude steel production Thousand metric tons	Cement production Thousand metric tons	Manufacturing employment Thousands
Brazil	8,555	4,436	7,281	2,120
Mexico	5,969	3,285	6,126	1,344
Argentina	5,836	1,552	4,213	1,320
Venezuela	2,455	860	2,437	181
Colombia	2,120	199	2,367	300
Chile	1,720	526	1,251	425
Peru	1,518	84	1,006	184
Cuba	1,255	—	835	—
Puerto Rico	1,119	—	1,525	100
Uruguay	477	8	506	—

UNITED STATES QUOTAS OF SUGAR FROM LATIN AMERICAN
PRODUCERS, 1972
(*tons*)

Dominican Republic	672,881	Venezuela	64,659
Mexico	595,080	Guatemala	62,031
Brazil	580,360	El Salvador	45,210
Peru	415,293	Panama	44,684
Ecuador	85,687	Haiti	32,594
Argentina	80,429	Honduras	12,616
Costa Rica	72,546	Bolivia	6,835
Colombia	71,494	Paraguay	6,835
Nicaragua	67,814		

INTERNATIONAL COFFEE COUNCIL'S EXPORT QUOTAS,
1971–72 SEASON

The individual basic quotas for Latin American producers are as follows, in thousand bags:

Brazil	17,364	Ecuador	622	Venezuela	376
Colombia	5,809	Peru	614	Trinidad	90
El Salvador	1,577	Nicaragua	456	Paraguay	70
Guatemala	1,494	Dominican Rep.	431	Bolivia	65
Mexico	1,460	Haiti	407	Panama	33
Costa Rica	913	Honduras	353	Jamaica	5

LATIN AMERICAN CACAO PRODUCTION, 1970–72 SEASONS
(*thousand tons*)

	1970/71	1971/72
Brazil	181·6	204·0
Ecuador	60·0	55·0
Dominican Republic	26·0	29·0
Colombia	21·0	21·0
Mexico	20·0	20·0
Venezuela	10·0	18·0
Costa Rica	3·9	3·4

References

MAPS

The Times Atlas of the World, edited by John Bartholomew, Volume V, 1957, with seven plates devoted to Latin America, gives the most up-to-date coverage of the area, most of the maps being on a scale of 1 : 5 million or larger. The index is especially valuable for location of recently significant place names.

For more detailed reference the American Geographical Society's *Map of Hispanic America* on the scale of 1 : 1 million is indispensable. These are in process of progressive revision, but inevitably some sheets lack modern information unavailable at the time of their publication.

Each of the republics has an active cartographic organization, but a relatively small area only has been covered by large-scale topographic maps. In Brazil this includes part of the coastal Northeast, southern Rio Grande do Sul and parts of São Paulo and Minas Gerais. In Argentina, the principal areas mapped on a scale of 1 : 50,000 or larger are on the boundary with Brazil and Uruguay, in the state of Córdoba, and in parts of the Argentine Andes. North Mediterranean Chile, including the most densely populated areas of the capital and Valparaiso, is mapped on a scale of 1 : 100,000. The northern third of Colombia is also covered on this scale.

The Directorate of Overseas Surveys is pursuing an active programme of publication of large and small-scale maps of the British Caribbean areas; and these maps on scales of 1 : 10,000, 1 : 25,000 and 1 : 50,000 are readily available.

An *Atlas of Mexico,* published by the Bureau of Business Research of the University of Texas at Austin (1970) gives an excellent impression of the distributional patterns of the Mexican people and their economy.

BOOKS

General

Latin America and the Caribbean: a Handbook (London, 1968), edited by Claudio Véliz is an excellent and most comprehensive treatment of the history, economy, politics and social background of the continent, with contributions from some eighty specialists on Latin America. It is an invaluable reference book of some 800 pages and is almost encyclopaedic in its coverage of Latin America. Preston E. James' *Latin America* (London, 1958) is the most useful treatment of the geography of the whole of Latin America. R. S. Platt's *Latin America: Countrysides and Related Regions* (London, 1943), giving sample studies of the major regions of the continent, is an excellent means of securing a fuller knowledge of the basic ingredients of those areas. The same is true of R. C. West and J. P. Augelli's *Middle America, its Lands and Peoples* (Englewood Hills, N.J., 1966). The two volumes of *Géographie Universelle*, vols. 14, 15, M. Sorre and P. Denis (Paris, 1927–28) unavoidably represent economic conditions of the 1920s, but the fundamental physical background, structural, climatic and bio-geographic, is the fullest analysis yet published. An excellent impression of landscapes can be obtained from the photographs (with notes) which comprise J. L. Rich's *The Face of South America: An Aerial Traverse* (New York, 1942).

The *South American Handbook* (London) is a splendid summary of the details of resources and settlements of all Latin America, and is revised and republished annually. The *West Indies and Caribbean Year Book* (London) more than adequately deals with Middle America in a similar way. A. C. Wilgus' *Latin America in Maps* (New York, 1943) and R. M. Schneider and R. C. Kingsbury's *An Atlas of Latin American Affairs* (London, 1966) are interesting portrayals in compilations of maps of some of the basic historical and economic information necessary to an understanding of the region's geography. A sound treatment of these aspects is H. Blakemore's and C. T. Smith's *Latin America: Geographical Perspectives* (London, 1971), and the best short interpretation of modern Latin American history is given by George Pendle's *A History of Latin America* (Pelican, 1963). *Concerning Latin-American Culture,* edited by C. C. Griffin (New York, 1940) contains chapters which provide essential background material for an understanding of indigenous and colonial contributions to Latin America. B. W. Diffie's *Latin-American Civilization* (Harrisburg, 1945) is a much more exhaustive analysis of these features. C. H. Haring's *The Spanish Empire in America* (Oxford, 1947) is probably the best study of the history of the colonial impact, while the five volumes of the *Handbook of South American Indians* edited by J. H. Steward (Washington, 1946–49) is an encyclopaedic analysis of the indigenous peoples. A condensed version of these volumes is J. H. Steward and L. C. Faron's *Native Peoples of South America* (New York, 1959). John Hemming's *The Conquest of the Incas* (London, 1970) is a recent masterly study of the indigenous occupance of the Central Andes.

The two most useful comprehensive studies of the historical, cultural and ethnic development of Latin America, including the modern period, are W. L. Schurz's *This New World* (London, 1956) and D. E. Worcester's and W. G. Schaeffer's *The Growth and Culture of Latin America* (New York, 1956).

For accounts of post-Independence history and modern economic developments A. B. Thomas' *Latin America* (New York, 1956), H. Bernstein's *Modern and Contemporary Latin America* (Chicago, 1952), S. G. Hanson's *Economic Development in Latin America* (Washington, 1957), and a fascinating two-volume treatment of the present socio-political background of economic development in the continent by Marcel Niedergang, *The Twenty Latin Americas* (London, 1971) provide a general picture of the basic foundations of the present setting. F. Benham and H. A. Holley's *A Short Introduction to the Economy of Latin America* (London, 1960), T. Lynn Smith's *Latin American Population Studies* (Gainesville, 1960), and the essays in the volume *Latin America: Evolution or Explosion*, edited by M. Adams (New York, 1963), are useful summaries of the principal economic, demographic and politico-social problems respectively. The Unesco publication (1963) edited by E. de Vries and J. Medina Echavarria on *Social Aspects of Economic Development in Latin America*, the collection of essays edited by Claudio Véliz, *Obstacles to Change in Latin America* (London, 1965), and the collection of *Latin American Issues: Essays and Comments* (New York, 1961), edited by A. O. Hirschman, are excellent analyses of some of the fundamental problems facing the continent. The Pan American Union's publication *Plantation Systems of the New World* (Washington, 1959) is a more limited sociological treatment; and A. B. Mountjoy's *Industrialization and Underdeveloped Countries* (London, 1963) has useful specific material within a Latin American context. A small booklet containing two studies of urban growth in the development of Mexico and Venezuela, entitled *Cities in a Changing Latin America* (London, 1969) is a most useful analysis of the contemporary urban scene.

M. S. Wionczek's *Latin American Economic Integration* is a collection of essays on this most important aspect of the future economic development of the continent.

Statistical

The United Nations' *Demographic Yearbook* and their monthly *Statistical Abstract* provide up-to-date information on population, vital statistics, economic production and financial aspects of Latin America. The United Nations Economic Commission for Latin America publish annual reports which contain useful analyses of contemporary trends. Technical reports on development plans and problems of individual republics are also an invaluable source of statistical material. The Center of Latin American Studies in the University of California at Los Angeles also publishes an annual *Statistical Abstract of Latin America* which contains demographic, social, economic and financial information together with a bibliography of source material for statistics.

Bibliographical

R. A. Humphrey's *Latin America: a Selective Guide to Publications in English* (London, 1958) is an excellent classified summary of the principal books available, and is indispensable as a guide to further reading either on general or regional lines.

Current Geographical Publications, published by the American Geographical Society, New York, and *New Geographical Literature and Maps*, published by the Royal Geographical Society, are valuable sources for locating recently published material on the continent. Similarly, the lists of geographical articles published from time to time in *Geography*, journal of the Geographical Association, are a useful supplement of new material. The feature, *This Changing World*, in the same journal frequently has up-to-date information on recent developments in the continent.

The monthly *Hispanic American Report* published at Stanford University, California, contains analyses of current developments in Latin America.

Regional

A selected list of some of the most useful references is given below:

Mexico

H. F. CLINE, *Mexico: Revolution to Evolution 1940–1960* (London, 1962).

C. SENIOR, *Land Reform and Democracy* (Gainesville, 1958).

A. J. BERMUDEZ, *The Mexican National Petroleum Industry* (Stanford, 1963).

G. M. MCBRIDE, *The Land Systems of Mexico* (New York, 1923).

E. N. SIMPSON, *The Ejido, Mexico's Way Out* (North Carolina, 1937).

N. L. WHETTEN, *Rural Mexico* (Chicago, 1948).

T. GILL, *Land Hunger in Mexico* (Washington, 1951).

G. C. VAILLANT, *The Aztecs of Mexico* (Penguin, 1950).

S. G. MORLEY, *The Ancient Maya* (London, 1947).

E. S. THOMPSON, *Rise and Fall of Maya Civilization* (London, 1956).

Central America

F. D. PARKER, *The Central American Republics* (London, 1964).

D. A. G. WADDELL, *British Honduras* (London, 1961).

V. CHECCHI, *Honduras: A Problem in Economic Development* (New York, 1959).

N. L. WHETTEN, *Guatemala: the Land and the People* (Yale, 1961).

C. WAGLEY, *Economics of a Guatemalan Village* (Wisconsin, 1941).

T. W. MCBRYDE, *Cultural and Historical Geography of South-west Guatemala* (Washington, 1945).

C. L. JONES, *Costa Rica and Civilization in the Caribbean* (Wisconsin, 1935).

S. MAY, *Costa Rica: A Study in Economic Development* (New York, 1952).

W. VOGT, *The Population of El Salvador and its Natural Resources* (Washington, 1946).

S. MAY and G. PLAZA, *The United Fruit Company in Latin America* (Washington, 1958).

448   *References*

The West Indies

M. DE YOUNG, *Man and Land in the Haitian Economy* (Jacksonville, 1958).
J. G. LEYBURN, *The Haitian People* (Yale, 1941).
M. J. HERSKOVITS, *Life in a Haitian Valley* (New York, 1937).
H. J. WIARDA, *The Dominican Republic: Nation in Transition* (London, 1969).
P. ABRAHAMS, *Jamaica, an Island Mosaic* (London, 1957).
F. HENRIQUES, *Jamaica, Land of Wood and Water* (London, 1957).
K. NORRIS, *Jamaica* (London, 1962).
R. B. DAVISON, *West Indian Migrants* (London, 1962).
W. L. BURN, *The British West Indies* (London, 1951).
D. SEERS (ed.), *Cuba: the Economic and Social Revolution* (Chapel Hill, 1964).
R. SCHEER and M. ZEITLIN, *Cuba: an American Tragedy* (Pelican, 1964).
C. T. JONES and R. PICÓ, *Symposium on the Geography of Puerto Rico* (Río Pedras, 1955).

Venezuela

E. WARD, *The New Eldorado: Venezuela* (London, 1957).
E. LIEUWEN, *Venezuela* (London, 1961).

Guianas

M. SWAN, *British Guiana, The Land of Six Peoples* (London, 1957).
R. T. SMITH, *British Guiana* (London, 1962).
D. B. FANSHAWE, *The Vegetation of British Guiana* (Oxford, 1952).
Colonial Office, *Report on the Sugar Industry of British Guiana* (London, 1949).

Colombia

W. O. GALBRAITH, *Colombia, a General Survey* (London, 1953).
J. J. PARSONS, *Antioqueño Colonization in Western Colombia* (Los Angeles, 1949).
J. D. MARTZ, *Colombia: a Contemporary Political Survey* (Chapel Hill, 1962).

Ecuador

L. LINKE, *Ecuador, Country of Contrasts* (London, 1955).
W. S. RYCROFT, *Indians of the High Andes* (New York, 1946).

Peru

J. A. MASON, *The Ancient Civilizations of Peru* (Pelican, 1957).
V. W. VON HAGEN, *Highway of the Sun* (London, 1956).
T. R. FORD, *Man and Land in Peru* (Gainesville, 1955).
E. R. OWENS, *Peru* (London, 1962).

Bolivia

G. M. MCBRIDE, *The Agrarian Indian Communities of Highland Bolivia* (New York, 1921).
O. E. LEONARD, *Bolivia, Land, People and Institutions* (Washington, 1952).
H. OSBORNE, *Bolivia: a Land Divided* (London, 1955).
UNITED NATIONS, *Report of the U.N. Mission of Technical Assistance to Bolivia* (New York, 1951).
A. G. OGILVIE, *Geography of the Central Andes* (New York, 1922).
D. J. FOX, *Tin and the Bolivian Economy* (London, 1970).
C. H. ZONDAG, *The Bolivian Economy, 1952–65* (New York, 1966).

Chile

G. M. MCBRIDE, *Chile: Land and Society* (New York, 1936).
M. JEFFERSON, *Recent Colonization in Chile* (New York, 1921).
I. BOWMAN, *Desert Trails of Atacama* (New York, 1924).
B. SUBERCASEAUX, *Chile: A Geographic Extravaganza* (New York, 1943).
G. J. BUTLAND, *Chile: An Outline of its Geography, Economics and Politics* (London, 1956).
G. J. BUTLAND, *The Human Geography of Southern Chile*, Institute of British Geographers Publication No. 24 (London, 1957).

Argentina

M. JEFFERSON, *Peopling the Argentine Pampa* (New York, 1926).
H. S. FERNS, *Britain and Argentina in the Nineteenth Century* (Oxford, 1960).
H. S. FERNS, *Argentina* (London, 1969).
R. J. ALEXANDER, *An Introduction to Argentina* (London, 1969).
A. D. LITTLE, *Industrial Development in Argentina* (Cambridge, 1961).
G. PENDLE, *Argentina* (London, 1963).
W. H. HUDSON, *Far Away and Long Ago* (London, 1939).
C. C. TAYLOR, *Rural Life in Argentina* (Baton Rouge, 1948).
I. BOWMAN, *The Pioneer Fringe* (New York, 1931).
I. BOWMAN (ed.), *Limits of Land Settlement* (New York, 1937).
American Geog. Soc., *Pioneer Settlement* (New York, 1932), includes also studies on Bolivia, Paraguay and Chile.

Uruguay

G. PENDLE, *Uruguay* (London, 1963).
R. H. FITZGIBBON, *Uruguay: Portrait of a Democracy* (London, 1956).
C. H. FARNWORTH, *The Agriculture of Uruguay* (Washington, 1952).

Paraguay

G. PENDLE, *Paraguay: a Riverside Nation* (London, 1957).
E. R. and H. S. SERVICE, *Tobati: Paraguayan Town* (Chicago, 1954).

J. W. FRETZ, *Immigrant Group Settlements in Paraguay* (North Newton, Kansas, 1962).

Brazil

G. FREYRE, *The Masters and the Slaves* (New York, 1946).
G. CAMACHO, *Brazil: an Interim Assessment* (London, 1955).
T. L. SMITH, *Brazil: People and Institutions* (Baton Rouge, 1954).
M. HARRIS, *Town and Country in Brazil* (London, 1956).
H. W. HUTCHINSON, *Village and Plantation Life in North-eastern Brazil* (Seattle, 1957).
H. W. SPIEGEL, *The Brazilian Economy* (Philadelphia, 1949).
S. H. ROBOCK, *Brazil's Developing Northeast* (Washington, 1963).
W. L. SCHURZ, *Brazil: the Infinite Country* (London, 1962).
H. HACK, *Dutch Group Settlement in Brazil* (The Hague, 1959).
C. WAGLEY, *Race and Class in Rural Brazil* (Paris, 1963).
G. WYTHE, *Brazil: an Expanding Economy* (New York, 1949).
T. L. SMITH and A. MARCHANT, *Brazil: Portrait of Half a Continent* (New York, 1951).
C. WAGLEY, *Amazon Town* (New York, 1953).

The publications of the Overseas Economic Surveys and of the Organization of American States, and the American Geographical Society's *Focus*, are sources of a considerable amount of up-to-date material on the individual republics. Recent publications in the latter series deal with Guatemala, the Bahama Islands, the Dominican Republic, Haiti, Jamaica, Mexico, Puerto Rico, Bolivia, Brazil, Colombia, Ecuador, Guyana, Paraguay, Peru and Buenos Aires.

The Revista Geografia of the Geography Commission of the Pan American Institute of Geography and History, published in Rio de Janeiro in June and December each year, specializes in articles on Latin American geography.

Glossary of Spanish and Portuguese Geographical Terms

altiplano: high plateau
audiencia: colonial territory
bañado: hollow, often near shifting watercourse (Argentina)
banco: bank, area above flood level (Colombia)
bandeirante: frontiersman (Brazil)
barranca: steep bank, often of loose material
blanco: white
bodega: warehouse, factory
bolsón: trough, depression
caatinga: semi-arid vegetation (Brazil)
caboclo: Portuguese-Indian mixture (Brazil)
cafuso: Indian-Negro mixture (Brazil)
caliche: nitrate ore
campo: country (rural)
campo cerrado: savana with many trees (Brazil)
campo limpo: grassland, mostly treeless (Brazil)
campos: savana, prairie
campos geraes: prairies (Brazil)
cañada: watercourse, swampy depression
cancagua: volcanic-derived soil, probably wind-blown (Ecuador)
Ceja de Montaña: mountain borderland of Peruvian Montaña
cenote: sink hole (Mexico)
central: central; also central sugar mill
cerro: hill
chancaca: partially refined sugar (Peru)
charqui: salted beef
chapada: scarp-bounded plateau (Brazil)
ciénaga: riverine lake (Colombia)
ciudad: city
colonia: settlement, often of small farmers
colono: small farmer, peasant
cordillera: mountain system
criollo: born in the Americas; unimproved cattle
cuchilla: undulating ridge of high land (Uruguay)
ejiditario: participant in community farm (Mexico)
ejido: community farm (Mexico)
engenho: primitive sugar mill (Brazil)

451

Entre Ríos: between the rivers (Argentina)
espigões: broad undulating watershed areas (Brazil)
estancia: large pastoral ranch
estanciero: owner of large pastoral ranch
estero: watercourse, usually seasonal
falda: zone, sloping fringe
falta de bracos: lack of labour (Brazil)
fazenda: coffee estate (Brazil)
frigorífico: meat-packing plant
fundo: farm, usually large
garua: Scottish mist (Peru)
gaucho: cowboy
hacienda: large self-contained farm-estate
hacendado: owner of large farm-estate
inquilino: peasant, farm labourer on estate (Chile)
jardim: garden, oasis (Brazil)
latifundia: system of large farm-estates
llanero: Venezuelan cowboy
llanos: savana grassland (Colombia, Venezuela)
mameluco: Portuguese-Indian mixture (Brazil)
mandioca: tuber of manioc (cassava)
mato grosso: large forest (Brazil)
matta: forest (Brazil)
matta de varzea: dense flood-plain jungle (Brazil)
mesa: tableland, plateau
mestizo: European-Indian mixture
milpa: forest clearing for subsistence farming (Central America)
minuano: cold south-west wind in South Brazil
minifundia: system of small, fragmented, and usually uneconomic land
    holdings
misiones: communal settlements for conversion of Indians
montaña: mountain
Montaña: Amazon forest of Peru
monte: woodland
monte alto: forest
monte bajo: scrub forest, thickets
mulatto: European-Negro mixture
municipio: municipality, district
negro: black
oficina: nitrate refining plant (Chile)
occidental: western
oriental: eastern
Oriente: Amazon forest of Ecuador
pajonal: an area with high tufts of grass
pampa: extensive plain

pampero: violent south-west wind (Argentina)
pantanal: alluvial plain, seasonally marshy (Brazil)
páramo: high alpine vegetation below snow-line
paraná: river distributary
pasto duro: coarse grass, indigenous (Argentina)
pasto tierno: tender grass, imported (Argentina)
patrón: master, landowner
Pé da Serra: piedmont zone (Brazil)
peón: tied farm labourer
planalto: tableland
playa: beach, marsh
potrero: cattle paddock
puerto: port
puna: high plateau, or bleak, arid, high mountain zone
quebrada: erosion valley with steep sides
rapadura: partially-refined sugar cake (Brazil)
real: royal, principal
Recôncavo: hinterland of Salvador (Brazil)
río: river
rio branco: river heavy with silt (Brazil)
rio negro: river coloured by vegetable débris (Brazil)
roça: burned-over clearing for subsistence farming
salar: salt basin
saladero: factory preparing salt beef
selva: hot wet forest
serra, sierra: mountain range
serra da rapadura: isolated plateau block (Brazil)
serranía: an area of hills and ridges
sertão: (plur, *sertões*). isolated, little-known area, remote from populated
  centres (Brazil)
siguane: sink hole (Mexico)
terra firme: land sufficiently high not to be flooded (Brazil)
terra roxa, tierra rosa: red soil, usually limestone-derived
tierra caliente: hot zone
tierra fria: cool zone
tierra templada: temperate zone
tosca: hard lime sub-soil pan
transversal: transverse
travessão: pastoral-agricultural boundary (Brazil)
Triângulo: pan-handle of Minas Gerais (Brazil)
usina: factory, especially sugar-refining
valle: rift trough, valley
vega: meadow, grazing area
Yungas: Amazon forest of Bolivia
zambo: Indian-Negro mixture (Brazil)

Conversion information and factors

INCHES TO MILLIMETRES
(1 in = 25·4 mm)

in	0·0	0·1	0·2	0·3	0·4	0·5	0·6	0·7	0·8	0·9	in
0	0·0	2·5	5·1	7·6	10·2	12·7	15·2	17·8	20·3	22·9	0
1	25·4	27·9	30·5	33·0	35·6	38·1	40·6	43·2	45·7	48·3	1
2	50·8	53·3	55·9	58·4	61·0	63·5	66·0	68·6	71·1	73·7	2
3	76·2	78·7	81·3	83·8	86·4	88·9	91·4	94·0	96·5	99·1	3
4	101·6	104·1	106·7	109·2	111·8	114·3	116·8	119·4	121·9	124·5	4
5	127·0	129·5	132·1	134·6	137·2	139·7	142·2	144·8	147·3	149·9	5
6	152·4	154·9	157·5	160·0	162·6	165·1	167·6	170·2	172·7	175·3	6
7	177·8	180·3	182·9	185·4	188·0	190·5	193·0	195·6	198·1	200·7	7
8	203·2	205·7	208·3	210·8	213·4	215·9	218·4	221·0	223·5	226·1	8
9	228·6	231·1	233·7	236·2	238·8	241·3	243·8	246·4	248·9	251·5	9

FEET TO METRES
(1 ft = 0·3048 m)

ft	0	1	2	3	4	5	6	7	8	9	ft
0	0·00	0·30	0·61	0·91	1·22	1·52	1·83	2·13	2·44	2·74	0
10	3·05	3·35	3·66	3·96	4·27	4·57	4·88	5·18	5·49	5·79	10
20	6·10	6·40	6·71	7·01	7·32	7·62	7·92	8·23	8·53	8·84	20
30	9·14	9·45	9·75	10·06	10·36	10·67	10·97	11·28	11·58	11·89	30
40	12·19	12·50	12·80	13·11	13·41	13·72	14·02	14·33	14·63	14·94	40
50	15·24	15·54	15·85	16·15	16·46	16·76	17·07	17·37	17·68	17·98	50
60	18·29	18·59	18·90	19·20	19·51	19·81	20·12	20·42	20·73	21·03	60
70	21·34	21·64	21·95	22·25	22·56	22·86	23·16	23·47	23·77	24·08	70
80	24·38	24·69	24·99	25·30	25·60	25·91	26·21	26·52	26·82	27·13	80
90	27·43	27·74	28·04	28·35	28·65	28·96	29·26	29·57	29·87	30·18	90

MILES TO KILOMETRES
(1 mi = 1·609 344 km)

mi	0	1	2	3	4	5	6	7	8	9	mi
0	0·0	1·6	3·2	·8	6·4	8·0	9·7	11·3	12·9	14·5	0
10	16·1	17·7	19·3	20·9	22·5	24·1	25·7	27·4	29·0	30·6	10
20	32·2	33·8	35·4	37·0	38·6	40·2	41·8	43·5	45·1	46·7	20
30	48·3	49·9	51·5	53·1	54·7	56·3	57·9	59·5	61·2	62·8	30
40	64·4	66·0	67·6	69·2	70·8	72·4	74·0	75·6	77·2	78·9	40
50	80·5	82·1	83·7	85·3	86·9	88·5	90·1	91·7	93·3	95·0	50
60	96·6	98·2	99·8	101·4	103·0	104·6	106·2	107·8	109·4	111·0	60
70	112·7	114·3	115·9	117·5	119·1	120·7	122·3	123·9	125·5	127·1	70
80	128·7	130·4	132·0	133·6	135·2	136·8	138·4	140·0	141·6	143·2	80
90	144·8	146·5	148·1	149·7	151·3	152·9	154·5	156·1	157·7	159·3	90

ACRES TO HECTARES
(1 ac = 0·404 686 ha)

ac	0	1	2	3	4	5	6	7	8	9	ac
0	0·00	0·40	0·81	1·21	1·62	2·02	2·43	2·83	3·24	3·64	0
10	4·05	4·45	4·86	5·26	5·67	6·07	6·47	6·88	7·28	7·69	10
20	8·09	8·50	8·90	9·31	9·71	10·12	10·52	10·93	11·33	11·74	20
30	12·14	12·55	12·95	13·35	13·76	14·16	14·57	14·97	15·38	15·78	30
40	16·19	16·59	17·00	17·40	17·81	18·21	18·62	19·02	19·42	19·83	40
50	20·23	20·64	21·04	21·45	21·85	22·26	22·66	23·07	23·47	23·88	50
60	24·28	24·69	25·09	25·50	25·90	26·30	26·71	27·11	27·52	27·92	60
70	28·33	28·73	29·14	29·54	29·95	30·35	30·76	31·16	31·57	31·97	70
80	32·37	32·78	33·18	33·59	33·99	34·40	34·80	35·21	35·61	36·02	80
90	36·42	36·83	37·23	37·64	38·04	38·45	38·85	39·25	39·66	40·06	90

MILES² TO KILOMETRES²
($1\ mi^2 = 2 \cdot 589\ 99\ km^2$)

mi²	0	1	2	3	4	5	6	7	8	9	mi²
0	0·00	2·59	5·18	7·77	10·36	12·95	15·54	18·13	20·72	23·31	0
10	25·90	28·49	31·08	33·67	36·26	38·85	41·44	44·03	46·62	49·21	10
20	51·80	54·39	56·98	59·57	62·16	64·75	67·34	69·93	72·52	75·11	20
30	77·70	80·29	82·88	85·47	88·06	90·65	93·24	95·83	98·42	101·01	30
40	103·60	106·19	108·78	111·37	113·96	116·55	119·14	121·73	124·32	126·91	40
50	129·50	132·09	134·68	137·27	139·86	142·45	145·04	147·63	150·22	152·81	50
60	155·40	157·99	160·58	163·17	165·76	168·35	170·94	173·53	176·12	178·71	60
70	181·30	183·89	186·48	189·07	191·66	194·25	196·84	199·43	202·02	204·61	70
80	207·20	209·79	212·38	214·97	217·56	220·15	222·74	225·33	227·92	230·51	80
90	233·10	235·69	238·28	240·87	243·46	246·05	248·64	251·23	253·82	256·41	90

CONVERSION FACTORS

To convert °F. to °C. carry out the following equation: (°F. − 32) × 5/9
To convert troy oz to kg multiply by 0·0311
To convert units/mile² to units/km² multiply by 0·386

Index

Abaco Is., 117
Acajutla, 102
Acapulco, 74, 75
Aconcagua Mt., 14, 238,
  291, 321
Aconcagua R., 293
Agrarian reform, 81, 84, 273,
  294, 301, 303, 412
Agua Caliente, 269
Aguanaval R., 51
Aguapey R., 327
Aguascalientes, 60, 62, 71
Agriculture,
  Antilles, 146–7
  Argentina, 326, 332–6,
    348, 350
  Brazil, 17, 388, 389, 401,
    402, 413, 415, 427, 431,
    433
  Central American Repub-
    lics, 92, 99, 100–1, 106
  Chile, 301
  Colombia, 222, 223, 228
  Cuba, 124
  Ecuador, 235, 241
  Guianas, 182
  Mexico, 41, 51, 54, 55, 62,
    64, 70, 72, 75, 81, 82
  Paraguay, 356
  Peru, 273
  Puerto Rico, 141
  Uruguay, 363–4
  Venezuela, 207
  West Indies, 117, 138, 130,
    155–6
Air transport, 53, 102–3, 158
Alacaluf Indians, 297
Alagoas, 390
Alajuela, 105
Alfalfa, 333–6
Alfredo Chaves, 413
Altiplano, 278–80, 315
Altitudinal zones, see tierra
  caliente, fria, templada
Aluminium Co., of America,
  180
Aluminium Co., Canadian,
  180
Amapá, 427
Amapala, 102
Amatitlán, 103
Amazon R., 16, 213, 227–8,
  237, 261, 268–9, 280,
  378, 423–30
Ambalena, 220

Amerinds, see Indians
Amuay, 193
Anáhuac, 64, 76
Anapolis, 422
Ancud, 297
Andalgala, 320
Andean Pact, 250
Andes Mts., 9, 14, 173, 189,
  193–200, 211, 220, 223,
  236, 261, 277, 280, 282,
  286, 288, 291–3, 315,
  319, 322, 343
Andros Is., 117
Añecon Grande, 343
Añegadizos, 225
Angostura, 200
Anta Plain, 266
Antigua (Guatemala), 103
Antigua (West Indies), 145
Antilles, 118–49, 164–7
Antioqueño colonization,
  222, 223
Antioquia, 223
Antofagasta, city, 289
Antofagasta, province, 286
Anzoátequi, 202
Apa R., 355
Apaches, 50
Apam, 64
Aracajú, 388
Araguaia R., 418
Araucania, 296
Araucanian Indians, 296
Arauco bay, 295
Arequipa, 266
Arica, 289
Artibonite valley, 128
Artigas, 367
Aruba Is., 149, 154–5, 193
Asiatics, 8, 428, see also
  Chinese, Japanese, East
  Indians
Asunción, 1, 309, 310, 312,
  354, 356, 357
Atacama, province, 286
Atitlán L., 94
Atuel R., 321
Avellaneda, 341
Ayacucho, 264
Aysén, 297
Azcapotzalco, 64
Aztecs, 3, 45, 64
Azua lowland, 128
Azuay knot, 237
Azuero peninsula, 105

Bagé, 411
Bahamas, 115–18, 155, 159
Bahia, 381, 386, 388, 391,
  392, see also Salvador
Bahía Blanca, 335, 346
Baja California, 56–7
Bajo Chocó, see Choco
Baker fiord, 297
Balboa, 106
Balsas R., 74
Bañados, 325
Bananas, 39, 41, 92, 98, 99,
  103, 104, 106, 135–8,
  147, 227, 236
Bancos, 225
Banda Oriental, 310
Bandeirantes, 327, 397, 411,
  412, 421
Barba, 94, 105
Barbados, 149–51, 155, 167
Barcelona, 200
Bariloche, 344
Barley, 67, 333
Barquisimeto, 196
Barranca, 330
Barrancabermeja, 219
Barranquilla, 226, 230
Bartlett trough, 119, 133
Basse Terre, 144, 145, 147,
  148
Batopilas, 53
Batuiité, 390
Baudó R., 224
Bauxite, 15, 133–5, 180
Beagle channel, 342
Beans cultivation, 39, 45, 64,
  70
Beet sugar, see Sugar
Belém, 423, 425
Belén, 320
Belize, 97
Bella Unión, 367
Belo Horizonte, 391, 405
Belterra, 428
Bení R., 282
Bermejo R., 324, 327
Bío-Bío R., 291, 294, 295
Bluefields, 99
Blue Mts., 133
Blumenau, 409
Bobures, 192
Bogotá, 211, 213, 214, 230
Bolívar, Simón, 174
Bolsones, 50, 319
Borborema plateau, 379, 383

Boyacá, 214
Branco R., 179, 426
Brasilia, 422
Brazil nuts, 427
Brazilian plateau, 15, 326, 355, 361, 365, 377, 418
Bridgetown, 151
Belize, 33, 91, 95–8, 109
British influences, 33, 41, 139, 369, 372, 415
British population, 8, 372
Brownson Deep, 115, 118, 119
Bucauramanga, 214, 216
Buenaventura, 223, 224, 226, 230
Buenos Aires, 309, 311, 313, 331, 336, 339–41, 351, 421
Buriticá, 224

Caatinga, 383
Caboclos, see mestizos
Cabo Frio, 394, 395
Cafusos, 7
Caicos Is., 115, 118, 159
Cajamarca, 263
Calama, 289
Caldas, dept., 223
Calera, 293
Calí, 223
Callao, 258
Camaguey, 121, 124, 125
Camaqua R., 408
Camargo, 51
Campeche Bank, 77
Campeche, state, 79, 80
Campina Grande, 390
Campinas, 400, 407
Campo cerrado, 420
Campo Grande, 420, 421
Campo limpo, 396
Campos, 15, 319
Campos geraes, 411
Cañadas, 330
Cañasgordas, 224
Cancagua, 237
Cañete, 258
Cap Haïtien, 131
Caqueta R., 227
Carabayllo, 258
Carácas, 194, 198, 200
Caravellas, 388, 389
Carcaraña, 322, 330
Cárdenas, 125
Carib Indians, 149
Caribbean 33, 88, 91, 92, 98
Caribbean Free Trade Area, 149, 158
Caroní R., 203, 205
Cartagena (Chile), 293

Cartagena (Colombia), 226
Cartago (Costa Rica), 105
Casiquiare R., 16
Castries, 148
Castro, 297
Cat Is., 115
Catamarca, province, 319–320, 323
Catamara R., 233
Cattle farming, 62, 64, 67, 310, 332, 333, 362, 401
Cauca R., 221, 223, 225
Cauquenes, 294
Caxias, 413
Cayman Is., 139, 159
Ceará, 379, 390, 391, 392
Ceboruco, 71
Celaya, 70
Cenotes, 77
Central American Common Market, 107–8, 114
Central Highlands (Venezuela), 194, 197–200
Cerro Azul, 258
Cerro de Mercado, 47, 51
Cerro de Pasco, 264
César R., 225
Chaco, province, 312, 324–8
Chañaral, 289
Chapada, 380
Chapada Diamantina, 394, 395
Chapada do Araripe, 380, 382
Chapala L., 63, 71
Chiapas highlands, 72, 78
Chiapas, state, 71
Chibchas, 3, 89, 213
Chibenga R., 238
Chicama, 255, 257
Chick peas, 70
Chiclayo, 257
Chicle, 79
Chihuahua, city, 52
Chihuahua, state, 51
Chilean Development Corporation, 301
Chili gorge, 266
Chillán, 294
Chiloé Is., 297
Chimbote, 257–8
Chinandega, 101
Chinese, 8, 152
Chiquinquirá, 213
Chira R., 254, 255
Chocó, 89, 224, 230
Choele Choel, 343, 346
Cholula, 67
Chone, 235
Chota, 238
Chuquibambilla, 268
Chuquicamata, 288

Cibao trough, 128, 132
Ciénaga, 225
Cienfuegos, 125
Ciudad Bolívar, 204, 228, 269
Ciudad Guyana, 205, 207
Ciudad Juárez, 52
Ciudad Madero, 44
Clarendon R., 133
Climate, 9, 14, 15
  Argentina, 317, 321, 323, 325, 330–1, 343–4
  Bolivia, 278–9
  Brazil, 382–3, 391, 396–7, 410, 420, 425, 426
  Central America, 88–9, 91, 104
  Chile, 286, 291
  Colombia, 214, 225, 227
  Ecuador, 234
  Guianas, 179, 180
  Mexico, 39, 48, 53–4, 59–60, 75
  Paraguay, 356
  Peru, 268
  Venezuela, 190–1, 194, 196, 201
  West Indies, 120, 130, 135, 140, 145, 151
Coahuila, 47
Coal, 18, 51, 55, 216, 295
Coatepec, 39, 77
Cochabamba, 281
Cockpit country, 133
Cocoa, 41, 76, 153, 199, 235–236, 388, 389, 431
Coffee, 17, 39, 41, 100, 101, 103, 106, 132, 194, 199, 222, 223, 228, 236, 269, 399, 402, 415–17
Colima, 57
Colón, 106
Colonia, 365, 411
Colonia Suiza, 364
Colonial divisions, 2–5
Colorado Delta (Mexico), 56
Colorado R. (Argentina), 332, 342
Comanches, 50
Comayagua, 102
Commewijne R., 180
Comodoro Rivadavia, 345, 346
Concepción, 294, 295
Conchos R., 49, 51
Concordia, 328
Conlara trough, 322
Conquistadores, 3
Constitución, 293
Continental islands, 149
Copper, 17, 50, 53, 55, 266, 279, 288, 289, 299

Coquimbo, 291
Cordillera Blanca, 261, 263
Cordillera Central de
Colombia, 211, 220–3
Cordillera Central de Costa
Rica, 104
Cordillera Central de His-
paniola, 128
Cordillera Corabayo, 280
Cordillera de Colonche, 233
Cordillera de Guanacaste,
104
Cordillera de Talamaca, 105
Cordillera Domeyko, 315
Cordillera Ecuatoriana, 239
Cordillera Occidental de
Colombia, 211, 236
Cordillera Oriental de
Colombia, 189, 211
Cordillera Real de Bolivia,
280
Cordillera Real de Ecuador,
236
Córdoba, city (Argentina),
312, 322–3, 341
Córdoba, province (Argen-
tina), 322–4, 333
Corinto, 101
Corocoro, 279
Coronel Oviedo, 357
Corrientes, city, 328
Corrientes, province, 326
Cortés, 3, 38, 60
Corumbá, 421
Costa Rica, 89–91, 104–6,
107, 108, 112–13
Cotahuasi gorge, 266
Cotton, 41, 45, 51, 67, 384–5,
403, 431
Cristóbal, 106
Cuantla, 72
Cuarto R., 322, 330
Cuba, 118, 119–27, 155, 158,
159–60
Cubatão, 407
Cuchilla, 361
Cuchilla de Haedo, 365
Cuchilla Grande, 362, 365
Cúcuta, 214, 216
Cuenca basin, 238
Cuernavaca, 72
Cuiaba, 421
Cuitzeo L., 70
Culiacán, 55
Cumaná, 200
Cundinamarca, 214
Cupica bay, 224
Curacão Is., 149, 154–5, 193
Curicó, 294
Curitiba, 414, 417
Cuzco, 266

Das Contas R., 394
David, 105
Demerara R., 180, 182
Desaguadero R., 278
Désirade Is., 145
Diamante R., 321
Diamantina, 398, 400
Diamonds, 180, 398, 400
Doce R., 394
Dolores, 333
Dominica, 145–9
Dominican Republic, 130,
132, 158, 161
Dulce R., 322, 324
Durán, 241
Durango, city, 51, 52
Durango, state, 47
Durazno, 367
Dutch influences, 3, 33, 178,
384

Earthquakes, 144, 321
East Indians, 152, 184
Economic factors,
Argentina, 348–52
Bolivia, 282–4
Brazil, 431–4
Central American Repub-
lics, 106–8
Chile, 299–303
Colombia, 228–31
Ecuador, 239–42
Mexico, 80–4
Paraguay, 358–9
Peru, 271–4
Uruguay, 368–70
Venezuela, 207–9
West Indies, 155–8
Ejidos, 34, 55, 62, 72, 79, 80,
84
El Bajío, 69–70
El Callao, 204
El Cardón, 193
El Dorado, 176
Eleuthera Is., 117
El Gran Chaco, *see* Chaco
El Mante, 41
El Romeral, 291, 295
El Salvador (Chile), 288
El Salvador, 87, 101–2, 107–
108, 110–11, 368
El Yunque, 140
Emigration, 82, 139, 142,
155, 390–1
Empedrado, 328
Encarnacion, 357
Enriquillo basin, 128
Entre Ríos, 327, 329–38, 335
Esmeraldas R., 233
Espigoes, 415
Espírito Santo, 392
Essequibo R., 179

Estancia, 344, 361, *see also*
Latifundia and Hacienda
Esteros, 330
Etang Saumatre, 131
Eten, 257
Ethnic characteristics, *see*
Racial composition
European immigration, 1, 8,
414
Exports and imports, 17, 18
Argentina, 341, 348–9,
352
Bolivia, 282–3
Brazil, 403, 431
Central American Repub-
lics, 103, 105, 106
Chile, 288, 289, 293, 298
Colombia, 228, 229
Ecuador, 236
Guianas, 182, 185
Mexico, 44, 57, 83, 86
Paraguay, 356, 359
Peru, 259, 271, 273
Uruguay, 366, 369, 370
Venezuela, 199, 207
West Indies, 123, 127, 130,
132, 139, 143, 146, 152,
156, 157

Faja de Oro, 41
Falcón dam, 45
Falda de Tucumán, 318, 324
Falta de braços, 176
Famatina, 319
Feira de Sant' Anna, 390
Fibres, 386
Fisheries, 57, 260, 290
Flores, 97
Florianopolis, 412, 414
Foot and mouth disease, 64
Fordlandia, 428
Forests, 53, 96, 179, 325, 402,
410, 417, 426
Formosa, city, 326
Formosa, province, 324
Fortaleza, 387, 391
Fray Bentos, 365
French Guiana, 178, 179,
182, 187–8
French population, 8, 33
Frontino, 224

Gamarra, 219
Garua, 258
Gaucho, 310, 361
Georgetown, 182
Germans, 8, 296, 412–14
Girardot, 220
Goiania, 422
Goiás, 418, 421, 422, 428
Gold, 50, 53, 62, 179–80, 229,
398, 400

Golfo Dulce, 105
Golondrinas, 47
Gonaïves, 131
Goyallarisquisga, 264
Granada, 101
Gran Colombia, 174
Grande Terre, 144, 145
Great Abaco Is., 117
Greater Antilles, 118–43
Grenada, 146–9
Guadalajara, 60, 71
Guadeloupe, 143, 144, 145, 165–6
Guaillabamba gorge, 238
Guaíra Falls, 326
Guajira, 227
Guanacaste lowland, 105
Guanajuato, 62, 70
Guano, 259
Guaraní Indians, 354
Guarapuava, 414
Guarello Is., 295
Guatemala, 87, 94, 98, 103, 107, 108–9
Guatemala, city, 89, 103
Guaviare R., 227
Guayaquil, 235, 241
Guayas R., 233, 235
Guerrero, 71, 74, 75
Guiana Highlands, 204–7
Guiana plateau, 15, 178–80, 204, 211, 377, 423
Gulf of Darién, 91, 92, 224
Gulf of Fonseca, 93, 100, 102
Gulf of Guyaquil, 235
Gulf of Honduras, 98, 100
Gulf of Maracaibo, *see* Maracaibo basin
Gulf of Mexico, 9, 46, 59, 76
Gulf of Paria, *see* Paria peninsula
Gulf of Reloncaví, 296
Gulf of San Marcos, 381
Gustavo A. Madero, 64
Guyana, 178–85

Habana, 119, 125
Hacienda, 34, 53, 55, 62, 298
see also Estancia and Latifundia
Haiti, 130, 131–2, 155, 158, 161
Henequen, 79
Heredia, 105
Hermosillo, 55
High islands, 145–9
Hispaniola, 118, 128–32, 158
Honda, 220
Honduras, 87, 94, 99, 100, 102, 106, 107–8, 111
Huachipato, 291, 295, 301
Huallaga, 263, 269

Huallanca, 257
Huancavelica, 263
Huancayo, 263
Huánuco, 263
Huaras, 263
Huasco, 29
Hurricanes, 14
Hydro-electric power, 47, 69, 133, 205, 299, 336, 346, 367, 392, 400, 407, 417, 422

Ibarra, 237
Iberians, 7, 8
Ica R., 259
Iguacú R., 409, 417
Iguazú Falls, 326
Ilhéus, 388
Illampú Mt., 280
Illimani Mt., 280
Immigration, 8, 337, 399–400, 412–15, 428
Imports, *see* Exports and Imports
Incas, 3, 248
Independence, 5
Indian population, 1, 3, 5, 6, 7, 8, 51, 53, 79, 248, 250, 276
Indo-America, 1
Industrialization, 5, 17, 18
  Argentina, 339, 350
  Bolivia, 283
  Brazil, 400, 403–4
  Central American Republics, 107
  Chile, 299, 301
  Colombia, 176, 229
  Cuba, 124–5
  Guianas, 176
  Jamaica, 138
  Mexico, 47, 65, 82–3
  Paraguay, 357
  Peru, 274
  Puerto Rico, 141
  Uruguay, 364, 368
  Venezuela, 176, 192–3, 202, 205, 207
  West Indies, 117–18, 157
Inírida, 227
Inter-American highway, 35, 46, 102, 108
Iquique, 289
Iquitos, 227, 268, 425
Irapuato, 70
Irazú Mt., 94, 105
Iron and steel industry, 18, 46–7, 205, 216, 259, 291, 295, 400, 404
Iron ore, 15, 47, 50, 51, 203, 204, 259, 291, 394, 400

Irrigation, 45, 46, 54, 84, 204, 266, 303, 321
Itabaiana, 390
Itabira, 401
Italians, 8, 399, 413
Ixtacihuatl Mt., 57
Izabal L., 98

Jachal, 320
Jacui R., 409, 410, 412, 413
Jaen, 263
Jalisco, 70
Jamaica, 118, 133–39, 163
Japanese, 8, 403, 440, 442
Jardim de Seridó, 385
Jauja, 263
Javanese, 8
Jequetepeque, 257
Jequitinhonha R., 394
Jesuit colonization, 228, 327, 354
Jivaros, 239
João Pessoa, 391
Jorullo, 57
Juanacatlán, 71
Juazeiro, 390, 394, 395
Jujuy, city, 318, 341
Jujuy, province, 317, 319, 324
Juluapán, 72
Junín, 335

Kingston, 138
Konawaruk, 179

La Boca, 341
La Ceiba, 99
La Dorada, 219
Lafaiete, 401
La Forestal Argentina, 325
La Gloria, 219
Lagoa Dos Patos, 409
Lagoa Mirím, 361
Laguna (Brazil), 414
Laguna de la Madre, 38
Laguna de Tampico, 38
Laguna district (Mexico), 51
Lagunillas, 193
Lambayeque R., 257
La Pampa, 288, 313, 322, 329–38, 344, 348
La Paz (Bolivia), 280, 283
La Paz Basin (Venezuela), 193
La Plata, city, 341
La Plata estuary, 310, 311, 312, 341
La Quiaca, 317
La Rioja, 319–20, 323
La Serena, 291
Las Flores, 333
Las Truchas project, 74

Las Villas, 121
Latacunga, 238
Latifundia, 5, 123, 273, 337, 362, 412
Latin American Free Trade Area, 250
La Unión, 296
La Venta, 45
Lead, 46, 50, 53
Lebanese, 8
Leeward Is., 143, 165
Lempa R., 101
León (Mexico), 60, 70
León (Nicaragua), 101
Lerma R., 57, 63, 69, 71
Lesser Antilles, 143–9, 164–7
Leticia, 227
Lima, 1, 3, 258
Limarí R., 291
Linares (Chile), 294
Linares (Mexico), 46
Llanos, 15, 200
Llanos de Mojos, 282
Loa R., 278, 288
Londrina, 415
Los Andes, 293
Low islands, 144–5

Macapá, 427
Maceio, 391
Magdalena R., 213, 216–20, 225
Magellan's Strait, *see* Strait of Magellan
Maguey, 64
Mahdia, R., 179
Maipo R., 291
Maize cultivation, 39, 45, 62–3, 64, 70, 194, 335–6, 431
Maldonado, 362, 364
Mamoré R., 282
Managua, city, 101
Manáus, 427, 428, 429
Manizales, 223
Manta, 235
Mantaro R., 263, 264
Manzanillo, 75
Mar del Plata, 333
Maracaibo basin, 189–93
Maracaibo city, 190, 191, 193
Maracay, 199
Marajo Is., 423
Maranhão, 391
Marañon R., 257, 260, 263
Marcona, 257, 259
Marie Galante Is., 145
Martinique, 145–9, 166–7
Massif de la Hotte, 128
Massif de la Selle, 128
Massif de Nord, 128

Matamoras, 44, 45
Matanzas, 121, 125
Matarani, 259
Mato Grosso, 349, 418, 421, 428
Matta, 396
Matta de varzea, 426
Maule R., 248
Maya Mts., 95
Mayapan, 79
Mayas, 5, 34, 45, 76, 79, 89, 96
Mazatlán, 55
Medellín, 222–3
Mejillones, 289
Melo, 367
Mendoza, city, 312, 321, 341
Mendoza, province, 320–2, 323
Mendoza R., 321
Mennonites, 358
Mérida (Mexico), 80
Mérida (Venezuela), 195
Mestizos, 7, 216
Meta R., 227
Mexicali, 56
Mexico City, 1, 3, 63–6, 69
Mexico, Basin of, 63–9
Milpa, 79
Minas, 362
Minas Gerais, 392, 398, 400, 401, 402, 407
Minerals, 15, 46, 50–1, 55, 62, 102, 106, 124, 157, 176, 193, 207, 248, 264, 267, 398
Minuano, 410
Mira Guaillabamba, 234
Misiones, province, 326
Misiones, 55, 56, 310
Misti, 266
Mitla, 76
Mixtec culture, 76
Moa B., 124
Moche valley, 257
Moctezuma, R., 57
Moengo, 180
Mollendo, 259
Monclova, 47
Montaña, 268–71
Montego Bay, 138
Monterrey, 44, 46, 71
Montevideo, 365
Montserrat, 146–9
Morelia, 60, 62, 70
Morelos, 60, 72
Morro Velho, 400
Motagua R., 98
Moyobamba, 263, 268
Mulattoes, 7, 46, 148, 388
Mundo Novo, 414
Muzo, 216

Nahuel Huapí, 344
Nassau, 117
Natal, 387, 391
National Maize Commission, 62
Nazas R., 50, 51
Nechi, 221
Necochea, 333
Negritos, 255
Negro R. (Brazil), 425
Negroes, 7, 46, 108, 131, 140, 148, 150, 388
Neiva, 219
Nepena, 258
Neuquén, 346
Nevis, 146, 148
New Providence, 117
Nicaragua, 87, 94, 98–101, 107, 111–12
Nicaragua L., 100, 104
Nicoya, 105
Niterói, 405
Nitrate, 289, 299
Norte Chico, 290–1
North-west District (Guyana), 184
Nuevitas, 125
Nuevo Laredo, 44, 45

Oaxaca, 75
Obidos, 427
Ocaña, 214
Oficinas, 288
Ofqui isthmus, 297
Oilfields, *see* Petroleum
Ollagüe, 277
Oracabessa, 137
Oriente (Cuba), 121, 124
Oriente (Ecuador), 233, 239
Orinoco R., 16, 200–4, 227
Orizaba Mt., 57
Oruro, 279, 281
Osorno, 296
Ouro Preto, 398, 405
Ovalle, 291

Pachitea R., 269
Pachuca, 62, 65
Paipote, 291
Paita, 255
Pajonal, 237
Pampa, see la Pampa, Humid Pampa
Panama, 104–6, 113–14, 174
Panama canal, 34, 104, 105
Panamá, city, 1, 89, 93, 106
Panama disease, 104
Pantanal, 419, 420, 421
Pánuco, 57, 63
Papa Coapan Development Scheme, 45, 77
Papantla, 39

Pará, 423
Paraguacú R., 381, 394
Paraguaná (Brazil), 412
Paraguay R., 16, 310, 354,
356, 418, 419
Paraiba R., 394, 395, 398,
399, 402, 407
Paraíba, state, 390
Paramaribo, 182
Paranaíba R., 395
Paraná R., 16, 310, 324, 326,
327, 328, 330, 335, 358,
394, 395, 396, 409, 417
Paraná state, 407, 412, 415,
417
Paranapanema R., 395, 410,
415
Pardo R., 394
Paricutín Mt., 57
Parnaiba R., 379, 381
Paso de los Libres, 328
Paso de los Toros, 367
Pasto, 174
Pasto duro, 331
Pasto tierno, 331
Pastoralism, 39, 41, 51, 278,
294, 319, 328, 332–6,
344, 348–50, 362, 366,
368, 401, 411, 412
Patagonia, 310, 312, 342–8
Patía R., 221
Paulo Afonso Falls, 15, 392
Paysandú, 365
Pé da Serra, 418, 420
Pedro Juan Caballero, 356
Pelée Mt., 144
Peraitepui, 204
Perené R., 269
Pergamino, 335
Pernambuco, 3, 390, 391
Petén, 95–8
Petróleos Mexicanos, 41
Petroleum, 41, 44, 152, 192–
193, 202, 203, 207–9,
219, 239, 255, 269, 283,
295, 298, 345, 388
Piassaguera, 404
Piauí, state, 391
Pichilemu, 293
Pilcomayo R., 324, 358
Pimentel, 257
Pinar del Rio, 121, 124
Pinos, Isla de, 124
Piracicaba, 403
Pisco, 258, 259
Piura, city, 255
Piura, dept., 254
Piura R., 255
Pizarro, 3, 174
Plaine de Nord, 128
Plaine du Cul-de-Sac, 128,
131

Playas, 321
Poas, 94, 105
Pointe-à-Pierre, 152
Point Fortin, 152
Poles, 8, 344
Pomeroon, R., 180
Ponce, 142
Ponta Grossa, 414
Poopo L., 278–9
Popayán R., 223
Popocatépetl Mt., 57
Population, 7–8, 20–3,
Antilles, 145, 147
Argentina, 337, 351
Brazil, 377, 390, 391, 405,
417, 428
Central American Repub-
lics, 95, 97
Colombia, 229
Cuba, 125
Guianas, 178, 184
Mexico, 35, 45, 51–2, 55,
56, 60, 63, 74, 77, 81
Peru, 273
Puerto Rico, 140–1
Uruguay, 365
Venezuela, 189, 207
West Indies, 131–2, 138,
147, 150, 152, 154, 155
Population pressure, 101,
103, 132, 133, 139, 140–
141, 150, 155
Port-au-Prince, 131
Porto Alegre, 391, 412, 413
Portobelo, 92
Port of Spain, 154
Porto Velho, 428
Portuguese colonization, 1–
3, 7, 383
Posadas, 327
Potaro R., 179
Potosí, 276, 281
Potrerillos, 288
Poza Rica, 41
Pre-Cordillera, 321, 322
Prospects and problems, *see*
Economic factors
Pucallpa, 269
Puebla basin, 67, 69
Puebla, city, 60, 67, 69
Puerto Ayacucho, 203
Puerto Barrios, 92, 98, 102
Puerto Berrío, 219
Puerto Cabezas, 99
Puerto Casado, 356
Puerto Chicama, 257
Puerto Cooper, 356
Puerto Cortés, 92, 99
Puerto de Hierro, 203
Puerto Ingeniero White, 335
Puerto La Cruz, 202
Puerto Limón, 104

Puerto Montt, 296
Puerto Pinasco, 356
Puerto Rico, 118, 140–2,
155, 164
Puerto Salgar, 219
Puerto Wilches, 219
Puna, 260, 281
Punta Arenas, 298
Puntarenas, 93, 105
Putumayo R., 227

Quebradas, 315
Queretaro, 70
Quesada, 3
Quezaltenango, 103
Quibdó, 225
Quilmes, 341
Quindío pass, 220
Quintana Roo, 80
Quito, 1, 174, 238, 241

Racial composition, 5–8, 89,
95, 125, 148, 151, 152,
158, 176, 184, 337, 388
Railways, 25, 55, 61, 71, 76,
314, 337, 390, 404, 421,
429
Rainfall, *see* Climate
Rancagua, 294
Ranco L., 296
Recife, 383, 384, 387, 391
Recôncavo, 384, 388, 390
Resistencia, 326
Ribeirão Preto, 398, 400, 407
Rice, 39, 41, 54, 182, 236,
413
Río Cuarto, 335
Rio de Janeiro, 391, 392,
393, 398, 405
Río Gallegos, 346
Río Grande, city, 411
Río Grande (Rio Bravo),
Mexico, 9, 45, 50, 51,
82, 395
Rio Grande do Norte, 390,
391
Rio Grande do Sul, 407, 411,
412, 413, 418
Rio Negro (Argentina), 346
Rio Negro (Uruguay), 361,
365, 367
Rios brancos, 425
Ríos negros, 425
Río Turbio, 346
Rivera, 367
Roads, 26, 46, 55, 215, 216,
230, 269, 390, 414, 428,
Roças, 385   [430
Rosario, 283, 335, 336
Rosas, 332
Rubber, 17, 427, 428
Rufino, 335

Saba, 145
Sabará, 398
St. Barthélemy, 145
St. Eustatius, 145
St. Lucia, 146–9, 156
St. Kitts, 146–9
St. Martin, 144, 145
St. Thomas, 143
St. Vincent, 146–9
Sajama, 277
Saladeros, 366
Salado R. (Argentina), 330
Salar de Coipasa, 278
Salar de Uyuni, 278
Salaverry, 257
Salina Cruz, 76
Salinas Grandes, 319
Salt, 227, 387
Salta, city, 312, 316, 318, 341
Salta, province, 315–19
Saltillo, 52
Salto, 365
Salvador, 383, 384, 390, 391
San Antonio (Chile), 293
San Bernardo, 294
San Cristóbal, 195,
San Felipe, 293
San Fernando (Chile), 294
San Fernando (Trinidad),
San Ignacio, 327   [154
San Jorje R., 225
San José (Costa Rica), 103,
    105
San José (Uruguay), 364
San Juan, city (Argentina),
    321, 324
San Juan, river (Argentina),
    321
San Juan, province (Argen
    tina), 320–2
San Juan (Puerto Rico), 142
San Juan R. (Colombia), 224
San Juancito, 102
San Luis, 322–4
San Luis Potosí, 44, 51, 52
San Pedro Sula, 99
San Rafael, 321
San Salvador (Nicaragua),
    102
Santa Corporation, 257
Santa R., 257, 263
Santa Ana, 102
Santa Catarina, 407, 412,
    414, 417, 418
Santa Clara, 124, 125
Santa Cruz (Argentina),
    343, 346
Santa Cruz (Bolivia), 282
Santa Cruz (Brazil), 413
Santa Fé, 331, 333, 335, 339
Santa María, 412
Santa Marta, 227

Santiago (Chile), 1, 3, 294
Santiago (Cuba), 125
Santiago R. (Mexico), 57, 71
Santiago del Estero, 325
Santiago de los Caballeros,
    132
Santo Domingo, 132
Santos, 402
São Francisco R., 15, 381,
    390, 392, 394, 395
São Francisco do Sul, 412,
    414
São Jerônimo, 414
São Joa del Rei, 398
São Leopoldo, 412
São Luis, 384, 391
São Paulo, 8, 64, 339, 391,
    392, 398, 400, 402, 404,
    405
São Roque C., 381
Saratún, 98
Segovia highlands, 196
Serra da Mantiqueira, 394,
    395, 402
Serra da rapadura, 418
Serra do Araripe, *see* Cha-
    pada do Araripe
Serra do Espinhaço, 394, 398
Serra do Mar, 395, 402, 408,
    409
Serra dos Orgaos, 395
Serra Geral, 409
Serra Grande, 379, 390
Serranía de Baudó, 224
Sertão, 385–92
Sheep farming, 298, 344,
    362, 372
Sicuani R., 266
Sierra de Aconquija, 316,
    317, 324
Sierra de Córdoba, 322, 329,
    332
Sierra de Cumaná, 194, 200
Sierra de la Ventana, 329
Sierra del Tandil, 329
Sierra del Cobre, 120
Sierra de los Orgános, 119
Sierra de Mérida, 189, 194–7
Sierra de Ocoa, 128
Sierra de Perija, 189, 211
Sierra de San Luis, 322
Sierra de Veragua, 104
Sierra Madre Occidental, 9,
    39, 47, 48, 49, 50, 52–3,
    55
Sierra Madre Oriental, 9, 36,
    46, 47
Sierra Madre de Chiapas, 76
Sierra Madre del Sur, 72,
    74–6
Sierra Maestra, 120, 124,
    133, 139

Sierra Nevada de Santa
    Marta, 226–7
Sierra Roraima, 178
Sierra Volcánica Transver-
    sal, 36, 39, 47, 57, 72
Sigatoka disease, 92, 99
Siguanes, *see cenotes*
Silver, 46, 50, 53, 62, 65, 102,
    276
Sinaloa, 54, 55
Sinú R., 225
Sogamosa, 213
Sonora, 54, 55
Sorocaba, 400, 407
Soufrière, 144
Spanish colonization, 1–5, 7,
    92, 120, 130, 140
Spanish Main, 33
Stanley, 372
Strait of Magellan, 297, 312
Sucre, 1, 281
Sugar, 17, 41, 55, 74, 97,
    120–3, 132, 135–8, 141,
    145, 150, 152, 182, 223,
    255–7, 301, 318, 384
Surinam, 178, 180, 182, 186–7
Swiss, 8
Syrians, 8

Tabasco, 38, 39, 41, 45, 76
Tacambaro, 72
Tacora, 277
Talara, 255
Talca, 294
Talcahuano, 293
Tamalameque, 219
Tamaulipas, 38, 39, 41, 45
Tampico, 38, 44
Tandil, 333
Taquarí R., 412
Tarapacá, 286
Tarija, 281
Tartagal, 324
Taxco, 74
Tectonic phenomena, 14,
    see also Volcanoes
Tegucigalpa, 102
Tehuantepec, Isthmus of, 75,
    76
Tela, 99
Temuco, 296
Tenochtitlan, 33, 60, 65
Teotihuacan, 34, 60
Tepalcatepec Commission,
    77
Tercero R., 322, 330
Teresa Cristina, 414
Terra firme, 426
Texas, 35
Texoco L., 63
Tiahuanaco, 279
Tibaji R., 415

Tierra caliente, fria, temp-lada, 38, 45, 89, 91, 93, 94, 100, 194–5, 212, 214, 238
Tierra del Fuego, 342, 346
Tierra rosa, terra roxa, 121, 399, 415
Tieté R., 395, 396, 400
Tijuana, 56
Tin, 17, 279, 281
Tingo María, 269
Tinogasta, 319, 320
Tipauni R., 229
Titicaca L., 278–80
Tlaxcala, 67
Tobacco, 39, 55, 123–4, 413
Tobago, 154, 168
Tocantins R., 418
Tocopilla, 289
Toltec culture, 45, 60
Toluca, 69
Tordesillas, Line of, 3
Torreón, 51, 52
Tosca, 330
Tourist industry, 83, 117, 127, 139, 157, 364
Transport, 46, 52, 55, 60, 158, 220, 223, 230, 269, 283, 414, *see also* Roads, Railways
Travessão, 389
Tres Arroyos, 333
Triángulo Mineiro, 421
Trinidad, 149, 151–4, 168
Trujillo, city, 257
Tubarão, 404, 414
Tucumán, city, 312, 318, 341
Tucumán, province, 315–19
Tulcán, 237

Tumac-Humac Mts., 178
Tumbes, 254, 271
Tunja, 213
Tunuyán R., 321
Turk Is., 115, 118, 159
Turrialba, 94, 105
Tuxtla, 39
Tuy R., 197, 198

Ulua R., 98, 100, 102
Unare, 200
Uncia, 281
United Fruit Co., 89, 92, 99, 103, 106
United States' commercial links, 18, 33, 41, 82, 89, 106, 121, 127, 140, 158, 173, 438
United States expansion, 9, 35
Urbanization, 64, 351, 405, 431
Uruapan L., 72
Urubamba, 266
Urucum, 419, 421
Uruguay R., 310, 327, 328, 361, 362, 365, 409
Usinas, 384

Valdivia, Pedro de, 3
Valdivia, 296
Valencia, 200
Valera, 195
Valle de Mexico, 57
Valles, 315
Valparaíso, 293
Vaupés R., 227
Veracruz, 38, 39, 41, 45, 76
Vichada R., 227

Victoria, 46
Vieques Is., 143
Villa María, 335
Villa Regina, 346
Villarrica (Paraguay), 357
Villavicencio, 228
Virgin Islands, 142–3, 165
Vitória, 398
Volcanoes, 39, 48, 57, 94, 100, 104, 144, 236–7, 266
Volta Redonda, 47, 400, 404, 414

Waini, R., 180
War of the Pacific, 250
Wetbacks, 82
Wheat, 51, 54, 67, 333–5
Windward Is., 143, 165

Xingú R., 425

Yaguarón, 356
Yanahuara, 263
Yaracuy, 197
Yautepec, 72
Yellow fever, 120
Yucatán, 77–80, 95, 115
Yungas, 16, 280

Zacatecas, 47, 48
Zambos, 7
Zapla, 324
Zapotec culture, 76
Zipaquira, 216
Zorritos, 255
Zulia R., 189, 216